The 1928
New York Yankees

The 1928
New York Yankees

The Return of Murderers' Row

Charlie Gentile

ROWMAN & LITTLEFIELD
Lanham • Boulder • New York • London

Published by Rowman & Littlefield
A wholly owned subsidiary of The Rowman & Littlefield Publishing Group, Inc.
4501 Forbes Boulevard, Suite 200, Lanham, Maryland 20706
www.rowman.com

Unit A, Whitacre Mews, 26-34 Stannary Street, London SE11 4AB

British Library Cataloguing in Publication Information Available

Library of Congress Cataloging-in-Publication Data

Gentile, Charlie, 1959–
  The 1928 New York Yankees : the return of murderers' row / Charlie Gentile.
  pages cm
  Includes bibliographical references and index.
  ISBN 978-1-4422-3598-4 (cloth : alk. paper) — ISBN 978-1-5381-1492-6 (pbk. :
alk. paper) — ISBN 978-1-4422-3599-1 (ebook)
  1. New York Yankees (Baseball team)—History—20th century. 2. Baseball players—
United States—Biography. I. Title.
  GV875.N4G44 2014
  796.357'6409747109042—dc23
                                                                    2014003086

This book is for my parents

Contents

Part IV: The Postseason

A Note on Sources

$\mathcal{G}$reat reliance was placed on www.baseball-reference.com for statistics on teams and players, unless where documented in the notes sections. Articles from ProQuest Historical Newspapers (American Periodicals Series Online) and Infoweb (America's Historical Newspapers) were used as primary sources for quotes and other information from major newspapers written before and up to the late 1920s.

The specific newspapers, magazines, and journals from these two sources fully referenced in the endnotes are the *Kansas City Star, Duluth News-Tribune, Hartford Courant, Morning Oregonian, Pawtucket Times, Chicago Daily Tribune, Fort Worth Star-Telegram, New York Times, New York Herald-Tribune, Baltimore Sun, Atlanta Constitution, Boston Daily Globe, Washington Post, Los Angeles Times, Bankers' Magazine*, and *Wall Street Journal*.

Information from other newspapers, magazines, and journals was gathered from microfiche, books, and interlibrary loan, mainly from the New York Public Library. Sources include the following, which are fully referenced in the endnotes: *New York Evening Post, New York Telegram, New York Morning Telegraph, Philadelphia Inquirer, Philadelphia Public Record, Philadelphia Public Ledger, St. Louis Post-Dispatch, Cleveland Plain Dealer, Detroit Free Press, Sporting News, Baseball Magazine, San Francisco Chronicle, Oakland Tribune, Literary Digest, Collier's*, and *Nation's Business*.

Weekday coverage of sports in the sports sections for most of the major newspapers ran, on average, three to four pages. Each paper had regular columns, with some devoted strictly to baseball and others to all things sport. The *New York Evening Post* featured "Cutting the Plate with Fred Lieb," a daily baseball column by Fred Lieb, as well as the "Listening Post," a regular column for other sports. Joe Williams commented on the sports world on a daily basis, and Dan Daniel on baseball, in his "Daniel's Dope" column for the *New York Telegram*. George B. Underwood authored "Fanning with the Fans" for the *New York Morning Telegraph*. John Kieran and James R. Harrison penned the "Sports of the Times" column for the *New York Times*. James Isaminger wrote "Tips from the Sport Ticker" for the *Philadelphia Inquirer*, which also featured sports commentary in "Old Sport's Musings." Ed Pollack authored "Playing the Game" for the *Philadelphia Public Ledger*. "Three and Two" by Bill Dooley, "Is Zat So" by Gordon Mackay, as well as a sports editorial, were regular columns in the *Philadelphia Public Record*. Albert Keane penned "Calling 'em Right" for the *Hartford Courant*. The *Boston Daily Globe*, *Cleveland Plain Dealer*, *Washington Post*, *Chicago Daily Tribune*, and *Los Angeles Times* all had similar columns.

When it came to daily reporting on game action, Richards Vidmer and James R. Harrison covered the Yankees and Giants for the *New York Times*; Hugh Bradley, Frederick G. Lieb, and Homer Thorne for the *New York Evening Post*; and Rud Rennie for the *New York Herald-Tribune*. James Isaminger covered the Athletics for the *Philadelphia Inquirer*, Bill Brandt for the *Philadelphia Public Ledger*, and Bill Dooley and Joe Dugan for the *Philadelphia Public Record*.

References to books are found in the bibliography and fully cited in the endnotes.

Preface

*N*ot quite fifty years after the fact, *The Greatest of All: The 1927 Yankees*, by John Mosedale, was published in 1974. The author states in his introduction that, "Surprisingly, not much has been written about the most dominant team in the history of professional sport. There are little more than a half dozen entries in the New York Public Library files." But one paragraph later, Mosedale writes, "This paucity seems about to be remedied, and books about the Yankees, in W. H. Auden's phrase, may soon rain on our defenseless heads."[1] Around the same time, *Where Have You Gone, Joe DiMaggio?*, by Maury Allen, and *Dynasty: The New York Yankees, 1949–1964*, by Peter Golenbock, were published. Both works, along with Mosedale's, were noncontroversial celebrations of sport's most dominant team.

The Yankees had been AWOL since 1965, but they were just beginning to crawl back onto the baseball scene after a group headed by George Steinbrenner bought a controlling interest in 1973. The team was playing in a blighted area in an old, decrepit stadium and had been losing badly in the popularity contest with the New York Mets.

With the relaxation of the reserve rule and the onset of free agency in 1976, the tone was set. The Yankees were going to spend money to remain at or near the top. Efforts paid off with a championship in 1977, bringing about Steve Jacobson's *The Best Team Money Could Buy* (1978). The book focuses on the high-profile free agent signing of Reggie Jackson. The subtitle, *The Turmoil and Triumph of the 1977 New York Yankees*, and a look at the table of contents, introduces a soon-to-be recurring theme. After another championship in 1978, there was *The Bronx Zoo* (1979), by Sparky Lyle and Peter Golenbock. Enough said.

This latest success by the Yankees was coming off the heels of the tumultuous, but successful, five-year run of the Oakland Athletics and their eccentric owner Charlie Finley. While winning three consecutive World Series and five straight division titles, they were one of the most colorful teams in the game's history at a time when baseball was in the midst of trying to reverse a long-term trend of losing popularity to the other three major team sports.

They were once, of course, the Philadelphia Athletics, and between that, from 1955 to 1967, they were the Kansas City Athletics, where Finley eventually gained control. There he ended the club's questionable deals with the Yankees, no longer acting as a farm club or allowing them to co-opt his promising young players. The Yankees, however, sought many, if not all, of Oakland's stars, still in their prime during Finley's later fire sales.

So, it was an accurate forecast. Books having the New York Yankees as their theme number well into the hundreds, if not more. The most dominant team in the history of professional sport is today, undoubtedly, the most written about and most dominant on sports bookshelves. Certain topics seem inexhaustible. It was written by one historian of the Civil War that it could possibly take decades to sift through the available material just to write about one state alone.[2] The New York Yankees don't quite go to that extreme, but there is a history of more than one hundred years, not necessarily one of unbroken success, within which there is still an ample supply of interesting subthemes to pick from among the more prominent.

This book is about the Yankees one year after their championship year in 1927. The team was on pace by Memorial Day to shatter the records of the year before. On July 1, 1928, in a season drenched with nearly a month's worth of doubleheaders, the Yankees swept the Philadelphia Athletics at Yankee Stadium to take a commanding fourteen-game lead in the loss column. But the Athletics, without ever falling below second place, went on a tear and, on September 8, after beating the Red Sox, briefly overtook the Yankees by a half game. These two teams together were the class of the American League from 1927, finishing either in first or second place five out of the next six years.

The 1928 New York Yankees contains fourteen chapters, in four sections, not all devoted strictly to the Yankees, or even to baseball. The introduction discusses what the experts and former players believed to be the most storied teams in baseball from the 1870s up to and including the 1927 Yankees. Chapter 1 departs from baseball somewhat and focuses on the character or frame of mind in our country one year before the Great Crash. Chapter 2 discusses the key steps involved in building the Yankee team and central figures behind the other three principal organizations that challenged the problem of Yankee, and even New York, dominance of baseball. The second part of the book, chapters 3 and 4, covers the offseason and preseason. Chapters 5 through 13 cover the regular season and are segmented according to the regional swings of the schedule. Chapter 14 covers the World Series.

ACKNOWLEDGMENTS

I would like to acknowledge the following people for their assistance. Christen Karniski of Rowman & Littlefield for considering my idea, her guiding me through the publication process and skillful content editing. Andrew Yoder at Rowman & Littlefield for alerting me to key corrections. I would also like to thank Patricia Kelly at the Baseball Hall of Fame photography section and the staff of the New York Public Library microfiche room.

Introduction: Baseball's Greatest Teams

> Still, we have now started baseball's sixth decade, and our
> present World's Championship team is among the top six of
> all time, so modern day fans ought to be fairly well-satisfied.
> Excepting in the single aspect of long-distance extra bases, Hug-
> gins's 1927 Yanks do not figure up very far.
>
> —J. Newton Colver, "Are the Yankees the Strongest Club of
> Baseball History? Part III," *Baseball Magazine*, January 1928[1]

*W*hat the Yankees accomplished during the 1927 season could not go
unnoticed by the contemporary baseball world. They were the first team to
win one hundred games throughout the course of a regular season during the
1920s, and only the fourth to do so in the past fifteen years. The last team to
win one hundred games during a regular season in the National League was
the Giants in 1913 and, in the American League, the White Sox in 1917.

The 1909 Pirates were the last mega world champion from the National
League, with a record almost identical to the 1927 Yankees. Three years after
the Pirates, the Boston Red Sox in the American League came to within less
than a percentage point of winning 70 percent of their regular-season games.
Their .691 was, until 1927, the highest for any World Series winner from the
junior circuit.[2]

The Yankees would be the first American League team to win 70 percent of their regular-season games with their record of 110–44. Although
it happens just about every year in football, basketball, and hockey, it has
become a rare benchmark in baseball, accomplished only three times in
either league since 1950. The Cubs and Pirates accomplished the feat twice
each in the early 1900s. Did the Yankees' super season in 1927 solidify
them as the greatest team ever? Just two years after baseball celebrated its

fiftieth anniversary as an organized sport, how did the Yankees compare to the great teams of the past?[3]

Baseball has benefited from a long and continuing interest in comparing and analyzing players and teams throughout different eras. Notwithstanding whether we believe the modern game to have begun during the 1890s or with the end of the Deadball Era in 1920, analysts and followers of the game during the mid- to late 1920s believed baseball at the professional level had built a history of at least fifty years.[4] Baseball scribes routinely dipped back to the 1880s and 1890s, as a follower of the game today would look back to the move west of the Giants and Dodgers, the first year of the adoption of the designated hitter rule, or the beginning of free agency.

Baseball Magazine considered Major League Baseball to be in its sixth decade, according to an article from its January 1924 edition. J. C. Kofoed attempted to compare the game's current star players to the stars of the late 1800s:

> There are few fans, we think, who can go back two decades and more and remember what baseball was then: who were the stars—and why they were rated as stars. . . . It is too bad that the records in those days were kept in such meager style, else it would be possible to check the players in many different ways and get a clearer line. . . . Fielding conditions were so entirely different forty years ago that it is manifestly unfair to compare the averages. The modern ballplayer has so big of an advantage here—what with perfectly manicured grounds, improved gloves, and the like that his average should look better than the old timer's.[5]

Fred Clarke began his Hall of Fame major-league career with the Louisville Colonels in 1894 and then became a lifelong Pirate. He made the following observations during the summer of 1925, when he made a comeback with them during their championship year as an assistant coach to manager Bill McKechnie:

> I never stopped to compare the present Pirate team with that of 1909. The 1925 outfit is a younger club. The boys ought to be good for ten years or more, and they ought to be up in the fight for years to come. Of course, the boys today have the advantage of all that has gone before, and they ought to improve by this knowledge. Ballplayers, as a rule, think that the growth in the game is due to them. I don't give them the credit. I give it to the magnates, because they have created greater facilities. That's why the game has grown. In the days when we had 15,000 seating capacity we could fill them, but we couldn't accommodate any more. Now they have 40,000 and 60,000 seating capacities, and they fill them. No, I don't think there is any perceptible difference in initiative today. On the whole, you'll find managerial methods more or less the same.[6]

During spring training in 1928, Yankee owner Jacob Ruppert reflected on his first few years with the Yankees, saying,

> This club of ours makes a striking contrast with the Yankee outfit [that] I saw train for the first time in 1915 at Savannah. Nobody is left. Bill Donovan is dead. Harry Sparrow, the secretary at that time, has passed away. Most of the players are out of the game. Baseball wasn't so big at the time; salaries weren't so high. The prices paid for players were rather modest, although just starting to soar.[7]

There were no highlight films, entire game replays, or altogether comparative statistical analysis. Attempts to compare different eras had to be done almost strictly on a qualitative basis, and many veteran players and managers, not to mention fans and writers, were in somewhat of an advantageous position of having participated in and seen firsthand what Clarke was referring to. They also witnessed the transition from the Deadball Era to the Lively Ball Era and the game's many administrative improvements.

When Ty Cobb told a reporter in June 1928 who he would put on his twentieth century All-Star team, he qualified it by saying, "I have designated this as a 'twentieth-century' team because I am not familiar, except by reputation, with the deeds of the nineteenth-century stars [like] Pop Anson and Ed Delahanty."[8]

Miller Huggins discussed how coverage of the game evolved with the *New York Telegram* in March 1928, stating the following:

> In the old days a club had only one newspaper man on the road with it, or at the training camp. He was one of the boys. Now we have anywhere from a dozen to fifteen correspondents. The player type is better, and he realizes that fifteen pairs of expert eyes are watching him closely. And then there are the high salaries and the need for clean conduct to get those salaries.[9]

But a few weeks after the World Series, Jim Nasium of the *Sporting News*, in a November 3, 1927, the article, made several references to the Yankees and Pirates and was critical of the influence "big money" was having on the "ordinary player" and its resulting in watered down talent. It was the classic, seemingly recurring theme that always seems to be critical of the modern player, while holding the players of previous generations in higher esteem:

> When two ball teams can permit their opponents to score an average of from four to five runs per game and make an average of [more than] nine hits per game throughout the season and still win the pennant in each league, it is the big tip-off on the general average of play produced by the other clubs in their league. When only one pitcher in the whole world of

big-league baseball can win as many as twenty-five games in a season and only six can win as many as twenty games, when pitchers who win fifteen games are rated as stars and paid salaries [of more than] $20,000, it is significant of the fact that the pitching in the big leagues is pretty much pop-eyed and has cost a lot of money for what it gave in return.

Today the club owners realize so much on their investment that they are able to reward the players more handsomely, while in those other days the owners were lucky to break even on the season, even at the low salaries they paid. Therefore, ball players of less merit are worth more to their employers than the stars of former years. Yet, there is little doubt but that this big money that is being paid to the players has had its effect on the playing end of the game.

The Yankees are now being hailed as one of the great ball clubs of all time, mainly because they far outclassed the measure of merit displayed by the other teams in both big leagues. But now pause long enough to look [at] the rest of the field and analyze what it was they outclassed—fifteen of the poorest ball teams that the two big leagues have ever displayed in any single season. While you are talking about the tremendous power of the Yankees attack during the recent baseball season, just stop and consider how it would stack up against the pitching of Young, Walsh, and Mathewson, and how it would compare with those old players who were born too soon to slam out a team batting average of .390, if it were possible to get them all on the same ball club in their best years.[10]

When the Yankees opened a big lead in early August 1926, veteran writer John B. Sheridan of the *Sporting News* believed that they were the "rottenest team I had ever seen to have a championship won on August 1." He also said the Orioles of 1894–1897 would have beaten them so badly in three games that they wouldn't show up for a fourth. As for the 1927 team, the "Yankees of 1927 are improved over 1926, but I am not at all impressed by their hollow victory in the American League race of 1927. On April 1, 1927, it appeared that, bar the Athletics, no team in the American League was better that a .500 team or second-division class."[11]

During a series in May 1928 between the Yankees and Athletics, Gordon Mackay of the *Philadelphia Public Record* pronounced,

> Babe Ruth stands without exception as the greatest batter who ever stepped to the plate. It is useless to compare him with Lajoie, Delahanty, and others, as the conditions under which the oldsters of the game played compared with those that govern the era of the Bambino furnish no satisfactory basis for comparison.[12]

Most spectacularly, there was a heated back and forth between John McGraw, Ned Hanlon, and Wilbert Robinson, all members and close friends while members of the Baltimore Orioles teams of the 1890s. During July

1927, as the Yankees were running away with the pennant, Robinson told Dan Daniel of the *New York Telegram* that he believed that the Yankees of the present day were the greatest team of all time. "We had seven .300 hitters, but no sluggers like Ruth, Gehrig, Lazzeri, and Meusel, and a couple of others," said Robinson. "We had heady ballplayers who would have outsmarted the Yanks at every turn. We had fast ballplayers. But I am sorry to say we had no pitchers to get those Yanks out." He added, "In other words, if the Baltimore Orioles were in the American League this year they would be licked by the Yankees because of a lack of pitching. We had to hit our heads off to carry our pitchers."[13] For a former Oriole and lifetime National Leaguer to profess that the Yankees the greatest of all, with two months still to play in the season, was treasonous. This could possibly be taken as proof that baseball of the late 1920s was vastly improved in comparison to that of the 1890s.[14]

John McGraw wasted no time in answering his former teammate, replying,

> The Orioles, in my estimation, were greater than the Yankees because they were smarter than the Yankees. The Orioles won ball games through smartness, as well as hard hitting, whereas the Yankees, it is my belief, depend upon pure power. In that respect the Yankees are a greater team.[15]

Ned Hanlon, who earned a ticket to the Hall of Fame as manager of those great Orioles teams, then seventy years old, wrote an op-ed that appeared in the *New York Telegram* on July 30, 1927. Hanlon asserted,

> So the New York Yankees of 1927 could have beaten my Baltimore Orioles of 1894 and succeeding years were they competing for the American League pennant!
> Not so you could notice it, Wilbert Robinson's statement to the contrary notwithstanding. When I see that old renegade again next winter in Baltimore I'll boil him in oil. He's the first of my Orioles to play traitor to the old cause. The Yankees of today are a wonderful club. But they haven't the mental poise or the resourcefulness [that] made my Orioles so dangerous.[16]

The *Baltimore Sun* actually requested that Hanlon personally make a trip from his cottage in Atlantic City to Washington during the 1927 season to chime in on the dispute and personally watch the Yankees play the Senators. He had praise for Wilcy Moore but felt that the Orioles' bunting and poke hitting would be too much for him to handle:

> Yessir, it's a great, straight-hitting club, but taken man for man, we would have had a big edge on them. I'll give Gehrig a slight edge on Dan Brouthers at first, because Dan was slowing up when he came with us, and

Lou is a fast mover and a great hitter. At second, short, and third, Lazzeri, Koenig, and Dugan, good players that they are, couldn't start playing ball with Reitz, Jennings, and McGraw, either in hitting or fielding.

In the outfield the Yanks have Ruth, Combs, and Meusel. Splendid gardeners. Ruth I consider a grand player in every way. But consider this trio as against Keeler, Kelley, and Brodie, all great ground coverers, fast, and splendid hitters.

Yes, Moore, Hoyt, Pennock, and the others are good pitchers. But do you think we'd stand up there and swing like a barn door in a windstorm? Huh![17]

Napoleon Lajoie, then fifty-one years old, began his career with the Phillies in 1896 and finished with the Athletics in 1916. Still considered by many to be the greatest second baseman ever, he was asked his opinion of the 1927 Yankees, and baseball, the following March. His answer went as follows:

What do you think of the Yanks? Why, what could anybody think of them? They rate with the greatest ball clubs the game has seen. When you consider the power alone, they may be the strongest team in baseball history. However, comparisons are complicated by one important factor. You know we didn't have the lively ball to hit at.

It is hard to say what some of the old boys would have done with the present ball and the present style of batting from the end of the handle.

You don't see much variety in hitting now; you rarely see a man choke his bat. They all like the giant swing. But I don't want to see anything taken away from the Yankees. They have strength down the line, which is more than we could have said about our great teams of the old days.

You remember we had two or three hard hitters. The outfielders, the first baseman, and the catcher were supposed to take care of the hitting. A shortstop batting .265 was a pretty hard hitter. Now the game demands power from the top of the batting order to the bottom. And the standard of play is pretty high, too. The pattern of the smart ball players has been lost.[18]

Lajoie expressed how he wished he were twenty-five years younger. He believed that he would have been even more successful hitting the lively ball, especially since he would be hitting in smaller ballparks. He went on to discuss the game's future and premier slugger:

Yes, the Bambino is a wonder, and I don't doubt he is in a class by himself in his specialty, but Jackson was an all-around hitter. He "socked" a mile 'n every park around the circuit. Didn't he hit the longest ball ever at the Polo Grounds over the clubhouse roof? I have no doubt that if Ruth went in for batting averages instead of home runs he would have hit .400. If he choked that bat and crossed up he'd paste many a ball to left and center.

But I guess he has dropped this thing out for himself. The money seems to be in the home runs.

Baseball sure is moving ahead in every way. Why look at the prices they pay for minor leaguers now. Look at the salaries the players get, and deserve, too. Why, when the Philadelphia club bought me from Fall River, and I looked pretty good even then, Geier, an outfielder, and I cost something like $1,500. The Philadelphia team wanted Geier, and I was thrown in.[19]

Comparing players or teams must inevitably involve the use of statistics. Records at a basic level were being kept as early as before the Civil War; a fresh batch of updates follows every pitch. Fortunately, no sport is more suitable to the use of records than baseball, and it no doubt adds to the game's popularity. Emphasis on statistics was on the rise in daily baseball coverage mainly due to the dramatic increase in extra-base hits.[20]

Grantland Rice printed a letter from a fan in his "Sportlight" column for the *Boston Daily Globe* just as the 1925 season was beginning. It demonstrates how people had a sophisticated grasp of the nature of baseball statistics:

> We have been asked often how many home runs Frank Schulte or Sam Crawford would have hammered out with the modern lively ball. It is always a complex matter to compare records where conditions change. For example, the following letter will be of interest to those who pursue the vital statistics:
>
> Dear Sir: Please note that for the four consecutive years of 1910, 1911, 1912, 1913, Cobb averaged .4027 (at bat 2,081, hits 838). For the four consecutive years of 1921, 1922, 1923, 1924, Hornsby averaged .4023 (at bat 2,175, hits 875).
>
> Please note further that the American League batting average (the average of all players) for the period during which Cobb hit .4027 was .259 (.242, .274, .265, .256). Cobb therefore averaged 144 points higher than his league for that period. The National League batting average for the period during which Hornsby hit .4023 was .289 (.289, .292, .286; 1924 not available). Hornsby therefore hit 113 points higher than his league for that period.[21]

Well aware they were not looking at the more or less apples to apples comparison we have today, writers and commentators at *Baseball Magazine* were making more use of charts and tables in their articles during the 1920s to help quantify the state of the game at different times. The same magazine began a three-part series beginning with its November 1927 issue called, "Are the Yankees the Strongest Club of Baseball History?" There was the following caveat:

> We do not mean now simply comparing the batting and fielding average of a ball team that sat on top of the baseball world back in the 1880s and 1890s with the master machines of 1925, 1926, and 1927. We cannot

simply take a table of figures compiled forty years ago and lay it alongside one of this day and age and say, "Read 'em and weep."

For back in the 1980s, ballplayers wore no gloves, and what would have been scored an error might then be a different thing from an error today. Then pitchers hurled the ball from only fifty feet away; the ball itself was deader and slower; the fields were larger and rougher. Scorers differed more in their personal interpretations of the rules in those days; the rules themselves have undergone many changes.[22]

The series was authored by J. Newton Colver and brought statistical analysis to a climax, while attempting to account for the aforementioned caveats. Only teams that won at least two consecutive pennants were considered. In addition, says Colver, "We followed the general rule of clustering the records of any team clear through a three-, four-, five-, or more year regime, while the general personnel of the team was intact."[23]

The first part of the series, written in November 1927, focuses on offense using five tests: runs per game, hits per game, total bases per game, stolen bases per game, and sacrifices per game. The December issue focuses on defense using three additional tests: errors per game, runs allowed per game, and hits allowed per game. These calculations were measured against league averages to get a better idea of a team's dominance. The January 1928 issue gives the final verdict using two additional tests, game winning efficiency and World Series performance.[24]

The final verdict placed the Yankees sixth, not even in the top third overall in a list of sixteen teams going back to 1880. Four of the six teams in the survey, which played during the nineteenth century, ranked in the top eight. The Chicago Cubs of 1906–1910 came out with the highest ranking, with the Baltimore Orioles of 1894–1896 the runners-up.[25]

An interesting survey was authored during the off-season by Dan Daniel for the *New York Telegram*, from January 23 through February 9. It lists each big-league city's greatest single year. The most engaging analysis was a fifty-six-year chronological survey of baseball printed in the *Sporting News*. The premier baseball weekly began a fifteen-part series with its October 27, 1927 issue called "MacLean Kennedy's Unusual Series: Greatest Ball Teams of History." The survey shuns statistics and rankings and is instead a verbal discussion of each team as it moved serially from the year 1871 to the Yankee team of the then present-day.

The series begins with the Boston Red Stockings, who participated in the National Association of Professional Base Ball Players when the southwest and most of the Great Plains and mountain states were still territories, and concludes with the Yankees since 1920. Kennedy includes ten teams from the National League, three from the American League, and one team from the defunct American Association, today's St. Louis Cardinals.[26]

In August 1927, with still more than a month and a half left to play in the season, Grantland Rice featured the Yankees in an article in *Collier's*. He writes, "Anyone desiring to add to the hubbub of modern sport can do so by coming out boldly and picking some one ball club as the greatest of all time."[27] Like Colver, and unlike Daniel, he chose to categorize teams during a span of a few years.

Babe Ruth is pictured in an oval with his arm around Lou Gehrig, while a photo of five of the old Orioles stands larger and more prominently to the upper right and center. Many of the active players in the American League were unanimous in their belief that the Yankees ranked with the greatest teams of all time, while opinions varied amongst the old-time fans.

Rice came to the same conclusion as Colver in leaning toward the Cubs of 1906–1910 as the greatest team ever. They won more games than any other team in a given five-year span, as well as four flags and two World Series. The Pirates of 1901–1903, Athletics of 1910–1914, and Boston Nationals of 1897–1898 may have been better in certain areas, but the Cubs had no weaknesses. The Yankees were grudgingly given consideration in "long-distance hitting," but many of the old timers believed that the players of earlier eras would have hit just as many long-distance blows if they played with the lively ball and thick-barreled bats and faced inferior pitching.[28]

I
THE BACKGROUND

We Live in a Marvelous Age

"I don't know how it is in this city of Los Angeles," Durant continued, "but in my city (New York) the attitude is one of cynicism and despair. To be in the swim you have to be a pessimist, and to be unpopular you have only to say you still believe in the progress of mankind."

—*Los Angeles Times*, January 8, 1928[1]

The Roaring Twenties is the subject of an enormous amount of literature and will doubtless continue to be an ongoing topic of study. The elimination of the age-old constraints of space and time was still being written about, especially with the great strides being made in aviation and communication during the latter portion of the decade. What was referred to as the "annihilation of space and time" began just after the Jacksonian Era, circa 1840, and extended into the pre–Civil War period with the railroad boom and the telegraph. The first fast-moving vehicle, three times as fast as the stagecoach, and the first means of electronic communication working in tandem, meant that for the first time in recorded human history it was no longer necessary for a person to physically carry a message to its recipient.[2] This development was a work in progress, witnessed and recounted by many as it occurred, as they continued to live and work in 1928.

Ed Barrow, one of the original architects of the Yankee dynasty, spanned the decades from the immediate post–Civil War era in 1868 to the nuclear age in 1953.[3] In his autobiography, Barrow described his own family's experiences as homesteaders around the time of his birth:

> Father planned to go on being a farmer, but not in Ohio. The war had uprooted him, and the young West beckoned. As soldiers who had

fought for the Union, my father and his brother were eligible for land grants in Nebraska of 160 acres each, and they decided to go out to work them. It was soon after he married my mother that they set off. They traveled West in four covered wagons, my father and mother, two of his sisters, his two brothers, and his mother. The horses pulled the wagons, and the cattle followed. It was a journey that lasted almost two years, the small wagon train moving slowly across country in the summer and laying up in the winter.[4]

From the kerosene-lit main street in his hometown just after the Civil War to the dawn of the space age, professional ballplayer, manager, and owner Connie Mack's life span from 1862 to 1956 allowed him to live through and experience the ever-quickening progress taking place.[5] From Mack's autobiography, *My 66 Years in the Big Leagues*, under the heading, *We Live in a Marvelous Age*:

> When I look around me and recall that I was here before most of our modern inventions, I begin to feel as old as Methuselah. I was here before the telephone, before electric lights, the talking machine, the typewriter, the automobile, motion pictures, the airplane, and long before the radio. I came when railroads and the telegraph were new. It was in my first year of professional baseball that somebody invented the fountain pen, and it was then that the first electric trolley cars began to run. I was playing with the Washington Senators when somebody invented the adding machine and photographic films. I was with the Pittsburgh Pirates when somebody invented photo engraving, and our newspapers first printed actual news photographs. Before that the only pictures we ever saw were old woodcuts or line drawings. It was quite a sensation to us when the horseless carriage came along. We were just starting to win pennants with our Philadelphia Athletics when the Wright brothers made their first successful flight in an airplane. It didn't create nearly so much excitement as our winning our first pennant. If anybody had suggested television to us then, we should have considered the person crazy.[6]

During the presidential election of 1928, the Republican nominee and then secretary of commerce, Herbert Hoover, opened his acceptance speech in Palo Alto, California, on August 11, on the theme of modernity:

> Mr. Chairman, you and your associates have in four days traveled three thousand miles across the continent to bring me this notice. I am reminded that . . . to notify George Washington of his election, Charles Thompson, secretary of the Congress, spent seven days on horseback to deliver that important intelligence 230 miles from New York to Mount Vernon. In another way, too, this occasion illuminates the milestones of progress. By

the magic of the radio this nomination was heard by millions of our fellow citizens, not seven days after its occurrence, nor even one minute.[7]

Hoover's acceptance speech from Palo Alto was broadcast over the largest radio chain ever; a total of 107 stations from throughout the country were expected to join together to carry his message. During the 1928 election, the main issues were prohibition, agnosticism and atheism, federal spending, our policy in Latin America, immigration, the causes of war, the struggling farm economy, labor relations, and managing our energy resources.[8]

MODERNIZATION

In an article entitled "America's Prosperity Reaches New Heights," published in the Sunday *New York Times* on November 27, 1927, Evans Clark described America's journey to modernity:

> The change is so vast, so difficult to reduce to comprehensive terms, that its implications—let alone its dimensions—are still undiscovered by the multitude. . . . The dividends of comfort and of culture are just as real, if more difficult to calculate, than the dividends of dollars that make them possible.[9]

It was, however, plain for everyone to see, even without super computers crunching reams of government data, the astounding expansion in use, and the ongoing development since the end of World War I to the eve of the Great Depression of the automobile, airplane, telecommunications, radio and motion pictures, electrification, and consumer credit. What is an afterthought today was just beginning to be taken for granted.[10]

According to the chairman of General Motors, the automobile was believed to be the basis of American prosperity, having surpassed the steel industry in volume in 1925. The industry's employment of 4 million people, together with their families, made up one-tenth of the country's population.[11]

The era of transocean flying had begun in 1927, with the first two transatlantic flights occurring within a month of one another during the spring.[12] The year 1927 was an important time in aviation, as records for speed, altitude, endurance, and distance were repeatedly broken. The output of planes for nonmilitary purposes would now account for the majority of production.[13]

Communication was also entering the teleconferencing age, as one scientist wrote in an article for the *New York Times* in April 1928:

> The spectacle of the officials of the Federal Reserve Bank, the Deutche Bank, the Banque de France, and the Bank of England traveling thousands

of miles to meet in New York or London will pass with other quaint and cumbrous customs of the early twentieth century. Even now it would be possible for twelve directors of a corporation in twelve widely separated parts of the country to hold a meeting in the New York office of the chairman of the board without leaving their desks.[14]

Consumers were holding off on buying radios in anticipation of the coming of television. Estimates of its availability ranged from within a year to twenty-five years. The televisions demonstrated at the radio show at Madison Square Garden later in the year were prototypes to excite the viewers. There was not yet a big enough screen and clear enough picture to make it feasible to sell. The latest technology in radios coming into the year was the house-current set, a unit you could plug into the wall for better reception rather than rely on batteries.[15]

At their annual spring sales conference in 1928, General Electric reported that in excess of 17 million homes were wired for electricity, and 4 million more were awaiting refrigeration. Since 1912, the number of customers paying for electricity outpaced the general growth in population by more than eighteen times.[16] By the middle of the decade, notable strides had been made in smaller towns and villages. It was believed that just about every community with a population between 1,000 and 5,000 people had electrical service, 50 percent of communities with a population between 250 and 1,000 had service, and 25 percent of communities with a population of 250 or less had electricity.[17]

More prosperity for a growing middle class meant a need for more financing. In November 1927, the National City Bank of New York, Citibank, became the first major bank to open a division specifically to make small, nonbusiness loans without collateral to consumers. It was approved by the attorney general of the state of New York since it was a much more desirable alternative to the evil tactics of loan sharks. All that was needed from the borrower was a list of assets, liabilities, and current employment. Six months into the program, the response was ten times greater than estimated, with five hundred, mostly new, customers on average per day applying for loans. The turnaround time for approval was usually only two to three days.[18]

To take advantage of the new options available, working people were just beginning to benefit from intangible things as well, including more time off from work and more affordable travel options. The number of people planning to get away from the workplace was increasing each year, using such resources as the Saving to Travel Association.[19] For their own reasons, more and more employers were supporting two days off for workers as a benefit to the private sector, since more leisure meant more consumer spending. The chairman of the Finance Committee for General Motors, John J. Raskob, along with Henry

Ford, predicted that electricity and inventions would give toilers two days off; in the case of most workers, these holidays would be Saturday and Sunday.[20]

The National Bureau of Economic Research estimated the total income of Americans at $90 billion, five times that of England, nine times that of Germany, thirteen times that of France, and twenty-two times that of Italy. From 1919 to 1926, income jumped 40 percent. Americans were also better off in real terms, as $2,500 just before the war was now worth $3,325, a 33 percent real increase in purchasing power. The world, especially Europe, devastated by the war and still trying to find a solid footing, watched the United States in awe. Factories were turning out goods about three and a half times greater than the growth of the population; however, the rising tide was not lifting all boats. U.S. agriculture was in a depression, and government employees, clerical workers, and unskilled laborers lagged behind in wages.[21]

The development of Wall Street did its part to keep pace with the increasing scale of business. This was the subject of a two-part series in the Sunday *New York Times* in April 1928, following a record-smashing March. The quality and quantity of finance had now dwarfed any attempt by any robber baron to dominate it. The aggregate market value of 1,097 traded companies was a little more than $45 billion, and the value of 1,490 bond issues was $37 billion. Companies now needed permanent legal departments following the great consolidations and battles with Congress earlier in the century. Investment trusts, the forerunner of the mutual fund, were introduced. There were more companies, with a declining proportion being railroads and many more investors. The branch offices of at least 80 percent of brokerage houses were now scattered throughout the country.[22]

There was now the ability to own stock in companies whose products were used on a daily basis. In a little less than thirty years, the number of shareholders of AT&T stock increased more than fifty-six times. Ten thousand dollars invested in General Motors ten years before had grown to $1.6 million, with dividends amounting to $292,880.[23]

THE GENERATION GAP

There was a definite awareness of the social, technological, religious, environmental, economic, and political trends taking place at the time. Issues within these categories were, in many instances, interrelated but always instantaneous. This was evident in a generation gap of sorts amongst the younger generation who would become the parents and grandparents of the hippies of the 1960s. Born around the turn of the century, their lives were divided almost in half between this country's fourth and fifth political party systems, from William McKinley to Franklin D. Roosevelt to Richard Nixon. Growing up, they witnessed four amendments to the U.S. Constitution, instituting the income tax, popular election of senators, prohibition, and women's suffrage.[24]

As adults living in a prolonged period of peace, prosperity, increasing free time, and technological progress, there was bound to be an effect on the popular culture. The radio, motion pictures, aviation, and the automobile, coupled with new opinions on acceptable social norms, gave rise to concern about loose morals, agnosticism, indifference to church, and companionate marriage. Just what kind of parents would the flappers make? The following is an excerpt from an article entitled "Youth's Questionnaire, Submitted to the Older Generation by the Intelligent Flapper and Her Boy Friends," from *Outlook Magazine* on May 30, 1928:

> We young people understand that we shock you elderly people by our candid disregard of established institutions [that] you revere. . . . Why should we take seriously a generation of adults whose combined wisdom the world over allowed the world to drift into what it became in 1914–1918, and what it has been since? Should we feel grateful to the generation that have saddled us with such enormous debts and taxes as a result of that war that, in America alone, more than two-thirds of the aggregate revenues collected by the Federal Government must be applied to liquidating the costs of past wars and present armaments?[25]

Another article, entitled "We Look at the Older Generation," by Helena Huntington Smith, came later in the year:

> A little while ago a friend of mine, watching her two-year-old son teetering around the room, was suddenly moved to speculate, "I wonder," she said, "what Geoffrey will be doing to shock his parents when he is our age." Later, because this had struck me as an entertaining angle of a very old question, I put it in reverse form to an attractive and discerning elderly lady of my acquaintance. "Can you look back to your twenties," I asked her, "and remember what were the chronic differences of opinion between you and your older relatives?" "We had them, of course," she replied. "But I can't remember any such startling differences as there are today. It seems to me the whole world has moved a hundred years in one generation."[26]

COMPANIONATE MARRIAGE

The institution of marriage was also undergoing scrutiny. Should companionate marriage or remaining single be acceptable? Many celebrities gave their opinions on this and other issues of the day. It was New York Yankees owner Jacob Ruppert's turn in the *New York Telegram* in a series of articles on the topic of bachelorhood in the summer of 1928. Betty Kirk informed her readers that Ruppert was a born bachelor, who, with a butler, maid, valet, cook, and laundress for his apartment alone, never felt a need for a wife:

> Lonesome? I don't have time! Besides, there are too many attractive girls in New York to ever allow a man to be lonesome. The city is full of them. The splendid thing is that the girls themselves prefer not to marry. They, too, value their freedom, which is the first thing that any married person gives up. I think that, one hundred years from now, there will be no marriages. The trend is toward that all the time, and it is right. The only way marriage can be a success is for the husband and wife to live separately and see each other only a few times a week.
>
> I've often been with married people who advise me to marry and tell me how happy they are together. . . . Then, invariably, when each of them gets me apart, they tell me not to believe a word of it, that marriage is a big failure.
>
> No girl is so charming as a married women. After marriage every wife gains in assurance and fascination. They're the most successful companions in the world—for the bachelors. But no matter how old and lonesome I get, I'll never get married. If it becomes necessary for me to find companionship I'll go to an old man's home.[27]

BASEBALL AND OTHER ORGANIZED SPORTS IN THE UNITED STATES

Organized sports and other forms of recreation were now growing and maturing businesses, with annual ticket purchases estimated at more than $200,000,000 for baseball, football, horse racing, and boxing. College football was estimated at $30 million, with 15 million paying customers. Baseball, the "best of America's organized sports," was calculated with a take of at least $50 million divided between the professional, semipro, and collegiate levels. Capital investment in new sports stadiums was also quite brisk.[28]

During spring training before the 1927 season, Jacob Ruppert discussed at length the game's progress at the major-league level during his twelve-year tenure as Yankees owner. Placing a value of $50 million on the sixteen big-league teams signified explosive growth, as well as genuine organic appreciation, since the two major leagues were completely static during this period. The Yankees were purchased for only $260,000, and none of the other teams outside of the Giants and Dodgers were thought, in Ruppert's view, to be worth more than $1 million at the time.[29]

Ruppert cited more leisure for all classes as an important factor, although there were no games played at night. He also mentioned that an investment in a star player, especially the more than $800,000 spent on Babe Ruth, would not have been possible twenty years before, when the game was not as popular. Ruppert believed that the caliber of play was much better, with more players taken from the college ranks, resulting in cleaner and more intelligent play, which had the effect of attracting more female fans to the games. The owner continued from an investment point of view, stating:

> The owners in baseball, too, have a different conception of the game. In former days, it very often happened that a man who could afford it and who liked the game bought an interest in a club as a whim to afford him some measure of pleasure and amusement. I confess that I entered baseball with much the same idea in mind. Then it dawned on me that baseball had wonderful possibilities. The business opportunity in it became apparent, and it wasn't long until I perceived that others had discovered the same thing and I knew that baseball was on the way to become a big industry. And it has. I still love the game for itself, but as a businessman I consider it a real industry. People speak of commercialized sports, but do so unthinkingly.
>
> Sports, baseball for one and probably as the best example, simply grew into big business because the people demanded it. We pay players high salaries. And why? Because the public demands the best, and the best always costs money. But, to my way of thinking, the commercial aspect is really a protection for the sport. You don't imagine for a minute, do you, that a man with a big investment in a baseball club, or eight or sixteen men and their partners with $50 million represented by their clubs, wittingly will permit anything crooked? Of course they won't. And you don't suppose that players who command big salaries, men like Ruth, Speaker, [and] Cobb are going to jeopardize their income by crookedness? No sir.[30]

Despite Ruppert's analysis, baseball, from time to time, had the perception that it was losing out to other sports. During spring training in 1928, incoming American League president Ernest Barnard, at the New Orleans base of the Cleveland Indians, on the final leg of his tour of his circuit's training camps, dispelled any concerns of a shortage of young recruits and the nation's youth defecting to the game of golf.[31] The golf industry was making sure it kept up with the times, marketing itself to the middle class and livening up the little white pill to where 250-yard drives were the norm and 500-foot drives were no longer unheard of.[32]

Barnard was not worried. He commented,

> Just go out to any golf course and toss a baseball and bat in amongst a bunch of caddies and see what happens. There is no use denying that

there has been a serious shortage of young ballplayers in the last few years, but that condition is nearly at an end. Another two seasons will see them coming up as fast as the major leagues can use them.[33]

He attributed the shortage to the war and the postwar industrial boom, which drew potential players to other higher-paying occupations, but that trend was reversing and baseball was beginning to look more profitable for young people. Barnard was encouraged by the American Legion's attempt to revitalize the game and estimated a pool of as many as 100,000 boys, of which a small percentage would supply the major leagues.[34]

During the winter before the 1928 baseball season, both major leagues voted a $50,000 fund to the American Legion. The first Junior World Series took place in 1926 but was abandoned the next year. The new infusion by the majors was an attempt to revive sandlot baseball and greatly expand the breadth of competition. Each of the 10,000 Legion posts in the country would field teams. Each state would have their own tournaments to decide the state champion, which would compete in six regional eastern and western competitions, followed by sectional and intersectional competitions, and finally a World Series.[35]

In a June 1928 interview for the "Baseball: Then and Now" column for the *Washington Post*, Ty Cobb said:

> Some writers try to tell us that golf and football and tennis have cut in on our game and are pressing it for honors as the "national pastime." I can't see it. Baseball is played throughout the country every day for six months, and more people are watching the game every year. It's increasing and not decreasing in popularity. The one time in my career when I went into the stands after a spectator was a few years ago, and only after his remarks became unbearable.[36]

For baseball, it was a matter of perception; the rising economy was lifting all recreation and entertainment boats. Baseball's popularity was not declining; other sports were by gaining a larger share of Americans' discretionary dollar. Business, for example, was very strong for A. G. Spalding, one of the country's premier sporting goods companies. The company reported another record year, ending October 1928 with sales of $26 million, which was an improvement in comparison with the $24 million of the previous year. Net profit was $1.8 million versus $1.33 million. They also had an unbroken dividend record for the past twenty-six years. In January 1929, the company declared a five-for-one stock split. Eighty percent of the products sold by the company in its stores came from its own factories.[37]

New York may have been the earliest version of a city claiming the title City of Champions. The Yankees won the World Series in 1927 and 1928; the Rangers won the Stanley Cup for the 1927–1928 season in the National Hockey League; the New York Original Celtics were champions of the American Basketball League that same year; and the football Giants were declared champions of the National Football League in 1927, with a late season victory over the Chicago Bears, while finishing the season with an 11–1 record.

The separation of the schedules for the four major team sports during the late 1920s was much more definite—and intentionally so. There was just a brief period from mid-November to mid-December when the two winter sports and football shared the stage. The New York football Giants began their 1927 season on September 25 and ended December 11. The National Hockey League's 1927–1928 season began November 15, with the Stanley Cup Finals ending on April 14. The American Basketball League began on November 19 and ended on March 26.

Baseball may have had an edge on football. An analysis in *Baseball Magazine* in January 1925 theorized that every fan of the gridiron was a baseball fan, but not every baseball fan followed football. Football rules committees were constantly changing rules, and, as a result, they were not absorbed by youth as easily as baseball rules. The demand for professional football though was somewhat underpinned by a curiosity amongst fans to see how the college stars would compete against one another if they continued their careers after graduation.[38]

Just after the Rangers clinched the Stanley Cup in 1928, Grover Theis wrote in the *New York Times*, "Though it came to New York two autumns ago, hockey has been received with favor, not only in this city, but in Chicago, Detroit, Pittsburgh, and Boston, where the arenas are crowded to capacity."[39] A good word for the game was written in the "Listening Post" column by Walter Trumble in late spring of 1928. Trumble states, "Hockey appears to have established itself firmly in this part of the country. The test of the game's hold on the fans is whether they talk of it in the off-season and we still hear enthusiasts conversing the Stanley Cup series and the glories of the Rangers."[40]

The increasing acceptance and appeal of the game of basketball at the institutional and amateur levels was important in developing basketball's future potential and staying power. There were several disjointed paid regional leagues during the first two decades of the twentieth century before the first national circuit, the American Basketball League, began in 1925.[41]

There were many who doubted the staying power of professional basketball, as described by John Kieran in January 1928:

One team in the "major league" professional basketball circuit has tossed in the sponge, which leads to the revival of the old query: "Is professional basketball strictly a small-town sport?" The Celtics are doing fairly well, at the Garden, but not well enough to carry the . . . league on their shoulders. Far from it. The Celtics have a great team, but, somehow, even such an outstanding basketball combination seems lost in such a big city.[42]

While professional football and basketball would be hindered by the amateur–professional barrier, baseball would remain firmly entrenched as the national pastime. Baseball was at the midpoint of its half-century of near-perfect stability. From 1903 through 1952, there were no additions, subtractions, or reorganizations in either major league, nor were their any relocations of teams to other cities. Major League Baseball consisted of sixteen teams in eleven cities, bound geographically to the District of Columbia in the Mid-Atlantic, Boston in the Northeast, and St. Louis in the West. These cities were in the top seventeen in population according to the 1930 census.

This is not to say that there were no stirrings for change. In 1926, there was talk of a third league that never made it much beyond the planning stage. Charters were supposedly already issued to teams in Pittsburgh, Cleveland, Detroit, and Baltimore, with Milwaukee, New York, Chicago, and Philadelphia competing for the final two positions. John McGraw estimated the cost of running a third eight-team league at $20 million, with stadiums at $12 million, administrative costs at $1 million, and $7 million for players' salaries.[43]

Since major-league teams only traveled long distance by rail, the schedule had to be structured a certain way if 154 games were to be played in just less than a six-month period. The eight teams in the American and National leagues were lumped together without any divisions. Each team played the other seven teams in its circuit twenty-two times, with no interleague play. The schedule was divided into sixty-six sectional or regional games and eighty-eight intersectional or interregional games. Individual series were not consistently structured strictly around the weekends, with two series scheduled during the work week, as is the case today. In addition, there was still a ban on Sunday baseball in effect in Philadelphia, Boston, and Pittsburgh.

An intersectional matchup was a team from a city on the East Coast— New York, Brooklyn, Philadelphia, Washington, and Boston—facing a team from one of the inland cities—Pittsburgh, Cleveland, Detroit, Cincinnati, Chicago, or St. Louis. Since each league had an even four-and-four sectional split, the schedule could be organized into a series of more or less half-month swings to minimize travel.

The American League was alternatively referred to as the junior circuit, since it was formed twenty-five years after the National League, the senior circuit. They were also named after their presidents, Ernest Barnard and John Heydler. Teams went by various nicknames: The Washington club went by the Nationals, Senators, or Griffs, after its president Calvin Griffith, or the Harrismen, after their manager Bucky Harris. The Athletics went also by the Macks, the Mackmen, or the Elephants. The Yankees went by the Hugmen, Ruppert's Rifles, or even the Manhattan Maulers. Although they played in the Bronx, they did not yet go by the Bronx Bombers. The Giants went by the McGrawmen, and Pittsburgh the Corsairs, the Bucs, or the Pirates.

• 2 •

One of the Best Cities in the Circuit

The one rumor which seemed to carry the most weight was that the new owners of the Yankees had come to an agreement with owner Joseph J. Lannin of the Boston Red Sox for a trade which would involve the transfer of one of the Boston left-handed pitchers to the Yankees. It is stated that the Yankees would probably get Vean Gregg, the former Cleveland southpaw, or Babe Ruth, the young pitcher who was a sensation with the Baltimore club early last season.

—*New York Times*, February 3, 1915[1]

With the first full generation of American League and National League baseball now complete, the Yankees were still a work in progress. The acquisition of Babe Ruth from the Boston Red Sox in January 1920 is what most people believe was the turning point that began the Yankees' long run of success. But the first building block occurred on New Year's Day 1915, with the transfer of ownership of the team to two men who were known as the Colonels. The prospective buyers of the team were Tillinghast L'Hommedieu Huston and Jacob Ruppert. Huston ran a successful engineering and construction company, while Ruppert assumed the reigns of his family's brewery.[2] Ruppert put it plainly:

I shall not start with a tail-end team and try to make a pennant winner out of it. I have made up my mind what to do if it is agreed to give me five new players and a manager. As to the Federal League proposition, I am not considering it at all. If I go into baseball, it will be with the Yankees.[3]

Another requirement was being allowed to lease the Polo Grounds for the first two years while constructing a new stadium in Manhattan.[4] Both

15

Huston and Ruppert were aware of the potential risks and enormous rewards ahead of them, as Ruppert explained:

> While we are convinced we will soon own the Yankees, there is no use of our taking over the franchise as matters now stand. As a matter of fact, we are being asked to pay considerable money out for merely the nucleus of a ball team that has no manager and is without a ballpark.
>
> We have insisted in these negotiations that we must get five more players and a manager before we would consent to take the franchise at the price named. New York is tired of having a losing club in the American League. It will be of benefit to the entire organization if we can produce a winner. We would be foolish, from our own point of view, to continue with a loser, and it would be equally foolish for the American League to longer permit conditions to exist as they have existed.[5]

The reported amount paid, $500,000, without a ballpark, was a record at the time.[6]

There was strong speculation with the dismantling of the Athletics that Connie Mack might be the next manager of the Yankees. Even after unloading four of its most highly paid stars, it was believed, with the team's lack of fan support, that their present cost structure could not be sustained. Mack was one of the highest-paid managers in the league and could possibly be succeeded by his understudy, Ira Thomas. Since Mack was a master at building teams, he was thought to be just the man to lead the Yankees and go head to head with John McGraw. It all proved to be a nonstarter, because just two years before, Mack had announced that he had become a half-owner with the Shibes of the Athletic team and Shibe Park.[7]

Both owners were in agreement and dead serious about building a championship team, but when they showed little progress during the next three years, playing at a .479 clip, with one fourth-place and two fifth-place finishes, a decision was made to fire Bill Donovan as manager after the 1917 season. Although the New York American League club had owners with deep pockets, they were still not making any inroads on the Giants.[8]

The process of choosing a new manager didn't go smoothly, but in the end, it would prove to be the second key building block. Huston wanted to hire his friend Wilbert Robinson, manager of the pennant-winning Brooklyn Dodgers, also referred to as the Robins, as manager, but, in 1917, Huston was away in France serving in the war effort. Ruppert leaned against bringing Robinson onboard and consulted Ban Johnson, who recommended the manager of the St. Louis Cardinals, Miller Huggins.[9]

In October, the conferences with Huggins led to a two-year contract. The agreement would remain a festering sore spot with Huston during his remaining tenure as owner. Johnson was elated, commenting,

Colonel Ruppert made the wisest possible selection when he picked Huggins for his manager out of the big field of eligibles for the position. I have known Huggins for a number of years and have admired him personally and as a baseball man. In St. Louis, he has got the most possible out of his material and has shown his ability to handle men. In New York, he will not be hampered by lack of funds, and he has learned by years of enforced economy how to make the most of the money placed at his disposal.[10]

Huggins would turn out to be a great choice, a classic "he'll never make it in the big leagues story." He began his major-league career with his hometown Cincinnati Reds, where he played second base from 1904 through the 1909 season. Before the 1910 season, he was traded to the Cardinals, where he was a player from 1910 through 1912, a player-manager from 1913 through 1916, and manger in 1917. It was reported that Huggins might be moved back to Cincinnati to manage and play for the Reds for the 1913 season, where current manager Hank O'Day had lost the respect of his players. The rumored trade would have sent Huggins and two other players to Cincinnati in return for seven Reds, a deal at which the Reds eventually balked.[11]

During his early years in St. Louis, the Cardinals were having issues with their current manager, Roger Bresnahan, who had the support of several of his players but wore out his welcome with the owners, the principle of whom was a woman. Bresnahan wanted to trade Huggins to the Reds, where he could enter the managerial ranks, for a promising outfielder named Mike Mitchell and give second base to Lee Magee, but Cardinals owner Helene Robison Britton nixed the deal. Her father, Frank Robison, passed away in 1908, but not before he handed the reins over to his brother Stanley in 1907. When Stanley died in March 1911, his niece, Britton, inherited the team.[12]

As widely anticipated, Britton fired Bresnahan after the 1912 season, during the fourth year of a five-year contract. Britton had wanted Huggins as pilot all along. In his first year as manager, the Cardinals won fifty-one games and lost ninety-nine, ending in last place. From 1914 through 1917, Huggins managed a .483 winning percentage, with a third-place finish, and a .539 winning percentage in his last year in St. Louis. Writing for *Baseball Magazine* in 1918, Al Munro Elias commented,

It is a fine record when one takes into consideration the conditions under which Huggins worked and the material he had at his disposal while with the Cardinals. Given an unlimited bankroll used in the purchase of players, it seems more than likely that Huggins may bring to New York its first American League pennant.[13]

Huggins turned down a generous offer from Branch Rickey to remain with the Cardinals, a reported $10,000 salary and 10 percent of the team's profits over $25,000. It was speculated that he signed a two-year deal with Ruppert for $12,000 per year.[14]

While the Yankees were at least spared being called the Robins, they would frequently be referred to in the press as the Hugmen. The new manager, himself, would be referred to in the press as the mite manager, the midget manager, Little Hug, or Little Miller.

Beginning his managerial career during the Deadball Era, Huggins emphasized all aspects of the game as being crucial to building a winner, especially a dominant pitcher in a short series. As a National Leaguer, he held John McGraw and the New York Giants as the standard of what a team should be.[15] But, as late as August during the 1927 season—with the Yankees a sure bet to win their fifth pennant—Huggins still failed to move the public the way John McGraw or Connie Mack had done. It would take Mack fifteen years to build another pennant winner after 1914, and McGraw had not won a pennant since 1924. It took Huggins just two years following the 1923 season to bring the Yankees back. The great sluggers of the Yankees overshadowed the manager who was content playing the hermit role.[16]

Skipping to the fourth significant move after the acquisition of Babe Ruth was the October 28, 1920, hiring of Red Sox field manager Ed Barrow as the team's business manager. When the Colonels' current business manager, Harry Sparrow, passed away in May 1920, there was a need to hire a replacement. Sparrow handled much of the grunt work that the two owners did not have the time to address or know how to take on, so they temporarily delegated his work to other employees.[17]

Barrow always had a talent for the administrative and organizational side of things, and growing up in the Midwest during the 1880s he became caught up in the growth of organized baseball.[18] He served in two capacities in a professional career that began in 1896 as manager and league president, serving as president of the Atlantic League in 1897 and 1898, and the Eastern League from 1911 through 1917, before managing the Red Sox in 1918 through the 1920 season. He also managed the Detroit Tigers in 1903, as well as various minor-league clubs. Under Barrow, the Red Sox won the World Series in 1918, followed by a sixth-place finish in 1919 and a fifth-place finish in 1920.

Barrow was featured in the *Sporting News* in early January 1928, after the Yankees' tremendous 1927 season, as one of the "Unsung Heroes of Baseball." According to Jim Nasium,

> Ed Barrow might have been rated a failure as a manager with the Boston Red Sox, and the reason is probably because his peculiar talent does not extend to the field of directing the strategy of play. But when it comes to

picking ballplayers, there is no keener or more accurate judge of playing talent in any man's league.[19]

The article gives Barrow much of the credit for giving the final "stamp of approval" to players like Gehrig, Combs, Lazzeri, Koenig, and Meusel, as well as the team's key reserve players.[20] The Yankees were still reaping dividends from trades it made with the Red Sox earlier in the decade. They were also getting tremendous production from players more recently signed in the open market from the minor leagues and college ranks.

Barrow's official title, business manager or secretary, was interchangeable, as listed by the Official Directory of Organized Baseball. They were the men, or woman, in the case of the Chicago Cubs, who acted as the bridge from the field manager to the owner or magnate, the forerunner of the modern general manager. The only team that used the official title of general manager at the time was the Cleveland Indians for Billy Evans.[21]

The final key development was the issue of dual ownership that had existed for eight years. It finally gave way in late 1922, following the Yankees' second straight loss to the Giants in the World Series, just prior to the winter meetings. If left to fester any longer, it would have profoundly changed the destiny of the team for the worse. Barrow was growing increasingly dissatisfied with working in an atmosphere of reporting to two feuding bosses and was seriously considering quitting the team.[22]

The New York papers tried to avoid any controversy and put as much of a happy face as possible on the eventual departure of Huston. "I'm old and tired," he told reporters in mid-December 1922. "The Yankees are a good team, and the stadium is nearly finished. It looks as if my work is about done."[23]

Ruppert attempted to smooth things over the next day, stating the following:

> We have had no serious trouble in our seven years together. Naturally, there have been arguments about certain points: Partners never agree absolutely. But Colonel Huston and I have got along splendidly. He simply wants to retire and enjoy himself, believing that he has reached the point where such an action would be most profitable. He has talked of going abroad, and also of devoting himself to other phases of his business.[24]

The market value of the Yankee team at the time of Huston's exit, without the stadium, was estimated at $3 million, with the stadium portion still mostly outstanding. Once constructed, it was believed that the value of the organization could rise to $5 million.[25]

In May 1923, Ruppert announced his $1.25 million buyout of his partner, who felt that the offer was too enticing but that he still had a moral interest in the Yankees. "In justice to myself, and family, I had to accept," said Huston. "Anyway, I wanted to take a rest. I've done a lot of work in my time, and I was beginning to get tired." Huston planned a trip to Hot Springs, Arkansas, followed by a tour of California with his family.[26]

The job of Miller Huggins became easier when Ruppert became sole owner. The only major trouble was the row with the Babe during the 1925 season, after which Ruth began to develop an appreciation for his manager.[27] The Yankee brain trust, and now stable front office, owner Jacob Ruppert, business manager Ed Barrow, and field manager Miller Huggins, would engineer the fundamental trades and signings of the Yankee players who would win on the field for the next decade. It would launch the great Yankee dynasty.

Much, if not all, of the credit for the great Yankee teams of the early 1920s, the first pennant three-peat, was accomplished via the trade and cash route courtesy of Harry Frazee and the Boston Red Sox. There would be seven transactions in all from July 1919 to January 1923, involving nine key players, six pitchers, and three everyday players that would cumulatively add to the team's success throughout the decade.

Five of the nine players acquired by the Yankees—Babe Ruth, Waite Hoyt, Joe Dugan, George Pipgras, and Herb Pennock—were still major contributors at the end of the decade. The second transaction, the big one, of course, was a January 3, 1920, New Year's gift in George Herman Ruth. On December 15, 1920, the Yankees acquired Waite Hoyt in a four-for-four deal described by the *New York Times* as "even-steven." The *Times* also describes the Yankee skipper as being "highly elated."[28] The pitching-conscious Miller Huggins particularly coveted the Brooklyn-born Hoyt as the key man in the trade.

Midway through the 1922 season, on July 23, the Yankees also acquired Joe Dugan and Elmer Smith from Boston for four players and cash. Dugan, originally with the Athletics, was unhappy in Boston, but he was a highly regarded infielder and much coveted by the Yankees. This was a timely arrival due to an injury to Frank Baker at third base.[29]

The following year rang in with the team acquiring Red Sox pitching prospect George Pipgras and outfielder Harvey Hendrick for third-string catching prospect Al DeVormer. Four weeks later, on January 30, deal number seven was consummated in the person of veteran left-hander Herb Pennock, the last player of the champion Red Sox team of 1918. This trade was questioned at the time, with the Yankees giving up three promising young players: Norman McMillan, an infielder; Camp Skinner, an outfielder; and George Murray, a pitcher.[30]

The other significant route of player procurement was the purchase of talent from minor-league teams. Manager Huggins became convinced about

Bob Meusel, a star with Vernon of the Pacific Coast League, during a trip to California in the winter following the 1919 season. By word of mouth from other Pacific Coast League players, and through conversations with Meusel, the skipper was anxious to see what he could do for the Yankees.[31]

The Yankees were also willing to go the college route with the signing of Lou Gehrig of Columbia and Mike Gazella of Lafayette. Gazella was more noted as a star football player, but he hit over .400 on the diamond. Gehrig, a pitcher and first baseman, and a sophomore at the time of the announcement, had a .440 batting average and a 6–3 record on the mound. He was regarded as the "Babe Ruth of the colleges," hitting several tape-measure home runs and being labeled the "best college player since George Sisler." College players were always a "pet peeve" of Huggins, who credited Gehrig's blossoming to the two years of seasoning acquired at Hartford of the Eastern League.[32]

On January 6, 1924, the *New York Times* reported that the New York Giants won an expensive bidding war for Wayland Dean, star pitcher for Louisville of the American Association, a Class AA minor league. The Yankees and Reds, and possibly the Robins and Indians, were some of the teams outbid by the Giants. The Yankees reportedly wanted Dean the previous summer; however, another sought-after star on the Louisville club was an outfielder named Earle Combs. Combs batted .344 and .380 in two seasons for Louisville. The article reports that the Reds were close to paying $150,000 for both players, while the Yankees offered four players, but not enough cash. With Dean gone to the Giants, the Yankees won the bidding for Combs. The reported prices paid for both players by the New York teams, believed to be $50,000 each, would have shattered all records for player sales from the American Association. The Yankees also sent two players to Louisville.[33]

Yankees owner Jacob Ruppert told the press that the Yankees were building for the future, but that Combs might make an immediate impact this spring. The Yankees also denied that Dean was their main man; it was actually Combs whom they had originally scouted last spring. He had a spectacular year for Louisville in 1923, batting .380, with a league-leading 241 hits, including 40 doubles, 15 triples, and 14 homers. In 1922, he homered off of Al Mamaux of the Brooklyn Robins during an exhibition game, raising some eyebrows. The future Hall of Famer immediately impressed Huggins during spring training that year.[34]

Some of the best trades that the Yankees made were the ones that never happened. The Yankees coveted thirty-six-year-old second baseman and future Hall of Famer Eddie Collins from the White Sox before the 1923 season and were willing to part with youngsters Bob Meusel and Aaron Ward, but the White Sox insisted on Waite Hoyt, who was a nineteen-game winner the previous two years. Huggins refused, and the deal was off.[35]

The next year, the trade was revived. The Yankees were now willing to part with Hoyt and Meusel, only now the White Sox changed their mind and insisted on twenty-six-year-old second baseman Aaron Ward. Ward hit 10 homers and drove in 82 runs, with a batting average of .284 in that first championship season of 1923. The Yankees considered him untouchable, and the deal was off again.[36] As it turned out, Ward's production would tail off during the next three years, and he would eventually be traded to the White Sox in 1927, in a less-publicized trade, while Collins was at the end of his long career, with his last great season coming in 1926. Meusel and Hoyt would go on to star and make huge contributions to the Yankees' back-to-back championship teams in 1927 and 1928, with Hoyt winning 45 games and Meusel driving in more than 200 runs and batting well over .300.

While the Yankees, as of the 2013 season, have won nearly one-quarter of all World Series and more than a third of all American League pennants, the three other teams that figured prominently during the 1928 season, the Cardinals, Giants, and Athletics, have accounted for the second and fourth most World Series appearances.[37]

Three of the game's great architects, all Hall of Fame inductees—Branch Rickey, Connie Mack, and John McGraw—were active participants in 1928. Branch Rickey was Ed Barrow's equivalent in the National League with the St. Louis Cardinals, with the more distinguished title of vice president and business manager.

Connie Mack was part-owner, treasurer, business manager, and field manager of the Philadelphia Athletics, and John McGraw vice president and field manager of the New York Giants. Both would be runners-up in the American League and National League.[38] The Cards, Giants, and Athletics, along with the Yankees, won nearly half of all the World Series and represent 42 percent of all pennant winners as of 2013.

The Cardinals, under Branch Rickey's guidance as president since 1917, were eight years into a process of building a full-fledged modern-day farm system, a system that was derogatorily known at the time as baseball's version of a chain store. While Ed Barrow had Jacob Ruppert, Branch Rickey had Sam Breadon, the eventual majority owner of the Cardinals. Under their leadership, using the chain system as a means of player procurement, the Cardinals' financial situation would markedly improve throughout the coming decades.[39]

With the efficacy of the chain-store system still a controversial subject and not officially sanctioned by baseball, the Cardinal organization did not overpublicize their investments, but, in the September 17, 1928, edition of the *New York Evening Post*, Hugh Bradley estimates the club's portfolio of teams as consisting of some 205 players in seven different farm teams.[40]

Miller Huggins was actually in favor of chaining and drew an analogy to what was taking place in industry and manufacturing. "Look at Henry Ford," said Huggins in December 1927. "How can Henry Ford produce a good car so cheaply? Because he owns the raw materials that go into the car. He owns iron mines and coal mines and steel works and a railroad, ore boats and what not. He had found out that to buy steel and coal and transportation from other companies was too expensive if he wanted to get out the lowest-priced automobile possible."[41]

Yankees owner Jacob Ruppert was not necessarily in favor of the chain-store system for baseball. The team was still reaping dividends from its trades with the Red Sox earlier in the decade and getting tremendous production from players acquired subsequently in the open market from the minor leagues and college ranks. He did not like the idea of buying minor-league clubs and taking their players late in the season, while they were in a pennant race, to help the Yankees. He believed this would hurt the greater good of the game. But Ruppert eventually warmed to the idea after realizing the mistake he and the other owners had made in signing an agreement with the minor leagues in 1921, allowing major-league teams only eight optional players after June 15. This cut the maximum number of players a team could control from forty to thirty-three, with twenty-five being regular roster players. Seven players representing an investment by the owners went into limbo at the June 15 deadline, as Ruppert explained to John Kieran in an interview in May 1929. [42]

Ed Barrow was not yet convinced of the need to either own or control a chain of minor-league clubs, and he remained cool to the idea when writing his autobiography in 1951,

> I don't favor the elaborate farm systems, the so-called chain-store baseball, as a means of building winning teams, although I have had success with both the farm system and the opposite free-enterprise system of buying the player you need, when you need him, in the open market. You can't win pennants with a farm system alone.[43]

The four-year span through 1926 was a period of unprecedented turn-over in the managerial ranks of Major League Baseball. The climax came before the 1926 season, when eight of sixteen helmsmen were replaced. Only the three New York-area managers and Connie Mack remained with the same teams.[44] Mack was in his mid-sixties, and John McGraw his mid-fifties. Although the former would go on to manage for a few more decades and the latter five more seasons, there was talk of, and a sentimental push for, one last pennant for both in anticipation of the two being at the end of their careers.

Both the Athletics and Giants were in a multiyear process of ramping up their payrolls, but paying promising minor leaguers, aging veterans, and current stars cost money and was squeezing many owners. Mack had been the Athletics' manager since 1901, and McGraw had been with the Giants as manager and a part-time player since 1903. Both baseball careers went back further as players to the late 1800s. Mack had a "lifelong knack of making people like him," which wasn't the case with McGraw, but both men had established extensive connections and contacts in baseball circles and developed a keen ability and respect for judging, coaching, and motivating players.[45]

Mack, who went by a trio of sobriquets—the tall tutor, the tall tactician, and the lean-leader—was striving to make the 1927 season the most successful one yet. He said the following on his sixty-fourth birthday, on December 22, 1926:

> I am aiming to make my sixty-fifth birthday a real birthday. I mean that I want to win the pennant next year. There won't be a single thing left undone to make next year the big year. We planned hard and tried our utmost the last two years, but next year we'll beat our utmost. Sixty-four birthdays are a lot of birthdays, but I want the sixty-fifth to be the finest of them all.[46]

The Athletics had been amongst the most well-balanced teams in the American League since 1923. Going into the 1927 and 1928 seasons, there was not much concern about having too many former managers on the club, as Ty Cobb's managerial ambitions seemed to be through, and Eddie Collins was not expected to cause any dissension.[47]

II

THE OFFSEASON
AND SPRING TRAINING

• 3 •

The Trade Embargo and
Baseball's Winter Meetings

He had been a baseball czar so long that he resented the new
czar, who had far greater powers than he ever had. He clashed
repeatedly with the new commissioner; the breach widened with
the years, until it became a case of Johnson or Landis. It ended
with the American Leaguer, crushed, beaten, and in ill health,
being forced from his post in 1927.

—Frederick G. Lieb, *The Baseball Story*[1]

The Yankees won the 1927 World Series after a wild pitch by John Miljus
in the bottom of the ninth inning of Game 4. The Pittsburgh pitcher was
overcome with grief following the game. He lamented, "Any other way but
that, any way at all but that way. A drive over the fence, a hit of any kind,
anything at all but that way." It was the first clean sweep since 1914, the third
overall, and the first with all four starting pitchers victorious.[2]

The sweep was a satisfying bookend for the embodiment of the American League. Ban Johnson cabled the following to Miller Huggins: "Hearty
congratulations to you, Manager Huggins, and the players. We like to destroy
the enemy in that manner. Four straight victories will have a wholesome effect upon the public mind and strengthen the position of professional ball."[3]

This was the first time a team from the Johnson circuit was able to win
in a sweep. The Cubs whitewashed the Tigers in 1907, and the Braves beat
the Athletics in four games in 1914. The Giant's four-game sweep of the
Yankees in 1922 included a game that ended in a tie.

The heretical Wilbert Robinson threw in his own critique, saying,

After my club got through with the Pirates, they weren't any good against
the Giants or the Yankees. Petty lost the first game of that last series in

27

Pittsburgh, 2 to 1, and we should have won. We took the next two, and we really won the last one, only the umpire was blind to a force at second base. I saw how that Pittsburgh club was going and I said to myself, "These birds aren't in shape to play the Yankees. They're going to be mauled." Well, I went out and said what I thought.[4]

Robinson was criticized for downgrading the National League when he stated, "What's the sense of kidding the public? The Pirates didn't fit, that's all. A great club, but not at the finish. Say, we would have made a better fight against the Yankees. Vance and Petty would have taken two, anyway."[5]

Jacob Ruppert wanted the Yankees to win every game decisively and win the World Series for at least the next ten years. He commented,

What kind of game do I like best? That's easy. I like those games when the Yankees win by seven and eight runs, when they score four or five times right away and the outcome is never in doubt. You keep those 2 to 1 and 1 to 0 games and those pitchers' battles. I don't want 'em even when we win them. The excitement is too much for me.[6]

The Colonel was frequently seen leaving games that went into extra innings. With the Yankees up three games to nothing against the Pirates, Ruppert could care less about the $100,000 that would have to be refunded if the Yankees closed out the series. He said, "They'll break my heart if they lose. I'd rather have the honor of owning a team that is good enough to beat a National League champion four straight games than all the money in baseball."[7]

The three previous series had gone seven games, and the 1923 series took six games; that year the gate receipts eclipsed $1 million. The joy the Colonel displayed about winning instead of the paltry $700,000 in proceeds and the original estimated sum of $100,000 he had to refund astounded many.[8] Ed Barrow took the same approach as his boss, saying,

Yes, we're giving it back—and much as I dislike refunds in a general way, it was a great thing for baseball, for the Yankees, for everybody concerned that we had no fifth game, and that we must give back thousands and thousands of dollars. Yes, over $150,000 going back, back to where it came from.[9]

Immediately following the series, as most of the team headed homeward, the twin sluggers, Babe Ruth and Lou Gehrig, went on a three-week, nineteen-state, countrywide barnstorming tour. Obliterating all previous records, the circuit covered 8,000 miles, 220,000 people. and 5,000 autographed baseballs. A total of twenty-one games were started and thirteen finished, with the highlight coming in front of a crowd of 30,000 in Los Angeles. Players were not allowed to barnstorm with the official team laundry. They performed as the Bustin Babes and Larrapin Lous. Notwithstanding, the Yankee brand name was born.[10]

Eight of the eleven All-Stars picked, including three pitchers, were from New York and Chicago; there was one Athletic and two Pirates. The National Leaguers outnumbered the American Leaguers six to five. Babe Ruth, Al Simmons, and Paul Waner were the outfielders. The infield selections were Lou Gehrig, Rogers Hornsby, Travis Jackson, and Pie Traynor. The catcher was Gabby Hartnett, and the pitchers were Herb Pennock, Charlie Root, and Ted Lyons.[11]

Barely two months after the Yankees made quick work of the Pirates, during the heart of the holiday shopping season, the genesis of a new season began. Major League Baseball's annual winter meetings were scheduled to open in New York City during the week of December 11. For the first time in recent memory, just less than a decade to be exact, the meetings were expected to be fairly mundane, due in no small part to the fact that the combative founder and only president the American League ever had known was gone, and with that the bane of Kenesaw Landis, the commissioner of baseball. The condition and administrative apparatus of baseball on the eve of the 1930s was not the same as when Ban Johnson founded the American League at the turn of the century.[12]

From the start, Johnson was a strong-minded entrepreneur and businessman who was just the right person to play hardball with the National League in the increasingly complex world of professional baseball. As the game began to stabilize and individual team owners began to prosper following the Federal League war and World War I, a dictatorial style was no longer necessary or even feasible. Basically ousted by his fellow owners and in failing health, Johnson submitted his resignation during the July league meetings in 1927, to be effective November 1, 1927.[13]

Ernest Barnard would be formally installed as the new president of the American League. Like his predecessor, he worked as a sports editor for a newspaper, the *Columbus Dispatch*, in the Midwest, and later as president of a minor-league circuit, the Western Association. Barnard then worked his way from secretary of the Cleveland Indians in 1903, to team president for six years. His contract as the new president had a term of three years.[14]

The fifty-three-year-old Barnard, although not a rubber stamp, would in no way clash and feud as Johnson did with the commissioner and other league owners. He was, however, an admirer of the league's founder and paid tribute to his accomplishments:

The American League has a rich inheritance in the high ideals created for it by a great leader, and the organization must keep these ideals constantly in mind as a guide in the successful conduct of its affairs. The rise of the American League from a humble beginning to its present strength and affluence has been largely due to Mr. Johnson's demand for clean, sportsmanlike conduct on the playing field and his vigorous handling of every situation that menaced the integrity of the sport.[15]

The Yankee run since 1920 was eight years old and, checking the histories of the past great teams, should have about run its course. On January 15, the *Los Angeles Times* reported that Howard Ehmke of the Philadelphia Athletics predicted that the Yankees would "crumble in 1928 and won't repeat," and he also said that, "great teams have been known to crumble and fall by the wayside . . . the old Athletic machine rated as one of the best slipped out of the picture in 1914."[16] There was, however, some concern throughout the league as to just which team or teams had the capability of challenging the Yankees, who had by now become too well entrenched as "one of the best cities in the circuit."

Connie Mack was constantly reminded of his 1912 club and was predicting that the same fate would affect the Yankees. He commented on these feelings, stating the following:

I have a feeling the Yankees won't win this year, in spite of the fact that on paper and past performances they unquestionably are the class of the league. If we don't beat them, either Washington or Detroit will. Somehow it's dangerous to make any team a standout favorite to win. Usually something happens between April and October to upset the dope.[17]

They would remain the team to beat in 1928, not just because of how they dominated the year before, but because the team's nucleus was still intact and in their prime. Babe Ruth, although slowing down at thirty-three years of age, still had 298 home runs left in his bat, and the careers of Lou Gehrig, Mark Koenig, and Tony Lazzeri were just getting started, while Earle Combs and Bob Meusel, at twenty-nine and thirty-one years of age, respectively, were the oldest of the other regular, everyday players. They were a team of young, tested veterans. The Colonel did not appear to have the same problem with nonattendance from his home crowd as Connie Mack had with his last great Athletic club. This was not attributed to Babe Ruth or the transient population of New York, but to the variety of their stars and the multitude of ways in which they won.[18]

Miller Huggins had just arrived in New York from minor-league meetings in Dallas, where he had made a deal for Bill Dickey from the Cotton States League. Huggins was under no illusions that any teams in the American League were willing to make his club any stronger. Nonetheless, the

Yankees were in the market for a top-notch pitcher, either George Earnshaw of the minor league Baltimore Orioles, Red Ruffing of the Red Sox, Ted Lyons of the White Sox, or George Uhle or Willis Hudlin of the Indians. The skipper was also asked about third base, to which he replied, "I may have talked about an infielder, but really I have given no thought to third base or any other position. I may shift my attention once I get that pitcher. But just now every effort is directed toward the hurler."[19] Huggins further explained his strategy as the major-league meetings got set to begin:

> I have a strong pitching staff. Hoyt, Pennock, Moore, and Pipgras make a fine quartet, and then there is Shocker, whom I have no intention of letting go unless somebody makes a good offer for him. But we must have another good hurler.
>
> Incidentally, I want to say that I have received flattering cash offers for many of my extra players, but we will not sell a man. If we let a player go, it will have to be in a deal. I have no desire to play Santa Claus to any other club. I do want to win five pennants in a row—at least five. Colonel Ruppert wants to score ten straight, but I expect the law of averages will knock us over before we reach number five.
>
> However, we will make every effort to keep the playing strength of the Yankees well above that of any other club in baseball. That's why I want another dependable pitcher. And that is why we are hot after Lyn Lary and Jimmy Reese of the Oakland club, for whom we have offered almost a fabulous sum. A pitcher like Uhle would help us a lot and would lift the strain off the effort to rush young hurlers. Uhle would come back strong with us. He still is quite a pitcher. There isn't a chance to get Hudlin away from Cleveland. I am very much interested in Ruffing, about whom I will see Bob Quinn and Bill Carrigan here on Monday.
>
> I think we have the players who will strengthen the Red Sox. There are other pitchers about whom I have had conversations, but it would not be fair to talk about them. There is such a thing as "tipping your mitt." In my effort to get a pitcher or two I have presented the names of two infielders, two pitchers, an outfielder, and a catcher. Who are they? Well, here again, you will have to dope the thing for yourself.[20]

The players the Yankees were using as bait were thought to be pitchers Myles Thomas, Joe Giard, and possibly Shocker; Ray Morehart and Mike Gazella were the infielders; Ben Paschal was the outfielder; and Pat Collins the catcher[21]; however, Bob Quinn, president of the Red Sox, would rule out trading Red Ruffing to the Yankees for benchwarmers. And Roger Peckinpaugh and Billy Evans of the Indians all but ruled out trading either Uhle or Hudlin to the Yankees. Huggins did not think anything would come of his conversations with Harry Grabiner of the White Sox for Lyons. He also failed to acquire Earnshaw while in Dallas and felt that he would certainly end up being sold to the Athletics.[22]

Huggins knew that acquiring a top-notch pitcher was a long shot, as he explained as the meetings concluded:

> I am told there is an embargo on trading with the Yankees. Well, it looks that way, doesn't it? But, do you see me crying? I have seen statements that this and that manager will not trade with me for benchwarmers. I have made no definite propositions to anybody. I have asked Carrigan if he would trade Ruffing. I have asked about other pitchers. But I have offered no benchwarmers. I have offered nobody. I do not like to be taken for a sucker, and I never try to make the other fellow out to be a sucker. I just have asked around, seeking information. Maybe I don't need anybody else.[23]

"I will not consent to a policy of standing pat or of reduction of Yankee armaments," complained Huggins. "We developed a club, and it is possible for others to do likewise. Let them take their chances on young players, go into the market for them, and rebuild instead of asking for help inside the league."[24]

The Yankee skipper knew he had a star in Lou Gehrig when he came out of Columbia. He took a flyer on Tony Lazzeri from Salt Lake City for $55,000 when other teams refused. Mark Koenig was well worth the $30,000 paid out by the Yankees. Meusel cost $30,000 from Vernon in the Pacific Coast League, and Earle Combs $25,000 from Louisville.[25]

The manager also discussed rumors that coach Art Fletcher was offered the managerial job with the Indians, stating,

> In so far as I personally am concerned, in so far as the New York club is concerned, there is nothing to the report that Arthur Fletcher is to leave the Yankees to become manger of the Cleveland Indians.
>
> I broached the subject of my telling him that if Cleveland did want Fletcher we would not stand in Art's way, but Evans did not indicate that Cleveland was interested in Fletcher. Arthur is a valuable man for us, and I would hate to lose him. But if he could advance himself, I certainly would not hold him back.[26]

He would also ultimately be correct in his belief that Roger Peckinpaugh would be the next manager of the Indians.

Huggins needed a lieutenant, or coach, following the club's loss to the Cardinals in the 1926 World Series. Many felt that the Yankees were one step behind the Cardinals and had lost some aggressiveness from the last western swing of the 1926 season. With only Huggins and his other assistant,

Charley O'Leary, James R. Harrison described the Yankee bench as "long on strategy but short on noise".[27]

Huggins first looked to former John McGraw understudies Hooks Wiltse and Fred Merkle but settled on another McGrawite, Fletcher. The purpose was to instill a fighting spirit in the Yankees. The move was lauded throughout baseball, as Fletcher was widely respected and recommended for two other managerial positions. The *Sporting News* described his job as "that of a fireman chucking coal into the furnace of a locomotive."[28]

With the exception of one blockbuster trade between the Tigers and Browns, the meetings were, indeed, uneventful. Both of these clubs believed that they needed an overhaul, and, on December 27, the Tigers traded Lu Blue and Heinie Manush to the St. Louis Browns for outfielder Harry Rice, infielder Chick Galloway, and pitcher Elam Vangilder.[29]

In late January, the *Sporting News* reported that the incoming president was reassuring the rest of the American League that they need not fear another runaway:

> The potential strength of the Yankees had not weakened the morale of the other clubs, but rather strengthened their ability to build up. The American League is fortunate in having the most aggressive ownership of its eight clubs in its entire history. If Colonel Ruppert and Miller Huggins can keep the Yankees up to their standard of the past two seasons, the American League is destined to give its patrons some great baseball, as the other clubs in the organization are determined to build up to the Yankees.[30]

The Yankees raised a firestorm just a few weeks before the *Sporting News* printed Barnard's comments. They outbid a few of the "other clubs in the organization," and the National League, by announcing the purchase of Lyn Lary and Jimmy Reese from Oakland of the Pacific Coast League, as well as Gene Robertson from St. Paul. The purchase price was $125,000 plus three players with a value of $30,000. A payment of $50,000 was to be made up front, with the balance due when the players reported. There was a provision in the contract with the Oaks that either player could report to the Yankees if any of the regulars were injured. Oakland wanted to sell the players together and turned down offers from the Cubs and Tigers for Lary and Reese alone. William Wrigley of the Cubs then offered $150,000 for the two stars but wanted the players to report immediately.[31] By selling the pair to the Yankees for delivery in 1929, the Oakland club had them for one more year.

These were three of the five most sought-after infield prospects in the minors. The two Chicago teams claimed the other two prospects, with the

White Sox paying a then-record $123,000 in November to the Portland team for Chalmer Cissell, while the Cubs purchased Freddy Maguire.[32]

Lazzeri and Koenig were both only twenty-three years old, and this raised concerns that a precedent was being set. Mainly due to money considerations, teams typically bid on minor-league talent to fill a current need on a major-league roster, not to stockpile players for future use or use as trade bait. It was hoped that the newly purchased Robertson would provide competition for Joe Dugan at third base, while still shopping the latter for George Burns.

In an interview in late December 1927, the Colonel explained his own ten-year plan:

> I think that, as the Yankees stand, with the possible exception of the pitching staff, they are good for five years more. Most of the players are youngsters. But much as I admire the efficiency of the team and much as I feel that they will be supreme for some time, I am not blind to the fact that ball teams have a habit of running down quickly, and I want the championship for at least ten years. That is the reason for my keeping my scouting staff at its highest efficiency.
>
> We lost Willis Hudlin to Cleveland by drawing the financial line a bit too fine. We passed up Paul Waner for a similar reason.
>
> But I am frank to say that I have adopted a new policy. The fans here want and are entitled to the best, and if it is possible to give it to them through a generous policy, I will do so. You cannot play ball entirely with what you have in the field. You must give the club ample protection, money and lots of it. Persistent reports to the contrary notwithstanding, we have not yet landed Lary and Reese. But I want to say that nobody is going to outbid us for the pair. They are coming to the Yankees.[33]

Huggins backed up his boss, stating,

> Of course, Koenig and Lazzeri look as if they would be good for many years to come. They are the youngest ballplayers on our club. But it was a good buy, nevertheless. Suppose Lyn and Reese should prove to be as good as we expect them to be. Think of the wonderful trading material we would have.[34]

The issue of stockpiling players for future use by a major-league club segued into the emerging reality of big-league ownership of minor-league teams within an officially recognized farm system for baseball. The issue of whether major-league teams should be allowed to own a chain of minor-league teams was reaching a climax during the late 1920s.[35]

Miller Huggins arrived back in New York from St. Petersburg, Florida, in late January to do a little hunting upstate. He then attended a meeting of baseball writers in New York on February 5. This was an annual event held before the teams departed for spring training. A pariah during any trade talks, he did not even bother to attend the American League meetings in Chicago on the Wednesday following the meeting, instead heading back to St. Petersburg to meet his players.[36] He narrowed his concerns to a reserve first baseman:

> My only worry is the infield. I want a first baseman to relieve Gehrig if Lou should get hurt. George Burns of the Indians is the man I have in mind. If the Indians can get Joe Judge from the Senators, Burns will be on the market, and I would like to have him.
>
> You may find it surprising that I want to strengthen such a strong position as first base, but my theory is that a ball club needs the most protection in its strongest places. What's the sense of reinforcing a spot that is already none too strong? If Ruth or Gehrig should be injured or get sick, it would be a very serious blow. I want the strongest understudies possible for them, and that's why I would like to get Burns.
>
> The rest of the infield I am not worried about. Gazella, Wera, and our new man, Durocher, will bolster up the other positions, with either Robertson or Dugan as additional help. I am going to keep both Durst and Paschal in the outfield. The pitching staff is okay, and I have no worries as to the catching. But I don't think the Yanks are going to have a runaway race of it. The Senators and Athletics will give us the strongest opposition. Connie Mack has a strong team; his southpaws, Grove and Walberg, are the best pair of wonders. The Senators have strengthened themselves considerably.[37]

The last two weekends of February were busy ones for the railroads as the teams that were headed south packed their bags and began the first leg of a new season. Five players led the first Yankee delegation, accompanied by even more newspapermen. The thumping twins, as Ruth and Gehrig were known, were among the quintet of players. Following were rookie infielder Leo Durocher, catcher Johnny Grabowski, and catching prospect Bill Eisemann.[38]

It rained for practically the entire trip southward. Part of the first contingent was expected to arrive in St. Petersburg on February 26. Naturally, Ruth and Gehrig were the players everyone wanted to talk to. "I'm just learning what it's all about," said Gehrig. "I'm still young, and I ought to improve steadily for the next three of four years at least. If Ruth hits sixty-one this year I'll be right up there close behind him, and we'll breeze in by almost as big a margin as last year, too."[39]

"I hope to crack out sixty-one home runs this season," said Ruth, "and I see no reason why I shouldn't do it. With Gehrig following me at the bat, most of the intentional pass stuff is eliminated, and as long as pitchers will pitch to me, I see no reason why I shouldn't break my record."[40]

Crescent Lake Park and the Trek North

They (the Yankees) are doing everything wrong, and they seem
to take no interest in the game. They look like the Phillies in late
September, and they try about that hard to win.

—Pat Robinson on the poor preseason record of
the Yankees, *New York Telegram*, March 29, 1928[1]

The Yankees had only five unsigned players as of the second week of February, of whom pitchers Waite Hoyt and Urban Shocker and second baseman Tony Lazzeri were of most concern. In January, Lou Gehrig signed a three-year total package believed to be worth $25,000 per year, nearly tripling his salary from 1927 of around $8,000. The Colonel would have liked to keep the terms of the contract a secret, but the news leaked out. With Earle Combs believed to have come to terms, and assuming Tony Lazzeri would sign, the Yankees' everyday lineup and reserve strength would remain intact.[2]

The Colonel had a much tougher time signing his stars before the 1927 season, when as many as sixteen players were holdouts as of late February.[3] Outfielders Babe Ruth, Earle Combs, and Bob Meusel, as well as pitchers Herb Pennock and Urban Shocker, held out until March before signing contracts. Ruth signed for three years at $70,000 per year. He had originally wanted a two-year contract at $100,000 per year. At the time it was believed that no one on the Yankees had a multiyear contract. Pennock didn't sign a three-year deal until late that month. Meusel signed a two-year deal mid-month.[4]

The Colonel's payroll for 1928 was approaching $300,000, which was easily a record. The "twin killers" accounted for nearly a third of the total. It was another indication of how the Yankees were breaking new ground. Just a few years before, a six-figure salary payroll was considered very generous.[5] In

January, Waite Hoyt returned his 1928 contract unsigned; the current salary of $16,000 fell about 25 percent short of what he wanted, which was three years at $20,000.[6]

The status of the team's pitching came under intense review in the aftermath of the loss to the Cardinals in the 1926 World Series. This caused the normally conservative Miller Huggins to take a closer look at his younger pitchers before the 1927 season. He commented, "This year experience isn't going to cut so much of a figure; a young arm sometimes is better than an old head. The whole thing is that the Yankees' pitching staff has reached the stage where I must gamble. These old fellows aren't going on forever."[7]

Huggins ended up squeezing one more year and a total of thirty-three wins out of Urban Shocker, Dutch Ruether, and Bob Shawkey in 1927. Hoyt led the team in victories, with twenty-two. Wilcy Moore and Herb Pennock tied with nineteen, while George Pipgras and Myles Thomas chipped in with ten and seven wins, respectively.

The subsequent release of Shawkey and Ruether at the end of November 1927, coupled with the uncertainty of Shocker's return, compounded the current holdout of pitching ace Waite Hoyt. With Shocker, it was believed that the team had deep enough pitching to allow them to go with a more youthful staff. Without him, the load would fall to the only proven starters, Herb Pennock and Waite Hoyt, and the developing George Pipgras and Wilcy Moore.[8]

In February, Shocker confirmed his decision that he was retiring from baseball to pursue a career in aviation or radio. Huggins wasn't expecting to hear that Shocker had retired but probably sensed or hoped he was bluffing:

> If Shocker insisted, that would be another cold spell for me. But we would try to do the best we could under the handicap. Shealy and Johnson, coming from the American Association, are supposed to be ready. They certainly will find no discouraging factors with the hitting support they are reasonably sure to get. Then I hear great things about Louis McAvoy, whom we bought from Chattanooga. These youngsters should help fill the shoes of Ruether, Shawkey, and perhaps Shocker. Coveleski also is not to be ignored. He's at Hot Springs and writes me that he is more encouraged than ever. We will have fifteen pitchers, and if Shocker makes good his threat there may be one among them to help make up for Urban's decision.[9]

The time had come for a little more than a slight overhaul, whether rookies or veterans or a combination of both. There was no modern-day free agency and, with the exception of the St. Louis Cardinals, no modern-day farm systems to develop and supply players. Even though each team had at least one affiliation with a minor-league club, it was not enough to overcome the limitations on how many players a team could effectively control. Pitching was a precious commodity, and the Yankees would have just a little more than two months to find some.

The spring training routine was not much different than today: Ten pitchers, four catchers, four infielders, and three outfielders were scheduled to report to St. Petersburg, Florida, on February 26. Among the infielders and outfielders were the "twin killers," Ruth and Gehrig.[10]

The Babe ordered a total of forty-eight forty-eight-ounce Claymore bats from Louisville. When a big truck arrived and unloaded them, the team's surprised trainer, Doc Woods, opened the box, saying, "It looks as if the big boy means business. He never before sent for so many bats. He'll try them all out, too, until he gets to hitting in a serious way. And then he will pick out just one playmate and go right on using it until he smashes it or perhaps gets into a little slump."[11]

Lou Gehrig thought it was three dozen too many:

> Say, that's a lot of bats. I have a dozen with me, and they ought to last for some time. But the Babe uses 'em up. He splinters quite a few, and he is sort of fickle with bats until he finds one [that] has the friendly touch. You know there's something in a good bat [that] makes you think there is a touch of the human in it.[12]

The Babe had come down from the fifty-four-ounce club last spring, after which he hit sixty home runs. Gehrig hit the ground running as he reported at his mid-season playing weight of 212 pounds.[13]

The rest of the squad was set to report about a week before the first exhibition game on March 12. The Yankees had ten games scheduled in St. Petersburg and one against the Cardinals at their facility in Avon Park. With no air travel, the next seven games would take place in seven different southern and Mid-Atlantic cities. The parks were arrived at via rail on the trip north for Opening Day. The preseason schedule ended with two games against the Robins at the Stadium and two more games at Ebbets Field.

The Yankee preseason schedule that was printed in the *New York Times* on January 4 varied slightly from the actual. In Florida there were six games scheduled with the Braves at St. Petersburg; one with the Cardinals at Avon Park and one at St. Petersburg; and one each with the Reds, Phillies, and Bisons of the International League at St. Petersburg.

Last season, from Avon Park, Florida, to Nashville, Tennessee, the Yankees split eight games with the Cardinals. The four previous years they traveled north with the Brooklyn Robins, winning the series each year, culminating in a twelve-game sweep in 1926. This year's seven-city trek north from

Jacksonville through Charlotte would be entirely against minor-league hosts. It was a deliberate business decision to avoid a 50-50 split of the proceeds with another major-league club. The Yankees were easily the greatest draw in baseball. From April 7 through April 10, the Yankees would face Brooklyn again to close out the preseason schedule.[14]

The team was elated with their state-of-the-art training facility. Crescent Lake Park was owned by the city of St. Petersburg and was in the process of being beautified. "We have here the finest training field in the country, bar none. Man and boy, manager and player, I've seen a lot of southern training parks." said Miller Huggins. "I've seen New Orleans, Shreveport, Jacksonville, Macon, and too many other places to mention now, but this field here, as it has been gradually improved each year, is the best in the south." James R. Harrison further described the facility for the *New York Times*:

> Crescent Lake Park, already generously proportioned, has been made larger and better than ever. The entire layout, infield and outfield, was generously restored with Bermuda grass and Italian rye, and now, from the backstop to the deepest point of center field, the eye is intrigued by a thick, luxuriant bed of beautiful grass, which looks so fat and inviting that it has been all Mr. Huggins could do to keep his athletes from lying down and taking a nap.[15]

Crescent Lake itself lay behind center field. The previous year, the park's left-field portion was drained in preparation for being decorated with various tropical plants, trees, and shrubs. Other improvements were planned as well. There was speculation that it was the Yankees' last year at the facility.[16]

Huggins began to survey his up-and-comers and what to do about third base. With Joe Dugan still considered expendable, Gene Robertson was getting close attention:

> I can't figure why he was ever sent down. He was the best third baseman in the minors last year, and I certainly am going to give Robbie every opportunity to show what he can do in his comeback. He has been around for a good number of years, but he still is a young man and has many more years of service ahead of him. It is apparent that Robertson is determined to stick, for he is showing me all his baseball wares. He is fast in the field, his arm is strong, and he looks good at the plate. I always did like him around third. With Dugan, Robertson, and Gazella, we certainly will be well-fortified at the last turn. Dugan is still a great ballplayer and isn't likely to let anybody come along and push him off the bag. Yes, it's an interesting situation.[17]

Robertson was formerly with the Browns, where he batted .278 in 1,553 at bats. His best year was 1925, when he hit .271, with 14 home runs and 76 runs batted in. But, as he explained it, he did not get along with team owner Phil Ball:

> He didn't like me, and I didn't care to continue on his club, so I was shipped to St. Paul. The trouble started in training camp in 1926. We had only one workout day. I used to order my breakfast while I was shaving and have the meal in my room. Ball didn't like that. He insisted that I was having breakfast in bed. And he ordered it stopped.
>
> Along the middle of the season I started to order breakfast in my room again on the road, and again Ball interfered. We had a little debate, and I told him I didn't care if I didn't play with St. Louis again. He promised to send me out of the league, and he kept that promise. But I am making a promise to stay up this time.[18]

Robertson took Julian Wera's spot with the Yankees' minor-league affiliate at St. Paul in the Class AA American Association during the 1927 season when Wera was shipped to the Yankees.

During workouts in late February, Leo Durocher made an almost immediate and positive impression on Huggins at shortstop. Hailing from West Springfield, Massachusetts, Durocher spent the 1925 season with Class A Hartford of the Eastern League, 1926 with Class A Atlanta of the Southern Association, and the 1927 season with the St. Paul club. He had one at bat with the Yankees in 1925. Said Huggins,

> Bob Connery sent Durocher back to me with the word that Leo was the greatest fielding shortstop in the country. Certainly Durocher was the best defensive infielder in the minors in 1927. Scouts brought very encouraging reports of the player, so I decided to take a chance on him and release Ray Morehart. Durocher is essentially a shortstop. He plays that position naturally. He has a fine arm and gets the ball away fast. However, he also can play around second base, so I am going to keep him for a double utility role. He will be ready to step in at either short or second.[19]

Huggins confirmed his starting lineup just a little more than a week into camp during an interview with reporters:

> After going over the third base problem very thoroughly within the last twenty-four hours, I have come to the conclusion that it would be folly to take Joe Dugan off the bag. Gene Robertson is an able ballplayer. He is bound to be of great help to me before the season is over, because I believe he is fit for second base, as well as third base, duty. But Dugan still is a great third baseman, especially for the first weeks of the season. Perhaps, as the summer comes on, Dugan's legs will bother him. But when we face the Athletics on April 11, Joe will be at the old stand.

Yes, we did offer Dugan to Cleveland, but that's all off now, and Joe is a definite fixture on the Yankees.

There will be no change in the Yankee batting order, and that takes in the pitching staff, as well as the fielders. There have been threats and ultimatums, but Hoyt and Shocker will be back, helping us get that very valuable April and May jump on the field. I hope to be able to keep Moore at his 1927 job and use him as a relief pitcher, with occasional starts against teams like the Athletics and Washington. You see, Shocker has trouble with Philadelphia and Hoyt with Washington. It is a tremendous advantage to have a pitcher like Moore in the bull pen. I don't have to go into that. Our 1927 experience explains that fully. A relief man like Moore not only saves a lot of games, but he saves men like Hoyt and Pennock from wear and tear in the bull pen. Moore's status depends a great deal on George Pipgras. If George can prove that he deserves a place on our big four, Wilcy certainly will not be moved from the relief corps.[20]

A decision was made early on to go with their two rookie pitchers, Al Shealy and Henry Johnson, and on other reserve positions as well. Huggins elaborated, saying the following:

Shealy, in particular, has made a fine impression. I am going to do with Shealy and Johnson what I did with Pipgras last year. They will get plenty of work once the season is underway, and some of the veterans need a little more time between starts. Robertson, Durocher, and Gazella will be the utility men. I may keep a fourth catcher, possibly Dickey, but I may decide to keep only my veteran backstops and carry a tenth pitcher. I am not likely to have more than five outfielders. In schooling the youngsters who have been out here this past week, and they are the finest gang of recruits we have had in my eleven years with the Yankees, we are concerned largely with the problem of getting five or six youngsters who are worthy of schooling in the higher minors. We are standing pat with Shealy and Johnson taking the place of Ruether and Shawkey, Durocher replacing Morehart, and Robertson filling the shoes of Wera.[21]

The week before their first exhibition game, efforts began to sign Hoyt and Lazzeri. Neither the players nor the team were budging, and the task fell to manager Miller Huggins to try his eloquence as a former lawyer to bring them to terms:

We are not trying to inveigle them into a bad contract. We are not trying to pay them less than they have earned. But we are offering them exactly what we think they are worth, and I see no prospect of the New York club going one stop beyond that figure. I will be glad to talk with Hoyt and Lazzeri, but I don't intend to retreat. If I can persuade them that their demands are unreasonable, well and good. If not, well, then the Yankees will have to stand pat and see what happens.[22]

Huggins also vehemently denied that the Yankees inferred World Series money when negotiating contracts:

> Never, never. We pay ballplayers what we think they are worth, regardless of the World's Series money. The Yankees have never underpaid a player, figuring that his World Series cut would be worth $4,000 or $5,000. That would be manifestly unjust. A player should be entitled to a fair wage for his season's work, and the World Series money should be regarded as a just reward for victory.[23]

As the second week of March approached, it became "get serious" time for playing baseball and all hands on deck. In camp for seven days, Babe Ruth shunned the team exercises and the diamond, playing a daily thirty-six holes of golf, albeit without a cart under a blazing sun.[24]

After hitting a line drive to left field instead of out of the park during his first workouts on the diamond, a sore Ruth explained:

> I would rather hit sixty-one home runs than hit .400 this year. You see, many hitters have done better than .400, but nobody has yet got sixty-one homers. I really think I can do it. I've got a splendid start, for I am in great shape. Oh, I'll start right after the sixty-one. You can't afford to lose any time when you're chasing a record like that. But I'll be in there playing the game for the Yankees too. When a chance to win by crossing the other birds presents itself I usually don't overlook it.[25]

Baseball drills took a bit more of a toll on the Babe than golfing, but he was just six pounds above his ideal playing weight of 218 pounds.[26]

From then onward, only Sunday was reserved for the links, as the manager demanded:

> I believe golf is a detriment to baseball. I think it is a dangerous game for any of our high-priced athletes. It's a cinch to throw out an arm, sprain a wrist, and, what's worse, dislocate your tongue in this game of good and bad lies. It wouldn't be so bad if all there was to golf was the playing of it. But golf entails a lot of talking. There is talk before the game, talk while it is being perpetuated, and more talk after it is all over. It encourages bragging, faulty arithmetic, an exaggerated sense of distance, unessential ditch digging, and, at times, mistakes regarding property. If any Yankee has enough pep to play eighteen holes, he isn't giving everything he has during the workouts on the ball field. If a man is a ballplayer, why, he should be a ballplayer. If he is a golfer, he should be a golfer.[27]

When Huggins was asked why he plays golf, he replied, "Oh, I am an exception. When a man reaches my age he likes those vices [that] golf envelops." Golf was seen to be a menace to baseball: Bucky Harris, John McGraw, and Wilbert Robinson all had bans in effect, while Connie Mack did not.[28]

Negotiations did bear fruit as far as Lazzeri was concerned: The Yankees inked the second basemen to another two-year deal on March 5, terms not disclosed. The manager broke the happy news, announcing, "Yep, Lazzeri is signed to a two-year contract, and everything is jake, and will you look at that Chapman digging them up out there at third? And I want to say for the benefit of all concerned that Leo Durocher is as fine a young shortstop as I've seen in a southern training camp."[29]

Lazzeri wanted more than two years but succumbed and signed for two years with a heady raise. On March 5, the regular Yankee infield worked out for the first time since the World Series. Recently signed Mark Koenig arrived at camp the same day. Herb Pennock arrived on March 4, along with Joe Dugan and Ben Paschal.

After glancing at a list of pitchers, Pennock noticed that he was the lone southpaw in camp. "Marooned again," he moaned. "Is it always to be thus? Take a look at this. Not another left-handed pitcher in the camp. Imagine a southpaw sentenced to spend weeks, yes months and months, in the company of a lot of goofy right-handers." He added, "I begged Miller Huggins to get me a left-hander to talk to. Think of it, fifteen pitchers on the list, and I am the only left-hander." Huggins promised that there would be a left-hander before the season opened.[30]

"I have had chances to pick up left-handers," said Huggins, "but they were just pitchers, with nothing in particular to recommend them. I do not intend to grab a southpaw just because he is a southpaw and we are supposed to be in need of a playmate for Pennock." There was strong speculation it was Walter Miller of the Indians. The Cleveland southpaw had some success pitching against the Yankees and, like Uhle, was tough on the Babe.[31]

In addition, Earle Combs and Bob Meusel were still no-shows. Rumors that Combs had not come to terms were addressed. "Combs hasn't signed, but he has accepted terms," said Huggins. "He will sign when he gets down here. Why he isn't here now I don't know. Maybe he had another load of hay to put away in the barn, or he may be painting his house."[32]

When Meusel arrived on March 8 and Combs two days later, the outfield was intact, allowing Ruth to start working out in the outfield. Combs's late arrival from his home in Richmond, Kentucky, was a mystery, but he was in playing shape, having worked hard during the winter. He also affirmed that he had signed and was pleased with his contract. Waite Hoyt, Stan

Coveleski, and Benny Bengough were expected to arrive on Sunday, March 11, from Hot Springs, Arkansas.[33]

The thirty-seven-year-old Urban Shocker actually had two stints with the Yankees. In one of his few errors in judgment and first moves as Yankee manager, Huggins reluctantly traded the pitcher and four other players to the St. Louis Browns before the 1918 season for prospect Derrill Pratt and forty-three-year-old veteran Ed Plank.[34] Shocker went on to become one of the premier pitchers in baseball during the next seven years, winning twenty games in four consecutive years from 1920 through 1923, during the Browns' only first division run. After winning sixteen of twenty-nine decisions in 1924, the Browns put him on the market and Huggins got him back, and he won forty-nine games in his three-year return against twenty-nine losses.[35] He had a reputation as a student of the art of pitching and used the daily box scores to analyze his opponents. He never feared facing the big hitters and used his spitter strategically. When he lost his fastball toward the end of his career, he used smarts instead.[36]

When the pitcher rejected the Yankees' final offer on March 8, he was removed from the roster and placed on the voluntarily retired list. "Naturally I could have used a pitcher like Shocker this year," said Huggins. "What's the sense of denying that obvious fact? But he is not indispensable, and his place on the roster will be taken by one of my young pitchers, who otherwise would have been farmed out so they could get regular work." He continued, "I'll probably make Wilcy Moore a regular starting pitcher, but I'm not sure of that angle of it. Maybe Johnson or Shealy will be worked into a regular job, with Moore to back them up if they weaken."[37]

Huggins persisted on the topic of Shocker and his pitching situation:

> As you know, Shocker is a good spring pitcher. If he delays getting into shape, and then decides to change his mind about tossing baseball and rushing into the radio business, his effectiveness would be reduced, and perhaps we wouldn't want him anymore. Delay will force me to look around for a possible trade. In my own mind there already is the certainty that Shocker has quit and that I must find a pitcher to do his work.[38]

Huggins continued to surmise that Shocker was bluffing and could not match in his new business what he made in baseball.[39]

The heat was becoming unbearable, and the manager wanted to lighten up on the workouts, as some of the older players were feeling the effects. The Babe was complaining about sore hands and having trouble gripping the bat, saying, "Either the 1928 ball is dead or the pitchers are putting an awful lot of stuff on the pill, but I don't seem to be able to knock it very far."[40]

Rookie right-handers Al Shealy, from the Yankee affiliate at St. Paul, and Hank Johnson, from Milwaukee of the Class AA American Association, as well as veteran spitballer Stan Coveleski, were the definite replacements for the pitchers that departed in 1927.[41] Milwaukee offered $30,000 to the Colonel, a record purchase coming from a minor-league club, for Johnson to be left with them on option before he was claimed by the Yankees. Ruppert responded, "I turned [them] down with the statement that if he was worth that much to Milwaukee, he was priceless to the Yankees, and I added that we still were buying and not selling ballplayers."[42] Two years before, Johnson had been plucked by Huggins from the Florida State League for nothing.

Although the twenty-two-year-old Johnson had more professional experience, Shealy, at twenty-eight, was considered riper. Shealy was born in Chapin, South Carolina, and signed out of Newberry College in his home state in 1926. He had a mediocre record of 35–34 in the minor leagues, but Gene Robertson, his teammate at St. Paul, believed that he was ready to help the Yankees.

The Yankees were giving up on adding Cleveland first baseman George Burns and, instead, groomed outfield reserve Cedric Durst to spell Gehrig. This would round out the corps of able substitutes in the infield. "Very likely we will not need him there, as Gehrig is one of those tremendously powerful men who know how to take care of themselves," said Huggins about Durst, "but we must guard against every contingency, and I regard myself as fortunate in having so good a utility man as Durst to call on."[43]

The Yankees were a loose outfit, watching the Babe take batting practice as they readied to take on the Braves. "Can you believe it," said Joe Dugan. "Out two days and smacking that pill as if he had been spending the off-season in the winter league in California. That bird is just a baseball genius. There's only one like him, and I don't think you will see his like again." About fifty cameramen were recording the show. "Will he hit sixty-one homers? Why not!" said Dugan. "If he made up his mind to hit seventy homers he would make them. Just a genius, that's all." Lou Gehrig was taking notice of rookies Henry Johnson and Sam Byrd, Herb Pennock was positive about Al Shealy, and Tony Lazzeri liked the purchase of Lyn Lary.[44]

During the off-season, Pennock was a fox breeder, and he also hunted them. He was born in Chester County, Pennsylvania, where his father was a representative in the legislature. He grew up hunting and fishing on a farm outside Philadelphia and was a big fan of the Athletics. He was first noticed in 1911, when he was eighteen years old and pitching with the Wenonah Military Academy in Atlantic City against the St. Louis Stars, a semipro Negro team. His battery mate was the son of Connie Mack. After pitching a no-hit 1–0 shutout, Pennock did not hesitate to promise Earl Mack to talk to the senior

Mack before any other team. The following May, he signed with the Athletics instead of attending the University of Pennsylvania, against his father's wishes.[45]

Pennock was still considered the backbone of the staff and felt he was a young man breaking into the major leagues at eighteen years of age. "In all honesty, I don't tire any faster or to any greater degree than I did ten years ago," he explained to Dan Daniel. "Yes, there is one difference. The day after I pitch I've got to warm up to keep from tightening up. My style is not a wearing and tearing one. For me, one year is like any other year."[46]

Waite Hoyt was studying to be a mortician and, although without a contract, was one of the first Yankees to begin training at Hot Springs, Arkansas, in February. "I haven't signed a contract, and that's all I can say," said Hoyt as of March 11. "What the trouble is I can't tell you. The whole thing may be adjusted tomorrow." There was a suggestion that he shoot a round of golf with his manager. Hoyt added, "What would be the sense of that? Once Huggins gets hidden in those palmettos, looking for his ball, a searching party could not find him."[47]

The problems were twofold: money and terms. Huggins conceded on a two-year contract during a three-hour talk with Hoyt on March 12, but the two were not in agreement on the $20,000 demanded. "We are still as far apart as ever. The two-year contract no longer is an issue, but the money offered is not up to my idea of my value," said Hoyt.[48]

"We had a little talk about things," said Huggins. "Yes, there was a good deal of kidding going around, and somehow we never did get to the main issue. It looks like we will have to sit down and talk this thing over again. The weather last night was propitious. It was rainy and Hoyt seemed to get hot under the collar." Huggins added, "But there need be no worry amongst our Bronx constituency. Hoyt will pitch again at the Stadium, as is customary."[49]

Hoyt countered, "I suppose Huggins must get my proposal before the Colonel."[50]

Hoyt had the Yankees over a barrel and forced the Colonel to crack first on the issue of duration to grant the pitcher a two-year deal. It was a big gamble using unproven rookies to make up for the thirty-three games won by Shocker, Ruether, and Shawkey in 1927, but Hoyt won twenty-two games and was desperately needed in the rotation. Hoyt wanted $20,000 per year, but the Yankees countered with $15,000.[51]

Hoyt was a product of Erasmus High School in Brooklyn. He was coached by Dick Elliffe. The school, along with St. Mary's in California and Holy Cross in New England, seemed to be a prime producer of major-league ballplayers.[52]

The following is how Hoyt furthered his case for a raise during an interview around the third week of January:

I rated first in winning percentage and second to Moore in the earned run column with 2.64 runs per game. I worked in thirty-six games, a total of 256 innings, and if the records speak the truth, I did pretty well. I feel that I am reaching a peak of a career and should be even better in the next three years. I don't want to be a holdout, because, as we players define that term, no man is a holdout unless he has failed to report on the Opening Day of the season, at least during the first week of training. I have no doubt that Colonel Ruppert and Ed Barrow will see the justice of my contention. But just now I stand in the position of a ballplayer who has returned an unsigned contract.[53]

He was ready to return home to Brooklyn from Hot Springs; however, the Yankees guaranteed his travel expenses to St. Petersburg.[54]

Ruppert and Hoyt talked again on March 13, and, as Harrison reports,

They were as one on such matters as companionate marriage, the Pennsylvania coal situation, Al Smith, the oil investigation, Nicaragua, and the high price of turnips in Albania. It was only when the topic of Mr. Hoyt's money value to the Yanks was brought up that the two conferees drew slightly apart.[55]

Through it all, both Hoyt and Coveleski were in uniform.[56]

Both sides finally came to terms on the Ides of March, as Hoyt signed his first multiyear term in his eight-year career with the Yankees. The amount was believed to be for $16,000, leaving Shocker the only unsigned Yankee. Both parties made concessions after forty-eight negotiations during a span of three days.[57]

The Brooklyn mortician put finality on the negotiations:

I guess I was a sucker to go to Hot Springs and get myself in tip-top shape. I knew I was in for a protracted gabfest here. I wasn't so much afraid of Colonel Ruppert. I was familiar with his generous style. But, frankly, I feared Huggins and that Cincinnati oratory of his. But I was in fine condition and finally got Huggins on the ropes at 10 o'clock last night. I knew I had him groggy when he telephoned down for ice water. He led with a final proposition, but I countered with revised terms and he gasped for air. I followed with a straight left to the two-year idea and hooked my dollar sign to Hug's swollen jaw. He went down for the count. The final terms suit me perfectly.[58]

Stan Coveleski, who arrived with Hoyt and catcher Benny Bengough, was cautious about his arm, stating, "My arm feels stronger than in several years. I hurt it last spring on the training trip and it was never right, but

I think the rest I've had and the baths at Hot Springs have restored full strength to my arm."[59]

The Yankees would be without a captain, a mostly symbolic status, for the sixth straight year. The Babe last held the position and wished to have it back again, but the mite manager refused the request, declaring, "We seem to be getting along pretty well without a captain. Ruth is playing better than ever just as an outfielder. Added responsibilities might affect his hitting. If I thought we ought to have a captain Ruth would get the job. Since he can't have it, no one else will get it."[60]

The Babe was becoming concerned that he may have overdone his training routine and it was affecting his play, and he was bothered by a sore hand due to blisters and callouses. They just redeveloped after the bandages were removed. "I just can't get hold of one, the ball sounds punk when I hit it." He continued, "Gosh, it looks like I'll have to wear these bandages from now on. When I grip the bat, it feels as if I'm holding a lighted match in my palm. I have been up against this before, but not so badly. No, I am not worried. It is not a chronic trouble." Many of the players thought that he was seeing the tough pitches that he would normally see during the season.[61]

The Babe sent for his favorite piece of artillery, known as "Big Bertha," the forty-eight-ounce bat that accounted for thirty-one home runs. None of the forty-eight sent from Louisville were to his liking. Ruth explained:

> The bat people used to save knots for me, but not one of the four dozen sticks they sent me has a knot. I have hit a few balls right on the nose, but they haven't gone very far. It's the wood, and maybe it's the ball. I hope they haven't put lead into the 1928 agate.
>
> Anyway, it looks as if I will have to bring Big Bertha into action. There's a bat [that] gave me that record last summer. I broke my first good broom handle in June after making twelve notches in it. I was afraid I wouldn't get another one like it. But along came Big Bertha and made poor Betsy look like a sucker. Yes, I've got Bertha, with a notch for every one of the thirty-one home runs she made and an extra deep one for number sixty. I'd like to save that bat—maybe give it to a baseball museum if they ever get one.[62]

The Colonel spoke with Dan Daniel just as his team got set to begin its exhibition schedule:

> Well, it certainly looks as if there might be still another World Series for the Yankees next fall. If we get the World Series we'll promise the fans quite an opening, for we will have close to 80,000 capacity. The steel for the new left wing of the Stadium already is up.

Miller Huggins just has assured me that we will have at least as good a ball club as we had last season. He thinks well of the young pitchers, and he believes that Gehrig, Lazzeri, and Koenig should be even better than in 1927. He says we will have better protection all around.

And that Ruth looks fine, doesn't he? We appreciate his efforts and his class now. But how Colonel Huston and I would have appreciated him had we had Ruth in 1915. I have learned a lot about baseball since the day Huston and I bought the Yankees.[63]

Taking somewhat of a backseat to the latest contract negotiations were the team's first three preseason games, two defeats to the Braves and a defeat at the hands of the Cardinals. The March 12 opener brought a capacity crowd of 3,500 to see three of the game's most popular players, Rogers Hornsby of the Braves and the Yankee slugging duo of Babe Ruth and Lou Gehrig. The Babe and the "Rajah," $110,000 worth of ballplayers, shook hands for the cameramen before the first game.[64]

Wilcy Moore pitched the first four innings against the Cardinals and gave up six hits, two wild pitches, and three walks, but just two runs. The Yankees felt that they were ready to start winning games after going winless in their first four tries, with two postponements. Huggins explained:

I am being joshed a lot about the fact that we have dropped two games to the Braves and one to the Cardinals.

We have a ball club made up of young players and older men, all of them businesslike and earnest. They know what is expected of them, and they will deliver it. I am not disposed to rush pitchers or fielders to unreasonable efforts. I never followed that policy, and I never would change my ideas, even under the pressure of losing a few meaningless exhibitions. The exhibition schedule is supposed to help condition the club. I never lose sight of that fact.[65]

With the deadline for releasing players approaching, the issue of Urban Shocker arose, and Huggins responded:

It must be that Shocker really has retired. He is not a headless youngster. He knows just what he can do and when he can do it best. In other words, Shocker knows that he must get in most of his victories before July 4, and that he requires a certain definite period in which to get into condition. This situation stresses the fact that the longer Shocker remains in retirement, the weaker does his chance of landing a contract with us become. In all sincerity, I am not worried over him. I think we have enough pitching class among the younger men to make up for Shocker's retirement.[66]

The losing and the errors were beginning to be a source of embarrassment to the Colonel, who was on the verge of walking out of a third loss to the Braves on March 20, and fourth straight overall.[67] The kidding and chatter about the early exhibition losses, which now stood at four, was making its way around the baseball world, while the Yankees tried to hold fast to an indifferent attitude. Losing early preseason games to the Braves, even a supposedly improved team, was not enough to cause panic, but losing three straight games raised questions. Huggins brushed it aside:

> I was hoping nobody would ask that question. That's our type of ball club. It's a great club, sure of its ability. No, not swell headed, but confident and not inclined to push the issue. The boys know that they are facing pitching two weeks ahead of their form.
>
> It is interesting to win these games, but not important. And it is impossible to rouse this type of ball club to feel that these types of games are important, even if I were so foolish as to want to create that feeling. Of course, if I were a pessimist, I might regard the present situation as forecasting a slow start for us this spring. That may be. I have seen this club act this way before, and then step out of it in one afternoon and keep smashing its way ahead.[68]

"We are not hitting," said Mark Roth, the team's traveling secretary. "When we hit, everything looks fine. Perhaps we should have a little esprit de corps. I'll see the manager and have it on the menu tomorrow."[69]

The manager, however, was not worried about the team's lack of hitting. "Pitching is my problem. I am not a bit alarmed at Gehrig's batting slump or Ruth's failure to knock them over the fence. I know both of them can hit. But I should like to have a little steadier pitching."[70]

Huggins answered the question of why the decision was made to release Ruether by stating, "We got Ruether in 1926 because we then were sorely in need of another experienced pitcher. If I had lost that year and not taken Ruether I would not have forgiven myself. As matters turned out we could have won that season without him."[71]

"There is every indication that Stanley Coveleski has regained his arm. True, the Braves nicked him for six hits and three runs in the three innings he worked yesterday, but I was more interested in his form, in his general conduct in the box and his stuff than I was in the safeties he yielded."[72]

Coveleski was one of the seventeen trick pitchers in 1920, eight in the senior league and nine in the junior, who were declared exempt from the trick-pitch rule outlawing the spitball. With Urban Shocker presumed retired, there were now only half a dozen left: Clarence Mitchell of the Phillies,

Bill Doak of the Robins, Burleigh Grimes of the Pirates, Jack Quinn of the Athletics, and Red Faber of the White Sox.[73]

"I've got a hunch about Coveleski," said Huggins. "Somehow I have a feeling that the spitter will be a big help to us. You will notice that he looks nice and free. He says his arm feels great, and Benny Bengough, who worked with him at Hot Springs, tells me that he, too, has that hunch on the Pole.

"Coveleski, in his prime, was the greatest of the spitters. He was what I would call the spitter of the spitters, throwing one damp fling after another," Huggins elaborated. "Most of the other spitters merely fake the ball. Faber didn't throw thirty real spitters a season but had that spitter threat in there all the time. Covey doesn't throw a dozen dry balls a game."[74]

Covey was pitching without a contract, and Huggins was quizzed about it:

> No, Coveleski does not expect or desire a contract at this time, and I am not ready to talk terms with him. He wants a more conclusive test, and I want to see more of his work. But his arm is back, or I don't know an arm when I see one.
>
> Possibly our exhibition schedule on the way to the Stadium will help him in an exceptional way, as we will be playing minor-league clubs which have seen practically no spitball hurling. Covey yesterday had his fastball working. He had his slow ball and his spitter. And he was free and loose. My hunch still stands. I think that Coveleski will be of great help to the Yankees before the pennant season gets very old.[75]

The pitcher himself was also confident. "I was as loose as I used to be three or four years ago. It was a great sensation to be in there pitching with stuff and form I had not been able to show since 1926."[76]

James R. Harrison reported on the Yankees' first preseason win on March 21, in the *New York Times*, writing, "Everybody get ready for a big shock, steadying yourself by taking hold of the back of a chair. Grasp a bottle of smelling salts, take a deep breath, and get ready for the startling announcement. The Yankees won a ball game."[77]

Waite Hoyt yielded two hits in four innings, and George Pipgras four hits in five innings, combining for an 8–2 victory. They were helped by a Joe Dugan home run, the team's first of the preseason. Huggins was upbeat after the team's first victory, announcing, "We are finally straightened out. Not that our defeats had worried me. But it is good to feel that we have won even if it is only an exhibition game. Colonel Ruppert had begun to feel as he used to back in the day when he bought the Yankees."[78]

In the final meeting with the Braves the following day, the second-line staffers were pounded. Stan Coveleski, Henry Johnson, Myles Thomas, and sloppy defense yielded six runs on a total of eleven hits in a 6–2 loss.

"There wasn't any more murder in murderers' row than there was in Mary's little lamb," wrote Harrison.[79] The Babe, the "Rajah," and the "Iron Horse" disappointed the fans with just seven hits in forty-nine at bats in the five games played.

"I'll get going. We aren't hitting nothing, and when you ain't hitting you look bad. I think it must be that fried egg up there that's bothering me," muttered the Babe, speaking of the hot Florida sun. Shealy and Johnson were looming as the margin of error for Pennock, Hoyt, Pipgras, and Moore. Many in baseball wondered how Moore would do as a starter and did not think that he would make a smooth transition from bull pen to starter.[80]

Wilcy Moore relished the relief role:

Well, I believe I'd just as soon keep right on doing what I did last year, although with an occasional rest. This business of being a relief pitcher has its advantages and funny angles. For one thing, I don't have to spend much time in the hot dugout.

I'm pretty much in the open, enjoying the breezes in the bull pen when I'm not pitching. You sit around in the bull pen thinking of the folks down home when somebody wakes you up and says, "There's the signal from Hug!" That means I've got to begin warming up. Sometimes I keep right on warming up, and the pitcher in the box gets straightened out. But very often Cy has to tote that sinker-ball into the box and begin saving a game.

Sometimes you don't get a chance to do much warming up. A pitcher goes like a house afire and sudden-like he loses everything. There's one thing about relief pitching. It's good, steady work. It helps keep your weight down, and it keeps the folks in Hollis and Mule Shoe, Texas, interested. Yeah, this relief work suits Cy to a T.[81]

The big Oklahoman had to overcome lapsing into nervousness on the mound earlier in his minor-league career. Opposing benches frequently tried to get an opposing pitcher's goat, and Moore was easily affected, but he followed his manager Earl Snapp from Ardmore to Okmulgee in the Western Association in 1923 and 1924, and the skipper worked with him to develop the steel nerves of a relief specialist.[82]

Following the 1927 season, Cy Moore began working on a curveball from his home in Oklahoma. Regarding his curve, he said, "The boys might not think much of it, but I'm fixin' to throw it plenty this year. Yes, and I'll fool a lot of them with it, just like I did today." He used it against the Cardinals in the preseason game and retired Frisch, Bottomley, and Hafey, but, as reported in the *New York Telegram*, maybe the Redbirds were laughing too hard to actually hit it.[83]

With less than a week before heading north, the team was still carrying eleven pitchers, one more than would make the regular squad. Yankee pitching and sloppy defense had given up six or more runs in three of six games, including the rain-shortened opener. Other teams were watching the Yankees' pitching situation very closely, hoping this would be the Achilles' heel.[84] For the most part, the Yankees still remained unfazed, or at least gave that appearance, about dropping five of six preseason games, four of five to the Braves and one to the Cardinals. Their skipper spent the final Sunday in Florida golfing, while the two sluggers went fishing.[85]

There was not any open cracking of the whip to the press by the Yankee owner, but there were closed-door meetings with Huggins after the recent setbacks, a reminder from the Colonel that he was paying high salaries and expecting another championship. The March 29 issue of the *Sporting News* focuses on the Yankee four-run loss to the Braves the week before as it attempted to get to the bottom of the team's preseason performance—at the time of writing, a record of one win in six games.

Miller Huggins again downplayed the defeat:

> I don't know that anything is the matter. These games in Florida don't mean a thing. We have had reverses in the south before and yet have come out on top, so don't start sending out pessimistic stories, because if you do the Yankees are liable to cross you up by going on one of their old rampages. They are a team of extremes. I must admit the Yankees are not hitting, but, as a whole, the hitting has been light through the belt where the major-league teams are training.[86]

As the team departed training camp, their record, which worsened to one win in ten preseason contests, was the talk of the baseball world. Lou Gehrig complained about the big ball in the Florida sky, stating, "You can't get your eyes open up there at the plate. When you try to bat you have to squint up your eyes like this. After we get up north where the glare isn't so bad, we'll start hitting. Don't worry about that." Earle Combs felt that the team wasn't yet interested:

> Everybody's loafing. There seems to be an undercurrent of confidence that anytime the Yanks want to win a game they can't lose. But we've tried to win them and haven't right here in St. Petersburg. Unless the club settles down to serious business within the next week it is going to find it difficult to get off on the right foot when the league campaign starts.[87]

A better showing had to be made during the upcoming seven-city minor-league tour and four-game series with the Brooklyn Robins. "It's hard to make a veteran team like mine snap out of it," said Huggins. He continued,

They know they're good and that there is nothing to be gained by knocking off a bunch of teams in the spring. But they may find it hard to step out when they have to. I'll admit they look terrible, but I'm not worrying yet, because I know the bunch is there and they'll produce the goods sooner or later.[88]

It seemed that only Joe Dugan and Earle Combs were performing in regular-season form. The Babe was nursing a sore hand, and Lazzeri a back injury, and none of the pitchers looked ready for the opener.[89]

The ten pitchers that figured to start the season were, from the previous year, Herb Pennock, Waite Hoyt, George Pipgras, Wilcy Moore, and Myles Thomas; the new faces were veteran spitballer Stan Coveleski and youngsters Al Shealy, Henry Johnson, Joe Marty, and Archie Campbell. They were still pursuing left-hander Walter Miller from the Indians and were willing to part with Ben Paschal, Cedric Durst, and Myles Thomas. To complete the battery were four catchers, three from last year, including Benny Bengough, Pat Collins, and John Grabowski. Future hopeful and Hall of Famer Bill Dickey saw much playing time and was waiting in the wings. The infield was unchanged except for the addition of reserves Gene Robertson and Leo Durocher. The outfield was identical. The Yankees headed north having compiled the worst-ever record in the preseason, losing four of five to the Braves, two each to the Cardinals and Bisons, and one to the Reds.[90]

While consistent in losing during the spring, managing one victory in fourteen attempts against major-league and Class A teams, the Yankees were just as definite in disregarding it. But the entire baseball world was taking notice, and the manager and players had to address their poor showing.[91]

Huggins felt confident with Hoyt, Pennock, Moore, and Pipgras as his main rotation. The question was replacing Ruether and Shocker. The question marks, Coveleski, Shealy, Thomas, and Johnson would provide the answer as to whether they would make up the difference. "Even if they don't," said Huggins, "I doubt that there will be a difference of eighteen games between the Yanks of last year and the Yanks of this."[92]

"This ends the barnstorming, and I'm glad of it," said Joe Dugan. He went on to say that,

> I think that when we get going with the major-league clubs we will break right into our stride and show the power that carried us to the pennant the last two years. You know we've been playing a lot of bad ball on this trip. We've been bad on the bases, running the wrong way on plays, hurrying our own ends instead of delaying them. That sort of baseball is not ours, and it won't go on.[93]

"It's a crime," said Rogers Hornsby. "These defeats down here do neither the fans nor the players any good. The southern fans, many of whom have never seen major-league ball, get the idea [that] their own players are better, and the big leaguers get into the habit of playing careless baseball." The "Rajah" was pointing fingers at the Yankees, saying, "In their case it may not mean so much because they are way ahead of the rest of their own league. But it looks bad for a world champion in any sport to be knocked off by palookas."[94]

Said Ruth,

Don't we look great, though? Don't I look great up there hitting through those slow curves that these bush pitchers are throwing to me? I've hit only about two balls all spring. That shot I got in Chattanooga was tagged, but the wind held it back and it just did the right thing by going over the fence. That ball in Nashville was a good line drive, and that's about all the hitting I've done so far. I'm not in stride yet and don't seem to be able to get into stride at all, but I've been just as bad in other springs and came through with good hitting when the season started. I expect to do the same thing this year. But the team! We've just been terrible. But I don't expect it to last. We've got all over any ideas about being good. Now we're trying to win, and by jingoes, we haven't been able to win.[95]

Colonel Ruppert remained confident:

The boys look very good to me. I saw them in the South, and while the Yankees have no impressive record in exhibition games, there is no good reason to be downcast. There is as much power as ever in the club, and it is just a matter of time until the boys begin to hit. The team has gained much experience, and the fact that virtually the same machine [that] won the pennant and World's Series last year will be in action again this season is an important factor. The boys will have a fine chance to win once more. The club is even stronger, and while the other teams doubtless have strengthened, the Yankees also have added power.[96]

The Yankees initially came back to cloudy, cool, and showery weather on Saturday, April 7. The first round of the interborough series at the Stadium went to Brooklyn in front of 20,000 fans. The Robins were having a decent spring, and their victory broke a fourteen-game losing streak against the Yankees. Brooklyn-born Waite Hoyt gave up seven runs in the first three innings. The Yankees took the second game in the Bronx. Wilcy Moore settled down after giving up two runs in the first inning and one in the second. The Yankees played little ball in the third game in Flatbush, as four sacrifices led to a 3–2 victory. Henry Johnson and Al Shealy split the action, each giving up a run. The Robins gained a split of the series by winning the final game, getting to youngsters Archie Campbell for five runs in the middle innings and Myles Thomas for one run in the seventh and eighth.[97]

The ballyhoo, slang for what we call controversy, was relatively subdued going into the 1928 season. The clamor following the 1927 season was described by Westbrook Pegler in the *Chicago Daily Tribune*:

> This spring's ballyhoo for baseball has been the best in the history of the trade. . . . It will be a point of pride with the proprietors, too, that the entire program of preseason advertisement was conducted without any assistance from the police, the district attorneys, or private detective agencies. . . . The fault of this harmless type of ballyhoo is always that it is likely to be boresome. Generally speaking, suspicion and rancor are more interesting than complete trust and goodwill.[98]

To grasp for straws, the gossip in the newspapers was about the trading for the second straight year of future Hall of Fame second baseman Rogers Hornsby. The second highlight was the Yankees' piling up of losses during the preseason.[99]

III

THE REGULAR SEASON

Epidemics of Cold and Flu
(April 11–May 2)

"The only time I ever worry," said Ed Barrow, "is when it rains."
He voiced the sentiments of every magnate when he uttered
those words.

—*Baseball Magazine*, June 1927[1]

The aforementioned quote came at a time when a team's sole source of
revenue was from ticket sales. Delayed games could not be pushed to later
at night, and every team was located in the northern and eastern quadrant of
the country. Will April and early May be cold, wet, and miserable, or balmy
and pleasant? What tended to be the rainier part of the schedule was also, according to F.C. Lane, the "haymaking season" for the weaker clubs. As teams
began to fade in the standings, so did attendance, along with revenue from
any postponements and fans staying away because of threatening weather.
This was particularly painful when the inclement weather occurred during
weekends and holidays. People also planned their vacations, something becoming much more available to the working class, and also took part in other
activities during the dryer, middle months of the season.[2]

The northeast, the country, and even the world had been experiencing
severe and unusual weather since the Mississippi floods in late 1926. The
Boston Daily Globe discussed this at some length on November 6, 1927:

> Will the year 1927 be written into human annals as modern history's "most
> terrible" twelve months of storms, earthquakes, and floods? It is impossible
> to arrive at any estimates of the total damage caused to property through-
> out the world, but addition of damage estimates from the great Mississippi
> flood, the Midwest tornado, and the floods in Polish Silesia, Central Ger-
> many, Belgium, Italy, France, and the Balkans exceed $2 trillion.

Within the last few days, New England has joined the long list of regions visited by destructive floods during 1927. With a million-dollar loss reported from one small city, another city threatened with complete destruction, railroads broken by washouts, and automobiles drowned on public roads, the November flood of 1927 will rank among the great disasters of the century.[3]

During the winter and extending through the first six days of March 1928, there were no zero-degree days, and the total snowfall total at nine and a half inches was the third lowest on record. Shortly thereafter, a storm hit, which added four more inches to the tally.[4] Would the mild winter in the northeast bring a pleasant spring and make a lot of hay for the baseball magnates?

The season began on Tuesday, April 10, with a single game in the nation's capital between the Senators and Red Sox. The sitting president in April 1928 was Calvin Coolidge. As vice president, he succeeded to the highest office after the death of Warren Harding in August 1923, and he was elected the following year. The incumbent made it official during the summer of 1927 that he wanted out of the White House. Citing the stresses of the office and being aware that there was only one living former president, William Howard Taft, Coolidge felt that ten years would be four too many, and he would not run as the Republican nominee.[5]

Playing out the string, "Silent Cal" once again accepted the honors to toss out the first ball for the home opener against Boston, missing only the 1926 debut due to his father's death.[6] It usually meant good luck. Walter Johnson blanked the Athletics during the 1924 World Championship year opener; Johnson and the Senators crushed the Yankees, 10–1, the next year, also a pennant winner; and, in 1927, Stan Coveleski beat Slim Harriss of the Red Sox, 6–2. But Shirley L. Povich, sports editor for the *Washington Post*, noticed a few bad omens: Neither team marched to the flagpole in center field, as was customary, and the president fired a perfect strike.[7]

Coolidge departed after the first inning, with the Senators in the lead by three runs. Another bad omen, the mercury hovered around freezing at game time, causing more than a quarter of the expected 25,000 fans to stay home. The Senator faithful who remained for the entire hour and forty minutes saw the Red Sox and Dan MacFayden hold their team to one run in the last six innings en route to a 7–5 victory.[8]

A full slate of games was on tap the following day. As many as 250,000 fans were expected, topping last year's seven-game benchmark of 227,660, which included 72,000 attendees for the Yankees opener at home against the Athletics. Baseball's burning question would initially be answered in the negative. Attendance was the smallest in six years, at around 200,000. The western clubs led the way in the junior circuit with 40,000 at Navin Field in

Detroit and 30,000 at Comiskey Park in Chicago. Temperatures in Boston, where 10,000 spectators turned out, were near freezing—not to mention wind and freezing rain, which threatened to cancel the entire series.[9]

A major initiative of the new American League president was to speed up the time it took to finish games. "Shorter and snappier games will be the watchword in that organization," said Ernest Barnard. "Two hours of baseball is all the ordinary fan cares for. He wants to see a good ball game and get home to a warm supper. This isn't a twilight league. If the players can't show a little snap on their own initiative, we will see to it that they do." Barnard announced the league's enforcement of the twenty-second rule, which stated that the pitcher must throw the ball within twenty seconds of receiving it back from the catcher or the batter will be awarded a ball.[10]

The twenty-second rule had been on the books for decades but was generally ignored. In May 1913, the Phillies protested the rule's application by umpire Bill Klem against the Cardinals. Tom Seaton of the Phillies had a 1–2 count on Ivey Wingo, with the bases loaded in the seventh inning. After Klem applied the rule and called a ball, Seaton grooved the next pitch, which resulted in a game–winning, two-run double.[11]

Likewise, the batter would be charged with a strike if he stepped out of the batter's box. "How is the umpire to tell when a batter gets a cinder in his eye, when he is hampered by sweat, or when he is bothered by some optical aberration?" asked Lou Gehrig. He added,

> I remember one afternoon last summer when I quit the box three times in facing Sam Jones. Once sweat got into my eyes. Then sweat got into my grip. When I finally got straightened out, Jones began to tantalize me, so I stepped out. Batters have troubles enough without being bothered by a rule such as that you say Barnard has laid down.[12]

The new president of the American League also wanted uniform ground rules in each park for each opponent. All inactive players were to be seated in the dugout or bull pen. The Babe or any other player could no longer dally on the sidelines or sit in or near the stands when his team was up to bat. No more than one batter could occupy the on-deck circle. These changes would move the younger circuit in sync with the National League, and the mite manager was pleased with the new ruling on the uniformity of ground rules. The home club had to post them in the clubhouses and dugouts and provide visiting players with a copy if requested. The rules had to remain unchanged throughout the year. The Yankees, in particular, felt that there was one set of rules for them and another for other clubs in visiting parks.[13]

Miller Huggins and Connie Mack had a different approach to managing on the field. "The Midget Manager, you know, makes the law of averages his

Bible," said George B. Underwood of the *New York Morning Telegraph.* "In times of sorrow and stress Miller always falls back on the law of averages." Either way, when a trend became too extreme, the law of averages would come back to haunt Huggins.[14] During a game in August of the previous year, when the Yankees made five errors against the White Sox with Ted Lyons the opposing pitcher and failed to lose, Huggins wondered if that long overdue slump might happen at the worst time in October.

"There is an element of danger in it," said Huggins the previous year on not being paid a healthy visit by "Sam Slump" during the first two weeks of August. He continued,

> While we are coasting, in the National League, teams are fighting themselves into shape. The Cubs, for instance, might whip us in the series before we wake up. On the contrary, the fact that we are walking in may help us to swamp a team [that] is tired after coming through a fight. There are precedents in both cases.[15]

Huggins knew he had smart, self-motivated players who were well aware that the slow preseason was an issue in baseball circles:

> There are no rules on this ball club, which the ballplayers have not made themselves. By that I mean that any rule we may have has been made necessary by their accounts. We have no checking in of men at nights, and I can't say that I regulate their habits too closely. But, on the other hand, I usually know what is going on. And if we take that the boys abuse the privilege of freedom, there will be a rule made. I try to make the fellows understand that it means as much to them to take care of themselves as it does to the club. And I must say I have had cooperation.[16]

The team brass was hoping that they would get off to a fast start in 1928, to deflect any carryover from the preseason. "In giving nearly all of the athletes long-term contracts," wrote Dan Daniel in the *New York Telegram,* "Colonel Ruppert, Ed Barrow, and Huggins played a big game. They took a gamble. I'm sure they'll win."[17]

While the Yankee players were left to their intuitions, Connie Mack, with his infamous scorecard, was constantly motioning to his players and pitchers. The Athletics also had a coterie of former managers, which many believed could have evolved into possible problems.[18] Then, there were reservations about the lean leader's reliance on his two forty-year-old outfielders, referred to as "Connie's Antiques." Ty Cobb and Tris Speaker, both also among the past managers, were not coming off particularly good years and were well beyond their prime. They were given hefty contracts that did not sit well with some of the other homegrown stars. Al Simmons, the "Milwaukee

Mauler," was also not pleased with being shifted to right field to make way for Speaker in center.[19] Dan Daniel quotes an unnamed source regarding the two antique outfielders:

> It is incomprehensible, but nevertheless true, that Connie Mack did not break even on the season. He ran his club for his players, with emphasis on Ty Cobb and his $65,000. He is making that mistake again. Cobb and Speaker mean more than $50,000 in salaries, but that's not the half of it. They mean poor spirit on the Philadelphia club.
>
> I visited the Athletics recently and sat talking with one of their players. Cobb and Speaker walked in, and this player sneered, "Well there goes our strength." Cobb without a doubt is through. He cannot throw, and his legs are very bad. He may force himself again, but he's making a mistake. Connie Mack is determined to get another pennant, but he is taking the wrong course. Has beens will not do it.[20]

Indeed, in early February, Cobb trained with the Giants in Augusta, his birthplace, and talked with team officials about a contract. According to Tris Speaker, Cobb felt he was too much a second fiddle to the Yankee stars and wanted to finish his career with the Giants. The "Georgia Peach" was actually not present with the team as the regular season approached, and his return to the Athletics was still a question mark until about ten days before the opener. There were rumors he cleaned up to the tune of $200,000 in the stock market.[21]

Wall Street had a record-breaking March, with 85 million shares traded, breaking the previous mark of 62 million set in December. There were sixteen straight 3-million share days when that was previously a rarity. The last week of the month saw a record of just fewer than 24 million shares traded, with a daily record of 48 million shares traded on March 26, when quotes were delayed for two hours and fifteen minutes after the close of the market. The market average advance was also a monthly record, breaking that set in July 1927.[22]

Cobb, a successful investor, denied the rumors, instead saying that he remained home with his wife, who was having minor surgery. He voiced that he had every intention of fulfilling his promise of playing another season for Mack if the manager so desired.[23]

As things turned out, the Athletics would be without Al Simmons, their star outfielder, for the season's first thirty-five games following an ankle injury, as well as another outfielder, Mule Haas, for the first twenty-five games of the season. Simmons was bothered by a bad back throughout the spring and played sparingly. Haas pulled a tendon during a benefit game while playing particularly well against the Phillies during the city series.[24]

With second baseman Tony Lazzeri out of the lineup for the opener, Huggins moved Joe Dugan up a notch and inserted Durocher seventh in the order. The battery was left-hander Herb Pennock and catcher Pat Collins. "Huggins could put his second team in the field and still win the pennant," Browns' skipper Dan Howley would later comment. "He's got a star in reserve for every position on his ball club."[25]

At 7:45 a.m. on the morning of Wednesday, April 11, a twenty-two-year-old painter named Earl Straddon arrived with his lunch pail at a newly refurbished Shibe Park for the season opener between the Athletics and Yankees. He said, "I took a day off, because I must see the opener. I wanted that one seat in the stands [that] is on a line with first base. It's the best in the park, and I don't often get a chance at it. That's why I came early, not to be the first one in, but to get that particular seat."[26]

Maybe Straddon had tailgating during a Giants–Eagles game in his plans since the mild winter was not translating into a balmy spring. Richards Vidmer opened coverage of the season for the *New York Times* by saying, "Cold, rain, and howling winds couldn't stop the baseball season from getting started here today. Some 25,000 shivering, shaking fans sat through as disagreeable baseball weather as conceivable, and the Yankees made them more miserable by walloping their favorite Athletics, 8 to 3."[27]

James Isaminger covered the Athletics all year for the *Philadelphia Inquirer*. On April 12, 1928, he wrote:

> It was cold enough to be uncomfortable, and the blustery wind only added to the unpleasant experience of the day, and yet that was not all. As a parting shot, a thick rain, almost sleet, fell in the final innings, and the big mob, cold and frozen, had a new quirk of nature to face before they could get out of the park. Of all the unlovely days that have greeted the Athletics on the season's opening, none in the twenty-eight years that the club has been knocking about has ever touched such low orbits of discomfort as yesterday's opener.[28]

The traditional Opening Day festivities, other than Mayor MacKay throwing out the first ball, were cancelled. There was no parade to the flagpole, and freezing lips made it just too cold for the band.[29]

It was, however, a new and improved Shibe Park. There was a new electronic scoreboard in right field, keeping the batters from being distracted by the white lettering. The batting orders were listed, and lights were used to track balls and strikes. There were also new water coolers in the clubhouses, dugouts, and umpires' rooms. Last, and not least, Connie Mack walked into a newly renovated private office.[30] There was also a call to replace megaphones with a public address system.

In a bit of superstition, the Athletics changed their uniforms, replacing the white elephant in the front with the "A," which was a throwback to 1914, the last year they won the pennant. The stockings were blue with two white bands. That prominent letter and team nickname was the oldest running in baseball, having its roots before the Civil War.[31] Mack opened the 1928 season with Max Bishop at second base, Ty Cobb in right field, Tris Speaker in center field, Bing Miller in left field, Mickey Cochrane the catcher, Joe Hauser at first base, Jimmy Dykes at third base, Joe Boley at shortstop, and Lefty Grove the pitcher.

The Yankees used the first three innings to relegate the exhibition season to the scrap heap. Grove lasted just nine outs, giving up five runs on as many hits and four walks. He had reportedly put the finishing touches on a curveball and changeup during the off-season, but they did not work too well amidst the gales at Shibe Park.[32] After sailing through the first inning, he walked Meusel, Durocher, and Collins to load the bases in the second, allowing Herb Pennock to drive in the first two runs of the season with a single. During Grove's final inning, he retired Koenig but walked Ruth, who took third on Gehrig's hit. Meusel scored the Babe and took second base on the throw to third, which failed to nab Gehrig. Super sub Leo Durocher scored both runners with a single to give the Yankees a five-run lead. The Athletics answered against Pennock with a run in their half of the third inning on Bing Miller's single. In the sixth inning, three singles and an out cut the deficit to two runs, but that was the closest the Macks would get. With President Barnard one of the freezing fans in attendance, Herb Pennock completely ignored the twenty-second rule as he scattered seven hits en route to a two-hour-and-twenty-five-minute, complete-game victory.[33]

The Yankees were bolstered by their Opening Day performance and eager to get back on the field the next day to dispel any leftover doubts about their preseason. "They're all right. I knew they would be," said Huggins with a smile. "They played with all their old dash yesterday, and with two of the main members of the cast out of condition. I'm satisfied that everything is going to be all right."[34]

"The feeling in the Mack camp was to discount the Wednesday defeat because the weather was not even fit for football," noted Isaminger. "Connie Mack declared that there was a lot in the Athletics team that did not come out Wednesday, and he hopes for better fortunes when the temperature steeplechases up the thermometer."[35]

The ice and snow, however, was way too much for the summer pastime and forced cancellations of all four contests on the eastern seaboard. Postponements, doubleheaders, and a cast of walking wounded were not something Huggins had to contend with in 1927. It was thought to be, like his own cold, nothing other than a short-term nuisance.[36]

Tony Lazzeri had a strained side but was expected back at second base shortly, and Mark Koenig was playing shortstop with a badly lacerated hand. Doc Woods, the team's doctor for eleven years and in the game for seventeen more, discussed the increasing investment value of professional baseball:

> When a player costs a hundred grand, more or less, he is too valuable to allow him to risk permanent injury. The player realizes that too, and hence baseball is more of a profession now than it was in the old days. They have no desire to be deprived of their meal ticket. But when I broke in, $5,000 was a big price for even a start, and things seemed different. If you hurt a finger, you simply stuck it in your mouth for a moment and then went on playing.
>
> Times have changed in that respect, as in many things. I never used to carry a fever thermometer, but now I have one, and it seems the fellows are so anxious concerning their health that I will wear it out within a few months.[37]

Play resumed on Friday the thirteenth, with Yankee coach Charley O'Leary making the decisions for the cold-ridden Miller Huggins. Nevertheless, the Yankees scored early and often against the Athletics. This time, the early barrage sent Ed Rommel to the showers in the second inning, and Jing Johnson followed him after the second inning. The Yankees built a six-run lead after three innings, with five runs in the second inning and two in the third. A line drive home run by Gehrig over the scoreboard and through an open window began the damage. Base hits by Meusel and Dugan, and a triple by Durocher, built a three-run lead, and Rommel was done. Joe Boley then misplayed Collins's grounder, allowing Durocher to score, with Earle Combs finishing the rally and right-hander Jing Johnson with an inside-the-park home run.

The lean leader summoned Ossie Orwoll to take on the pitching duties in the third inning, and he gave up a triple to Gehrig and a home run to Meusel, bringing the score to 7–0. The first-year, combination first baseman/pitcher calmed the Yankees down after that, allowing only one run on four hits in the last six frames. That single run proved to be the winning run in the seventh inning, when Ruth's single brought Combs home to make the score 8–3.

The Athletics chipped away at the Yankee lead throughout the game, with single runs in the third and fifth through seventh innings. Cy Moore started and pitched well enough, scattering ten hits in seven innings, but he was a victim of bad luck. On his third putout attempt, a ground ball to Gehrig in the fifth inning, he was badly spiked after leaving his foot on the bag too long. With the Yankees leading by a score of 8–4, Moore subsequently labored in the eighth inning, allowing the Athletics to cut the deficit to two runs after two runs scored on a triple by Joe Hauser and a home run by Mickey Cochrane.

O'Leary called on Al Shealy, and the rookie's major-league debut was a short one. With still no outs, he gave up a double to Sammy Hale and a walk to Eddie Collins, who was pinch-hitting for Joe Boley. Another call to the bull pen went out to Waite Hoyt, who forced Sammy Hale on Ossie Orwoll's bunt, struck out Max Bishop, and retired Ty Cobb on a pop fly to end the inning. Joe Hauser's second blast of the afternoon in the ninth inning off Hoyt came with no one on base as the Athletics fell short by a score of 8–7.[38]

The final game of the season-opening series on Saturday was rained out, resulting in an early season blow to the treasury of the Athletics. It was a second total washout for the eastern teams, with snow in Chicago also cancelling the White Sox game against the Browns. New York Giants officials were especially unhappy, as a large Saturday showing of 40,000 was anticipated at the Polo Grounds for the "Rajah" and the Boston Braves.[39]

It had to be encouraging for the Yankees to open the season by pounding their strongest rival and their best pitchers on their home field. It also had to be a bit disconcerting to those celebrating the Yankees' terrible preseason. "In short, the Yankees haven't clinched the pennant by their two victories in Philadelphia, but they have shown they know the difference between shadow-boxing and real fighting," said John Kieran in his "Sports of the Times" column.[40]

Some additional pitching help was possibly on the way. Stan Coveleski was reportedly close to beginning his pitching duties, and the re-signing of Urban Shocker was anticipated shortly thereafter. Tony Lazzeri was recovering nicely from his back sprain during the preseason and being given further incentive by the stellar play of Leo Durocher.[41]

The Yankees continued their early-and-often scoring in wintry, windy Boston in a five-game series that was scheduled to end with a Patriot's Day morning–afternoon doubleheader, one of four twin bills officially slated for the year. Harry Frazee and Bob Quinn tried on many occasions to get Bill Carrigan back as manager since his resignation in 1916, at the age of thirty-two. He had managed the team to two straight world championships when he quit to go into the banking business. "My signing a Red Sox contract was just as much a surprise to me as you folks," said Carrigan, "I got talking baseball, and before I knew it I was manager of the Sox again. I can't tell you how it happened unless it was because they didn't tell me what I would have to do if I took the job."[42]

For the second year of his second stint, Carrigan initially decided to abandon plans of fielding a veteran club and had only three players older than thirty in training camp as of the first week of February, with the average age being twenty-four. Carrigan was still of the opinion that a player could be developed at the major-league level without a resort to chaining.[43] But the outfield Boston ended up with was thirty-four-year-old Ira Flagstead and thirty-eight-year-old Ken Williams, with Doug Taitt the youngster, at twenty-five, while taking a wait-and-see attitude with the team's youthful, all right-handed pitching staff.[44] The oldest starting pitcher was thirty-year-old Slim Harriss, followed by Ed Morris at twenty-eight, and then Dan Mac-Fayden, Red Ruffing, and Jack Russell in their early twenties. Said Carrigan on his first year back,

> I remembered the hitting weaknesses and the strengths of some of the veterans who had been in the game before I left. It did not take me long to correct pitching to those veterans. There were some funny instances connected with that too. We talked things over, and I found that some of our men had been pitching wrong—that is, to the strength of some of the veterans for years. We had to change that and did. This year we'll start off with the initial advantage—and it is a big one—of knowing the proper way to pitch to almost all of the regulars in the league.[45]

Dan MacFayden lasted just three innings as Lou Gehrig continued his torrid start in the second inning with his second home run to the opposite field over the fence in left field. But the game was broken open in the next inning with five runs. The bottom five of the Yankee order—Meusel, Durocher, Dugan, Grabowski, and starter Pipgras—had eight of the ten Yankee hits. George Pipgras went the distance, giving up only five hits in a 7–2 victory.[46]

The pattern of playing every other day continued, as the second game in Boston was called due to the cold weather. In New York, both the Giants and Robins were frozen, as well as snowed out, and for a third time, all the eastern clubs were shut down.[47] The first full week of baseball concluded with sixteen of fifty-five games being cancelled, eight in each league. Three-quarters of these occurred in the coastal cities, where the rain and cold shut things down on three separate days.[48] Half of the pitchers in both leagues completed their games, reversing a trend since the lively ball. The only team to score double digits was the Cardinals during their 14–7 drubbing of the Pirates on Opening Day.[49] The second week began with Washington and Brooklyn, along with the Yankees, reaching double digits in runs, while Cincinnati tallied nine.

Lousy weather kept attendance to 5,000 as the series resumed at Fenway Park. Each Yankee regular hit safely in a 10–7 triumph, while once again scoring at least five runs by the fourth inning. The only home run of the game came in the ninth inning by Red Sox outfielder Ken Williams, who at one time was believed to be the next Babe Ruth. Leo Durocher, the native of West Springfield, Massachusetts, who was "supposed to be a weakling with the willow," continued to be a pleasant surprise with six hits in sixteen at bats and five runs batted in for the season.[50]

The play every other day pattern was finally broken, but scattered heavy showers put a damper on what was hoped to be a much-enjoyed, sports-filled Patriot's Day in Boston. Sandwiched between the morning–afternoon doubleheader was the American marathon of the Boston Athletic Association, the Boston Marathon. A record 280 participants were expected for the Thursday, noon-time start. President Barnard, who seemed to be everywhere, witnessed the action as well. Attendance during the 10:30 game was kept down to 4,000, but they were the lucky ones who saw their team overcome a six-run deficit to defeat the unbeaten Yankees. Al Shealy and Cy Moore combined in the loss.

The Yankees took the nightcap, which was a rain-shortened six-inning affair. A large crowd of 32,000, many of whom attended the marathon, jammed Fenway for the 3:30 start. The Yankees jumped on Boston pitching once again, scoring five runs by the third inning after failing for the first time that year in the first game. The big thrill for the crowd came in the fifth, when the Babe launched his first blast of the year into the right-field bleachers. Shortly afterward, the heavens opened, causing one of the worst jams ever, with fans rushing for the streetcars at Kenmore Square and Boylston Street.[51]

Bob Meusel was on pace for a career year and led the Yankee regulars with a .560 batting average, .880 slugging average, and 10 runs batted in. The lanky Californian could have been motivated by competition from Ben Paschal and Sam Byrd, and he was also in the final year of his two-year contract. Lou Gehrig was batting .391, slugging at .783, and had 5 runs batted in. Leo Durocher, the rookie, was batting .435, with six runs batted in.[52]

The Bronx was the home of the Yankees. The borough had a population of 872,200, according to the New York census of 1925, and 926,100 as of July 1, 1927. Estimates closer to the year 1928 recorded a population greater than 1 million. The Bronx was the fastest-growing borough and was classified as the country's sixth-largest city by the U.S. Census Bureau. Building and development in the borough during the first seven years of the decade amounted to nearly $1 billion and quintupled that of the entire previous decade. In 1926 alone, development eclipsed that of the previous decade. The assessed value of real estate was 200 percent higher than that of 1910.[53]

While the Yankees were finishing their series in Boston, the big city was being battered by wind gusts of as much as sixty miles an hour, causing many injuries from flying glass, planks, and debris. Amidst the elements, the Yankees won five of the six games played, with three postponements. They were tied with the Senators for second place and trailed the surprising Indians by one game. The conditions for the opener were fair but cold, with a total of at least 200,000 expected for the three-game weekend series against the Mackmen.[54] This was the twenty-fifth anniversary for the Yankees, and the team was a striking contrast from the one led by Clark Griffith in 1903, which opened before a crowd of 16,293 in rickety Hilltop Park.[55]

Work had begun at the Stadium after the Christmas holidays, which increased the distance down the left-field line from 299 feet, 7 inches to 310 feet. Boxes that had jutted onto the field were eliminated, giving the facility a cosmetic lift, in addition to increasing the capacity to 75,000, although it still ranked as having the shortest left field in the league by two feet, remaining even shorter than Shibe Park.[56]

The Yankees and Giants moved up the starting times for their home games from 3:30 to 3:00. Seventeen years earlier, the games began at 4:00, supposedly out of convenience for the Wall Street crowd, as the market closed at 3:00, while in Washington games started at 4:30 to accommodate government office workers. But fans still complained about getting home too late for dinner. The 3:30 starting time was still in deference to commuters, but it was discovered that most of them were going home to the suburbs rather than the ballpark and were outnumbered by the transients and tourists who would rather take advantage of an even earlier starting time.[57]

The Yankees were the last team to debut at home, and the game was attended by 55,000 freezing and faithful fans—well below the previous year's crowd. Included in the pregame festivities were Commissioner Kenesaw Landis, Yankee owner Colonel Ruppert, league president Ernest Barnard, and New York mayor Jimmy Walker. The commissioner presented the Yankee players with their diamond championship rings, and the league president presented to Lou Gehrig a diploma signifying the Most Valuable Player Award, worth $1,000. Walker proceeded to throw out the first ball—or two—as the mayor, possibly thinking of the new twenty-second rule with the league president next to him, hurriedly tossed a wild pitch.

With the last of the festivities out of the way, it was time to face a hungry Athletics club—the only winless team in baseball. The Athletics had twenty-seven hits in their first three games, but their opponents scored thirty-two runs. Jimmie Foxx was batting .429, Ty Cobb .412, Joe Hauser and Mickey Cochrane .375, and Sammy Hale .364. But Jimmy Dykes, Joe Boley, and Tris Speaker were all hitting below .150, with Max Bishop at .222. The big four of Connie's staff, Lefty Grove, Ed Rommel, Rube Walberg, and Jack Quinn, each shared in the team's four defeats.

A leadoff walk by George Pipgras to Jimmy Dykes on four pitches was of no consequence. The Athletics were hitless until there were two out in the sixth inning, when Bishop hit a bloop single, Cobb rocked one by Gehrig, and a single by Speaker past Durocher scored the game's first run. The Yankees tied the game in the seventh on a sacrifice fly by Collins. Cy Moore relieved Pipgras for a pinch hitter in the seventh inning and in the ninth inning gave up the winning run. Ty Cobb led off the inning with a triple and scored on a single by Speaker. Both antiques atoned for gaffes in the field, with Speaker's misplay of Durocher's fly ball in the seventh leading to the tying run. Grove went the distance for the Athletics, fanning seven on five hits.[58]

After winning twenty of thirty-three decisions during his third season in 1927, many thought this could be a breakout year. Grove walked 232 batters in 455 innings in his first two seasons. This improved to seventy-nine walks in 262 innings the previous season. Grove and Walberg were considered the most dependable pitchers on the Athletics staff.[59]

When asked how he felt about the Yankees being out of the lead, Huggins replied, "Oh, that doesn't mean a thing. It isn't where you are in April so much as where you finish in September that counts. We haven't settled down yet." The manager also responded to the fact that the Babe wasn't in full stride, and Lazzeri was not yet in the lineup:

> There's something in that. But we haven't got our form as yet. We are losing games on account of trivialities—little breaks [that] would go our way if we were straightened out. Take that beating we got from the Athletics yesterday 2 to 1. Two little breaks cost us two runs. One real break cost the game for us. Know what it was?
>
> And in the ninth Ty Cobb got a triple because Earle Combs misjudged the ball in the sun. Speaker followed with a fly, and the game was won. Just two trivialities and we were licked. Still, the little things that make baseball. By the way, I told you weeks ago that Cobb and Speaker would make the Athletics much tougher, didn't I? Well, I think I had the right dope. This man Cobb would be a dangerous ballplayer if he had only one leg.
>
> We had the hard luck to run into Grove when he was invincible and Boley playing a game he never showed before. But it wasn't all tough for us. Pipgras looked pretty good, didn't he? For five innings he pitched about as pretty a game as I have seen in some time. Then came Bishop's hit in the sixth, and he became unsettled. We'll come along all right, but we haven't settled down yet.[60]

The second game of the early season showdown was not one of the day's four rainouts. The skies opened much too late, permitting the Yankees to play their third straight scheduled game, but the inclement weather kept the Saturday crowd way below expectations, at 15,000. Another Athletic left-hander did a number on the Yankees, while Athletic hitters did a number on Yankee pitching. Doing some of the swatting was Rube Walberg, the author of the 10–0, complete-game drubbing, with a home run in the sixth inning. Henry Johnson issued seven walks and as many hits in eight innings but held the Mackmen to three runs before the Macks put up a crooked seven against Arch Campbell in the ninth inning.[61]

The Athletics had handed the champions their first home series loss since 1926. Connie's antiques continued to pay early dividends. Tris Speaker, ranging well in the outfield, drove in both runs in the first game and the first run in the second game. Ty Cobb had hit safely in all six games thus far, with a .444 batting average and five runs batted in. The Yankees were hearing raspberries from the home crowd for the first time in two years, and it was no doubt music to the visitors' ears. For two games, the famous slugging Yankee duo was a combined one for sixteen, but Tony Lazzeri received a warm welcome back into the lineup and responded with a double to right field. More importantly, the poor performances by Johnson and Campbell gave some hope that the Yankees would make a panic move to acquire more pitching.

"The Yanks admit that their pitching situation is serious," commented James Isaminger. "They haven't the staff of experienced flingers that they enjoyed last season. Ruether and Shawkey were released, while Shocker is a holdout and now on the ineligible list for not reporting. Moore is not the pitcher he was last year." Cy Moore was charged with two of the team's losses, with both coming in relief.[62]

Three weeks into April and where was the spring? New York fans lost out on the choice of a day at Ebbets Field to see the Giants play the Robins or the Yankees avoid a sweep against the Athletics. Rain, wind, and cold continued to bedevil baseball treasuries, victimizing Ruppert's team for the fourth time and confining people to indoor activities. The Athletics left town with a little less of the gate share than they hoped, but also with a two-game sweep.

Miller Huggins and the Yankee brain trust used the rainout to brainstorm the need for another pitcher to take some of the eventual pressure off Pennock, Hoyt, and Pipgras, while at the same time putting a happy face on Henry Johnson's eight walks, eight hits, and three runs against the Athletics.[63]

The name of Urban Shocker, to whom an ultimatum from the team was set to expire in late April, was again on the radar screen. Shocker did an about face just before the season opened and announced that he was leaving the radio business and was ready to get back into baseball. Two weeks later, Shocker and the Yankees began finalizing terms of a contract. Huggins made it clear, however, that there would be no checks until the pitcher worked into shape and began throwing for real.[64]

"I finally decided to let Shocker get into shape at his own expense, and he agreed," Huggins explained. He added,

> Just as soon as he shows me that he is fit and ready to take his turn, he will get a contract. But not before that. It wouldn't be fair to the other players who went to training camp and worked hard were I to greet Shocker as the return prodigal and put him right on the payroll. He should have had his training when the training season was on.[65]

Shocker replied that it would not take him longer than a week to get ready. Within the next few days, Shocker would sign for $15,000.[66]

The Washington Senators, having recently dropped two games to Boston, were the Yankees' next opponent for three games, beginning Monday, April 23, but for the fourth time all eastern games were cancelled. The Yankees had played eight of thirteen scheduled games.

Player-manager Bucky Harris, hobbled by an injured foot, blamed the weather for his Senators' injuries and illnesses, particularly his pitchers, Sam Jones, Bump Hadley, and Milt Gaston. Harris believed early in the preseason that he had the deepest staff in the American League, even though right-handers Jones, Hadley, and Gaston thus far had only mediocre careers, along with left-hander Tom Zachary. His hopefuls were Garland Braxton, Lloyd Brown, and Horace Lisenbee.[67] The boy manager then discussed the Yankees:

> I regard the position of the Yankees as being much less favorable than it looked before the start of the season. It isn't so much that the New York club has lost a few games and isn't in its accustomed place at the top of the standings. And I am not trying to be a killjoy for the fans of New York.
>
> A gang like the Yankees is likely to break out any day and keep right on slugging. I am not kidding myself, and I am not underestimating the power of Miller Huggins's outfit. But events thus far have shown me that the Yankees miss Shocker and Ruether, and it will be some time before the young pitchers gain the confidence to step into the breech.
>
> As you know, the Yankees last year sort of overawed some of the other players by rushing out in April and murdering all opposition. This had a strong psychological effect on the Yankees and on their rivals as well. But that effect is missing today. And we all know—the Yankees included—that we are to have a real race. You don't see things like the Yankee runaway of 1927 happen two years in succession.
>
> Bad weather has hampered the New York club, but it has rained on us and on the rest of the league, as well as on the Yanks. And if they have got colds, so have the rest. The Yankees are not getting pitching. Even Hoyt was plastered the other day by the Red Sox. One of these days the

Yanks will begin to kill the ball. But even then they will be handicapped in the box. We are in for a real fight, and I think we have as good a chance as anybody else.[68]

The Babe got down to business the next day, hitting his second and third home runs of the season off Horace Lisenbee. The press was already starting to track this year's pace to the previous year's record of sixty home runs; after nine games in 1927, the Babe had hit just one homer. Herb Pennock gave up three scratch hits and no walks for his third victory, a 4–0 shutout. It was the third straight loss for the Senators and the beginning of a rapid free fall in the standings.[69] Commented Ruth,

Lisenbee tried to shove a fast one past me with two strikes and two balls in the third inning. I knew it was coming, and when it came, boy! I needed no invitation. In the seventh I knew he would change his tactics. I thought he would try to shove a slow one by, and he did. I was in there laying for that one, too, and I put everything I had on it. Still, I am not hitting the way I should. I am down to 218 pounds when I should weigh 225. I am too light, and I feel light.[70]

When asked if he was thinking about going back to the hot dogs, Ruth answered, "Well that may come. I've got to get some heft on my skeleton."[71]

With the season still in its infancy, a Wall Street firm wagered $1,000 even money that the Bambino would not hit fifty home runs for the year. The odds also shifted to the Yankees and Cardinals meeting in the World Series.[72]

Many players were feeling the effects of the unfavorable weather. For the following game against Washington, George Pipgras had to pitch for Waite Hoyt, who was nursing the flu. Cedric Durst got the call in center field for Earle Combs, who was recuperating from a head cold. In addition, pitcher Myles Thomas was in the hospital with a bad cold, and Charley O'Leary was now making the managerial decisions since Miller Huggins was home with the flu.

The Babe mentioned that he felt the twinges of aging:

We haven't got a thing on those flyers who are frozen in up there in Canada or Spitsvarden, or wherever they may be. This is the coldest spring I can remember, and I am getting to be quite a veteran, man. I feel the twinges of old age out there when the wind blows the way it has been singing recently. Yeh, I am getting to be an old man, as old as men go in this business.

One of these days, I suppose, I will have to step out and let some fresh kid step in. I thought for sure I had one off Marberry in the third. It was a ball just to my liking, but I didn't cut at it right and got nothing but a toe-timer. Better than nothing for an old man.[73]

There was a little less hay in Mr. Ruppert's coffers since only a paltry 3,000 decided to show up and watch the champs score a season-high dozen runs. The Yankees routed the Senators and starter Fred Marberry and, for a second straight day, claimed first place on a percentage basis, although still trailing Cleveland by half a game, having played three fewer games. George Pipgras allowed the Senators four runs on eleven hits, nearly half of those to Goose Goslin and third baseman Ossie Bluege.[74]

Pipgras was a player Huggins always had high hopes for. He initially had control problems, issuing forty-four walks and eight wild pitches in forty-eight and two-thirds innings in 1923 and 1924. Patience finally paid off after two years in the minor leagues, mainly under the tutoring of Bob Connery at St. Paul in 1926.[75] Speaking about the hurler, Huggins said,

> I think that my faith in Pipgras, my feeling that he could step right in and take his place as a regular starter, has been justified. George had hard luck against the Athletics last Friday. With a fair break he would have gone the route and won.
>
> Yesterday I understand he worked a pretty game, and would have pitched much tighter ball but for the fact that with a big lead he eased up. Pipgras pitched out of turn too. It was Waite Hoyt's game, but Waite is in bed nursing one of the many colds we have on our ball club.[76]

Players on the other clubs, however, picked up on when he was going to throw his knuckleball.[77]

According to a story by Frank Graham in the *Sporting News*, George Pipgras was down to his last dime and nickel after being released by an unidentified team in Minnesota and risked being arrested under that state's tough hobo laws. He gambled on the nickel and called a friend, who hooked him up with a team in the South Dakota league. His friend had the manager wire him sixty cents for the fare to the city of Madison. That was the beginning of Pipgras's journey to major-league stardom. Once property of the Yankees, he was farmed out four times because of control problems.[78]

The Red Sox left Shibe Park in last place, having lost eight of their first twelve games. They began a three-game series at the Stadium. Their latest defeat was a 3–2 loss to Lefty Grove, but it was the first game their pitching held an opponent under five runs.

Dan MacFayden relieved starter Merle Settlemire in the third inning and nursed a one-run lead going into the eighth inning, which ended up a five-run deficit. Walks, singles, sacrifices, advancing runners, and a two-run double by Bob Meusel off Slim Harriss accounted for the scoring deluge. Al Shealy went the distance, winning his first major-league game. He gave up nine hits and struck out seven.[79]

The Babe had an off day, and for the first time in a few years, he heard about it from the crowd in right field. Two times he struck out, once in the seventh inning with two runners on. Twice he made infield outs with the bases loaded, but in the bountiful eighth inning he managed a sacrifice fly. "I don't mind it," said Ruth. "They weren't the regular customers. I didn't recognize any of my constituents. They must have been cold weather substitutes. For a time I thought they were the graduating class for some correspondence school for razzing who had got in on passes."[80]

With the mite manager still nursing a cold, the leadership fell to Charley O' Leary and Art Fletcher. The former descended from the famous Mrs. O'Leary and poked fun at some of the Boston pitchers:

> I thought there was a rule [that] says you can't use freak pitching. Carrigan used nothing but freak pitching. First we saw a left-hander with a name like Merle Claypool Settlemire. Well, when we settled Settlemire, Carrigan shoots this MacFayden with his specs and the look of a guy who is in the big city for the first time. If this MacFayden isn't a freak, what is he? Well, we knock Mac loose from his specs, and in comes this long, lean Harriss. And if he isn't a freak, then what is? When that guy pitches, you think the flagpole is throwing the ball. If he gets in line with the pole you can't see Harriss at all, at all.[81]

O'Leary did have a heads up on the rookie pitcher, stating, "Keep your eye on this Shealy, even if he isn't an O'Brien."[82]

"We have a great ball club," said Huggins. He went on, commenting,

> It looks funny when we lose a couple. And a team like the Red Sox makes us look bad. The boys get careless, feeling they can go out and win any time they choose. That's got to be driven out of them. But we really have a great ball club. And I don't think the Senators will bother us this year. They look dead already.[83]

The two remaining games with Boston were cancelled and were Friday and Saturday haymaking affairs. The seven cancellations in April, four at home and three on the road, were giving the Colonel second thoughts about cancelling the team's rain insurance three years earlier after paying out approximately $37,000 more than they took in. On the business end, Ed Barrow couldn't help but notice the Cub scores coming in on the ticker with only one postponement all year.

Taking a different position was manager Huggins, whose pitchers Waite Hoyt, Stan Coveleski, Urban Shocker, Myles Thomas, and Henry Johnson felt under the weather and needed the rest. The thirty-seven-year-old Shocker's reinstatement was still pending approval by Commissioner Landis and the team's requirement to get into pitching shape by May 23. Huggins felt no need to rush him into action with Johnson and Shealy pitching satisfactorily. Leo Durocher for Tony Lazzeri at second base, and Cedric Durst and Ben Paschal platooning for Earle Combs in center field, were batting an even .500.[84]

The Giants now had nine of their first seventeen games postponed. "I hardly remember a spring as bad as this one," said John McGraw. Continuing on the topic, he said,

> We have played less than half the games scheduled—only eight out of seventeen. This is the worst spring in a great many years. The miracle is that our players are in as good a health as they are. Playing in cold, damp weather, with chilly winds blowing, is likely to bring an epidemic of colds and flu, but the Giants, in that respect, at least have been lucky.[85]

The "Scribbled by Scribes" column in the *Sporting News* of May 3 stopped short of calling it the worst start for baseball, saying, "The weather has been rotten, without a doubt, and its rottenness has been widespread, on the Pacific Coast, the South, and in the Far East, meaning that distinct section of the United States known as New England. And it has to be put up with."[86]

To shift the beginning and end of the schedule would only cause a conflict with football season,

> It is well enough to argue that the interest in the two games would not conflict, that baseball fans would go to baseball games, while football draws a following that is not greatly interested in baseball anyway. But the facts as they have been demonstrated destroy the argument. Indeed, the minds of a very considerable proportion of baseball fans begin to turn to football with the opening of the colleges in September, long before the big gridiron games start.[87]

Fred Lieb, in his "Cutting the Plate" column, liked the status quo, stating,

> After a month or so in the semitropical climate of Florida, it is no fun spending an afternoon in a refrigerator. And sniffles is the order of the day in the baseball racket. Whether the start of the season is April 12 or 20 doesn't make a great deal of difference. The baseball men are just as liable to get good weather on the first named date as the second.[88]

As April came to a close, the Athletics were riding a five-game winning streak, outscoring their opponents by a margin of thirty-six runs to nine. With one exception, the outfield combination of Cobb and Speaker each hit safely in the team's last five games. They were beginning to look more like the great all-around team that was expected. The current infield was beginning to remind fans of the famous $100,000 group of fifteen years earlier. More importantly, Grove, Quinn, and Walberg were displaying their authority on the mound.[89] The Athletics would be forced to play eleven games in eight days because of six rainouts. The stretch would begin on May 21 and consist of six games against the Yankees and five against the Senators.

"There is no use worrying over the loss of money you never had." Connie Mack was quoting the late Ben Shibe as he lamented about the financial hit from the recent postponements against the Yankees and Senators. Many of the Athletics players used their three straight days off to study the stock pages as they traveled to the circuit's northernmost city of Boston.[90]

The Hugmen closed out their first sectional round in the nation's capital for four games. The forecast beginning on Sunday, April 29, finally called for fair and warm conditions. Washington was in the midst of a five-game losing streak. "This time I am out of the lineup until my foot has entirely healed," said Bucky Harris. "In a half crippled condition, I am not of much use to the team and am just taking a chance of further injury." Jackie Hayes would take his place. Milt Gaston was still looking for his first victory but saved three games; Bump Hadley, a key pitcher in 1927, made just one abbreviated appearance all season; and catcher Muddy Ruel was nursing a sore arm. Harris was forced to use the injured Goose Goslin because of his hitting but had to take him out of games when they were not close since he had to relay throws back to the infield.[91]

The Yankees and Athletics were beginning to make their move, somewhat at the expense of Washington. During the past nine days, the Nationals had dropped two games each to the Red Sox and Yankees and were then routed by the Macks before the rain thankfully rolled in. The five-game skid left them one game under .500 after eleven games.[92]

While still in the heart of haymaking season and with the Senators playing at home against the champions, a crowd of 20,000 showed for the Sunday opener. While the weather finally cooperated, the Yankees did not. They swung back into first place on a percentage basis in their early season battle with the Indians with a 7–5 victory, after pounding last year's sensation, Horace Lisenbee. The Babe hit the first pitch to him in the fifth inning for his fourth home run of the season, with two on base, to make it a 5–1 game. Lisenbee, an eighteen-game winner the previous year, had given up three of

Ruth's four blasts for the year. Herb Pennock matched Ruth's home run total with his fourth victory against no defeats.[93]

Lisenbee started playing baseball when he was nearly twenty years old and was twenty-seven during his rookie year in 1927, when he beat every team in the American League at least twice. His most amazing feat was beating the Yankees five times. His toughest opponent was the Red Sox. "I beat them, but they always gave me a battle," said Lisenbee. "They may not be as strong a club as others, but they're deceptive. They may seem a little dead at times, but they'll come to life at a moment's notice when you least expect it. They bothered me much worse than the Yankees." No one, however, including Lisenbee, thought he could ever replace Walter Johnson.[94]

The month ended with the Yankees handing the Senators their seventh straight defeat. George Pipgras and Cy Moore split the pitching duties, limiting the damage from eleven Washington hits. Untimely hitting would plague the Harrismen all year. Milt Gaston failed to make it past the fifth inning. Charley O'Leary remained behind the bench, but the mite manager was reportedly on his way south.[95]

There were only 4,000 in attendance on an overcast May Day to view the heavy artillery of the Yankees pound out an 8–5 victory. The heart of Murderers' Row—Ruth, Gehrig, and Meusel—combined for 9 hits, 18 bases, and 7 of the team's 8 runs. Fred Marberry bore the brunt for Washington. Al Shealy threw goose eggs for six innings for his second win. Miller Huggins was reportedly somewhere in the vicinity of Baltimore.[96]

Former Yankees Sam Jones and Garland Braxton salvaged the final game of the series, which was the first of the year completed without a postponement. Another small crowd registered attendance for the four games to a disappointing 33,000.[97]

In a column in the *New York Evening Post* on May 1, Hugh Bradley told the story of the old man who couldn't decide whether to sleep with his head under the covers or above them, because something would always happen to make him change his mind. American League managers were faced with the same situation regarding whether to throw left-handers or right-handers against the Yankees. They had faced seventeen right-handers and twelve left-handers, with two of their three losses coming against southpaws. With Herb Pennock being the only left-hander, there was no one to practice against.[98]

There were some questions as to why Harris did not start any southpaws against the Yankees, where they showed some weakness:

> Of course, with three of three games lost, I can now "second guess" and see where the left-handers might have done better, but you have only one guess in this game.

Late last season, I so arranged a series that Tom Zachary would both open and close against the Yankees, and that knocked "Zach" from under his hat on both occasions.

With Braxton needed for relief purposes this year, Burke and Brown inexperienced, and Zachary, in my mind, not effective against New York, I figured it was best to stick to my right-handers.[99]

The Yankees routed the Cadets on an off day at West Point before 6,000 fans who did not get to see a home run from the Babe. This year, their first intersectional batch of games was at home, four games each against the White Sox, Indians, Tigers, and Browns.[100]

· *6* ·

Haymaking Season (May 4–May 20)

The Yankees are bound to face stronger opposition in the next few weeks, but the chances are that they will meet it with a heavier attack. They still look as though they would finish somewhere above second place.

—*New York Times*, May 3, 1928[1]

"*There* will be a welcome sigh of relief heard around the double major-league circuit when the month of April has passed into the misty shades of months gone by," wrote Homer H. Metz in the *New York Morning Telegraph*, adding "Seldom, if ever before, have the big leagues experienced such a deplorable month in the matter of weather conditions and attendance."[2]

Despite the weather, during the first ten days of the season, there was no noticeable difference in the time it took to complete games or umpires enforcing rules for the players to step it up. Games were averaging between one and a half and two hours. Teams were more concerned about winning than finishing the games on time, and any orders from league headquarters fell on deaf ears. Even fans seemed unperturbed about the lousy weather as they sat through the early games.

The "Casual Comment" column in the *Sporting News* at the end of April contains the following observation regarding the time in which teams were to complete games:

We merely desire to note that the fans, with the weather at its worst, and hot dogs with little less, have sat out some games that would seem long beyond reason from the time limit angle, yet they held their seats, regardless of time, cold, or what the good women might hand them when they got home. . . . And we would say that so far, no ballplayer whose work we have put a spyglass on has acted as if he had any idea of time or tide—if he could just do something or other that would put the old game in the won column.[3]

In 1927, the Yankees won fourteen games against Detroit, seventeen against the White Sox, and twenty-one against the Browns, which was a rate of nearly 80 percent. The Indians provided the stiffest challenge, winning ten of twenty-two contests. Beating the lackeys was what Miller Huggins felt was key to the Yankees' success. Huggins commented, "Mack's team usually plays pretty well against us, but we can knock off the second-division clubs much better than the Athletics."[4]

McGraw agreed:

Persons not so close to baseball often mistake the importance of winning games from the second-division clubs. They believe that the so-called crucial series between the contenders decide pennants. Usually they don't. When two or three clubs are well matched, they usually play each other to a standstill, or one may get a 12–10 edge on the other. When teams are matched that way, the club [that] wins the most from the second-division clubs will win the championship.[5]

The Yankees were averaging more than six and a half runs per game with the best winning percentage in baseball, but opponents were putting up fairly impressive numbers against Yankee pitching, scoring seventy-one runs and averaging nine hits per game. It was speculated that the Yankee skipper, now fully recovered from cold and fevers, remained back in New York attempting a deal for a pitcher, as Charley O'Leary was winning seven straight games as a fill-in.[6]

The revamped Browns and Indians were unexpected occupants in the first division, with the Tigers and Senators surprise disappointments in the second division. Detroit already had nine more losses than the Yankees, and eight more than Philadelphia. The standings sometimes listed teams in order of winning percentage, not games back, which, either way, would not take into account the wide distortions in games played (see table 6.1).

Table 6.1. American League Standings, May 3, 1928

Team	Won	Lost	GB	Pct.
Yankees	11	4	—	.733
Indians	13	7	0.5	.65
Browns	12	9	2	.571
Athletics	7	5	2.5	.583
Senators	6	9	5	.4
Tigers	9	13	5.5	.409
White Sox	7	12	6	.368
Red Sox	5	11	6.5	.313

Nearly a third of the eastern teams' games were postponed, including five separate days of total washouts. The western clubs in both leagues saw only postponements at a rate of slightly more than 11 percent. The Indians played eight more games than the Athletics and five more than the Yankees, while the Tigers twenty-two games played to the Athletics twelve was the largest disparity. With eight postponements, the twelve games the Athletics played of the twenty scheduled was the fewest in baseball. The lean leader used the off days to buy time for his antique outfield tandem of Ty Cobb and Tris Speaker to welcome the warm weather. More importantly, the injured Al Simmons and Mule Haas were still nursing injuries.

Connie Mack knew that there was still a long way to go but discussed the season's progress:

> If we get the pitching, we will be a hard team to beat. We have power, and that will cut quite a figure in a long race. I should like to see the clubs in our league bunched up a little better so that there would be a contest from start to finish, and we will be willing to take our chances with the best of them. Simmons is supposed to be out and able to walk around a little, but I do not expect that he will be able to play with us for another month.[7]

In late March, Edward Burns of the *Chicago Daily Tribune* did not mince any words about the Yankee's first western opponent.

> The White Sox, full of synthetic enthusiasm and vigor, through the medium of routine practice, today sought to iron out some of the terrible things that are wrong with the organization. Aside from the circumstances that Mr. Comiskey is somewhat shy of young persons who can play baseball in big-league fashion, the greatest grief has resulted from the fact that when pitchers are pitching, hitters are not hitting, or vice versa. This highly technical quirk now is responsible for what shreds of optimism still exist around Sox headquarters.[8]

The situation remained much the same twenty games into the season. "There seems to be a unanimity of opinion regarding the White Sox," said Don Maxwell of the *Chicago Daily Tribune*. "The club that hasn't finished out of the second division for eight years is as poorly a balanced team as a management could provide. . . . Of course, the White Sox were hit hard by the scandal of 1919, but Chicago's fans rate more than an eighth-place team nine years afterward.[9]

Manager Schalk's club was off to a slow start losing twelve of nineteen games with a total of two home runs hit by relief pitcher Charlie Barnabe and starting pitcher Tommy Thomas. They were one of the teams most encouraged by the Yankees poor preseason.

The four games between the Yankees and White Sox beginning on Friday, May 4, went off without a hitch, much to the disadvantage of the White Sox, as they were manhandled in each game and outscored 29–11. The whitewash of the White Sox began and ended with their second-best pitcher, Tommy Thomas. The Yankee scoring barrage was no doubt helped by the absence of Ted Lyons, who was back in Chicago with the flu. Thomas pitched well in all but one of his six previous decisions against the pinstripes during the past two seasons, but they were all losing causes. Both Herb Pennock and Tommy Thomas were going for a league-leading fifth victory in the opener won by the Yankees. The big blow was a first-inning grand slam by Joe Dugan, who had a perfect day, driving in five runs and lifting his average to .355. "Jumping Joe" was actively shopped around during the off-season, but he had hit safely in fourteen of sixteen games, making Huggins thankful that he didn't trade him.[10]

Connie Mack discovered Dugan while he was at Holy Cross. He played for the Athletics for five years, from 1917 through 1921. Just how did he get the nickname "Jumping Joe"? James S. Collins wrote the following in the *Washington Post*:

> On the slightest provocation, or none whatever, he would pack up his things and go home to mother, without even bidding his boss good-bye. Dugan developed this reputation early in his career when he jumped right from Holy Cross to play for Mack during the Athletics' early days of despair. The lean leader's high hopes for him faded, and he was moved to the Red Sox, closer to his home. But this didn't cure anything, as Boston later sold him to the Yankees.[11]

Nice weather finally ended a long string of rainy weekends, bringing thousands out to area beaches, parks, and other outdoor venues for the first time that spring. George Pipgras pitched the team's second shutout on Saturday, and on Sunday, a crowd of 55,000 cheered on the Yankees and the transatlantic flight crew of the *Bremen*, special guests of Colonel Ruppert. Thirty-eight-year-old spitballer Stan Coveleski opposed thirty-nine-year-old spitballer Red Faber of the White Sox. Covey gave Huggins six and one-third innings, allowing just five hits before weakening in the seventh inning. Cy Moore pitched scoreless ball the rest of the way.[12]

Al Shealy combined with George Pipgras for the victory to close out the Chicago series. The Yankees were impressed with the high-priced Chalmer Cissell. He came into the series batting .347 and finished at .355, hitting safely in each game. The rookie played flawlessly in the field on sixteen chances and made a particularly great play in the first game, robbing Bob Meusel of a hit on a ball hit behind third base.[13]

One week into May, a sharp distinction was emerging in the Barnard circuit between the teams in the first and second divisions, although the possibility of a three- or four-team race remained. Helped somewhat by a disparity in games played, three teams already had at least ten more losses than the front-running Yankees.[14]

The Cleveland Indians came into Yankee Stadium in second place and a team wracked with the flu and other assorted injuries, but their fifteen wins tied them with the Yankees for the most in baseball. Their earned run average was the stingiest in the league, at 3.09, with the Browns a close second at 3.21.[15]

Their front office had been completely overhauled during the 1927 off-season, after the team slumped to 66–87, and a new corporation formed, with Alva Bradley as the team's president for Ernest Barnard and former umpire Billy Evans as general manager. Despite rumors in December that the Indians hired Art Fletcher, they chose Roger Peckinpaugh as their new manager instead. "We've simply got to win for this fellow Peck," said one veteran on the team just before the season began. He added, "He's having his big chance, and we've got to help him make good. And I swear that if I find any man loafing at any time during the season, I'm going to punch that man's nose out through the back of his head."[16]

At the age of twenty-three, Peckinpaugh was the youngest manager in the history of baseball when he took over the reins from Frank Chance as manager of the Yankees for the final twenty games of the 1914 season. The Yankees were forced to trade him after the 1921 season because the Babe was pushing for him to replace Huggins as manager.[17]

What really lifted the spirits of the Cleveland players was a decision by Bradley to raise every player's salary at the beginning of the season. The new slogan invented by Evans was, "Victories from contented ballplayers." The key was to get their three top starters, George Uhle, Willis Hudlin, and Joe Schaute, to click during the same year. If Uhle and Hudlin won twenty games apiece, and Schaute and Garland Buckeye a dozen each, while the rest of the staff chipped in with twenty, then eighty-four wins might just be enough for the team's goal of fourth place.[18]

Miller Huggins compared the 1928 Indians to the White Sox at the same time in 1927, who won fourteen of their first twenty-five games and were then in second place, two games behind the Yankees.[19] Huggins did not believe the Indians were the real thing:

> The flowers that bloom in the spring, tra la, have nothing to do with the thing. Who's going to make trouble for me? Here I am still nursing a cold, and Tony Lazzeri is suffering from a dozen charley horses, and Joe Dugan

has the pipp or something, and Herb Pennock isn't feeling well, and you come here and ask if the Indians aren't going to make trouble for me!

Don't count them out yet. Give them a little time. Wait until some of those birds strike their real levels. I still say that the club we will have to beat is Connie Mack's gang. The Indians remind me of the White Sox of last spring. They went like a house afire, and one morning they walked in here and were burned to the ground.[20]

He was also unimpressed with the salary and other perks that the players received, stating, "Well most of the clubs are being run for the benefit of the players." Continued Huggins,

But the Brotherhood League once tried that stuff, and it didn't work. That slogan "Victories from contented cows," which Billy Evans has hung up, will operate until the cows get discontented on account of losing a few ball games. There is nothing [that] will discourage a lot of young ballplayers like losing a few ball games in a row. I really wish the Indians the best of luck.[21]

The next three series had the possibility of being pivotal for the rest of the season. There was speculation in the Cleveland press that the Yankees might have a tough time pulling away from the rest of the pack, having not yet faced the deeper staffs of the Browns or Indians, compounded by the piling up of doubleheaders.[22] Although it was coming to an end, it was still haymaking season.

The Yankees would face George Uhle on Tuesday, who had been bothered by a sore arm for much of the previous season and was thought by Huggins to be on the market. Nonetheless, he had had the Yankees' number during the previous two seasons, having lost only three of twelve decisions while holding the Hugmen to two runs or less in the course of eight of those wins. Uhle was the product of a flourishing system of semipro clubs in Cleveland, where he was born. From there, at the age of twenty-four, he jumped straight into the majors with no college coaching or minor-league training.[23]

The Cleveland ace shut out the Yankee scoring machine, 3–0, on four scattered hits. The Indians had had Pennock's number for the past few years and continued the unfriendly trend by bunching four of their ten hits in the second inning for two runs, handing the Yankee starter his first loss of the season.[24] The Yankees' fifth loss of the year matched that of Philadelphia. As of the second week of May, there was still a semblance of a possible race in the American League. The top three teams in both leagues were separated by three losses. In addition, the Yankees (15–5) and Athletics (11–5) still had to make up a four- and eight-game discrepancy on Cleveland (16–8).

After nine days of smooth sailing, the weather intervened, and cold, wet grounds cancelled all four games in the American League. None of the games were postponed in the National League, where the western cities were hosting the eastern teams.

The official reason for the Yankees–Indians postponement was wet grounds, and the Indians were not at all pleased with the decision by Huggins to call the game. Home teams, and not the umpiring crew, were responsible for making the call to play or not play, and decisions were oftentimes based on momentum or resting players.[25]

As of Wednesday, May 9, the Yankees were just one-seventh of the way into the season and had played only twenty of twenty-eight scheduled games. This prompted a separate schedule of eight doubleheaders to begin with the next eastern batch of games.

May 21 at Yankee Stadium against Boston
May 22 at Yankee Stadium against Boston
May 24 at Shibe Park against Philadelphia
May 25 at Shibe Park against Philadelphia
May 29 at Yankee Stadium against Washington
June 19 at Yankee Stadium against Philadelphia
June 30 at Fenway Park against Boston
July 14 at Yankee Stadium against Cleveland[26]

These were in addition to the four regularly scheduled holiday doubleheaders—the Patriot's Day twin bill already played in Boston in April, Memorial Day at home against Washington, Independence Day in Washington, and Labor Day at the Stadium against Boston. The Athletics had nine washouts, four at home and five on the road.

Even before the season began, Miller Huggins was somewhat concerned about his frontline pitchers holding up. Twenty games into the season, Herb Pennock had started six games, George Pipgras five, and Al Shealy four. Waite Hoyt, still recovering from a head cold, only had two starts, while Coveleski, Johnson, and Moore each had one. Moore led the staff with five relief appearances, followed by Pipgras, with two. The status of Urban Shocker was still an uncertainty.[27] Although Shealy, Moore, and Coveleski had one-third of the Yankee wins, there was a slew of doubleheaders looming, and Huggins was still concerned about having to rely on three regular pitchers. The situation was not much better for the Athletics, who had played a lower ratio of sixteen of twenty-five scheduled.

Following Uhle's shutout, Cleveland right-hander Willis Hudlin two-hit the Yankees through five innings when singles by Earle Combs and Mark

Koenig in the sixth inning set the stage for a two-out, three-run homer by the Babe to left field. As the Yankees came into the dugout before the big inning, the mite manager reminded them that their Colonel was in the hospital with a high fever, and it was Ed Barrow's birthday. George Pipgras won his fifth game of the season against no defeats.[28]

The final game of the series resulted in a tough 7–6 loss for the Indians. Both managers pulled out all the stops in a game that featured four of the game's top pitchers, Waite Hoyt and Herb Pennock for the Yankees, and Joe Schaute and George Uhle for the Indians. Schaute won twenty games for the sixth-place Indians in 1924, but he slipped to 27–38 during the span of the next three years because of poor conditioning. It was rookie Al Shealy who would ultimately be credited with the win, his fourth against no losses. The loss temporarily dropped the Indians to third place behind the red hot Athletics.[29]

In the May 13 installment of the *Los Angeles Times*, John P. Gallagher discussed the prospect of pennant races in both leagues. While the National League was behaving according to plan, five teams in the American League were on the verge of having ten more losses than the surging Yankees. Most of the grumbling, without surprise, was coming from Chicago, St. Louis, Detroit, and Washington. Fans in Washington were beginning to scream for Harris's scalp, even though the team was plagued with injuries. Browns fans weren't showing up at the park for games despite the team's decent performance. The White Sox had just concluded their series with the Red Sox, which saw both teams knock one another in and out of the cellar, with Boston ending up the seventh-place occupant.[30]

The Tigers would face the Yankees next and were off to a disappointing start, already eight and a half games behind and in sixth place. Their fans, and the players as well, were discouraged with their club already being twelve losses in the hole and the team's front office and manager fining and suspending players for "indifferent play." They were still regarded by baseball experts as the best of the western clubs and gave the Yankees a tough time at the Stadium in 1927, winning five of eleven games.[31]

The series that began on a Saturday and ended on Tuesday was a disaster for the Tigers' second-year manager, George Moriarty, as his club dropped four straight games and, by May 15, had fallen hopelessly out of the race. The Yankees scored thirty-four runs on fifty hits, but the Tigers went to their bull pen just four times to the Yankees' three. The Hugmen had to play catch up twice against Owen Carroll and the loser Lil Stoner in the opening game, once in the third inning from a four-run deficit, and again in the seventh inning from a two-run deficit. Lou Gehrig's fifth home run with the Babe on third kick-started the first comeback. Ruth's eighth home run in the seventh tied the game, setting the stage for Gene Robertson's pinch-hit, game-winning sacrifice fly in the ninth inning. Al Shealy won his second game in relief in two days.[32]

The season was, thus far, going just the way the Colonel liked it. The Mother's Day crowd of 50,000 on Sunday, May 13, was treated to the Yankees' familiar pattern of jumping ahead early and coasting to victory. Herb Pennock won his sixth game of the year, beating every team but the Indians.[33]

Both the Athletics (13–7) and Indians (18–10) were trailing the Yankees (19–5), who began the workweek by becoming the first team to win twenty games, while three other clubs lost their twentieth. Another Yankee victory against the Tigers dropped Detroit to 12–20, the White Sox fell to 9–20 after losing to the Senators, and the Phillies' defeat at the hands of the surging Reds in Cincinnati dropped their record to 5–20. George Pipgras was not sharp but won his sixth game. The Babe's ninth home run off Elam Vangilder in the seventh inning kept him three games ahead of the previous year.

The Babe discussed hitting home runs:

> Old friends are the best. Now there's Big Bertha over there. I just put another notch in her—twenty-seven marks in all—every one of them standing for a perfectly healthy home run. I got eighteen of them last season, finishing with Big Bertha after I had broken Big Betsy's back on nothing more than a humpbacked liner. Yeah, old friends stick by you. Yesterday I went to bat three times with some new lumber I have picked up lately. Twice I walked, and then I struck out. That made me sore. So I grabbed hold of Big Bertha in the seventh, and away went my ninth home run of the season into the right-field bleachers.
>
> Yeh, I sort of liked to get that homer. It was off this Vangilder, and I didn't get one off him all last season. I remember I picked one of his fast ones in the last series in St. Louis in 1926, but I never did sock one off him all through 1927. Old friends sure are the best. I had intended to save Big Bertha for a baseball museum or something, but it looks like she will have to do duty out there until she, too, busts that back of hers for the old Yankees. It's funny how you get attached to a bat. After a while it seems as if the piece of wood were human, a pal of yours. You hate to see it splintered.
>
> But sentiment doesn't carry you very far in this game of ball. Once in a while you face a pitcher who you know is on the ragged edge. You know that if he is knocked out he will get a ticket to the minors. But you go right out and knock him for a loop. Yeah, old friends are the best. Come on, Bertha, into your cage. I don't want you kidnapped like Betsy was last season by those burglars from St. Louis.[34]

The Yankees' final game with Detroit was a twenty-run, twenty-eight-hit slugfest. Hoyt won his second game with a save from Shealy. The Babe homered twice, giving him five in his last seven games and eleven for the season. The team expected to give the Yankees and Athletics trouble was in big trouble. The Tigers lost all seven games played on the current swing. Their sixteen and fourteen more losses than the Yankees and Athletics, respectively, was a deficit next to impossible to overcome, even at this stage.[35]

The oldest pitcher in baseball, Jack Quinn, blanked the Indians for his second shutout and fourth victory of the year. The win put the Mackmen firmly in second place. As of May 15, the top two slots in the American League would remain the same for the remainder of the season, with third place left to linger for a few more days.

The St. Louis Browns were the last of the western invaders for the first intersectional swing. Team president Phil Ball and manager Dan Howley nearly overhauled the team's entire roster during the off-season. The most notable move during the winter meetings was the sale of George Sisler to the Senators. The thirty-four-year-old Hall of Famer had been with the team since 1915. There were hopes to trade Sisler for another star, but there were no takers.[36]

In a surprise move, the Browns acquired John Ogden from Jack Dunn's Orioles of the International League. Dunn once refused $50,000 from Connie Mack for the right-hander. Ogden won 191 games during his eight years in Baltimore.[37] Also acquired were shortstop Ralph Kress and second baseman Otis Brannan. Both played for Tulsa of the Western League, with whom the Browns had an affiliation, and were believed to be excellent prospects. Kress was the youngest player in the starting lineup, at twenty-three; Brannan was twenty-nine but had only two years in the minor leagues.[38]

The Browns had a little momentum built up against the Yankees after beating them on September 11, in their final meeting of 1927. Prior to that game, they dropped twenty-one straight to the Hugmen.[39] Dan Howley spoke after the Yankees beat the Browns for the fourteenth straight time in 1927. "When I complained about the Yankees being in the same league with the rest of us in May, I knew what I was kicking about," said Howley. "Something will have to be done to assure anything like a race in 1928. I am in favor of passing a rule forbidding the Yankees from acquiring any new players."[40] A clean sweep of any team had never been recorded. The Red Sox of 1904 and Athletics of 1911 came within two games of having perfect seasons against the Senators and Browns.[41]

The box score of the opening game of the series on Thursday, May 17, looked like some sort of binary code, with the Yankees scoring single runs in four innings and the Browns single runs in three innings. The Babe once again upped his record pace of last year to nine games with his twelfth round-tripper. Lou Gehrig also smacked his sixth home run, and Stan Coveleski won his second game of the season. Huggins felt vindicated about Coveleski:

Sometimes it pays to listen to Old Man Hunch. I had a hunch that Stanley Coveleski would come back and win quite a few games for the Yankees. Common sense, which sometimes is foolish in this game of ball, tried to talk me off Covey. But I harkened to the hunch— and now he is paying dividends. We'd be in a very bad way if it wasn't for Coveleski. It's bad enough even with the old spitter pitching a six-hit game, as he did in beating the Browns on Thursday. But it would be terrible without this old bird. He still has a lot of stuff—and he has the noodle.

Yeh, it pays to listen to Old Man Hunch every now and then. It was a hunch [that] led me to take Herb Pennock from the Red Sox, without the cost of a dime to the New York club. I was told he could not go more than six innings. That was in 1923. But I had a hunch. The first year we had him he won only nineteen games, with an earned run average of close to three. I am sorry to see Pennock suffering with a bad arm, but he'll come around in a few days—be all ready for the Red Sox when they move into the Stadium on Monday. He never carries around a sore arm very long— just a sweet pitcher, that's all.[42]

Rain postponed every game in the American League on Friday—where all four games were taking place in the east—and the games at the Stadium and Fenway Park on Saturday. The backlog of doubleheaders had reached ten. Miller Huggins was heartened by the performance of his spitballer but concerned about the loss of Herb Pennock and Wilcy Moore with sore arms, in addition to Urban Shocker, who was nursing a wrist injury. Waite Hoyt was still feeling the effects of the cold weather and had only started four games as of the middle of May, going the distance only once. This was the worst shape that the Yankee pitching staff had been in since 1921.[43]

Connie Mack's frontline pitching was working on all cylinders: Lefty Grove, Rube Walberg, Ossie Orwoll, Ed Rommel, and Jack Quinn contributed to the team's stingy earned run average of 3.15. Grove, Walberg, and Quinn had not lost a game in more than a month.[44]

Huggins discussed the upcoming series at Shibe Park with Dan Daniel, stating,

Those half dozen contests will have a very important bearing on the race. Just now Mack's club looks to have the edge over us. But our pitching may tighten and his loosen up by the time we land in Philadelphia. Nobody else figures. Connie, penniless since 1914, is battling with an inspiration, and he will be tough, very tough. We are hitting .322, but the Athletics are going at a .310 clip—and their defense averages at least a run per game better than ours.[45]

The rain held off on Sunday as George Pipgras got the nod over Urban Shocker and ran his victory count to seven without a defeat. After blasting four home runs in his last three games, the Babe was held to a mere single by three St. Louis pitchers, but it did not stop the Yankees from winning their eighth straight game. Ten makeup games and four-fifths of the regular-schedule remained before the second batch of sectional games, when Commissioner Kenesaw Landis cleared the way for Urban Shocker to return to the Yankees. There was also progress regarding Waite Hoyt and Cy Moore's recovery from a twisted elbow, and further contributions were expected from Stan Coveleski.[46]

• 7 •

The Makeup Games Begin
(May 21–May 31)

Up the walls, over the barbed wire entanglements, climbing the flagpole, charging the doors and smashing through the police lines came the real throng, which saw the Athletics and Yankees battle yesterday. The largest crowd in the baseball history of Philadelphia.

—Philadelphia Inquirer, May 25, 1928[1]

The American League race was coming apart at the seams; five clubs already had at least ten more losses than the Yankees. "The pennant race in the American League now looks like there are six teams battling for third place," wrote James Isaminger. "Only the Yanks and the Athletics have a chance for the pennant. So far both of these clubs have outdistanced their rivals, and, by July 4, they should be so far in front that none of the other clubs can ever overtake them."[2]

"There would be no great surprise if the American League race ended with the standings of the clubs arranged very much as it is now," John Kieran confirmed, adding, "but there are bound to be many changes in the National League standing."[3]

For the third straight year, the Yankees had an excellent opening against the west, winning twelve of thirteen games and gaining substantial ground in the standings. The previous year on the road, they won ten out of thirteen, and, in 1926, they took twelve out of fourteen at home. The eastern clubs in the Barnard circuit won two-thirds of the first set of interregional matchups, with only the Senators having trouble, losing nine of fourteen games. After a 6–9 trip out West in 1927, the Athletics nearly kept pace with the Yankees by winning ten of thirteen games.

95

Cleveland emerged as the lone inland team in the first division. They were the only successful visiting team in either league, although they lost four and a half games in the standings. They were playing great defense, but the team's hitting was beginning to falter, and their record of twenty-one wins and thirteen losses would prove to be the high-water mark, as a totally disastrous one-month home stand loomed. The Browns lost nine games in the standings, the White Sox lost seven games, and the Tigers plunged nine and a half games; these three clubs lost twenty-nine of thirty-eight games on their itinerary.

A fan in Detroit posed the following thoughts to Fred Lieb, which he printed in his "Cutting the Plate" column:

> How long is the present condition in the American League going to last? We are getting exceedingly tired of New York domination of everything. We are getting tired of seeing the Yanks in first place, year after year. We also are getting pretty tired of your Al Smith and his brown derby. And a lot of us are going to take great joy in kicking it for a row of bathhouses. Returning to baseball and the American League. I come from Detroit, and Detroit is the best ball town in the country. But interest out our way already is decidedly on the wane. By the Fourth of July, Navin may have to hire people to go to his games.
>
> The truth is, with the season just started, interest in the American League race already has been killed except in New York, Philadelphia, and Cleveland. Cleveland will flop quickly enough, and once the Indians slide the town will turn its back on them. Cleveland is a poor ball town. Philadelphia may hold up longer, but the Athletics will crack before mid-summer. The Yankees probably will win by twenty-five games again.[4]

The postponements from April against the eastern clubs would now begin to be worked into the original schedule to address the large disparity in games played. The twenty-seven games played by the Athletics as of May 21 was still the fewest in baseball, with the Yankees, Giants, and Red Sox not far behind. The Tigers' thirty-six games played was the most in the American League. The Reds and Cubs played thirty-seven and thirty-six games, respectively, in the National League, compared with the twenty-eight games played by the Giants.

For the Yankees, beginning Monday, May 21, fourteen games and four doubleheaders would be crammed into what was originally three games at the Stadium against Boston, four games at Shibe Park, and a single game and doubleheader in the Bronx against the Nationals. The additional four games would take care of two of the three rainouts against the Athletics, one of the three against the Red Sox, and the single postponement against the Nationals.

The players used the recent weather interruption against the Browns to analyze the picture in the American League and came out feeling prematurely confident and somewhat complacent about the competitions' ability to represent a challenge. They were aiming for a wider margin of victory than in 1927. The only team viewed capable of putting up a fight was Philadelphia, a team that the Yankees handled with relative ease the past two years. But even there, it was felt competition from the other teams would hold the Mackmen back. With the exception of the Indians, the rest of the league had already fallen too far behind, and Cleveland did not have enough hitting to go along with their capable pitching. The caucus was a little puzzled at the performance of the Tigers but expected them to improve; and the same was forecasted with the Senators once their injured players returned to health. The Red Sox and Browns were believed to be playing above their heads and would soon fade into the second division. There was no mention of the White Sox.[5]

The Colonel felt that a two-team race was all but signed, sealed, and delivered, but that it would not necessarily have a negative effect on baseball. While in Atlantic City for a brief rest, he reaffirmed his skipper's opinion, saying, "In my opinion, the race for the pennant this year will be between just two teams, and they are the Athletics and the Yanks. Of course, I have faith in the Yanks."[6]

The streaky Red Sox found themselves in fourth place. They had won seven of their last eight games and six in a row, and were within two games of breaking even. For this current run, Ed Morris, Red Ruffing, and Jack Russell each had a pair of victories, with a single win going to Slim Harriss. They were getting great hitting from their outfield tandem, from left to right, of Ken Williams, Ira Flagstead, and Doug Taitt, as well as first baseman Phil Todt. They had just taken two in a row against the Tigers, whose skipper, George Moriarty, was impressed. Miller Huggins paid Red Sox manager Bill Carrigan a compliment:

> Listen, don't laugh at the Red Sox. They will be tough for us. They will be tough for anybody as long as their pepper and spirit holds out and they get any kind of pitching. The fact that they have climbed into the first division for the first time in eight years will give them a psychological impetus which will make them dangerous. Perhaps that impetus will carry them into third place. You can never tell about such things at this time of year.
>
> The Browns, who lost three straight in Boston, tell me that Bill Carrigan has a really formidable ball club which is fighting for every break and is getting plenty of opportunity. Bill Carrigan, a smart manager, finally has the boys playing the game his way—and that means the right way. But of course I am not worried about the Red Sox in so far as the ultimate result

is concerned. When I think of September opposition I still have in mind only the Athletics.[7]

Although ten games back as of Sunday, May 20, this was the best showing for the Red Sox this early in a season since 1924, when they won sixteen of their first twenty-seven games and were a game and a half out of first place. Boston would be put to the test, however, as another round of games was approaching against the equally hot Yankees and Athletics.

The outcome of the first makeup doubleheader was a split. Al Shealy lasted five innings and took his first loss of the year against Ed Morris, who won three of his first four decisions, all complete games. Huggins once passed on Morris and did not like it when bad decisions came back to haunt him.

The Red Sox missed a chance to draw even for the season as Waite Hoyt bested Red Ruffing in the nightcap. Ruffing made one bad pitch in the sixth inning, after issuing walks to Ruth and Gehrig, when Bob Meusel blasted his third home run into the right-field stands, erasing a two-run deficit. The Babe had only one hit all afternoon but made a game-saving catch in the ninth inning off the bat of Doug Taitt.[8] Following Monday's split, the offense made things easy for Stan Coveleski with a twenty-two-hit attack for thirty-eight total bases and a 14–4 victory. Bill Carrigan used only two pitchers amidst the barrage.

The Yankees finished off the Red Sox on Wednesday. Henry Johnson had no problems with his control, previously issuing thirteen walks in twelve and a third innings. The two passes this day came in the eighth inning, when he eventually got out of a bases-loaded jam. Boston right fielder Doug Taitt was caught trying to steal home in the seventh and was cut down at the plate again in the ninth on a failed squeeze attempt.

Meanwhile, the Athletics dropped the Nationals to the basement after sweeping the series. The Athletics got a superb effort from rookie Bill Shores. Tris Speaker recorded his 222nd triple while his mate, Ty Cobb, recorded single number 3,000. The real coup of the game came when Eddie Collins caught the Griffs batting out of order in the third inning and the bases loaded, resulting in a run being disallowed.[9]

The stage was set for a six-game showdown at Shibe Park between the two clubs known all along as the top contenders for the American League flag. The Yankees, with twenty-six wins, were exactly twenty games over .500 and three and a half games ahead of the Athletics, with twenty-one wins.

What was originally a four-game Thursday through Monday series had the two makeup games from the season-opening series added. The worst case for the Mackmen would be a split, but the Babe reminded those in attendance at a Knights of Columbus meeting the day of the first game of the series that although the Athletics had a great team, they would finish in second place and be pushing the envelope if they thought they would finish ahead of the Yankees.[10]

Shibe Park, opened on April 12, 1909, could be used as a model for baseball's progress since it was built. The park's original capacity was 23,000; the grandstands held 10,000, and the bleachers 13,000. Pricing was along the quarter and fifty-cent model for the bleachers and grandstand that existed in the American League, and approximately 2,000 reserved seats cost one dollar. By 1928, the Park was changed beyond recognition, with a capacity of an additional 10,000. What was left of the bleachers, now just 6 percent of total seating capacity, cost fifty cents, and the better seats fetched one dollar. The lot of the working man in the greater Philadelphia area improved, and with it the cost of living.[11]

The total attendance for the Thursday, May 24, showdown was guesstimated at 45,000 for a park that still held 33,000. It was estimated that attendance could have easily been 75,000, as fans from the surrounding counties of Lancaster, Montgomery, and Bucks clamored to see the games. "In short, there were spectators everywhere a human being could sit, stand, kneel, or crouch," wrote Richards Vidmer.[12]

"It was not entirely a Philadelphia crowd which made Shibe Park the Mecca of its baseball pilgrimage," wrote Stan Baumgartner of the *Philadelphia Inquirer.* He continued,

> The farms, villages, and cities of upstate counties and sister states of Pennsylvania yielded up a tremendous part of the mob which swept down upon the citadel of baseball like a huge tidal wave. Maryland, Delaware, New Jersey, and the District of Columbia contributed their quotas to the vast throng. Even from the far off Shenandoah came a plaintive note which reflected the great interest which gripped upstate baseball fans.[13]

Fans who had bought their tickets earlier in the morning and returned home found that they could not get into the park when the games started that afternoon.[14]

"There was never anything like it before," said John Shibe. "Fans came in with wire cutters and actually cut wires to get to the roofs. We found two big sledges left behind in the park, and they certainly didn't belong to us. Whoever heard of men carrying sledges to a ball park."[15]

One fan wrote a letter to Joe Boley, who was born in Mahoney City, Pennsylvania, stating, "Everyone who has a machine has left town for Philadelphia to see you and the rest of the boys take the Yanks over the hurdles. Two large funerals were to have been held Thursday, but there are not enough cars left to make up the cortège."[16]

A column in the *Sporting News* describes the afternoon of May 24 as the most historic day in the history of Philadelphia baseball. It reads: "There was never anything to approach it in Philadelphia baseball history, and the occurrence showed that Shibe Park, enlarged two years ago, is not big enough to accommodate the crowd on big days."[17]

The efforts to control the crowd reached the danger point when an official in charge of the electric scoreboard called the police out of fear that it would collapse under the weight of the fans. As usual at Shibe Park, reserved seats were sold in advance, with the other seats sold on a first-come, first-served basis. The commotion was such that as soon as the gates opened at 10:40 a.m., the fans who arrived after 8:30 could not get to their reserved seats.[18] Bill Dooley of the *Philadelphia Public Record* could not get to the press box and had to be helped through a clubhouse window by four players. When access to the park was closed at 1:00 p.m., other reporters also had difficulty reaching their posts.

There were tens of thousands of fans outside still attempting to get in. Many fans, from ages five to sixty-five, climbed the walls to sit on the scoreboard, and many ended up suspended on barbs after their coats became caught. The activity of the fans, climbing the walls and falling, being shoved over the wall in right field, or dropping onto the field and running toward the grandstand, took away much of the attention of the games themselves. Ty Cobb was cheering on the audacious fans from his vantage point in the outfield. The police force of Philadelphia was not prepared for such a fury but was reinforced from nearby districts after the first game. There were injuries and several fistfights that threatened to turn into riots. Toward the end of the game, fans began to hurl cushions from the upper decks, some aimed at Babe Ruth.

"Calm, placid businessmen who had never thought of themselves as tightrope walkers or human flies forgot their dignity and the wife and children at home to hang their life in the balance as they walked and hung on narrow ledges," wrote Baumgartner. Close to 3,000 fans sat atop the roof of the left-field pavilion, while others smuggled in ladders to scale the lower barbed-wire walls in right field.[19]

Athletic fans were hungry for another pennant, and a World Series atmosphere was already apparent. Miller Huggins was just beginning his managerial career in the National League when Connie Mack won his sixth and last pennant in 1914. Not quite fifteen years later, Huggins was on pace to draw even with the tall tutor. One of the two would add to their flag count with a two-team race all but a sure thing.[20]

The first game was a thriller. The matchup of rookie Al Shealy opposing Lefty Grove was not in Huggins' favor. Shealy ended up pitching seven and a third innings, while Grove went eight innings before he was removed for a pinch hitter with the Athletics trailing by two runs.

Grove got out of a first-inning jam by striking out Ruth and Gehrig with Combs on third and one out. He also came away unscathed the next inning after yielding a leadoff double to Meusel. The Mackmen left runners on first and third in the first at bat off Shealy. In the third inning, Grove was not so fortunate, as two lucky hits by Shealy and Combs, and a misplay by Joe Boley at shortstop, placed runners on second and third. This was followed by a two-run single by the Babe.

Mickey Cochrane led off the fourth inning for Philadelphia with a triple, and he scored on Walter French's groundout. The Macks tied the score in the next inning, when Cobb singled and took third base on a hit-and-run with Speaker and scored when Lazzeri booted Cochrane's grounder.

With the score tied at three runs apiece in the seventh inning, Grove struck out Shealy and then issued passes to Combs and Durocher. After striking out the Babe for the second out, Gehrig singled Combs home, Meusel walked, and Lazzeri singled two more home to put the Yankees ahead by three runs. Al Simmons' pinch-hit single drove in Speaker in the Athletic half of the inning.

Jimmie Foxx pinch-hit for Grove in the eighth inning and failed to get a hit, but Moore relieved Shealy after Bishop walked and Cobb singled. Speaker cut the Yankee lead to one on a groundout that scored Bishop. The Yankees seemingly put the game away with three runs against Ike Powers and Howard Ehmke in the ninth inning.

With a 9–5 lead, last year's premier relief specialist began the Athletics' ninth inning by giving up a single to Mickey Cochrane, who stole second and third. Then Moore walked Haas and threw a wild pitch to score Cochrane. After striking out Hale, he was relieved by Hoyt after going two balls and no strikes on Jimmy Dykes. Hoyt walked Dykes and then Bing Miller to load the bases. With one out, Max Bishop hit a screamer to Gehrig for the putout, but Haas scored to make the score 9–7. With runners on second and third, it was up to Ty Cobb. The veteran hit a line drive back to the box that Hoyt knocked down and picked up just in time to nail Cobb for the final out.

In the second game, rookie left-hander Ossie Orwoll outdueled George Pipgras to gain a split for Philadelphia. Orwoll had lost his last three decisions to Boston, Cleveland, and Chicago and was the one possible chink in the Athletics' pitching armor. Pipgras had won all seven decisions and was pitching on three days' rest. Orwoll turned the tide with his arm and bat, collecting two hits and scoring two runs. The Yankees failed to bunch their six hits, managing no more than one in any inning. In the third inning, Ruth struck out, and Gehrig popped out to Speaker with runners on second and third.[21]

After the first game, Wilcy Moore was sure that something was not right with his arm. After being examined in the clubhouse, he departed for Rochester for treatment by renowned osteopath Dr. Harry Knight. The pitcher told Huggins that he had injured his arm during preseason in Nashville.[22]

A sports editorial in the *Philadelphia Public Record* congratulated President Ernest Barnard for the "terrific speed' with which the games were completed during daylight savings time. A reference to a need for ballparks to install lights is even mentioned. "Yesterday's great contests were a shining example of the manner in which the umpires, quick to obey the mandate of their boss, managed the games with such expedition that the opening tilt of the doubleheader only took about two hours and three quarters to play."[23] The first game lasted two hours and thirty-eight minutes, and the second game just a little more than two hours.

Connie Mack had Yankee nemeses Rube Walberg and Jack Quinn ready to go in the next doubleheader, while Miller Huggins was in favor of holding back on using Pennock. The veteran southpaw advised that he did not feel any pain, but, at the same time, he was not getting anything on the ball. Wilcy Moore was sent home to Oklahoma, possibly for the remainder of the season, following his visit with Dr. Knight.[24] A reliable bull pen was something that the mite manager needed going into an important six-game series on the road against their main rival.

"It is almost unbelievable how a crowd could work itself into such a state of emotion so early in the season," reported Fred Lieb. "It was cold and blustery up among Mr. Shibe's rafters yesterday, more like a fall day in September than a late May afternoon. And one had to pinch himself to make sure that it was late May and not late September." Lieb had never seen a crowd as worked up as the one in Philadelphia.[25]

To no one's surprise, the two undisputed contenders in the American League had split their first six engagements. All signs pointed to at least a split for the six-game series consistent with the previous four games. The Yankees had beaten Grove in two of three decisions, and they also beat Ed Rommel once. The Athletics took advantage of Moore and Johnson and most recently beat the previously unbeaten George Pipgras.

The third makeup doubleheader was played the following day in front of another capacity—but not overflowing—crowd. The final results, however, ended in the Yankee's favor and signaled a turning point in the American League race. Herb Pennock dueled Howard Ehmke for five innings and came away with his seventh victory.

The Yankees broke open a one-all tie in the top of the sixth inning when Gehrig took Ehmke the opposite way for his eighth home run. The blast followed a single by Combs and a walk to Ruth and put the Yankees ahead by three runs. Speaker later drove in Dykes in the eighth inning, which made the final score 4–2.

The Yankees jumped out to a seven-run lead after the third inning of the nightcap as revenge was enacted against Rube Walberg. The final score was 9–2. The Athletics' lefty had his six-game winning streak snapped and lasted just three innings, giving up six runs on six hits. The Babe started the rout with a three-run blast in the first inning, followed by Joe Dugan's solo home run in the second and another three-run clout in the third inning. Ruth's second homer was a solo shot in the seventh inning. The Yankee right fielder and third baseman accounted for all the team's nine runs, while Hoyt held the Athletics to two runs on eight scattered hits.

The crowd might not have been as large as the previous day's, possibly just under 40,000, but the police and park officials had their hands full with rowdy, profane, and confetti-hurling fans. After the fans lost interest during the second game, papers and a lemon were hurled at the Babe as he was going after a fly ball in left field, and at Miller Huggins around the dugout. Both Athletics lefties, Grove and Walberg, had identical 6–2 records, with three of the four combined losses coming at the hands of the Yankees.[26] The two contenders had played one another eight times, with the Yankees winning five. There were the following observations from the *Washington Post*:

> Although the baseball season is barely on its way, with four-fifths of the schedule still to be played, the otherwise staid city of Philadelphia worked itself into a state of frenzy this week over the appearance of the New York Yankees for a six-game series. Reputable chroniclers of such events report that not even in the days when the Athletics were World Series heroes have such scenes been witnessed. Inhabitants of the Quaker City clung from the rafters in the ball park, risked their lives by climbing a twenty-foot fence, and roosted precariously on the roof of the grandstand . . . to view the contest. Theories cannot alter facts. Whenever such occasions arise as the one now being offered in Philadelphia, the huge grandstands will not begin to accommodate the crowds. The question, therefore, is whether it is baseball of itself or the desire to back a winning team that generates the enthusiasm which the American public shows for the game. Circumstances indicate that the latter factor is the ruling one. If there is a way of reversing this condition, any owner with a team below third place in the league would be grateful for the information.[27]

According to the *Philadelphia Public Record*, "Certain ease of manner and latitude of expression are permitted to spectators at any great spectacle. But where liberty ends and license begins, where exuberance is merged into pestiferousness, the line should be drawn."[28]

The observations from the "Tips from the Sport Ticker" column were as follows:

> The scenes at Shibe Park on Thursday never had a parallel in Philadelphia baseball history. If the Athletics had the accommodations of Soldier Field in Chicago or Wembley Stadium in England, they would not have had the room to seat the hordes that swept into their plant from all directions. As many were turned away from Shibe Park as entered, and it is easy to understand that the local plant will never be able to meet the demand on big days, even if thousands of seats were added to it in the last few years.[29]

Not taking any chances, an increased police presence was posted in the upper pavilion of Shibe Park to try to curb the rowdiness, including a promise of five-dollar fines. The public address announcer read the crowd the riot act, announcing a trip to the police station and a fine of twelve dollars and fifty cents for offenders—easily one week's worth of groceries. The umpires also threatened to call the game if necessary. An even higher authority than the umpires bedeviling these two teams all year threatened the game as the tarpaulin had to be placed on the field. At noon, the dark clouds gave way to the sun, and the game was played.[30]

The elder statesmen of each staff, spitballers Jack Quinn and Stan Coveleski, natives of the coal regions of Pennsylvania, attracted a crowd of 30,000—not quite capacity—but then again, this one was just a single game. "Talk to 'Em, Connie," reads the memo above the box score in the May 17, 1928, edition of the *Philadelphia Inquirer.* Thirteen hits, combined with six Philadelphia errors, four by third baseman Sammy Hale, made it almost impossible for the Yankees to lose. Quinn was gone after the second inning, and so was his five-game winning streak after he gave up five runs—four earned—on seven hits. The Yankees scored early and often, once again, with two runs in the first inning and three in the second inning, when they disposed of Quinn.

Covey realized his fourth victory, but he had to be rescued with two out in the sixth inning. The Yankees' four-run lead began to look tenuous after three singles scored a run. Al Shealy relieved Covey and walked pinch hitter Simmons to load the bases. This brought Cochrane out of the dugout to bat for Rommel, but Gehrig backhanded his drive down the first-base line to end the threat. Shealy held the Athletics without a hit for the rest of the game. The final result was a 7–4 victory for New York.[31] This spurt of three straight wins against the Athletics gave the Yankees a 6–3 advantage for the season.

"One by one, Mack's pitching idols, who enjoyed smart runs of prosperity, are toppling off pedestals," wrote Isaminger. "Lefty Grove and Rube

Walberg, with six victories to their credit, tumbled earlier in the series, and yesterday Jack Quinn's winning streak of five conquests collapsed when he was stormed off the tee in two innings."[32]

The Sunday baseball ban in Philadelphia briefly interrupted the series for an exhibition game between the Yankees and the York team of the New York–Pennsylvania State League while the Athletics traveled to the nation's capital. The Yankees used the game as an opportunity to try out a new pitcher named Roy Sherrid. Sherrid scattered ten hits in a 9–2 victory. He pitched as Sherid Richards in the New York–Penn League while attending college to keep his amateur standing and won thirteen of seventeen decisions. The Yankees fought the Cardinals regarding which team had the valid option, and the Yankees won. The game attracted an overflow crowd of 4,000.[33]

The record attendance for the first three days of the series at Shibe Park, estimated at 115,000, was more than enough to pay for the $60,000 in combined salaries of Ty Cobb and Tris Speaker. The lean leader invested an estimated $300,000 in the players currently under contract and $150,000 in players who failed to come through. The Giants continued to be the biggest draw, however.[34]

The banner above the box score in the May 28, 1928 copy of the *Philadelphia Inquirer* screams, "Hey! What's the Matter?" The Mackmen dropped their fourth consecutive game—a real contest—in Washington. The Nationals snapped a nine-game slide after a two-hit game by Bump Hadley.[35]

The race in the Barnard circuit further deteriorated, as Cleveland's loss to St. Louis gave the Tribe seventeen losses on the year, leaving the Athletics as the only club with fewer than 10 more losses than the Yankees.

The two foes got back to business to begin the workweek, with the Yankees thrashing the Mack's again by a score of 11–4. The pitching matchup was once again in the Athletics' favor, with Lefty Grove facing Henry Johnson. But the ace of the Mackmen could not stop the quartet of Durocher, playing shortstop for Koenig, Ruth, Lazzeri, and Dugan. These men alone accounted for eight of the team's runs.

Al Simmons made his debut in left field and blasted his first home run of the season in the third inning to put the Mackmen ahead by two runs; nonetheless, the banner atop the box score in the May 29, 1928, issue of the *Philadelphia Inquirer* laments, "Woe, and More of It." The Yankees erased the deficit, battering Grove for five runs in the fifth inning. Johnson and Combs singled, and Durocher reached on Hauser's error. With the bases loaded, the Babe then drove in two runs with a single. After Gehrig struck out, Meusel's groundout forced Ruth but scored Durocher with the third run. Lazzeri's blast over the scoreboard brought in Meusel with the next two runs for a 7–4 lead.

Henry Johnson outlasted Grove, who was taken out for a pinch hitter in the sixth inning. Wildness victimized the rookie, who had to be relieved by Arch Campbell in the seventh inning, with the Yankees still leading. Campbell pitched two and two-thirds innings of shutout ball. The Yankees tacked on two more runs in the eighth inning on hits by Combs and Durocher, and a two-run home run by Joe Dugan in the ninth inning.[36]

It seemed to be coming apart at the seams once again for Connie Mack's pennant ambitions. With a split in the six games against the Yankees and a victory against Washington as a worst-case scenario, the Athletics would have knocked half a game off what was a three-and-a-half-game deficit. But a much more disastrous scenario unfolded and the Athletics found themselves staring at a seven and a half game deficit. Most upsetting to the lean leader was the collapse of Grove, Walberg, and Quinn after building so much momentum. The Yankees averaged seven runs per game for the six games.[37]

A repeat of the previous year was evident, and in his column "Is Zat So," Gordon Mackay nearly wrote a swan song:

> T'was the acid test, and the Yankees met it in their might and strength. The five games which have been played between the world champions and the Mackmen carry but one message to anybody whose vision is clear and whose judgment is unbiased. The Yanks are absolutely the greatest ball club in this country—one of the greatest, if not the mightiest, in the history of baseball . . . few of the loyal are willing to admit now that there is a chance of any pennant flying at the halyards of Shibe Park. Nothing save a railroad accident, earthquake, or assassination seems likely to wrest the flag from the champions in this year 1928.[38]

The Yankees yet again appeared to be a roadblock to one last pennant. "Once again it appears that the Yankees have stepped between Connie Mack and his rocking chair," wrote John Kieran. "Connie wants to retire. He has been working at this trade of baseball, man and boy, for more years than he cares to remember. He's a wee bit tired of arguing with umpires, waving a scorecard at outfielders, and traveling 12,000 miles a year."[39]

But Kieran admitted that there was still much baseball to be played, as did Huggins: "I'd like to wait until we make a swing around the West before I commit myself. A road trip is the best test of a team. I'll know more about my young pitchers then." By that time, the Yankees were hoping to increase the lead by another third to possibly a dozen games.[40]

The Athletics did have an announcement, however. Connie Mack had finally landed George Earnshaw from the Baltimore Orioles of the International League. Born in New York City, on February 15, 1900, and reared in

Philadelphia, Earnshaw was very pleased, saying, "It has always been my ambition to pitch in the major leagues, and I know I can win for the Athletics."[41] After disappointing their fans, the Athletics packed their bags for Fenway Park and would not see Shibe Park for nearly a month.

Huggins tried to take the latest successes in stride:

> Well, it looks like a nice tight race. Yes it is a race. Any lead of less than ten games always is in jeopardy. Sickness, flood, famine, measles, mumps—anything may happen. Suppose the Babe stepped on a broken bottle? Or Gehrig fell off his roof while doing a job of painting the shingles? Yes sir, I still insist that we are in a real contest. We went into Philadelphia and what happened? We lost a game! Now we have lost seven in all and have won just thirty-one. The Athletics, with that great pitching staff and their punch, are bound to be heard from.
>
> Well, the Senators seemed to have perked up and are in the midst of a winning streak. We play them two today, two tomorrow, and one on Thursday, and then leave for Detroit, where we work on Saturday. The Senators may knock us over and stretch our losing streak to eight complete games. Yes, it is quite a race, quite a race.[42]

Both the Colonel and the business manager were not concerned about any decrease in attendance, as the team was once again making a shambles of the race. What was more important was putting a winner on the field.[43]

The Senators occupied each rung of the American League ladder in 1928, sharing first place for just one day back on April 16. Since winning five of their first six games, they were, after the Phillies, the worst team in the major leagues, winning only one-third of their games.

A three-run triple by Leo Durocher was the key hit during a 3–2 victory in the Yankees' first game against the Senators. George Pipgras went all the way, allowing six hits. The Yankees were without regulars Mark Koenig, Bob Meusel, and pitcher Cy Moore. Milt Gaston and Lloyd Brown were pounded in the nightcap, 12–3. The twin sluggers each had two home runs, as well as one for Combs.[44]

As of May 29, the Yankees were at one of the high-water marks of the season, having won thirty-three of their first forty games and boasting an eight-and-a-half-game lead on second-place Philadelphia. The champions were playing at an incredible .825 clip, scoring seven or more runs twenty-five times. Going back to the previous year's rampage, including the postseason, during a span of nearly 200 games, they won 147 games and lost 51, good for a .742 clip. There was additional commentary from Alan Gould in the *Los Angeles Times* on what a shambles the Yankees were again making of the race. With a bigger lead over Philadelphia now than they had mustered this time last year, should Connie Mack concede the race, as he had done last June? Gould wrote,

> It began to look a bit interesting in the American League this year after the Athletics displayed signs of being a distinct menace to the world champions. But it hasn't lasted long. By taking five out of six games from the Athletics, the Yankees have just about ruined Mack's prospects and jumped into a bigger lead than they had at this stage of the race a year ago. Connie Mack admitted last year that the pennant race was settled in June. He may be forced to make the same admission again.[45]

A huge Wednesday, Memorial Day crowd of 70,000 for a regularly scheduled doubleheader was disappointed by the results and the rain as Senators lefty and former Yankee Garland Braxton shut out the Yankees on three hits. This was his thirteenth appearance of the year but his first start. He had five saves, three losses, and four relief appearances. The complete game shutout lowered his earned run average to 1.64. Urban Shocker pitched the final two innings and gave up three hits and no runs during his only appearance of the year.

Braxton's debut for Huggins came at the tail end of the down year of 1925, after being purchased from Springfield of the Eastern League. He beat Ted Lyons and the White Sox, 7–6, in a cold, empty Yankee Stadium. After the 1926 season, he was traded to the Senators, along with an outfield prospect, for Dutch Ruether.

The Yankees began to exact revenge on Horace Lisenbee in the second game, when they scored seven runs before the second inning was over, but a higher authority stepped in and washed away what looked like a certain victory for Stan Coveleski.[46] As of the final day of May, the only Yankee regular who remained injured for any extended period of time was second baseman Tony Lazzeri. That was until Leo Durocher, at shortstop, had to fill in for Mark Koenig, who had been out of the lineup since May 21, and Cedric Durst for Meusel in left field since May 29. Each of Huggins' four reserves, including Robertson and Paschal, were batting over .300.

This probably had little to do with the fact that the Thursday post–Memorial Day crowd was less than one-tenth that of the day before. As it turned out, Durst's home run in the second inning was the only scoring needed for Herb Pennock's second shutout and eighth victory of the year. Both shutouts were 4–0 scores against Washington.[47] Following the game, Pennock mentioned that he had nothing on the ball during the last three innings and complained of an aching arm, pitching, as Fred Lieb describes, "with heart and head, saving his best stuff for the pinches."[48]

**Table 7.1. Yankee Postponements after the
Second Sectional Batch**

Date	Opponent	Makeup Date
April 12	@Athletics	May 24
April 14	@Athletics	May 25
April 17	@Red Sox	
April 22	Athletics	
April 23	Senators	May 29
April 27	Red Sox	May 21
April 28	Red Sox	
May 9	Indians	
May 18	Browns	
May 19	Browns	
May 30	Senators	

The second go-round against the eastern rivals, which included four makeup games, went nearly unscathed as far as postponements (see table 7.1). The games-played disparity had almost been closed as the Yankees headed west, with only two fewer games than St. Louis and Detroit, and one fewer than Cleveland and Chicago.

Yawning Spaces in Grandstands (June 2–June 17)

> The Yanks may break or may batter the race as they will—but a
> gent named Babe Ruth will draw them in still.
>
> —*New York Evening Post*, June 13, 1928[1]

*H*opes of anything more than a two-team race in the American League were fading. The players on the Athletics were in good spirits, however, and nowhere close to throwing in the towel, even as they trailed by seven and a half games with more than half a season to play. They were still the lone challenger in the American League. But earplugs could not mute the gossip in the baseball world that they had no "guts" after losing five of six games at home to the Yankees.[2]

The holler was growing, nonetheless, that something had to be done to weaken the Hugmen. The Colonel let it be known:

> Let the other American League clubs go out and buy high-class players as we have done! We couldn't win pennants until we spent money in the open market for championship material. We had to take chances, and it must be remembered that we didn't get a single player from a rival club for nothing.
>
> It is Colonel Ruppert's desire to give New York the best team in baseball, and he intends to peruse that policy as long as the Yankees need strengthening and star players are available. The other American League clubs will have to outbid us whenever we seek promising youngsters. They shouldn't kick because the Yankees win pennants and world championships. For eighteen years, the American League failed to have a championship team in New York, which now is on top.[3]

In the June 2, 1928, *New York Telegram*, Pat Robinson compares the Yankees to the old Orioles, saying,

111

The Yanks today are the most confident, struttingest team that ever trod on a ball field. The old Baltimore Orioles, with such noted strutters as McGraw, Jennings, Robinson, and Keeler in the cast, probably could not have matched the Yanks in their confident disdain of all rivals. To hear the Yanks tell it, the race is practically over, and they are only playing out the schedule.[4]

The inferiority of the American League would become a stark reality four decades later, but the question was then being raised as to whether it was a lack of great players, especially great pitchers, in the junior circuit making the Yankees look better than they really were. Were they lucky to face the Pirates rather than the Cardinals or Giants in the Fall Classic?

This was all the more remarkable as Yankee reserves had to be called to duty. The injured included third baseman Joe Dugan, who was suffering from a mashed finger; outfielder Bob Meusel, who was out due to a charley horse; and shortstop Mark Koenig, who had been benched because of a bad hand. Gene Robertson, Cedric Durst, and Leo Durocher, respectively, were the fill-ins. Not having Cy Moore available was not much of a concern either with Urban Shocker and Arch Campbell in the wings.[5] Pat Collins and John Grabowski were handling the catching chores for Benny Bengough, who had a split finger. The Yankees ranked third, behind the Red Sox and Athletics, in defense, even though Miller Huggins was using his reserves in the infield.[6]

The Yankees were aiming to win a dozen of the sixteen matches out west, or three of four in each series. This would at least match the Athletics, if not better their performance and increase their lead. They began June by entertaining a Friday crowd of 8,000 in Toronto on a Friday with the leading team of the International League, before moving on to Detroit for four games. This would be followed by three series of four games in Cleveland, Chicago, and St. Louis during a stretch of sixteen days, ending on June 17.

Detroit is the city where it all fell apart twenty years ago, almost to the day, for the Yankees, as recalled by the team's traveling secretary since 1903, Mark Roth, to Hugh Bradley of the *New York Evening Post*.[7] The Highlanders, as they were known during the epic pennant race of 1908, were in the thick of it, just a half game back as they took off for the west. They gained a split with Cleveland and took the first game in Detroit on June 9, but managed only one more victory during the swing's remaining twelve games.

The tailspin continued as the team, managed by Clark Griffith and Kid Elberfeld, lost sixteen of their next nineteen games and landed in last place, seventeen games behind. The western clubs dominated the first division that year, with Detroit, Cleveland, Chicago, and St. Louis finishing in order. The Highlanders ended that year with 103 losses. Twenty years later was a much different story, with any chance of a 1908-type pennant race being an impossible scenario.

Detroit fans were not happy about their team's lack of competitiveness, as described by James R. Harrison for the *New York Times*:

> Detroit critics are particularly exercised over the situation. They demand that Babe Ruth be curbed by a constitutional amendment, that Lou Gehrig be traded to the Red Sox or somebody, that Tony Lazzeri and Earle Combs be allowed to play only every other game, and that Herb Pennock be made to retire to his farm, where he may devote his days to the improvement of the breed of silver foxes. In effect, the experts demand that the Yanks pick on somebody their own size.[8]

Ty Cobb had a decent managerial career with Detroit for six years, with the team's record improving in each of his first four years, beginning in 1921. The Tigers last competitive season was 1924, when they were within a half game of first place in mid-August. Cobb blamed the team's failure on the tightwad president, Frank Navin, who refused to purchase Johnny Neun from St. Paul for the stretch. He also urged George Moriarty not to give up on pitching prospect Carl Hubbell.[9]

Harrison also reported that reliable sources claimed that only three teams made money in the American League last year, the Yankees comfortably and the Athletics and White Sox just barely. The five clubs in the red were caught in a vicious cycle since they couldn't spend money they were not making. But it should be remembered that free agency was still a half-century in the future, when rich clubs could steal away players established by poorer clubs, and teams were now in about the second inning of copying the Cardinals' model of owning a network of farm teams.[10]

In the first game of the series between the Yankees and Tigers, George Pipgras was locked in an extra-inning duel with Detroit right-hander Elam Vangilder but won his ninth game of the year. The righty was in and out of trouble throughout the entire game. The Tigers stranded thirteen base runners and were not getting the timely hits this year.

With one out in the tenth inning, the Yankee bench came through. Singles from Cedric Durst and Gene Robertson off Vangilder came after walks to Ruth and Gehrig. The Tigers had Ruth nabbed at the plate on Durst's hit, but Tiger backstop Mervin Shea dropped the ball as he made the tag, and the Babe badly twisted his ankle in the process; Gehrig scored on the play as the ball rolled to the backstop. Robertson singled, scoring Durst from second for a 5–2 victory.[11]

The second game was on a Sunday, and one of the largest crowds in the history of Navin Field, estimated at 40,000, came out to see what their

Tigers could do with the best team in baseball. The scene was somewhat reminiscent of what took place in Philadelphia, with the Detroit police getting involved. Still without Koenig and Meusel, the Yankees had to replace the Babe during the fifth inning due to his badly swollen ankle. For a second day, the seventh inning was the undoing for Detroit: The Yankees scored five times on three hits, two walks, and two errors to break a two-all deadlock. The latest setback gave the Tigers exactly twenty more losses than the leaders. "I have the greatest collection of six-inning pitchers in the world," said the Tiger skipper. "Unless the Yankees run into a train wreck soon, this race is going to be all sewed up by July 4."[12]

Following a relatively full schedule of play for the entire month of May, the game nearly had a two-day retreat due to rain and wet grounds, wiping out the last two games in Detroit. Only three of a full lineup of sixteen games scheduled for Monday and Tuesday were played. The inclement weather turned out to be a timely break, as an x-ray on Ruth's ankle showed only a bruise—although a painful one—and he was considered day-to-day.[13]

Since the previous autumn, many observers had been questioning whether the thirty-three-year-old Ruth was slowing down. It seemed that he was not getting to fly balls he would normally get to, especially in the latest series in Detroit.[14] Ruth answered his critics:

> What's all this I hear about losing some speed? Some of the boys around here tell me that while I was away on business in the west some of the newspapers said that I was slipping. Well, if this bird is slipping he should be the first to know about it—and he hasn't noticed it yet.
>
> What's the matter with twenty-five home runs in fifty-five games? Has anybody gone any further than that? Once they tell you they have noticed that you have started to slip you begin to watch out for waivers. But ten will get you twenty if you think about that in the next month. I won't make those birds change their stories. I'm slipping, eh?[15]

The *Los Angeles Times* also speculated on June 19 that the Colonel and his skipper were worried that the Babe was slowing down in other departments as well, even though he was on a pace to break his single-season home run record. Fans, scouts, rival players, and writers had all noticed that Ruth had slowed down noticeably since the previous fall. During the spring, he was not going very far for balls, and the thought was that he was just relaxing, but recent play in the outfield confirmed otherwise.[16]

"Babe could and would easily hit 100 home runs if he got a fair break in pitching," said Joe Sewell,

> I have never seen a man who hits with the power of Ruth. It is impossible to predict definitely what he would do if pitchers would pitch to him as

they do me and the average league player, rather than issue passes. Believe me, I know how hard this Ruth hits a ball. When he happens to smash one my way, it almost puts gray hairs on my head, the pill comes so hard and fast. It's worse than facing a cannon.[17]

The two-day layoff was also an opportunity for manager Huggins to chat with the press about the race in the National League, since there was virtually none in the American League. He had predicted the last two champions and thought the Giants would prevail this time, saying, "It would be sort of foolish for anybody to come out with a flat prediction about the National League race at this time. It's all scrambled together, and five or six teams are trying to cut one another's throats. They all have a chance, but I think the Giants are going to win."[18]

Huggins also announced that the Yankees were standing pat on any trades, although the team could use another catcher and southpaw hurler but were not rushing into any deals:

I have another catcher in Grabowski. He isn't hitting so much, either, but what difference does that make? The rest of them are going pretty good, aren't they? And we're winning, aren't we? Furthermore, where could I make a deal if I wanted to? Didn't everybody avoid me as if I were a leper when I wanted to talk trade last winter?

Say, if some unforeseen emergency arose where I had to have a catcher immediately, I have two pitchers I could use. Shocker was a catcher long before he ever threw a spitter, and Archie Campbell had pitched only eight games in his life when Frank Isbell signed him for Wichita Falls. In fact, Campbell thought Isbell had signed him as a catcher.

Would you believe it, that fellow Campbell wants me to use him as a catcher right now? To tell you frankly boys, I could use another left-hander if some angel would present me with one, and I might find a place for a top-notch receiver, but I know that Connie Mack isn't going to send me Grove or Cochrane.[19]

Base running was not the first thing that came to mind when discussing the Yankees, but, according to an article for a rainy day in the *New York Post* on June 5, they were a team that knew how to manufacture runs. "If there is any truth to the old saying that the race is always to the swift, it is just another reason why the Yankees seem destined to win the pennant this year," wrote Hugh Bradley. Although they did not steal many bases, Earle Combs, Mark Koenig, Bob Meusel, Babe Ruth, and Leo Durocher ranked among the top base runners in the game.[20]

Huggins addressed the Yankees' base-running strategy just before the season began, commenting,

People have an idea that we won't run much. It's true that we don't run as much as the Tigers or Senators, but, then, we don't have to run as much as they do. You wouldn't expect Earle Combs, for instance, to do much base stealing when he has such hitters as Koenig, Ruth, Gehrig, and Meusel coming up behind him. That's why Earle stole only ten bases last year, although he is one of the fastest men in the game.

Don't let anyone tell you we haven't plenty of speed. Combs, Paschal, Durst, Meusel, Koenig, and Lazzeri are all pretty fast, and for big men, Ruth and Gehrig are about as speedy as they come. Big fellows like Gehrig don't seem to be going so fast as the short-striding little fellows, but they cover more ground in one jump than a little guy does in two.

Gehrig also might surprise a lot of outfielders that think they are fast. We weren't the slowest team in the league last year. We stole ninety bases last year, and that's as many as the White Sox or Browns stole and more than the Red Sox. The Athletics stole only ninety-eight, which, if I remember rightly, is exceeding the number Ty Cobb stole in one year a few seasons ago.[21]

The western swing resumed at League Park, in Cleveland, on Wednesday. Along with Detroit, this was a city that was very much a part of an optimistic, industrial United States. Its population increased from twenty-five souls in 1800 to 381,000 one hundred years later. Featured as "Opulent Cleveland" in the "Our Changing Cities" series in the *New York Times*, it now stood at 1 million proud, all living between the statues of its two "prophets," Mark Hanna and Tom L. Johnson. The soot blowing out of the blast furnaces from the Cuyahoga River did not detract from its cultural appeal, emphasizing music and the arts, helped along in no small part by its Community Fund. In addition to more than 3,000 industrial plants, there were also renowned museums and educational institutions.[22]

The Cleveland Indians were reeling after reaching their high point of the season, at 21–13, on May 21. They lost nine of twelve games, with the slide beginning with a pair of 4–3 loses in Chicago to begin the third week of May, and they didn't help themselves with sloppy defense. Cleveland management felt that the team might turn around with George Uhle on the mound and elected to play on a cold, threatening Wednesday, but the result was defeat.

The Tribe got to Herb Pennock for five hits and two runs in the first three innings, and one run on two hits in the last six, as the Yankees won, 8–3. It was only Pennock's second win against Cleveland since 1926. He had yet to be relieved this year in ten starts, with nine victories. With their just-concluded loss, Ernest Barnard's old club joined the others in his circuit—with the exception of the Athletics—with at least fifteen more losses than the Yankees.

The makeshift Yankees again beat the Indians the following day, with George Pipgras going the distance for his tenth win. In the ninth, with two on, the Babe hit his twentieth home run into right field and onto the roof of someone's house, followed by an even longer clout by Gehrig, his twelfth, capping an 8–2 victory. Gehrig was just one home run behind his 1927 home run pace, while Ruth was five games ahead. "Jumping Joe" Dugan was batting .348, and it was not going unnoticed by the mite manager:

> The fans in the stands may not realize his worth to the Yankees, but all of us on the club know that Joe Dugan is about the most important bird we have. When Joe is going great, like he has been all year, the Yanks are almost a sure bet to win. Joe is up there with the .340 mark, but best of all is he is driving in a lot of runs. Any pitcher in the league will tell you that Joe is about as tough to pitch to in a pinch as anybody you can name.
>
> I suppose the baseball writers will say a lot about those homers Ruth, Gehrig, and Lazzeri got off Schaute yesterday, but they were not as important as Joe's work. The break in that game came when Joe made that marvelous stop with the bases full and turned it into a double play. If that ball had gotten by Joe, as it had every right to do, Schaute would have been away out in front, and the boys might never have had those homers.[23]

General Crowder, let go by the pitching-rich Senators, bested Lefty Grove as the Browns beat the Macks for a second straight day. With Philadelphia now an even ten games out of first, the race in the Barnard circuit had become a dead issue (see table 8.1). The seventh-place team in the National League was only a half game worse.

The Yankees got back to business against the Indians following their fourteenth postponement and won their sixth straight game. Once again, the seventh inning was the lucky frame, with the Indians leading by one run, and the undoing of the loser, Jake Miller. The reserves played a big part once again, with Durocher singling in Combs after his leadoff triple. Gehrig's thirteenth homer of the year in the ninth inning made the final score 7–3 and improved Waite Hoyt's record to 7–1.

The specter of another runaway by the Yankees, which seemed to be where things were headed, was bringing more predictions of doom for the

Table 8.1. American League Standings, June 7, 1928

Team	Won	Lost	GB	Pct.
Yankees	38	8	—	.826
Athletics	27	17	10	.614
Browns	24	24	15	.500
Indians	24	24	15	.500
Tigers	20	28	19	.417
Red Sox	16	24	19	.400
Senators	16	27	20.5	.372
White Sox	17	30	21.5	.362

junior circuit. Hopes that the Athletics would at least pose a challenge were fading.

"American League leaders are in trouble over the situation," wrote John F. Wray in the *St. Louis Post-Dispatch*,

> The Yankees have been in the saddle too long for the good of the league. No city can compete with the Yankees in finance, and so none can compete with them in spending money for talent.
>
> How to combat the situation is not yet apparent. The only city that might enter the field and make it a two-team monopoly, instead of one, is Chicago. Alas, the head of the club there is asleep at the switch, while his pocketbook is suffering from acute stringency of the outlet.[24]

The Yankees played at a .674 clip after the first forty-six games of 1927. Not too many people would have expected that just after spring training in 1928 they would actually improve to winning more than 80 percent of their games. The 31–15 record of the Yankees in 1927 was identical to that of the Cubs during their 1906 record-breaking season, when they won 116 games. The 1928 Yankees were on a pace to win 127 games, but even a .745 clip from this point onward would surpass the Cubs. By the late 1920s, winning, or even losing, at a 70 percent rate, even during a third of a baseball season, had become very difficult at the major-league level.[25]

There was a pressing concern amongst the other owners in the circuit that the deep pockets of the Yankees would increase their staying power and lengthen their cycle of dominance. A local Cleveland paper believed that the Yankees' success was based on luck and money after rumors arose that the Indians were about to trade Willis Hudlin or Joe Schaute for Yankee reserves Gene Robertson or Mike Gazella. Huggins replied that other teams had the same opportunity, as only Ruth, Hoyt, and Meusel were left from the early 1920s. "Plenty of other owners spend money, but we get results," he said. "If you think anybody has gone around offering the Yankees any bargains you are vastly mistaken. We know what we want, and we get it."[26]

Later in the season, in the *New York Morning Telegraph*, Homer H. Metz estimated just how much money the Colonel would have realized if orders went out by the American League for him to begin selling off his stars to other clubs. The Babe alone would have been worth the unheard of sum of $500,000. During the off-season, the Indians had offered the Yankees $175,000 and George Burns for Lou Gehrig. Tony Lazzeri was considered by many to be the best second baseman in baseball, and worth at least $150,000 to other teams. Bob Meusel could have been helpful to a club on the upswing and might have been worth $100,000. Mark Koenig had a price tag of $75,000, and Earle Combs possibly as much as $100,000. Without even mentioning the pitchers, Yankee players could have fetched their boss close to $1 million. In the end, the Colonel did not give in and meant what he had previously said about his desire to see the Yankees win, and win big.[27]

The Athletics took over second place for good in mid-May and were trying to break out beyond ten games over .500 after forty-six games. Cleveland's recent loss to the Yankees, coupled with a St. Louis victory over the Athletics on June 9, solidified the first three slots in the American League for the remainder of the year. The Browns were at breakeven after fifty games, with the Indians a half game worse, with one less victory.

Connie Mack made a second key move after signing George Earnshaw by shifting his outfield. Bing Miller permanently replaced Tris Speaker in center field on June 8, with Al Simmons moving to left field. Speaker may still have been feeling the effects of a collision with Miller in early May. Ty Cobb remained in right field.[28]

The Yankee players were divided on the pennant race but confident that they would lose no more than thirty-five games while on a pace to lose only thirty. As for who would finish behind them and the Athletics, the Tigers and Browns would probably round out the first division.[29]

After the Yankees' Opening Day victory against the Athletics, the Babe predicted that they would win forty games before they lost ten. They had thirty-nine wins against eight losses after forty-seven games going into Comiskey Park on Sunday, June 10, and they got there without a six-game winning streak. For his part, the Babe had only seven hits since May 28, and he saw his average drop more than thirty points.[30]

More importantly, the team had a double-digit lead on the rest of the league, with the second-place Athletics ten and a half games behind. The lack of a race and poor weather was a major problem for the owners in the Barnard circuit and had major financial ramifications. The various circumstances that collapsed Connie Mack's last great team were not in place for Ruppert's Yankees, and the several big weekend dates that were postponed with the Yankees were a much bigger blow for Philadelphia.

This observation was made by James Isaminger in his "Tips from the Sporting Ticker" column,

> The season is still young and an unexpected slump on the part of the Yanks or a series of injuries that cost them the services of their heavy hitters for a considerable period would change things, but that is all a negative and a visionary prospect. Today the Yankees are so far ahead in first place that it is preposterous to imagine that any of the other clubs will collar them unless these things happen.[31]

On Sunday, June 10, the White Sox revealed to 40,000 of their fans that the Yankees could be beaten, giving them a taste of their own medicine with a late inning rally. The Babe clouted two more home runs, raising his total to twenty-two—six games ahead of his 1927 pace. During the game, he was pestered by two lady fans who had balloons shaped like bats and another requesting that he sign two baseballs.

Stan Coveleski could not hold a two-run lead against Red Faber when he walked the bases loaded in the seventh inning. Al Shealy was summoned from the bull pen and greeted by a game-tying single from left fielder Alex Metzler. Three more Chicago runs the next inning put the Yankees in a three-run hole. Ted Lyons got credit for his sixth win.[32]

Ted Blankenship, always trouble for the Yankees, would have recorded a shutout the next day had it not been for an error by outfielder John Mostil. For the first time in the season, Herb Pennock failed to pitch a complete game, lasting only three innings in a 6–1 losing cause.[33]

With Mark Koenig out of the lineup, Leo Durocher, his replacement, continued to impress his teammates with his scrappiness and cockiness. As of May 2, he had hit .419 in twelve games while subbing for Lazzeri at second base, and .286 while in for Koenig at shortstop in twenty-one games as of June 11. He was converted to the left side of the plate from a switch-hitter.[34]

The following game, the Yankees snapped their first two-game losing streak since their home opening series in April and raised their record to 40–10. George Pipgras won his eleventh game against one loss. Lou Gehrig was the hitting star in a fifteen-run onslaught, with a home run, two triples, five runs batted in, and five runs scored.[35]

By breaking out into big leads during the past two seasons, the "800 percent" Yankees put a dent in the turnstiles at American League ball parks. The decrease in attendance was becoming more and more noticeable. Hugh Bradley stated,

> Traveling through this portion of the country, where great open spaces have been noticed in the grandstands quite frequently during the past two years, the young men who write for the papers hear frequent tales of sorrow. It is even reported that more than one pillar of the game is fearful of being down to his last Rolls Royce if the fans, who make the turnstiles go round, do not take more interest in what is laughingly called the race.[36]

Before gaining a split at Comiskey Park, the 1928 Yankees had beaten their western foes in seventeen of eighteen games. It was a pace that was impossible to maintain against one team, let alone any four. Waite Hoyt and Ted Lyons had off days, being tagged for twelve and fifteen hits.[37]

A fan wrote the following letter to Joe Williams of the *New York Telegram* on June 7:

Sir; You say in your first return article that nothing has changed in the sports world. You're right. Even the sportswriters are still raving about the Yanks. One calls them the "Juggernauts of Baseball." Another calls them the greatest team of all time. A third says they won't be beaten for three or four years. I'm willing to admit that the Yanks are good, but at the same time I think they are playing in one of the weakest and worst balanced leagues baseball has ever known. No wonder the Yanks are running away with the championship. Wouldn't Reigh Count do the same thing in a field of seven selling players? Answer me that!

The quickest way to stop the Yanks would be to drop them into the National for a full season's test. They'd have a tough time winning, I think. And in a best seven out of nine test, wouldn't the Reds beat the Indians, the Cubs the White Sox, the Cards the Browns, the Pirates the Tigers, and the Braves the Red Sox?[38]

Williams replied,

Perhaps the American League isn't as strong this year as it had been in the past, but it is still a pretty fair league as leagues go. There is certainly no reason to believe that it is generally weaker than the National, and this seems to be what all the shouting is about. . . . The evidence to the contrary is not convincing. The National League is obviously better balanced this year, but that doesn't mean it is a better league.[39]

Williams continued the debate two days later:

I don't see how anyone who knows a base hit from a press box yawn can deny the native greatness of the Yankees. The team has tremendous power. On this alone it could go a long way. But in addition it has about everything else a team needs, including a gay, competitive spirit, to be great or reasonably great. There is no way, actual or physical, to prove that the Yankees haven't been beating a lot of cheap ball clubs in a cheap league. The American League is probably no weaker or stronger than it has been for the last five or seven years. The superlative power of the Yankees probably makes the rest of the league look weak.[40]

The Yankees' .826 percentage as of June 7 included three losses to the Athletics, two to the Red Sox and Senators, and one to Cleveland, the only western team to defeat them. Williams also points out Wilbert Robinson's comments and an unnamed umpire in Heydler's circuit who said that there were three leagues, the National, the American, and the Yankees.[41]

At the same time, there was an ongoing mock debate by John Kieran taking place in his "Sports of the Times" column between the National League and American League. The Athletics were the only team remotely close to the Yankees, according to "N.L.B." (National League Baseball), and they were led by two worn out veterans, Cobb and Speaker. The American League countered with the fact that the front-running Reds were led by such players as Carl Mays and Wally Pipp, waived from their league. Joe Harris was an American League castoff and a key in the Pirates rotation in 1927; George Sisler waived as well and was expected to help the Braves.[42]

How much longer could the league survive with one team dominating? The nature of the Yankee dominance since 1921 took on a different character than that of previous teams. The Colonel did not believe in the law of averages as much as his manager and made it clear that he wanted to win for ten more years. In actuality, the Indians had the richest ownership, but because of lack of players to offer other clubs, they were at a disadvantage.[43]

Was the dominance of the Yankees the result of the caliber of play in the American League being beneath that of the National League? With the exception of the likes of George Uhle, Ted Lyons, and Lefty Grove, there was some belief that there was nothing else to compare to the talent possessed by Brooklyn, Chicago, Cincinnati, and St. Louis in the National League; in addition, it was believed that the American League leaders were also lucky to have met the Pirates in the World Series the previous year rather than the Cardinals or Giants. There was also a question of whether Ty Cobb and Tris Speaker, so relied on by the Athletics, would even make a National League roster.[44]

Sid Keener of the *St. Louis Times* wrote about the unfortunate situation of the Athletics being in the American League. They were better than any team in the senior circuit and would make a lot more money if they played there instead, but much of the consensus was that the Macks were not a gutless team, as some had claimed, but would make a race after all.[45]

The "Our Changing Cities" series in the *New York Times* now featured "Sturdy St. Louis," saying:

> It was, and still is, hard to tell whether St. Louis was a northern or a southern city. The opinion at present seems to be that it is southern and also western in its conception of hospitality, and just now possibly a little northern and eastern in its new spirit of enterprise. The southern flavor makes it agreeable to visit; the northern has arguments for the investor.[46]

The improved play of the St. Louis Browns and Boston Red Sox was giving some ray of hope to the American League. In the middle of June, one month after haymaking season, Dan Howley's team was in a position to challenge the Athletics for second place, and Bill Carrigan had Boston just four games from the first division.[47] The Browns were a much tougher team than in 1927, and they beat the eastern clubs seven of the last ten times they faced them. The pitching roster of Sam Gray, Jack Ogden, George Blaeholder, General Crowder, and Lefty Stewart was also pitching well.[48]

The Yankees opened the last leg of their western swing in front of a Thursday crowd of 12,000 in St. Louis with a 4–3 victory. A run-scoring single by Gehrig and a three-run home run by Lazzeri off of Sam Gray handed a three-run lead to Pennock that held until the home half of the eighth inning, when he escaped a bases-loaded jam after two runs had crossed.

Tony Lazzeri was thought by many to be the best all-around player in the game, with base-hit streaks during the year of five, eight, and eleven to go with his current string of nine games. They weren't just singles, but ten doubles, seven triples, and four home runs. He was batting .363 as of June 14; was among the league leaders in runs batted in, with forty-one; and was playing peerlessly in the field.[49]

General Crowder was in and out of trouble the next day but pitched a complete game, while Otis Brannan was the hitting star for the Browns. The Babe's twenty-fourth home run, a two-run shot over the right-field roof, made the score 3–0. But wildness and base hits, including a bases loaded double by Otis Brannan and a home run by Red Kress, got the better of the Yankees' Henry Johnson in the fifth inning, as he allowed the Browns four runs and a 5–4 victory.[50]

With ten makeup doubleheaders looming, Miller Huggins was increasingly worried about having to rely on three pitchers. During the month of May, question marks Shealy, Coveleski, and Johnson won eleven of twenty-four games for the Yankees, with Pipgras winning five and Hoyt and Pennock four each, but it was the big three only for the eleven victories through June 17. A fourth starter was needed, and hopes were still being pinned on Henry Johnson.[51] The rookie had an excellent hits per innings pitched ratio, but he had twenty-six walks in just fewer than forty innings.

Cy Moore's dislocated ligament in his elbow was snapped into place with the one caveat that he could not throw curveballs anymore, a curveball he received much kidding about from his teammates and manager. The Babe also made a wager with Moore in the preseason that he wouldn't get a hit all year, and Moore was still without one.[52] Moore had six hits in seventy-five at bats in 1927, with two multihit games.

The Yankees' first trip out West proved to be more challenging. George Pipgras was let down by poor throwing from catcher Pat Collins during his first bad start of the season and was relieved by Shealy in the fourth inning. Brown starter Dick Coffman held the Yankees in check the entire game.

An interesting observation was made by Harrison on the state of fan sentiment in St. Louis for its two teams: "A lot of the rooters, we suspect, came out to the ball game merely because they could get a rapid report on the Cardinals' contest in Brooklyn. The posting of the glad tidings of a Red Bird victory brought bedlam in its wake."[53]

For a third time, the Yankees, fifty-five games into the season, avoided their first three-game losing streak of the year as Waite Hoyt won his ninth game against one defeat. It was a Sunday game at Sportsman's Park, and possibly the largest crowd ever to see the Browns, estimated at 30,000. A complete game from Hoyt and home runs from the slugging twins was the winning formula. The Babe's twenty-fifth home run did not come until the sixty-ninth game in 1927.[54]

The top two contenders in the American League completed their second intersectional round with victories as they headed to Yankee Stadium for their eleventh matchup of the season, where Philadelphia would have an opportunity to close an eight-and-a-half-game deficit and address the issue of a lack of "guts." For the Yankees, injuries were not proving to be a minor, temporary nuisance as in 1927, but so far the reserves were coming through.

· 9 ·

A Painful Contrast (June 19–July 4)

The general prediction early in the season was that the Yankees would slip across the American League goal line with the Athletics in pursuit at some uncertain distance. Also that the National League affair would be a wild tangle through August and early September, with four of five clubs packed around the top.

—*Boston Daily Globe*, May 30, 1928[1]

The Washington Post printed an editorial, "The Two Leagues," on June 18:

Many doleful predictions are being made as to the future of the American League. Some pessimists even say that unless the domination of the New York Yankees is ended, every other team in the league will show a loss at the end of the season. In following out this line of reasoning, it has been suggested that Colonel Ruppert, owner of the New York team, should scatter his stars among the other teams . . . to restore the proper balance.

It is additionally annoying to the American League magnates under such circumstances to consider the race in the National League. Only six games separate the first five teams, and anyone familiar with baseball will tell you what that means in enthusiasm and big crowds. No team is sure of the lead. New York, Brooklyn, Cincinnati, and St. Louis have all been in and out of leadership.

The contrast is painful in the American League. Each year the eight team owners have combed the minor leagues in the hope of finding players suitable for a team to break the Yankee spell. . . . The New York team is almost a mathematical certainty today. There will at any rate be no suspense. The race will be a runaway affair. The fight will be in the National, and it is the fight that pays.[2]

The Yankees, with all their dominance, were believed to worth around $7 million. Dismantling them would just hand supremacy to the Athletics and not necessarily help the American League. The National League was believed to have superior pitching, as minor leaguers just called up were hitting better in the junior circuit, but the Yankees would probably hit just as well.

Jacob Ruppert remembered his original cost with Huston of $480,000 in 1915. He was successful in most of his endeavors, and it stood to reason that he should not be penalized and watch his huge investment in baseball be voluntarily collapsed. "Don't let folks worry too much about the Yanks winning too many times," Huggins said, trying to put everyone at ease. "Nature and the law of averages always attend to clubs like ours. We will keep plugging up gaps, but nature and the old L of A no doubt will find a way."[3]

There were rumblings in Chicago, Detroit, and Washington in order of vociferousness for a change in managers. Tiger fans, and possibly the players themselves, were becoming disinterested in baseball, with the patrons coming to the games to razz the players, and the players doffing their caps in return.[4]

Detroit Tigers owner Frank Navin continued to stand by his manager and instead blamed the team's problem on pitching. Letters from fans were demanding that George Moriarty be fired. They wanted a manager like Dan Howley or Joe McCarthy, one who seemed to be able to better motivate their players.[5] White Sox fans were largely standing behind manager Ray Schalk, blaming their cheap owner. Even when Charles Comiskey spent money, he seemed to spend it unwisely.

Bucky Harris's popularity had been waning since 1925, but it seemed to perk up when the team began playing well. They had the best swing in the American League, paced by three wins in relief from Fred Marberry, two each from Tom Zachary and Sam Jones, and one each from Horace Lisenbee and Garland Braxton. On offense, Goose Goslin topped the .400 mark with three hits against Cleveland on June 10, while increasing his average from .384 to .418. The Senators made the most progress, climbing out of the cellar and now challenging the Tribe for the first division.

After the abbreviated sweep of the Tigers and Indians and splits of the two four-game series against the White Sox and Browns, Miller Huggins read the riot act, fully aware that a ten-game lead this early could quickly evaporate. The nine victories out of thirteen on the latest swing, however, was one game better than the Athletics.[6]

The Tigers landed in seventh place and the White Sox in last place, as both clubs were tied for the most losses in the league, with thirty-five. The Indians managed to hold on to fourth place by barely a thread, one half game over the surging Senators, having lost eighteen of twenty-three games since the first eastern swing. Roger Peckinpaugh tried shifting his lineup around,

but it was the pitching that collapsed. The Tribe's earned run average bal-
looned to 4.16 on June 18, from 3.52 on May 20, as George Uhle suffered
from a sore arm and Willis Hudlin was ineffective.[7]

The Yankees virtually had first place locked up by July 4, which, even
in 1928, was recognized as an indicator for the standings at the end of the
season. Huggins gave his views on the current situation:

> Well, it looks as if we will have to lead the American League on the morn-
> ing of July 5. You know, they say that the club [that] is on top on the night
> of July 4, wins the pennant. Of course, I like to set the pace, but I do hate
> to have my players get the idea that anything is settled. Nothing ever is
> settled in baseball until you have grabbed the mathematical certainty and
> put it in your trunk. We came back here with a lead of eight and a half
> games. But what guarantee is there that this won't be hammered down to,
> well, let us say, seven before another month is out? Everybody all around
> the circuit has taken up the holler that we are a monopoly in restraint of
> competition and should be busted up. How do they get that way?
>
> Let me tell you that the boys are getting tougher. That series we start
> with a doubleheader tomorrow with the Philadelphia Athletics will be
> no picnic. Connie Mack's club has been coming along in great shape and
> may take the best part of the series. The St. Louis Browns, whom we took
> for twenty-one out of twenty-two last year, are no pushovers. Nor are the
> White Sox, now that Ted Lyons is back in form. And watch the Senators
> and the Red Sox. I think the Washington club will keep climbing from
> now on, and I have a hunch it will make trouble for us. In fact, I see noth-
> ing but trouble before me—lots of it. And we are getting fair pitching.[8]

When asked what would be the catalyst, Huggins humored, "Mark Roth
looks very tired, and Eddie Bennett, the bat boy, is two pounds underweight."[9]

Huggins also discussed the highlight of the western trip, saying,

> The work of our reserves. We left here with Bob Meusel and Mark Koenig
> out of the game and Joe Dugan getting over an injury. Meusel still is out
> of the game, but Durst has done fine work in his place. Durocher played
> a wonderful game in Koenig's spot at short, and from time to time Rob-
> ertson stepped in and gave a corking exhibition of fielding and hitting in
> Dugan's place. As for old Joe himself, he never looked better.[10]

Huggins reiterated that the trade embargo placed on the Yankees last December was still in force. The Indians offered Johnny Hodapp for Gene
Robertson, and then Mike Gazella, but were turned down.[11]

The Yankees were preparing to face their eastern rivals for the next two
weeks, both home and away, beginning with the Athletics, before hosting
the western clubs. The consensus was that they would increase their lead of

eight and a half games, but beginning around the end of June, the Athletics would be at Shibe Park for a month-long stretch.[12] The backlog of makeup doubleheaders was ten, three each at home and on the road against western teams, and three at home and one on the road against eastern clubs.

The absence of Meusel and Koenig for the entire trip and Dugan the last three games was somewhat compounded by the Babe's hitting slump. During the same period in 1927, he was getting base hits, but not home runs; however, on the recent swing, six of his nine hits were home runs and the rest were singles. The Babe's batting average topped out at .372 on May 17, and he was hitting at a .273 clip since then, dropping his average to .323. On the latest western trip, the Babe only batted .200, but the team was picked up by Robertson, who paced the Yankees with a .478 average, followed by Lazzeri (.418), Gehrig (.413), and Dugan (.366). Waite Hoyt (8–1) paced the Yankee pitchers, winning four decisions on the latest road trip.[13]

After batting .285 during the regular season in 1927 and .500 in the World Series, Mark Koenig found himself making way for Leo Durocher after the reserve filled in so well during Koening's spell with lower back pain. Koenig was off to his best start ever both at the plate and in the field before he was forced to leave the lineup on May 21, with a .330 batting average. The shortstop went from the goat of the 1926 World Series to hero in 1927. He handled all fourteen chances in the field with ease and had nine hits in eighteen at bats, with two doubles and three runs batted in. His speed and daring on the base paths against the strong arms in the Pittsburgh outfield were crucial to the Yankees' success. His double in the first game was a crucial factor in the game-winning rally. In a game that the Yankees won, 5–4, he also scored two runs. The Yankees were held to six hits and could have gone either way. Koenig had three hits in the second-game victory and three hits in the game-four clincher, as well as a perfectly executed sacrifice in the ninth-inning, game-winning rally.[14]

Durocher subbed admirably for Lazzeri earlier in the season and hit well above expectations. He was a favorite of the mite manager. "I suppose if he falls off in his hitting I'll put Koenig back," Huggins confided to Fred Lieb. "But how can I take him out now? He is playing the best shortstop in the American League, and he is my type of a ballplayer."[15]

Durocher had one plate appearance since Lazzeri returned on May 2. Shortstop was his position until he stopped hitting. After twenty-six games, he finally gave way following two losses in St. Louis, where he went hitless in nine at bats and his average dropped to .297 from .419. The super sub managed just five hits in thirty-two at bats in Chicago and St. Louis.[16]

The Athletics' second series at the Stadium was originally scheduled as four games in four days, but one makeup game was added to the opener on

Tuesday, June 19, from the April 22 rainout. Persisting rainfall postponed the doubleheader, necessitating bonus dates for Wednesday and Thursday and a single game on Friday. These were financial blows to the Athletics more so than the Yankees. A record crowd was expected for the Saturday, April 14, rainout at Shibe Park; the Sunday rainout at the Stadium on April 22 nullified an expected turnout of 60,000 fans, and the crowd the day before was kept down by threatening weather. The most recent postponement turned away an estimated 20,000 to 30,000 patrons.[17]

Players on both teams were primed to go, especially the Babe, who had just nine hits in his last forty-six at bats. Six of those hits were home runs, just three less than the entire White Sox team. Said Ruth,

> It sure gets a guy, how rain sometimes interferes with the best-laid plans of men and mice. Here I was all set to knock a few pailings off the bleacher fence today, and then it has to pour. A guy ought to have a "pull" with this fellow that tells it when to rain. I understand this Rickard bozo who promotes the fights has a drag like that. Maybe he'll put me wise to how he rates it, sometime.[18]

Bob Meusel was expected back in the lineup in this series after missing action since suffering a charley horse on May 28 in Philadelphia.[19]

The Athletics were in no way conceding their chances for first place, although still smarting from their last six games at home with the Yankees. They were a great road team and had beaten the Yankees in their only two meetings at the Stadium. They had eleven games in the next seven days, but team captain Eddie Collins was confident that the Yankees would concede four of the five games and turn the race in the Athletics' favor.[20]

The tall tutor explained:

> It was a severe disappointment to us when the Yankees beat us five out of six on our own field last month; however, if our boys were disappointed in that series, they never let down. Right after that we went to Boston, and although we caught the Red Sox when they were playing their best ball in years, we won the entire series.
>
> We had a good trip in the west, winning all of our series except in St. Louis, where we lost three out of four. Howley has a fighting aggressive team this year. I see that he also gave Huggins a little opposition, and the Yanks did all they could do to break even. We recognize what we are up against. It is pretty hard to gain on a team [that] proceeds along at a gait near .800. However, we again have a big batch of games with Huggin's team just ahead of us, and we are hopeful of making a better showing than when we last met the Yankees.[21]

Huggins reiterated his belief that the Yankees would have to win at least 100 games,

> I know a lot of fun has been poked at me because I haven't claimed the pennant by about twenty games. I am not exactly alarmed at the situation, but if we had an ordinary second team to beat it would be a breeze. But Connie Mack has a pretty powerful team himself. He should win at least ninety-five games, maybe one hundred. If we win no more than ninety-one games—our record in 1926—I do not believe we can win. Mack won ninety-one games last season but should do much better this year.[22]

After the first intersectional batch of games, the talk of the baseball world was about the Yankees topping last year's margin of victory, setting additional team and individual records, and again attaining a 70 percent won–loss percentage. The Yankees winning the pennant was a foregone conclusion. Two swings later, as of June 19, the gap in the American League was four games wider, at eight and a half games, compared to a four-and-a-half-game lead in 1927. The lead widened by four and a half games during the 1928 season, after the Yanks took five of six in Philadelphia in May, and increased another half game after the western trip. There was continued speculation on how much the rest of the league was suffering financially and even how an All-Star team would fare against the conquerors.[23]

A large crowd of 35,000 watched the Athletics blow the first game open during their final time at bat. The Yankees reached Jack Quinn for five runs in the third inning and a three-run lead. The Macks, however, came back with four runs off of Pennock in the sixth inning, with Quinn driving in Boley and Cochrane with the tying and go-ahead runs, prompting Moore from the bull pen.

The Athletics scored four more runs in the ninth inning, three earned off of Moore, to win the game, 10–5. It was the Macks' third win without a loss at the Stadium and a gritty performance by Quinn, who was on the ropes five times en route to his eighth victory. The Babe was not pleased about being hit by Quinn his first time up to the plate, and after being hit again, the two almost came to blows his next time up to bat.

The Yankees used the late innings to win the second game. George Pipgras and Ossie Orwoll were locked in a one-all tie going into the home half of the seventh inning. Tony Lazzeri led off the inning with a single and took third on Gene Robertson's single, which set up a home run by John Grabowski to left field.

The Mackmen got two runs back in the eighth inning, but the Yankees broke the one-run contest open with five runs in the eighth inning. Gene Robertson hit a sacrifice fly to score Lou Gehrig with the bases loaded. John

Grabowski drove in his fourth run of the game with a double, and hits by Earle Combs, Mark Koenig, and Babe Ruth accounted for the last three runs off of Ed Rommel. George Pipgras pitched a complete game but was on the ropes from the start. One of the most important developments of the year was the emergence of Pipgras as the top pitcher on the Yankees.[24]

Huggins sang the praises of Jimmie Foxx and other blessings in disguise for Connie Mack:

> Suppose I tell you that the nineteen-year-old Jimmie Foxx is the spark plug of the Athletics. Connie complains that he has been forced to make shifts because of an epidemic of batting slumps. Well, it looks to me as if those slumps came as a blessing in disguise. Hauser's ineffectiveness at the plate led Connie to replace him with Foxx, normally a catcher. And I want to go on record right here with the statement that this kid has made the Philadelphia club.
>
> Bishop's falling off in hitting brought Jimmy Dykes to second base, and Tris Speaker's troubles sent Bing Miller into center. Speaker, in form, would be an improvement over Miller, but at that Bing is hitting .340. Those slumps haven't done the Athletics a bit of harm, and they have brought this park into the daily picture.
>
> It isn't often that I envy another manager over the possession of a ballplayer, but I sure like Foxx, as a hitter and as a first baseman. Connie will have a hard time dislodging this lad from the bag, as he is one of the finest natural hitters I have seen in years.
>
> Too bad I missed landing Foxx when he was in the Eastern Shore League. Frank Baker tipped me off to Foxx, who was only sixteen at the time, but before we could rush a scout down there, Mack had grabbed him for next to nothing. Yes, Foxx is the real thing.
>
> Incidentally, that was quite a ball club we beat in the second game yesterday, 9 to 3. And it was quite a ball club [that] walloped us in the first one 10 to 5. I know all about our lead of eight and a half games, but don't let anybody tell you anything is a certainty, with a team like the Athletics chasing us. Right now, Mack has everything.[25]

The first matchup for the Thursday twin bill, again, did not appear to be in the Yankees' favor. For the second time in 1928, it was the rookie Hank Johnson going against Lefty Grove. The game was scoreless until the fifth inning, when Tony Lazzeri, batting .405 against Athletic pitching, hit his sixth home run with no one on base. The Yankees scratched out another run in the next inning, when a Ruth liner handcuffed Jimmy Dykes at second base and scored Earle Combs. In the seventh inning, a two-out double by Koenig scored Combs and Collins. For his part, Johnson scattered nine hits and walked only one for a 4–0, complete-game shutout and the finest game of his young career.

Grove took his fifth loss of the year against eight victories, but four of his defeats came against the Yankees, and the other against the Browns. Miller Huggins was naturally all smiles about Henry Johnson, stating, "I told him all along that he could pitch like that. He has everything. All that he needed was confidence. That game should give it to him. With our teeth behind him, he should be as good a pitcher as Pipgras."[26]

Huggins was trying to avoid his top pitchers going up against Grove and Walberg, and he was frustrating Connie Mack by stealing games the Mackmen were supposed to win. The Athletics began hammering Hoyt in the second game, until Mother Nature saved the day. The game was called in the third inning, just as Al Simmons doubled Cobb home, and he and Cochrane were on base with Jimmie Foxx due up next.[27]

What was originally a four-day, four-game series became five games in four days. Additional rain on Tuesday compacted it to five games in three days. In the final analysis, with still more rain on Thursday and Friday, the Yankees and Athletics managed to play just three games in four days. Five of the first eight postponements through May 9 were made up, but ten additional cancellations after that increased the backlog of makeup games to eleven. Four of the seven games scheduled between the Yankees and Athletics at Yankee Stadium were postponed. Through it all, the Yankees gained a game in the standings.[28]

The Red Sox followed the Athletics for three games in two days, as they would spend nearly the entire month of June away from Fenway Park. The series included a doubleheader to make up for the April 28 postponement. Their pace had slowed considerably to .320 since they last challenged the breakeven mark on May 21. They dropped six of seven games to the Yankees and Athletics after May 21.[29]

The Yankees felt that the Red Sox could be a tough club if they got some pitching, and Bill Carrigan was hoping to build his pitching staff around Ed Morris and Red Ruffing. But Huggins was backing his rookie, Henry Johnson. "Morris? Just a fair pitcher, Bill," he said. "He's just a flash like Ruffing. But if you want to see the real thing in pitching sensations, watch that Henry Johnson of mine. You should have seen the kid shut out the Athletics on Thursday—beat them with nine hits and allowed two safeties in only one round."[30]

Carrigan was ready to send Morris back to the minors, but the Mobile team didn't want him. Huggins wanted him, but Carrigan gave him another chance. The Yankees offered Boston $50,000 for Ruffing in 1927. Huggins selected Johnson from the Florida State League when he was just a little more than seventeen years of age and just graduated from Bradenton High School.[31]

The Red Sox surprised the champions and 20,000 fans by sweeping the Saturday doubleheader, beating Hoyt and Pennock. A grand slam by Boston's second baseman, Bill Regan, broke a tie in the first game, and Dan MacFayden shut down the Hugmen on three hits in the nightcap. "Now that this incredible event has taken place," reports James R. Harrison, "your correspondent would not even be mildly surprised if Pennsylvania went Democratic or if it should develop after all these years that Paris is really the capital of Rumania, and not a large city in France."

It also happened to be Leo Durocher Day at the Stadium, and the event brought a delegation from Durocher's hometown and the Springfield, Massachusetts, Chamber of Commerce. The super sub was presented with checks worth $1,500 and two traveling bags but did not play in either game. The Boston gifts of long ago, Waite Hoyt and Herb Pennock, took the losses, with Hoyt seeing his eight-game winning streak come to an end. The Babe's twenty-sixth home run in the first game, and twenty- seventh in the nightcap, kept him fifteen games ahead of last year.[32]

Herb Pennock had lost three of his last four starts, with the setbacks coming against the White Sox, Athletics, and Red Sox. The recent pitching of Waite Hoyt and relief work of Wilcy Moore was also looming as a concern.[33]

George Pipgras pitched a three-hit shutout before a crowd of 20,000 the following day. He retired seventeen straight, while not allowing any member of the Red Sox to reach third base. The game was over for Boston, and starter Jack Russell in the first inning, when an easy grounder by Gehrig skipped past second baseman Bill Regan, the hero of the previous day, with the bases loaded, scoring Koenig from third and Ruth from second.[34]

The Athletics came into their final series at home with the Yankees trailing by ten games, having dropped four straight to the Nationals, but they did manage to make up a half game in the standings since June 10, while the Yankees were coming back to earth, splitting their last fourteen games. Miller Huggins still believed that the Macks would win one hundred games, meaning that they were capable of playing at, or better than, a 70 percent clip the rest of the year. This meant that the Yankees needed to play at least at a 60 percent rate.[35]

Losing four straight to the Senators at Griffith Stadium was not the way Connie Mack wanted his club to prepare for the Yankee finale at Shibe Park. Said Mack,

> I know just where we stand. I thought I had a great club last year. I have a great club, but the Yanks are the sort of club that come along once in a generation. In an ordinary year, my club would go right through to a pennant, but we're up against a team that combines too much power with fine fielding and plenty of pitching.

We have had some bad breaks in luck, or the race would be much closer. I have felt right along that if we could only stay so close to the Yanks that they would have to worry and play their best every time they went on the field, we might have a great chance.

As it is now, they are so far in front they don't have to worry much. Huggins can afford to experiment with his young pitchers, and I must admit, his experiments have been a success. Even so, we won't quit fighting, no matter how this series comes out. You never can tell about baseball. I think the Yanks will have a much harder going on their next western trip, but so will we, so we can't expect to gain much that way. We do as well against the rest of the league as the Yanks do, but they have beaten us off, so we have only ourselves to blame.[36]

Huggins slated Johnson, Hoyt, and Pipgras, while Mack depended on Grove, Walberg, and Ehmke for the Tuesday through Thursday games.[37]

The maulers from Manhattan took two steps forward and one back, and for a second time in one week and the third time during 1928, Henry Johnson bested Lefty Grove. With their regulars back in the lineup, the Yankees rolled a three in the first inning and a four in the eighth. Grove got off to a rough start, giving a two-run triple to Gehrig after an infield hit by Koenig and a pass to Ruth, with Lou ending up scoring on the same play as a result of a bad relay from Boley.

The Macks got a run back in the bottom of the first inning and took the lead in the fourth inning, when a three-run rally was capped by a bad throw to first base by Koenig on a Dykes grounder, scoring Bing Miller. From there, Lefty sailed into the eighth with the Athletics leading, 4–3. Then came the bombardment. Combs led off with a double, followed by a Koenig triple, a Ruth single, and a Gehrig walk, forcing Grove to walk to the dugout. After Meusel popped out, a wild pitch advanced the runners, but Cochrane made a wild throw, which scored the Babe and sent Gehrig to third. The fourth run scored on Lazzeri's comebacker to Orwoll, who threw too late to the plate to get Gehrig.[38]

The Yankees recorded their tenth victory in fourteen tries over the Mackmen, with half of them coming against their ace. The Yankees' record against Grove during the 1928 season is one of those hidden statistical anomalies in baseball given his overall record. He won three of five decisions against the Yankees in 1927, won four of five in 1926, and split six decisions in 1925.[39]

Connie Mack was reaching the breaking point with certain of his pitchers:

It just seems that when Grove can't beat the Yankees, nobody can. How long has it been since he beat them? It doesn't seem to do any good, how I work them.

I give them plenty of rest. I tell them what to do, but I can't do it for them. And that's what a lot of them seem to need—somebody else to pitch for them. I've done almost everything I can think of to get them straightened out. I'd like to get them working in some kind of rotation. Quinn has pitched well for us but really needs five days of rest between games. Grove and Walberg can pitch every fourth day but are better with four days off. Ehmke—I'm lucky to get a game out of him once in seven days.

Orwoll was good for a time. I thought I had a reliable pitcher in him. But of late he has been the same as the rest. The only thing left now is for me to try to get Earnshaw into shape. If we don't get some pitching soon we won't even finish second.[40]

The Babe continued his torrid pace against Rube Walberg and George Earnshaw with his twenty-ninth and thirtieth home runs, already half way to last year's sixty after just the sixty-third game. The second homer landed on the roof of a building and prompted a woman to open her window to see who was throwing rocks. The Babe remained confident that he would break his 1927 home run record, saying, "I'll beat that sixty, and I'll lay anybody odds that I come nearer to seventy than sixty. The season is not nearly half over, and I've got half as many homers as I had last year."[41] Ruth continued,

Funny thing about Walberg. He used to be pretty tough on me, but he's sure my coz now. Another funny thing, the last three times he's pitched against us, I've got a homer off him in the first inning. I would have had two off him this last time if that single I got was just a foot higher at the fence. I'd be surprised if I don't make seventy round trips this year. Somehow I got a hunch. I can always tell when my timing is right for those long ones and I feel I'm right.[42]

Walberg lasted two innings, giving up five runs on eight hits; his last defeat came more than a month earlier against Hoyt at Shibe Park.

The Yankees once again scored five runs by the third inning, with three in the first and two in the second. George Pipgras won his fourteenth against two losses, while extending the Athletics' losing streak to six. Gene Robertson was looking like the Yankees' handyman version of Jimmy Dykes, getting three hits and two runs batted in and robbing Bing Miller of a single.[43]

The banner above the box score in the June 30, 1928, edition of the *Philadelphia Inquirer* read, "Well, It's About Time."[44] The last hope for the American League was fading fast. The Athletics desperately needed to salvage the last game to avoid their deficit in the standings from hitting the teens. The six-game losing streak was snapped by Howard Ehmke, with help from Grove. The slumping Herb Pennock had not fully recovered from a sore arm since the rains of mid-May, but he ended up pitching a complete game.

He gave up fourteen hits, but only three of the Athletics' six runs were earned. His record slipped to 10–5 during the month of June, after winning nine of his first ten decisions. While the Yankees made a mockery of the Athletics in their own park, winning all but two of the eleven games played, the third-place Browns were making a move on second place.[45]

The original schedule called for a single game in Boston to close out the month of June for the Yankees, but the added April 17 postponement brought a less than expected 25,000 to Fenway Park as rain again threatened. The Yankees, behind Shealy and Coveleski, avenged the previous week's sweep by the Red Sox at the Stadium by taking a pair at Fenway. The Red Sox were clinging to a chance at a better than .500 season and came into the day's twin bill seven games under the breakeven mark. The crowd that began filing out for the nightcap missed a four-run comeback fall one run short, as George Pipgras finished the last two innings for Covey.[46]

The perplexing inability of the Athletics to beat the Yankees continued as the imaginary July Fourth marker approached. "Two More Gone" is the bold message above the box score in the July 2 issue of the *Philadelphia Inquirer*, and it might as well have read "Season Gone."[47] The original schedule called for another single-game series at the Stadium on July 1, but a double-header took place to make up one of the two home games, with the Athletics still pending. A double setback ensued for the Macks before a huge Sunday Stadium crowd of 60,000, dropping Philadelphia to fourteen games behind in the loss column, officially thirteen and a half in the standings.

The Athletics lost six games in the standings from June 23 through July 1. Four of the eight losses in the team's last ten games came against the Yankees, whose lone loss in their last eight games came against the Athletics. Any and all semblance of a pennant race in the American League was gone. While the Yankees and second-place Athletics were separated by fourteen losses, the Athletics and the last-place Tigers were separated by thirteen losses. The race had become a battle between the Athletics, Browns, Indians, and Red Sox for the first division.

Connie Mack used Joe Bush and George Earnshaw to oppose Henry Johnson and Waite Hoyt, and each pitcher ended up figuring in the wins and losses for the games. Only five hurlers were used in both games, which saw a total of forty-five hits and thirty runs. But it was the Yankees who doubled up on the visitors in both games by scores of 12–6 and 8–4.[48]

In his "Tips from the Sporting Ticker" column, James Isaminger referred to that "one big inning" by the Yankees that allowed them to put away their opponents. His interview with Mark Roth led to the issue of Yankee dominance:

> The public forgets that the Yankees had many lean years in baseball. Why they never won a pennant until 1921. Prior to that year they finished last

in two seasons and seventh in one. They finished in the second division ten out of eighteen years prior to 1921.

Should the Yankee be begrudged? Everybody declared that the Yanks were foolish when they paid more than $100,000 to the Red Sox to acquire Babe Ruth. Yet, he proved to be the biggest bargain in baseball history. It is true that a closer race would mean more money all around yet the Yanks partly offset this by drawing heavily in every city they appear. In this way they make money for all the other clubs. The Yanks are going ahead and will try to win every game they can. If they surpass their field, why, that's the fault of the other clubs. Let them go out and get the players to beat the Yanks.[49]

The Athletics were all but mathematically declared out of the race. The Athletics dropped to thirty-nine wins and thirty losses on the season and were hopelessly behind the Yankees (see table 9.1).

Table 9.1.   American League, First Division, July 1, 1928

Team	Won	Lost	GB	Pct.
Yankees	52	16	—	.765
Athletics	39	30	13.5	.565
Browns	37	33	16	.529
Indians	33	38	20.5	.465

Harrison's latest synopsis of the pennant race after the latest sweep was as follows:

If you have been lying awake at night racked with worry as to whether the Yanks were going to win the pennant or not, retire to your couch tonight and enjoy a deep and unbroken slumber. The pennant race is all over but the shouting, and there isn't any shouting to be done. The Yanks, winning their thirteenth game of the season from the Elephants, are now thirteen and a half games ahead of the languid Philadelphians with less than half the season played.[50]

One of the Yankee players was puzzled about the performance of the Athletics during the 1928 season. Answered another Yankee,

There's nothing wrong with them, except that Connie shifts them around too much. One day he's got Hauser at first. The next day it's Dykes. The next day it's Foxx. The next day it's Orwoll. You see Bishop at second one day, and you can't find him again for a week. Hale has been on and off third base half a dozen times. That guy Foxx played almost every position on the club. I expect to see him come out with a whiskbroom and start umpiring any day now.[51]

The Athletics lost thirteen of eighteen games against their main foes with four games remaining between the two clubs in September at the Stadium, a series that included one makeup game. Their deficit on July 1 was the largest ever in the American League, and it was only topped by the fourteen-and-a-half-game advantage enjoyed by the Giants in 1912. One factor working in favor of Philadelphia was that they were in sole possession of second place.

Four of the five leading hitters in the American League as of July 1, 1928, were Yankees. Goose Goslin led the league with a .412 average. Similarly, the Red Sox would dominate the individual statistics at their nadir of the 1978 season.

When the Colonel was asked his opinion of the pennant race, he replied, "It's great, as thrilling as I ever want to see." When he was reminded that there was no race, he answered, "Sure! That's what makes it a great race to me. I can't stand those close ones." His idea of a perfect season was the Babe hitting one hundred home runs and the Yankees going undefeated. He explained that Ruth, Gehrig, and Lazzeri were the dominant force in baseball and that he would rather kill off competition than be killed by it.

When the issue of too much dominance hurting attendance was raised, Ruppert replied, "Well, they say there's no competition now, but I've had to enlarge my ballpark. I didn't do that just to keep skilled laborers from having a summer vacation at the seashore." The fact that other teams were not drawing after the Yankees left town was none of the Colonel's concern, and he felt it was the other magnates' problem.[52]

The July 5 edition of the *Sporting News* threw out the white flag for the Athletics, saying,

> The Mackmen have indefinitely postponed their campaign against the league-leading Yankees. The serious reverses, not only at the hands of the Yankees themselves, but also those handed by Washington, spoiled all Connie Mack's plans to make a drive for the top. It now looks, to a man up a tree, that the business of the Mackmen, for the time being at least, is to hold second place against the oncoming St. Louis Browns.[53]

Ten days earlier, the Macks had felt that the Yankees would finally go into a slump when they picked up two games in one day as a result of doubleheader sweeps. The deficit was cut from nine and a half games to seven and a half.[54]

The Yankees followed the sweep with a loss in the nation's capital, which prompted the following wit from James Harrison: "The Yankees went into another bad slump here today and lost a ball game to the Senators, 4 to 3. This tightened up the American League race considerably, and the Yanks are only about twelve games ahead now."[55]

The team began a four-game series the next day at Griffith Stadium. The Senators, behind Garland Braxton, beat George Pipgras in a back-and-forth, nearly two-hour affair. Before the game, the Babe shook the hand of the assistant secretary of war at home plate and signed fifty-one baseballs that would be awarded to the best players in the citizens' military training camps.[56] Braxton, a direct descendant of Carter Braxton, a signer of the Declaration of Independence, became the first pitcher to beat the Yankees twice during 1928, and teammate Sam Jones would become the second two days later.[57] Frank H. Young of the *Washington Post* raised the issue of the Yankee's pitching depth, especially during the slew of doubleheaders.[58]

During the next game, the lead changed four times, with the last time going in favor of the Hugmen. Both starters, Herb Pennock and Bump Hadley, went the entire eleven innings. The Yankees played a horrible game in the field, a fact that was overshadowed by eighteen hits and seven runs.[59]

The hottest day of the year, July 4, at eighty-nine degrees in the New York City area, brought forth statistics that read like a battle zone. Thirty-eight deaths, including reports of twenty-one people drowning, as approximately 3 million patrons jammed local beaches and resorts. Four of the deaths and two hundred injuries came as a result of fireworks, as well as four casualties and eleven injuries on the roads. The heat and humidity resulted in a heavy thunderstorm with winds gusting as fast as eighty miles per hour.[60]

Nonetheless, doubleheaders were on tap in the major leagues for the Fourth of July. The Yankees were at Griffith Stadium, while the Athletics were home against Boston. Sam Jones beat Al Shealy in the first game, which was settled in the first inning by the first three batters, when Rice and Hayes both singled, followed by a three-run inside-the-park homer by center fielder Red Barnes. Between games, the tarp was taken out at Griffith Stadium, and there were concerns of a possible tornado.

The second match between Hank Johnson and Lloyd Brown went off as scheduled and was not settled until the sixth, when the Yankees broke a scoreless tie with five runs to win, 5–4. Gehrig's base hit that inning, which drove in Paschal, placed him ahead of the Babe for the team lead with his seventy-fourth run batted in. The Babe left the game in the fourth inning with a sore shoulder from an injury suffered in the first game of the series.[61]

The Hugmen closed July Fourth the previous year with a record of fifty-three wins and twenty-one losses and had increased their lead to eleven and a half games over Washington and twelve and a half over Chicago. This year's split gave them a record of fifty-four wins and eighteen losses and a twelve-game lead over Philadelphia. There was a long stretch of games ahead with intersectional rivals that included six makeup games going into the heart of summer.

A Fine Kettle of Fish (July 6–August 7)

The Mackmen still have an excellent chance to win. If Ruth
contracts yellow fever, Lazzeri breaks his leg, Lou Gehrig comes
down with sleeping sickness, and George Pipgras suffers complete paralysis of the right arm, the Mackmen will have a fine
chance to gallop through.

—*New York Times*, July 2, 1928[1]

$\mathcal{A}$s of July 1, the second-place Athletics were closer to last place than first,
and the dominance of the Yankees continued as a front and center topic in
baseball. In the June 30 installment of the *Washington Post*, Alan J. Gould asks,

Do the Yankees get the breaks? Yes, and how, you will hear it said around
the rest of the American League circuit with pronounced accent. But the
metropolitan experts who peek intently at the proceedings in the Yankee
Stadium attribute the team's "luck" to good management.

Probably there's a little of both. It was a break last season, for example,
to have Wilcy Moore blossom forth in his first season, first as the best
relief hurler in the league and then as a full-fledged moundsman. It was a
break for the league that Ruth and Gehrig were able to put on a home run
act that helped divert customers when they had nothing in the pennant
chase to keep them around.

This year George Pipgras has stepped into the box to fulfill all the nice
things predicted of him after the way he curved the Pirates to a standstill
in the last World's Series. George has filled not only one, but two or three,
gaps in the Yankee pitching staff. His success is attributable more to good
handling and natural developments than any breaks. So it was with Lazzeri, Koenig, Gehrig, and the others who have become important cogs in
this championship machine.[2]

James R. Harrison reported:

Although the American League race may be an artistic success, it is developing into a bust financially. The Yanks are twelve games ahead at the halfway mark; also, there is no home run race between Ruth and Gehrig to whet the appetites of the jaded clients. At least half the teams will lose money, and it wouldn't be surprising if five of the eight went into the red at the end of the fiscal year. The only solution seems to be to have a split season, starting all over again on July 4—or to rule the Yanks off the turf on the grounds that they are a monopoly in restraint of trade.[3]

The St. Louis Browns appeared to be the best of the western clubs. Nothing much was expected of the White Sox, or the Indians, who faded after a surprisingly good start. The biggest disappointment of the western teams was the last-place Tigers. Interest in Detroit was believed to be at its lowest level since 1922. As of July 4, the Tigers were twenty-six games behind the Yankees, but they were still only five and a half games out of fourth place. Nevertheless, fans viewed the situation as a glass half empty, as attendance was suffering, hurting the coffers of visiting teams as well.[4]

Huggins was reminded that his club was a half game better at the July 4 break of this year than in 1927:

Well, I had hoped that you would not put that question to me. As everybody knows, there is nothing to that July 4 bunk. I have seen it made to look foolish many a year. Some team may come along with a lot of fight in the second half and tear the league to pieces.

But I do want to take this opportunity to get in a boost for this Yankee club. Last winter, many competent critics, experienced baseball men, came to me and said, "Hug, your Yanks will not repeat; they are going to beat themselves. Some of your athletes already have swelled heads. The factor [that] broke up the old Athletics in 1912 will tear your team apart." I smiled because I knew my ball club, and they didn't. But to make safe, I got ready a plan of action in the event there was an outcropping of that head swelling. There hasn't been the slightest hint of it. My men are just as ambitious now as they were two years ago. They are out for more records, especially that mark of 116 victories held by the Cubs of 1906.

Some of the critics told me that it was a fatal error to give so many long contracts to a club riding as high. I was warned that while I had the best players in the league, the old ego and the carelessness [that] comes with excess, would beat us. No matter whether we win or not, my tribute to the players stands. They are a levelheaded, hard-working gang, and the veterans are just as ambitious as the youngsters.[5]

The schedule deviated slightly for July and August. According to the original version, the Yankees were essentially to oppose their western foes for forty-two games, with six games against Boston and five off days thrown into the mix. From Friday, July 6, through Sunday, July 22, the Browns, Tigers, Indians, and White Sox traveled east for separate four-game series.

The four-game series with the Browns that was scheduled to begin Friday, July 6, included the two makeup games from May 18 and 19. Yet, more rain meant that six games had to be crowded into three days instead of four. The rain temporarily broke a severe heat wave, with temperatures plunging from eighty-five degrees to sixty-seven. The relief came at a cost, as more than five inches of steady rain fell in Plainfield, New Jersey. There were heavy downpours in other surrounding suburbs as well, causing rockslides and mudslides.[6]

Opined Fred Lieb,

> While their Giant brethren will be obliged to fight every moment during their invasion of the west, the Yankees are in the pleasant position where they can coast along for the remainder of the season. An even break from now would be sufficient to put the Yankees into another World Series in October.[7]

The always cautious Miller Huggins somewhat concurred as he began to doubt whether the Athletics could reach the century mark in wins after they were swept on July 1. Treading water would give the Yankees ninety-five wins, four more than in 1926. But Huggins also reminded his players that they almost blew a ten-game lead that year and not to get overconfident.[8]

The earlier postponements could not have come at a better time for the Browns. Since then, they had taken advantage of a month-long home stand, lasting from the tail end of May through almost the entire month of June, by winning eighteen of twenty-seven games to give them a firm hold on third place.

The three straight doubleheaders with the Browns had Huggins worried. He stated,

> A fine kettle of fish, with Pennock fatigued and Hoyt right in the middle of his busy season in the undertaking business in Flatbush. Mark my words, here's where our lead is whittled down to maybe ten games. Six games in three days and Ruth has a bad shoulder and a crick in the back, and Dugan's floating rib still refuses to drop anchor. Mark my words, we'll lose two of those contests unless we snap out of our hitting slump.[9]

Even though nine Yankees were batting better than .300 and six players were above the .330 mark, Huggins was thinking ahead: "Yes, some of the boys are hitting in spots, but we should be hitting at least .315. A fine kettle of fish. Here we are all nervous from breaking even in Washington and we are handed another crucial series with St. Louis."[10]

The Yankees announced the release of Urban Shocker on July 6, due to poor health, after pitching only two innings thus far in the 1928 season. Huggins discussed the release of Shocker and the signing of Fred Heimach,

> Shocker has gone because he could not get into shape to pitch. He ignored his big chance while we were down in Florida. He is essentially a spring pitcher, and once behind in his work he could not catch up.
>
> I wish him lots of luck. He may need it. But we are not sending in for a replacement. That would not be fair to the young pitchers we now have. Heimach apparently is due to come back. But we have men like Shealy, Thomas, and Campbell who deserve to get occasional opportunities to earn their salaries.[11]

In the *Washington Post*, Frank H. Young explained that he didn't believe that Huggins had a thing to worry about—it was just a matter of whether the Yankees would break the Cubs' records of the early 1900s:

> As a matter of fact, not only are the Yankees apparently just the same as in, but they stand an excellent chance of equaling the modern record of winning two consecutive seasons with a percentage of .700 or better. . . . A .700 performance in the major leagues is as rare as a Dodo bird. The 1927 club is the only team [that] has done it in the junior circuit, while it has only happened four times in the National League since 1900. . . . With exceptional reserve material for practically every post, there seems to be no chance that the Yankees will slip in the present runaway. It is only a question of how many games they'll win, and their pace to date points to another percentage well in excess of the .700 mark.[12]

There was similar talk during the previous season of the team breaking records. With sixty-seven games remaining, no one thought any team would catch the Yankees. The one jewel was to break the Red Sox mark of 105 wins set in 1912. With ninety-eight home runs in ninety-four games, they were on pace to break the old mark of 140 set by the Chicago Nationals in 1884, not to mention their own of 134 in 1921.[13]

The St. Louis Browns were still within striking distance of second-place Philadelphia, trailing them by five games as of July 4. They also kept a winning record well beyond haymaking season. The team, or, more definitely, their manager, "Fearless" Dan Howley, was the talk of the baseball world. During the winter meetings two years ago, his first year as manager, Howley told the paper that he would find what kind of club he had, saying, "I'll keep the players hustling, and if we all keep working we will win many a game. If they don't hustle, I'll get some players who will. I did it in Toronto, and I think I can repeat in St. Louis." The results of 1927 were not good, and during the winter meetings the following year, the team was, of course, almost completely revamped.[14]

Three straight days of doubleheaders beginning on July 7 resulted in a wash. The Yankees swept the Browns on Saturday, only to have Dan Howley's men return the favor on Sunday. The Browns took advantage of the vulnerable part of the Yankee staff—Arch Campbell, Al Shealy, and Myles Thomas—who took a pasting in the first game, with the red hot General Crowder cruising to a 9–1 record. Manager Huggins flipped the slumping Meusel and Lazzeri in the batting order for the second game. Meusel had been batting at around a .280 clip for the past two months. George Blaeholder went the distance for the victory against Henry Johnson. The timing couldn't have been worse for President Barnard, who "was one of the wilted and perspiring thousands" who had to endure more than four hours of baseball.[15]

On Monday, Herb Pennock's six-hit, complete-game shutout was followed by a twenty-hit, twelve-run outburst against three Yankee pitchers. Stan Coveleski lost his first game of the year in the nightcap, lasting just four outs. Wilcy Moore was charged with four runs, and Arch Campbell three, in a 12–6 loss.

When the Tigers and Yankees took the field on Tuesday, they were greeted by a garden-variety thunderstorm that canceled the first game of the series. The slumping Tigers had won only twelve of their last thirty-three games since they last met the Yankees.[16] Temperatures had previously hovered at or above ninety degrees in the northeast for forty-eight hours. Around noon, the Charity Organization Society on 103 East 22nd Street was hit with pleas from 2,500 families, encompassing about 7,500 children, for ice, milk, and fresh produce.[17]

The storm gave the city a brief reprieve from the sweltering heat, which had claimed forty-five lives since Sunday. Coney Island had its largest weekend crowd ever, estimated at 400,000, while the Rockaways and other beaches saw 350,000 people.[18]

The latest postponement forced yet another doubleheader. This would be the sixth since the twin bill with Boston on June 30, all during an extreme heat wave. The Tigers had been buried in last place for sixteen straight days and had yet to spend one day of the 1928 season in the first division. The descent into the basement and a sub .400 won–loss percentage began at the start of a home stand on June 23, against the White Sox. It had become a foregone conclusion that George Moriarty would be replaced at the end of the season, probably by Bucky Harris, who was in the final year of a three-year contract making $33,000 for the Senators.[19]

Huggins expressed the surprising performance of the Tigers:

How many of you would have taken a bet last February that on July 11 the Tigers would be in last place? None of you would have dreamed of so terrific a flop for the Tigers. It preaches a moral. It shows you why the New York club is leaving no stone unturned in an effort to keep plugging up gaps and providing against losses of personnel and effectiveness. Unless you keep plugging, a ball club will go to pieces. You've got to make some young men feel that if they don't deliver there is a lad on the bench or a kid in Sacramento who will get the job.[20]

The Colonel stuck by Huggins after the team finished in seventh place in 1925. This was a time when owners, for the most part, dealt directly with their managers. Huggins was in the same position during the 1925–1926 off-season that Bucky Harris, Donie Bush, and George Moriarty would face after 1928.

"If he has supported me it is because he has confidence in my judgment, and that my judgment has been influenced by the fact that we run a dollar club in New York and not a five and ten club [like] they run in some other places," said Huggins. Clark Griffith paid lip service to Bucky Harris, and Frank Navin to Moriarty, but only Donie Bush would remain with Pittsburgh for another year. Huggins bore out Ruppert's confidence in him as the team restocked with new players.[21]

The Yankees were coming to terms with their own disappointment regarding Wilcy Moore. Last year's league leader in earned run average had been all but given up on. "If anyone had told me down at St. Petersburg last spring that Moore would be of no help to us, I guess it would have worried me considerably. I had counted on him heavily in this year's campaign," said Huggins. "Yet, in the first half of the season, we've hung up a tidy lead without Wilcy, and I guess we will have to go through the season without getting much help from the big Oklahoman." Moore never impressed any scouts, having pitched mainly in the lower minor leagues, but he had impressed the Yankees with his sinker in early spring training of 1927.[22]

As play resumed against the Tigers, George Pipgras sailed into the seventh inning of the first game with a two-run lead, but after getting the first out, the Tigers scored four runs to win the first game. Ken Holloway shut out the Yankees on six hits after a shaky first inning, with Elam Vangilder pitching a scoreless final three innings. Herb Pennock rescued Waite Hoyt in the ninth inning of the second game to save a 6–5 victory. The Babe's thirty-third home run in the seventh inning turned out to be the game winner and put him fourteen games ahead of 1927.[23]

Another storm threatened a single game the following day. The Yankees second-line staffers held up well until the ninth inning, when the inability to find the plate once again victimized Henry Johnson and then Cy Moore in relief. The team scratched out what they hoped was the go-ahead run in the eighth inning, when Meusel's single scored Koenig, but the cloudburst the Yankees were hoping for came in the form of a three-run Tiger outburst in the ninth inning.[24] The final game against Detroit on Friday was rained out, placing the Yankees under .500 against the west on the home stand.

When the Tigers arrived in Philadelphia, they were one and a half games in the basement. They used the day off to contemplate their prospects for turning their season around. They were within striking distance of the first division and still had an outside chance for third place. The race in the American League was amongst the bottom five clubs, and of the top five clubs in the National League (see tables 10.1 and 10.2).[25]

Table 10.1. Battle for the First Division, American League, July 13, 1928

Team	Won	Lost	GB	Pct.
Browns	43	41	third place	.512
Indians	38	44	fourth place	.463
White Sox	37	45	1	.451
Senators	36	46	2	.439
Red Sox	33	45	3	.423
Tigers	33	48	4.5	.407

Table 10.2. Battle for First Place, National League, July 13, 1928

Team	Won	Lost	GB	Pct.
Cardinals	53	30	—	.639
Reds	47	35	5.5	.573
Giants	43	33	6.5	.566
Cubs	47	37	6.5	.560
Robins	42	36	8.5	.538

Tiger manager George Moriarty believed that his club was coming around:

We have had a lot of luck all year, and all of it has been tough. We never had one break in our favor, but lately things have turned out for the better. When our pitchers braced, we started to do better. I was proud of the way the Tigers played at Yankee Stadium. Their backs were against the wall, and they just turned on the champions and clawed them down in two games out of three.[26]

Yankee business manager Ed Barrow had to call off a Saturday, July 14, doubleheader against Cleveland that included the May 9 postponement, nullifying a large weekend crowd of 40,000 and forcing five games in three days. When the Indians last left the Stadium in May, they were six games over .500. They had since dropped to six games below and lost seventeen games in the standings. Ed Morgan from Tulane University was one bright spot, batting .343 in thirty-nine games and playing several positions, but the high hopes for the pitching staff that were in place at the beginning of the season failed to materialize.[27]

The Yankees' recent slippage suddenly began prompting questions as to whether they could continue to be compared with the 1927 team. In his coverage in the *New York Times* on July 15, Harrison observes that the Yankees were equal or better in all aspects except pitchers Moore, Campbell, and Coveleski, who were underperforming. Moore's earned run average was nearly two runs higher, at 4.54, than at the same time in 1927, while Campbell's earned run average was more than seven. Coveleski had won five of six decisions; however, the Yankees were averaging seven runs per game during his starts, and his earned run average stood at 5.69.

Harrison's assessment of the team continued,

> Mr. Huggins or Hudland points to the fact that the Yanks have won as many games as last year and are as far ahead, and this is a rather convincing answer, although it wouldn't necessarily prove that the Yanks of 1928 are as good as their 1927 variety.
>
> Ruth and Gehrig aren't hitting as well as a season ago, nor, we fancy, is Combs. The pitching is long of quality but short on quantity. Moore, Thomas, and Coveleski have done little or nothing, leaving the matter up to Pipgras, Hoyt, Pennock, Johnson, and Shealy.
>
> On the other hand, Lazzeri, Koenig, Dugan, and Robertson are all better than in 1927, and the Yanks' reserve strength is magnificent. A few outstanding things about the Yanks are these: Cy Moore's notable failure to deliver anything, the passing of Shocker, the steady rise of young Hank Johnson, Pipgras's entrance into stardom, and Gehrig's failure to measure up to 1927.
>
> Also Ruth's slump in hitting, aside from home runs; the rejuvenation of Joseph Aloysius Dugan; Robertson's splendid showing; steady improvement of Lazzeri and Koenig; the amazing skill of Leo Durocher, the best fielding shortstop in baseball; and the new quality of catching.[28]

Huggins then announced that Myles Thomas would step into Moore's former relief role:

> I expect to use Thomas a lot from now on. He looked as though he would develop into a regular winner for us in 1926, and I haven't weakened on him. He was quite ill early in the present season, and it took him some time to regain his full strength. For that reason I gradually nursed him along, letting him pitch to batters, and in exhibition games. I called him three times in the Browns series, and he did real well. Thomas is a smart pitcher; he has a good change of pace, and I still entertain a lot of hope for his future.[29]

Thomas was used in mainly mop-up roles for eight and two thirds innings against the Browns and had not given up a run. Were there some leaks in the ship?

The rain left the Yankees, their manager, in particular, the chance to ponder their mid-season malaise:

> Whatever might ail them might do them a lot of good. They are taking a very beneficial midsummer tonic, which is good for that tired feeling and is an admirable preventive for enlargement of the hat size. It creates mid-afternoon insomnia and stirs up jaded nerves.
>
> But, seriously, nothing is wrong with the Yankees. Some of the boys are a little tired and banged up, and the pitching staff is showing the effects of the doubleheader schedule, which set in at Washington on the Fourth. Once past the two games today, we will have a chance to give the hurlers more rest, and it will be easy sailing. If it doesn't keep on raining and piling up doubleheaders.[30]

In reality the Yankees had only three established pitchers in Hoyt, Pipgras, and a tiring Pennock. Henry Johnson was trying to be too fine with his pitches and missing the plate. The doubleheaders were also hindering some of the injured infielders and Ruth's shoulder from healing.[31]

Saturday's postponement made way for a Sunday bonus game, enticing a crowd of 45,000. The Yankees took the lead in the first inning of the first game on a sacrifice fly by Ruth. In the bottom of the sixth inning, Herb Pennock aided his thirteenth victory with a bases-loaded single to left field off of the loser, Joe Schaute, good for two runs and a three-run lead. That was all the scoring, and Pennock's second shutout in a row. The Babe drove in Mark Koenig with his thirty-fourth home run in the first inning of the nightcap, which paced the lone victory and decision for Myles Thomas for 1928. Ruth's thirty-fourth home run in 1927 did not come until the ninety-seventh game.

The loss knocked the Indians out of the first division by a single percentage point after the White Sox swept Boston.[32]

With the next-nearest team, the third-place Browns, having eighteen more losses, three-fourths of the league was essentially done for the 1928 season. True to the haymaking pattern, the large weekend crowds in St. Louis for the Browns and in Cleveland shrank as the season wore on, and South Side Chicago fans defected en masse from the massive 55,000-capacity Comiskey Park to Wrigley Field. Hope was gone in Washington, and in Detroit they had even lost interest in the World Series.

Would Yankee fans lose interest the same way Athletic fans did during the 1914 season if the pennant race was no longer a contest? Would they have to unload expensive stars like the Red Sox in 1920? John P. Gallagher of the *Los Angeles Times* believed that the Yankees were actually already losing money due to such a large lead.[33]

The *Hartford Courant* suggested adopting a split season,

> When a single pennant race drags its length from April to October, it is not at all unlikely that some one team will dash away in the lead and widen the distance between itself and the other contenders so that the race ceases to be interesting—as in the American League in this year of 1928. As a safeguard against this probability, various minor leagues adopted split schedules for this year.[34]

Another solution to bring the owners checkbooks in parity and sink the Yankees would be to deaden the ball again.[35]

"The Yanks' idea of Paradise," said Harrison, "is merely a place where one plays the Cleveland Indians a doubleheader every day." The Yankees took the next three games by sweeping another doubleheader on Monday and winning a single game on Tuesday. George Pipgras improved to sixteen wins and four losses in the opener and also had three hits and one run batted in. Henry Johnson won his seventh game against four defeats in the nightcap.[36] The next day, Al Shealy followed the sweep, beating Yankee killer George Uhle, who was betrayed by his fielders and gave up a solo home run to Shealy in the second inning.

Sixteen days into the month of July, the Yankees had played eight doubleheaders, beginning with the sweep of the Athletics. They won four, divided three, and were swept in one. The backlog was reduced to six, with two games to make up in Detroit, one in Cleveland, and three at home against Detroit, Washington, and Philadelphia.

The Yankees would face the White Sox next. Ray Schalk had become the second managerial casualty of the season on July 4, following Jack Slattery's dismissal by the Boston Braves on May 25. The White Sox had just taken four of five games from the Browns when he was let go. Schalk was popular in Chicago and had caught more games than any other catcher up to that time. He was one of the good guys during the 1919 scandal and replaced Eddie Collins before the 1927 season.[37]

The White Sox began making their move after beating Cleveland in the nightcap of a doubleheader on June 21. They went on to win twenty of twenty-nine games to move from last place to fourth place as of July 18. Lena Blackburne's appointment was the fifth managerial change since 1923, and his was expected to be an interim appointment, with Tris Speaker possibly being next in line. They now had their sights set on second and third place, trailing the Browns by five and a half games and the Athletics by ten. Blackburne did not make any changes to his predecessor's lineup and was also reassured by Charles Comiskey that his position was permanent.[38]

The White Sox had Ted Lyons this time around against the Yankees, and he opened the series against Waite Hoyt. A pitcher's duel never materialized and, instead, a seventeen-run, twenty-five-hit slugfest took place, with the Yankees prevailing by a run. The Yankees blew a five-run lead after the fifth inning, thanks to six errors, three by shortstop Mark Koenig. Waite Hoyt was replaced by Cy Moore in the eighth inning, leading 6–3 when Chicago tied the score. Koenig muffed an easy grounder with Alex Metzler on base and then Hoyt served up a three-run home run to Bibb Falk. It was just the club's seventeenth home run of the season.

The fielding woes continued in the ninth inning as misplays by Mike Gazella and Mark Koenig set up a two-run single by Buck Redfern and a two-run Chicago lead. In the Yankee half, Earle Combs singled, and Koenig doubled after two were out. The White Sox could pass on pitching to the Yankee right fielder and take their chances with the first baseman. They pitched to Ruth, and all hell broke loose. It was always worth the price of a ticket to see the Babe hit a home run, but a ninth-inning, come-from-behind, walk-off homer resulted in bedlam. Home run number thirty-six went to right field, and hundreds of fans mobbed the field.[39]

Two more blows by the Babe and untimely hitting by the White Sox powered the Yankees to their seventh consecutive win. Ruth's thirty-eighth blast did not come until his 114th game in 1927, against the White Sox on August 17. Said Babe,

> Yes, sir, that Al Thomas certainly is a first cousin of mine, right from my old Baltimore home, too. Usually I don't mind an afternoon off at this time of the year. But after the way I socked Cousin Thomas for those two home runs yesterday I deplore—that's the word, isn't it?—I deplore the little vacation, for I am rarin' to go.[40]

Ruth thought a new home run record was all but a done deal. He added, "With thirty-eight home runs in eighty-eight games, I can't see how I can miss a new record this year."[41]

Mike Gazella, a former algebra student at Lafayette College, figured that at his current pace the Babe would hit sixty-seven home runs. Ruth responded,

> I never died for old Lafayette, Mike, but that's how I figure it out in my noodle. I think I ought to hit about sixty-five. That would be just right. And don't let anybody tell you I won't try to hit as many as I can. Might as well sock 'em while the socking is possible. Old age is creeping up on the Babe. If they keep shooting Cousin Thomas at us, I might even hit more. Yes, he's a great cousin, is Al, from my old hometown, Baltimore.[42]

Since 1926, the Stadium had been a house of horrors for the White Sox, losing twenty-five of twenty-nine games. "Gaze upon the two games we have lost and you will find evidences of occult interferences with us. The stars and the planets are against us in the Bronx," said catcher Moe Berg. It was the eleventh consecutive setback for Thomas against the Yankees. Pennock was not sharp, giving up thirteen hits, and he had to be rescued by Cy Moore in the ninth inning after a leadoff single and walk with the Yankees ahead by two runs. Moore finished off the Chisox with a double play and groundout.

The Babe's sister was at the game; in addition to hitting two home runs, both with Combs on base, he presented her with a jeweled wristwatch in a signed baseball-shaped case. Knute Rockne and Pop Warner were also in attendance.[43]

The Yankees were twelve games ahead of Washington after eighty-eight games in 1927, and they were leading the Athletics by the same amount in 1928. The team's record of 65–23 was still two games ahead of the previous year. At this time during the previous year, Lou Gehrig had thirty-one home runs to the Babe's thirty, whereas this year the Babe had thirty-eight to Gehrig's nineteen.[44]

During the spring, many people, including Miller Huggins, predicted that pitching would be the team's undoing, but as one former National League owner stated,

> I regard Miller Huggins as one of the greatest managers in the history of baseball. You watch him work those pitchers, and see what he does at critical times during a game, and you will note the mark of a very efficient leader. He has the Yanks playing his type of ball. The fan in the stand will say, "Why, that club could run itself. Look at the players Huggins has!" Well, it might run itself for a while, but that's another tribute to Hug's managerial genius.[45]

"He eats and sleeps and thinks, just lives baseball," a veteran on one of the western clubs said. "Huggins is the best manager in the American League, and nobody even comes close to him. Not even Mack gives Hug a close fight. There isn't a moment when that little fellow hasn't a pitcher ready to go to the rescue."[46]

In the following game between the White Sox and Yankees, Ed Walsh Jr., son of the great future Hall of Fame spitballer Ed Walsh, gave the Yankees all they could handle in a tough pitcher's duel. Walsh was just a month off the campus of Notre Dame, but he held the Yankees hitless and scoreless through five innings. In the seventh inning, the young pitcher got behind in the count to the Babe, who took him out for his thirty-ninth home run. Ruth was now twenty-eight games ahead of his 1927 pace. Walsh later balked in the second run, which was more than enough for Pipgras, who was sharp in tossing a four-hit shutout. But the rookie was loudly applauded by the fans on his way to the clubhouse after being removed for a pinch hitter in the eighth inning. After the game, Wilcy Moore shouted to Pipgras to give him his sinker back.[47]

Huggins was hoping that the team could piggyback on the Babe's assault on his own record and was not concerned about the team consciously trying to hit home runs:

> If the Babe betters his home run record this season—and I have reason to believe he will—the big fellow will pull the whole Yankee club to another mark for hitting circuit drives. You will note that we are out for home run no. 100 today. With sixty-six games to go, we should pass the record of 158, which we made last year.
>
> No, our men get those home runs in stride. True, Ruth keeps on trying to pull the ball into the right-field stand, but there are times when he, too, is just swinging for his hit, although hoping that the hit will be a homer. There is no danger connected with the Yankees in any department. We seem to have gotten over our relapse.
>
> Don't forget this—the opposition has been showing the Yankees some fancy pitching. Great pitching! We have had some pretty good pitching ourselves, but the western clubs have spilled wonderful hurling. The heat seems to have oiled up the pitchers to remarkable efficiency. Yes, it looks like another great home run year for the Yankees—and I'd like to see Tony Lazzeri back in there to help. He'll return within a few days.[48]

A doubleheader conquest by the Mackmen over the Browns and completion of a five-game series sweep were described by Bill Brandt in the *Philadelphia Public Ledger* as being done in Yankee fashion. Lefty Grove and Jack Quinn were the arms, while Al Simmons, Joe Hauser, and Jimmy Dykes were the bats. The victories put the Athletics twenty games above the .500 mark for the first time in 1928, and opened a ten-game hold on second place.[49]

The Yankee win streak was snapped at eight in their final game with the White Sox by the pitching and hitting of Urban "Red" Faber. In the eighth inning, with the score tied with runners at second and third, two easy strikes were issued by Cy Moore. Faber switched to the left side of the plate and hit a clean single to center field, scoring two runs to win the game.[50]

The schedule then made its fluky shift on Monday, July 23, to Boston for two games. The first game was settled after the fourth inning, as Al Shealy and Myles Thomas combined to put the Yankees in an eight-run deficit. The Babe's fortieth home run was one of the longest ever at Fenway Park. It traveled about 450 feet to left-center field. Otherwise, the Yankees could do nothing with Dan MacFayden. The Babe was nearly a month ahead of his 1927 pace. Ruth didn't hit his fortieth home run in 1927 until August 22, but he would have a tough time topping September, when he hit seventeen.[51]

Boston righty Jack Russell cruised into the final inning with a 3–1 lead when the Yankees just missed batting around, scoring four runs. Herb Pennock gave up three runs in the first inning but held Boston until the eighth inning, when he was removed for a pinch hitter. Boston attempted a comeback against Moore in their last at bat. The premier reliever of 1927 walked the first two batters and was replaced by Hoyt, who saved a 5–3 victory.

The original schedule now swung to intersectional play for fourteen games, first in Detroit for three, followed by Cleveland for four, St. Louis for three, and Chicago for four. The team felt that they were in good shape physically outside of Waite Hoyt's neuritis and Tony Lazzeri's shoulder. They arrived in Detroit with an eleven-game lead at 1:25 p.m., on July 25, the day of the doubleheader. What was originally a three-game series included two make up games from June 4 and 5.[52]

The Tigers were in the basement by half a game. They had occupied that space for all but two days since June 25. But, exactly one month later, Detroit fans took a keen delight in seeing their last-place team defeat the leaders twice and cheered for the Athletics on the scoreboard. They had beaten the champions in four of the last five meetings.

George Pipgras began to tire in the sixth and fell apart in the eighth with the Yankees ahead, 2–0. He walked first baseman Marty McManus and then allowed a single to second baseman Charlie Gehringer that set up a game-tying triple by Sam Rice. Cy Moore was summoned and promptly gave up the winning run on a single to left fielder Al Wingo.

The more vulnerable part of the staff let Huggins down in the second game, with Henry Johnson lasting just one-third of an inning. The Athletics' sweep of the White Sox brought their deficit to fewer than ten games for the first time since June 25.

The next day, Waite Hoyt stopped the bleeding in the first game of the doubleheader in what turned out to be an unusual 12–1 victory. Bob Meusel's third home run of the year off Vic Sorrell in the sixth inning broke a scoreless pitcher's duel, but pinch hitter Pinky Hargrave tied the score for Detroit in the bottom of the ninth off of Hoyt with his fourth home run. Both pitchers worked into the twelfth inning, when Sorrell fell apart. Fifteen Yankees came to the plate as the team scored eleven runs on two triples, three doubles, and five singles.

Miller Huggins used Johnson, Campbell, and Moore, with a brief appearance from Pipgras in the second game in what was an ugly loss. The Yankees cut into a 10–2 Tiger lead with five runs in the sixth inning but ended up losing, 13–10. Huggins took extreme measures by juggling his lineup, moving Meusel to second, Lazzeri to fifth, and Koenig to the sixth slot.

The split with the Yankees, coupled with the Indians' sweep of the Red Sox, lifted the Tigers out of the basement for the remainder of the season. Moriarty's club was predicted to be a possible dark horse to challenge the Hugmen; instead, they had twice as many losses, with fifty-six, and a .404 won–loss percentage.[53]

The final matchup with the Tigers was postponed, while at the same time the White Sox bid farewell to the Athletics after having been decisively swept by them and dropping two notches, to sixth place. Meanwhile, the deficit crept downward to eight games.

The Yankees closed the month of July with five games in Cleveland against a team that they had beaten the last ten times. The Indians did sign Roger Peckinpaugh for the 1929 season, in the midst of their worst slump of the season in late July. The players responded positively to the confidence placed in Peck by Alva Bradley and swept the Red Sox in four games at League Park. The series with the Yankees began with the eleventh doubleheader of the month, which made up for the June 8 rainout.[54]

Herb Pennock won the first game as poor defense plagued George Uhle. Al Shealy didn't make it past the third inning in the nightcap, with Stan Coveleski giving up five runs in relief. Willis Hudlin recorded a complete-game victory, even though Cleveland was just as sloppy in the nightcap, if not more so, than in the first game. Fortunately for Hudlin it wasn't bad enough to overcome Cleveland's nineteen hits and nine runs.[55]

It was not verified at the time whether it was the worst defeat in Yankees history, but the 24–6 loss to the Indians on Sunday, July 29, would have been considered lopsided even if it were a football game. Cleveland put up eight runs in the first inning, nine in the second, six in the sixth, and one in the third inning for good measure. The blame only partially belonged to the vulnerable portion of the pitching staff, since nine Indian runs were unearned. The Yankees trailed by twenty-one runs when they scored three runs in the ninth inning against starter Joe Schaute. Three of Huggins' pitchers hit the showers before the second inning was over. Pipgras should have benefited from a double play that was muffed by Koenig, but he was gone before he could retire a batter. Archie Campbell was the one bright spot, blanking the Tribe in the last two and one-third frames on four hits.[56] "While the Athletics were constructing their seventh unbroken win on western soil," wrote James Isaminger, "the Yanks again flopped in Cleveland, and now only five and a half games separate the two teams."[57]

The Yankees' stumble in Detroit and Cleveland was costly. For the seven days ending July 30, the lead dwindled to five and a half games from ten and a half. They were not playing consistent baseball and were performing erratically in all phases of the game. Mark Koenig led the team in errors, with fifty-two in 1926, and forty-seven in 1927, and he was having a tough time in 1928.

Cleveland followed the previous day's shellacking with another victory, handing the Yankees their first three-game losing streak of the year. Miller Huggins juggled his lineup once again, taking Combs out of the leadoff spot for the first time in two seasons and moving him to the second slot and inserting Mark Koenig. The Babe accounted for the only Yankee runs in the sixth, with Combs on base when he hit his forty-first home run.[58] Meanwhile, the Macks won a ninth-inning squeaker over the Browns and Sam Gray. The winning pitcher, Rube Walberg, got the last out in the seventh inning in relief of Rommel after the Browns tied the score, and helped his own cause with a leadoff single in the top of the ninth.[59]

With the lead down to five and a half games, an editorial in the *Philadelphia Public Record* signaled the complete reversal of fortunes in the American League:

> The Yanks are on the verge of collapse. The pitching staff has sagged and bent, and not even the strident hitting can overcome such rotten hurling. . . . Foxx, Haas, Cochrane, Orwoll—lads who have strength and speed and color and abilities—now have their head and are rushing ahead like Man o' War in the stretch. . . . The race is NOT OVER YET. We may still fly the grand old rag in Shibe Park in brown October.[60]

The Yankees managed a victory in the final game against Cleveland, but it was not a pretty sight. Twelve runs would usually be more than enough for three games for Waite Hoyt. Cleveland battled back twice, once successfully, from five-run deficits. They pounded the mortician for seven hits and seven runs in four and two-thirds innings, and Moore for five hits and two runs in two and a third innings before Pennock barely calmed things down in the last two sets. Yankee pitchers were not completing games, nor was Tony Lazzeri or Mark Koenig's fielding helping them out.

Earle Combs, however, had a fantastic month of July. After the first game of the July 1 doubleheader against the Athletics, his average dipped to an even .300, but he hit safely in all but six of the next thirty-four games and lifted his average to a season high of .326. Combs believed that he got a bum rap on his throwing arm and that his hitting was underappreciated. He felt at home playing center field, however, and covered far more ground than Ruth or Meusel. Combs stated the following in 1927:

> My arm was never more than moderately strong. I could name at least a dozen outfielders in the American League whose throwing arms are not a little bit better than mine. You never hear of them however. I have to compete with Babe Ruth and Bob Meusel, and, of course, I simply don't class with those fellows. Even one glaring fault will queer a fellow in the Big Leagues.
>
> Leading off as I do, I am bound to lose a couple of hits [during] a season's length. It's difficult to estimate how many, but I think I'd be conservative to claim that the leadoff man suffers at least fifteen points in batting average. Here's one illustration. Three times this season I've been robbed of a hit because Shocker was on first base and couldn't make second. A faster man would have had the base easily. And there never was a chance to get me at first.
>
> Besides, the very percentages, I believe, work against a leadoff man. The average number of the batting list will be up say four times. The leadoff man is very often up at least five times. The extra time will go against you much more than an even percentage.
>
> You do more running in center than at either of the other positions. But that doesn't bother me now. Perhaps if I were ten years older I would feel it. And there are advantages in playing center. For one thing you're not so apt to be in the sun field. Then again you don't have to worry about the different fields that you visit on the circuit. Outfield fences cut into the right and left fielder's territories and give them something to think about. But center field is about the same old job anywhere.[61]

Combs led the league in hits and triples but believed that his speed helped him more in stretching singles into doubles rather than getting triples. He felt his equilibrium was around the .330 to .340 mark.[62]

The Yankees weren't exactly collapsing, having won eighteen of thirty-three games during that span. Instead, it was due more to the spectacular surge of twenty-four wins in thirty games from the Mackmen, the same record that the Yankees had begun the season with. The Athletics needed to trade wins and losses with the Yankees, inch a little closer, and beat the front-runners in their final head-to-head competition. This was something they had not been able to do, having lost thirteen of eighteen matchups.

Working in Connie Mack's favor was the pitching situation. The Yankees had three tired regulars in Pennock, Pipgras, and Hoyt, with four makeup doubleheaders left. The Athletics had six performers, Grove, Walberg, Ehmke, Quinn, Orwoll, and Earnshaw. Mack's twirlers threw twenty-three complete games in July, which was nine more than the Yankee starters. The Yankees used more than two pitchers ten times during the month, compared to five for the Athletics.

Huggins also did not have a catcher like Mickey Cochrane. In addition, the lean leader's strategy in mid-July to bench his two antiques and permanently go with a set lineup of younger players—mainly Jimmie Foxx at third base, Ossie Orwoll at first base, and Mule Haas in center field—came with immediate results.[63]

The Yankees showed signs of their early season form with a lopsided victory as they opened a three-game series in St. Louis to begin the month of August. Henry Johnson beat Browns ace General Crowder, who had lost his previous two decisions to the Athletics. Johnson collected five of the Yankees' sixteen hits for a perfect day with the bat. Bob Meusel hit his ninth home run with two men on, and the Babe crushed number forty-two. Miller Huggins had to look to his bench to Gene Robertson to fill in for Tony Lazzeri, who was out indefinitely with a sore shoulder, this as the regular second baseman had ten hits in his last eighteen at bats and was batting .356.[64]

Herb Pennock was unbeaten in five decisions during the month of July, but, "dog tired and wearied by heat and his labors of fourteen innings," he lost a tough game the next day against the Browns, and the Yankees lost another game in the standings as the Macks crept to within four and a half games of the lead.[65]

Pennock was still on the mound with the score tied in the fifteenth inning when Lu Blue singled and went to third on a double by Frank O'Rourke. An intentional walk to Wally Schang set the stage for Walter Stewart, the second pitcher of the day for the Browns, who dropped a bases-loaded, no-out single to left field. The Babe made a great try to grab it, but to no avail. Tony Lazzeri checked into St. John's Hospital in St. Louis for treatments on his shoulder by the club physician for the Browns and Cardinals.[66]

"Murderers' Row is as rough and ferocious as an affectionate little kitten," reports Harrison. The Yankees were shut out in the finale in St. Louis and had not scored a run in twenty-one innings. The eight runs scored by the Browns came in every inning but three of them. Sam Gray held the Yankees to six harmless hits, while Brown bats knocked Hoyt out of the box in the fifth inning leading. It was the eighth setback for the Hugmen in the twelve games played west of the Alleghenies. They were now in a pennant race.[67]

Comiskey Park was next for four single games to close the first week of August. The White Sox would be the only club that the Yankees would not have to play a makeup game against in 1928. The Yankees took the opener for the third straight series to maintain their lead at four and a half games. Ben Paschal was the hero, batting for Leo Durocher, as he doubled in the go-ahead runs in the tenth inning. The Babe lined his forty-third home run of the year in the fifth to keep him twenty-one games ahead of his 1927 pace.[68]

The Yankees finally made a deal for former Athletic Fred Heimach from their affiliate in St. Paul of the American Association, as the champions were grasping to find an answer to the incredible rush of the Athletics. The twenty-seven-year-old made a comeback after suffering a serious shoulder injury during spring training in 1925, and he had been one of the best pitchers in the American Association, with a record of eighteen wins against ten losses and a 2.76 earned run average. Similarly to Orwoll, he was a combination first baseman and pitcher with the Athletics. It was reported at the beginning of June that the White Sox considered paying $100,000 for Heimach.[69]

The Hugmen were prevented from gaining any traction by the popular right arm of young Ed Walsh. The White Sox, in front of a Sunday crowd of 35,000, built a picket fence in the first three innings against young Henry Johnson, only to watch the Yankees respond with single runs in the fourth and fifth innings. Chicago added two more runs in the eighth inning to take a 5–2 lead. The Yankees attempted a comeback with two runs in the ninth, but the two-out rally fell just short.[70]

Lefty Grove cooled down the Tigers, striking out eleven and allowing just three safeties en route to his fifteenth victory. The Macks were now within three and a half games of the top with four games remaining with the Yankees.[71]

Willie Kamm was the hometown hero on Monday, as the Chicago third baseman connected on a George Pipgras curve and lined a two-out triple to left field, driving in Bibb Falk. These heroics took place in the bottom of the fifteenth inning, with the score tied at four, after three hours and thirty-four minutes of play. At the same time, the Athletic juggernaut hit a snag as the Tigers solved George Earnshaw following his shutout in Cleveland for an 8–5 victory.

The Yankee record of ten wins in twenty-two games since July 17 gave the illusion of a collapse. John Kieran commented as follows:

The recent collapse of the Yankees was something like the clattering apart of the famous One Hoss Shay: "All at once and nothing first, Just as bubbles do when they burst." The hitters stopped hitting; the fielders began kicking the ball around like a lot of soccer players; the pitchers showed nothing except a remarkable aptitude for bouncing two-baggers off enemy bats.[72]

The problem was the second-line pitching putting pressure on the infield, which was compounded by the loss of Tony Lazzeri. With Joe Dugan in and out of the lineup, Mark Koenig was having a hard time getting used to an unsettled infield.[73]

The team gained ground on the Athletics for the first time in two weeks. Herb Pennock bested Ted Lyons, 6–3, in the finale at Comiskey Park. In an article for the *New York Times* on August 8, Harrison wrote,

Your correspondent, who is rather psychic about such matters, has a feeling that the nightmare is over, that sunlight lies directly ahead, and that the Yanks have turned their faces toward a bigger and better life. In fact, history may record that the turning point in the 1928 race took place on the afternoon of August 7.[74]

The Macks could not solve Owen Carroll and dropped a 4–1 decision behind Rube Walberg.[75]

The Athletics had initially picked up steam in early June, when Al Simmons returned to left field. Subsequently, the original plan to depend on Ty Cobb and Tris Speaker as regular outfielders was scrapped, making Bing Miller the permanent right fielder and Mule Haas the regular center fielder. There was also the decision in late July by Connie Mack to go with a set lineup of younger players instead of constantly shifting his lineup around. He may have been looking, in part, to the 1929 season, but the changes had the effect of pushing the team back in the race. Ty Cobb was permanently removed from the lineup on Thursday, July 26. The previous day, Ossie Orwoll took over first base, and the previous Friday, Jimmie Foxx was given third base.[76]

Pictured from left to right: two of the game's great sluggers, Jimmy Foxx of the Athletics and Babe Ruth of the Yankees, and two of the game's great hitters, Lou Gehrig of the Yankees and Al Simmons of the Athletics.

National Baseball Hall of Fame Library, Cooperstown, N.Y.

Most of the Yankee twirlers of 1928, from left to right: rookie Henry Johnson, veterans Waite Hoyt, Tom Zachary, George Pipgras, Rosy Ryan, Fred Heimach, and Myles Thomas. Those missing from the picture who finished the season as Yankees are Herb Pennock and Al Shealey.

National Baseball Hall of Fame Library, Cooperstown, N.Y.

Wilcy Moore, who was considered by many to be the most valuable player in baseball in 1927 as a relief pitcher, was plagued by a sore arm in 1928.

National Baseball Hall of Fame Library, Cooperstown, N.Y.

Third baseman Joe Dugan frequently came up as trade bait during the offseason and tailed off in 1928 after a fast start. This would be his last year as a Yankee.
National Baseball Hall of Fame Library, Cooperstown, N.Y.

Waite Hoyt held out for more money before the 1928 season and justified his demands by winning twenty-three games against seven losses.

National Baseball Hall of Fame Library, Cooperstown, N.Y.

Miller Huggins played the hermit role among the Connie Macks and John McGraws but built his legacy with six pennants and three World Series victories.

National Baseball Hall of Fame Library, Cooperstown, N.Y.

Earl Combs played his entire twelve-year career with the Yankees and was inducted into the Base-ball Hall of Fame in 1970 with a .325 lifetime batting average.

National Baseball Hall of Fame Library, Cooperstown, N.Y.

Tony Lazzeri was one of the team's inspirational leaders but he felt he missed too many games during the 1928 season to be given the most valuable player award, saying instead it should go to Mickey Cochrane.

National Baseball Hall of Fame Library, Cooperstown, N.Y.

Shortstop Mark Koenig was one of the team's most consistent hitters during 1928 for batting average, finishing the season at .316.

National Baseball Hall of Fame Library, Cooperstown, N.Y.

Bob Meusel began with the Yankees in 1920 from Vernon of the Pacific Coast League and finished his major league career with the Reds in 1930. He had a lifetime batting average of .309 and drove in more than 1,000 runs.

National Baseball Hall of Fame Library, Cooperstown, N.Y.

Rookie right-hander Al Shealy was counted on in 1928 to pick up some of the wins from pitchers let go after 1927. An injury while playing football at Newberry College deadened his right index finger, causing him to pitch with virtually three fingers.

National Baseball Hall of Fame Library, Cooperstown, N.Y.

Henry Johnson won fourteen games during his first full season in 1928; more importantly, he out-pitched Lefty Grove in four head-to-head matchups.
National Baseball Hall of Fame Library, Cooperstown, N.Y.

Herb Pennock won seventeen games and lost six for the Yankees during the 1928 season, with an earned run average of 2.56. This would be the last quality season for the Knight from Kennett Square before he ended his Hall of Fame career in Boston (A) in 1934.

National Baseball Hall of Fame Library, Cooperstown, N.Y.

Give Me Pennock and We'll Win
(August 9–August 27)

> There is, of course, the time-honored tale of the gentleman who fell out of a window on the twentieth floor and, passing the tenth floor level, reported that he was all right so far.
>
> —*New York Times*, July 31, 1928[1]

The Yankees were not playing bad baseball; their longest losing streak of the season was still just three games, and the wear and tear of a baseball campaign eventually affects the hurling staffs of every team. The Athletics were certainly capable of playing at better than a .750 rate during an extended period of time, and, since July 4, they had clipped seven and a half games off of what was a twelve-game deficit.

Miller Huggins was worried during the first week of August in the 1927 season when the Yankees were getting ready to face the Tigers. That happened to be the anniversary of the team's slump that began in 1926, against the very same opponent, and the team almost went on to blow a ten-game lead to Cleveland. But during 1927, just two and a half games were shaved off of a peak lead of fourteen games reached toward the end of July, and a serious threat was never mounted.[2]

This year was turning out differently, and Connie Mack could not help but be pleased with his team's play as they prepared to open a home series with Washington, where large crowds were expected. The Athletics were inwardly confident that they would overtake the Yankees by September 2.[3] While in Detroit, the lean leader confided to George Moriarty how the changes he made to his lineup were a pleasant surprise, even to him:

> I have tried to believe that for years, and I hope I am not kidding myself now. To have Haas, Foxx, and Orwoll come through at one time is a

great stroke of fortune. Usually a manager is tickled to have one player blossom out in an emergency. Haas, however, impressed me last spring when he played so brilliantly in the Philadelphia city series. Orwoll as a first baseman frankly surprises me, as I figured he would make an excellent outfielder. Foxx has fine possibilities as an infielder. Our club has started uphill at a rapid clip with these three players in the lineup.

We have a chance if our boys will just play the game. That's all I am asking of them. Tightening up till it becomes a state of mental pressing is the real danger a ball club faces in a crises. I think our whole club sensed their opportunity the day we won the doubleheader in Chicago about a week ago, because the Yankees dropped two games on the same day.[4]

The Yankees' winning percentage had tumbled from a high of .813 on June 10, to .676 on August 8, but it was still, by far, the best in baseball. Nonetheless, the lead had slipped from thirteen and a half games to four and a half games, with the momentum completely in Philadelphia's favor. The Macks were presently on a pace to win 106 games. The talk of the Yankees breaking records, split seasons, and the Yankees distributing their players throughout the league had suddenly ceased.

There was a tight battle in the American League amongst the teams in the second division. Only three losses separated the fourth- through seventh-place clubs as of August 7, with the last-place Red Sox eight losses behind the fourth-place Indians and White Sox. The Tigers were still in seventh place after mowing down the east at Navin Field (see table 11.1).

Table 11.1.   American League Standings, August 9, 1928

Team	Won	Lost	GB	Pct.
Yankees	74	35	—	.679
Athletics	69	39	4.5	.639
Browns	57	54	18	.514
White Sox	50	59	24	.459
Indians	50	59	24	.459
Senators	49	62	26	.441
Tigers	46	60	26.5	.434
Red Sox	40	67	33	.374

The 6–10 western swing of the Yankees was getting a great amount of attention, but it was noted by John Kieran that the Giants performed similarly on their last trip west and managed to recover:

That's it exactly. The Yankees are a good team. Everybody knows it. They should win and win rather handily. If they don't win, human reason will stagger in devising a punishment to fit the crime. They had an overwhelming lead. They had, and still have for that matter, a good infield, a fine outfield, three Grade-A pitchers, a strong attack, and the biggest ball park in either league as a setting for a World's Series.[5]

The two-month stretch of intersectional games was briefly interrupted a final time as the Yankees traveled to Boston for three games beginning Thursday, August 9, with the two teams traveling back to New York for one game that Sunday. Boston had been hemorrhaging, winning just eleven of their last forty games.

The newest Yankee, left-hander Fred Heimach, shut down the Red Sox on four hits, while allowing one run. Heimach got off to a rough start, giving up a run on one hit and two walks, but he shut out Boston for the rest of the game, retiring fifteen straight hitters after the first inning.[6]

The Red Sox had George Pipgras on the ropes the following day, but the Yankees won, again maintaining their four-and-a-half-game lead. The Yankees beat Boston a third time on great pitching and clutch hitting. Waite Hoyt earned his first win since the opening series against Detroit on July 26. As James R. Harrison wrote, "When the scoreboard showed the A's beating the Senators in the ninth, the silence on the Yankee bench was thick and clammy."[7]

The two clubs shifted to the Bronx, where things got worse for Bill Carrigan's crew, losing 8–0 on only three hits. The crowd of 25,000 that welcomed the Hugmen was treated to Herb Pennock's fifth shutout of the year. Production had been decent offensively from the catching core of Benny Bengough, Pat Collins, and John Grabowski, but the team decided to recall Bill Dickey from Little Rock.[8]

The win increased the lead to five games, as the Athletics and Senators were rained out. Tony Lazzeri had been out of the lineup since July 30 and was gradually working his injured shoulder into shape by taking only six throws a day. He expected to be back in the lineup in ten days.[9]

The Yankees were scheduled to play twenty-four of their next twenty-seven games at home, which began with thirteen games against the western clubs. Fred Heimach began the long home-stand start against the White Sox on Tuesday, August 14. For Huggins, the season had been an emotive roller coaster:

> I think we have started to turn the tables on the Athletics. A week ago the A's were putting the pressure on us. Now we're putting the pressure on them. We're winning, and they have to keep step or fall behind to the point where their prospects are almost hopeless. With the Yanks finally headed on a winning streak, one little misstep on the part of the A's may prove disastrous. In other words, they will have to keep up the powerful pace that they have been setting, and, frankly, I don't think they can do it.

Of course, they may be like the Braves of 1914, who nobody or nothing could stop. But the Braves are the exception of baseball history. They are the only team that started to win and kept on winning without having a reaction or slump. Another thing about the A's is that they play their last game at home on August 31, whereas the Yanks don't play in New York until September 12. The Yanks, I feel have had the one bad trip that every team has in the course of a season; the A's still have a bad slump coming to them. And I think they'll get it.[10]

Yankees players were getting a thumbs-down from their fans since the rest of the clubs in the Barnard circuit lifted their veil of dominance. "The crowd will always follow the winner. . . . You find this detestable feature of herd philosophy prevalent in all phases of life," wrote Homer H. Metz in the *New York Morning Telegraph*. He added, "But in the sporting world it is brought to the attention more often than any place else."[11]

Both teams were no doubt watching the scoreboard. The Athletics watched the Yankees as they were in a dead heat with Chicago, and, likewise, the Yankees followed their rivals as they trailed Detroit, with the final result being blown opportunities for both sides. Heimach was locked in a one-all duel with Grady Adkins until the Chicago eighth, when the White Sox nickel and dimed the new Yankee left-hander for two runs en route to a 5–2 victory.[12]

The Yankees and Athletics were beaten for a second day. The White Sox roughed up George Pipgras, Hank Johnson, and Wilcy Moore with Huggins' regulars in the lineup and in their usual batting order. Old Red Faber went the distance for Chicago, hitting a home run and singling in a run as well. Pipgras had won just five of twelve decisions since the end of June, when his record stood at fourteen wins and only two losses. The lead remained four and a half games as the Tigers beat the Athletics, handing Jack Quinn his first loss since June 25.[13]

Connie Mack couldn't help but feel that his club had the advantage in the remaining schedule, with six more games than the Yankees against the Red Sox, three additional contests against the White Sox, and one more game against Cleveland. The Yankees had more games to play with the Tigers, Senators, and Browns, teams that had improved as the season progressed. The lean leader believed that his club would possibly catch the Yankees by the time the two teams met at the Stadium on September 9, especially without Tony Lazzeri and with a ragged pitching staff.[14]

The Yankees of late were described quite aptly like the "little girl with the curl." They played like champions, crushing the White Sox, 11–1, in the series finale. Larrapin' Lou continued his torrid pace, with three doubles, five runs batted in, and three runs scored. He was batting .473, with twenty-three runs batted in, during the first fourteen games in August. Waite Hoyt improved to 15–3 on the year and just missed a shutout, coasting to an easy four-hit victory. The Yankees played spoiler with their victory, knocking Chicago out of the first division and into fifth place. Catching prospect Bill Dickey saw action for the second straight game and had three plate appearances.[15]

White Sox outfielder Bibb Falk was picking the Yankees to prevail:

These fellows will win, but they've got to get out and hustle more. No fooling. They've had things too easy. They haven't had to fight for a long while, and sometimes you forget how to do it, which is tough if it so happens that you run into a real fight. Anyway, suppose they had a few accidents. They have only three reliable pitchers. Maybe one of them might bob up with a bad arm. Their reserves aren't so hot, and what would happen if Ruth were hurt? These birds have been on a good club so long, they don't know what it is to win one ball game, because one ball game never has meant anything to them. But it means a lot to a guy who is trying to land a job or to a team that doesn't win a game very often. The less you win, the more one victory means to you.[16]

About the Athletics, Falk commented:

They sure have been busting along, haven't they? But, believe me, we'll try to set 'em back on their heels. We're out to do all we can against any team, of course, but off the field we like the Yankees, and we aren't exactly in love with the Athletics. I don't know why it is, but you might say we take more pride in beating the Yanks, but we get more pleasure out of beating the Athletics. That is, when we do beat 'em.[17]

The Tigers left Shibe Park shell-shocked after losing by twelve runs, but also with a split of the series. Al Simmons broke out of a five for twenty-four slump with a home run and two singles, and George Earnshaw was once again within one game of drawing even for the season, with five wins and six defeats.[18]

The opening game of the series with Cleveland, on Friday, August 17, was postponed, as was the Athletics' opener with St. Louis. Postponements this late in the season during the preflight era could be a potential problem, because the rules stated that any make up games had to be played in the visiting team's ball park if that is where the two teams had any remaining games on the schedule. The Athletics were unbeaten against the Browns at home in nine games and wanted to complete their three games against them in Philadelphia. They had only two more days left with the Browns at home, and, for the sake of the pennant race and financial reasons, they did not want any rainouts to be transferred to St. Louis. The Athletics and the Browns would play a doubleheader that Saturday.[19]

The downswing that began for the Yankees one and a half months before is encapsulated by the following observations from Harrison:

> All of Mr. Huggins' thoughts are not of this year. He is looking forward to a lot of winter housecleaning. It is safe to say that three or four prominent members of the cast will be traded or relegated to the bench.
>
> Mr. Huggins has had some bitter disappointments. His reserve strength, for one thing, failed to materialize. When Lazzeri was hurt, the infield collapsed for lack of capable substitutes. Durocher can field, but he is a miserable hitter. Cy Moore has been worthless, Meusel has disappointed, and the catching has been decidedly minor-leaguer-ish.
>
> People who said the present Yankee team was good for five more years realize now that changes will have to be made this very winter if the Ruppert colors are to be kept aloft next season.[20]

The president of the Washington Senators raised the ire of Ed Barrow when he predicted that the Yankees would not outlast the Athletics. Clark Griffith actually made the prediction when the Yankees had their biggest lead at fourteen games:

> I told you so. The Yankees are through, and Connie Mack's team will represent the American League in the World Series. Huggins lacks the necessary pitching strength to hold first place, and several of his stars are fading rapidly. His team is weak behind the bat, and the batting order lacks its old punch. The Athletics are playing faster ball than the Yankees. Mack has the best pitching staff in the league and a powerful batting lineup. His team is coming while the champions are going. When the contenders go west again next month, I look for another New York losing streak and the loss of first position.
>
> Beating the Yankees out of the pennant will be a good thing for our circuit. It will help all of the other clubs and arouse new interest next year. So long as the Yankees held their overwhelming lead the pennant race was considered a farce, but now things are different, and the coming triumph of the Athletics will serve to encourage the other clubs to redouble their efforts to get high-grade players.[21]

Barrow replied:

> Griff's prophecy is amusing. He has been wrong many times in picking pennant winners, and his present forecast is not an exception to the rule. We have not lost the lead yet. It's true, we haven't played our best game lately, but that is nothing to worry over. The crippling of Lazzeri has been

a drawback, and the inability of Wilcy Moore to repeat his remarkable pitching of last season has hurt our team a lot.

The Athletics deserve credit for their fight to overhaul the Yankees and for making the final stages of the race exciting. But, in my opinion, they cannot keep up their fast gait. It isn't in the cards for the Yankees to remain in a slump for the rest of the way. They have the experience, the hitters, the fielders, and enough pitchers to carry through when the real pinch comes. We are not alarmed by the present situation. The Yankees are sure winners.[22]

The Saturday box score showed all goose eggs for Cleveland except for one crooked five in the seventh inning that put a significant dent in what was a seven-run deficit. This only blemish on George Pipgras's twentieth victory was more than offset by the eight runs scored by the Yankees. The last two Cleveland runs in the seventh inning were allowed by Cy Moore.[23]

Ed Barrow put two games on sale for $1.00 for a Sunday doubleheader. The Yankees did not wish to disappoint the crowd of 65,000—the largest of the year—which made up for Friday's rainout. The result was a split, with three Cleveland pitchers—Joe Schaute, Willis Hudlin, and Bill Bayne—combining to beat Fred Heimach in a tight ten-inning duel.

The Yankees got back to their early season form in the second game, scoring three runs in each of the first two innings to take a six-run lead. Henry Johnson held the Tribe to six hits in a 10-2 rout. Cleveland starter George Uhle fell to 11–16 on the season, lasting only two innings.[24]

The team was finding some solace in the fact that the race in the American League was treading water during the month of August. The margin remained at five and a half games three weeks into the month, but without Herb Pennock, it was not a very comforting one for Miller Huggins. In hindsight, they were playing above their heads, winning four out of every five games with only three steady pitchers and average backstopping, and they had also been without their regular shortstop and second baseman for a good part of the year.[25]

Miller Huggins reassured everyone that there was nothing wrong with Pennock, just a slight attack of neuritis in his pitching arm. Huggins said that he should be available for his next start against the Browns. He was very pleased with Heimach's three outings since joining the team, stating, "Heimach is going to do us a lot of good. He has had to pitch every minute of the three games he worked for us. The boys wanted to get him off to a nice start, but so far they haven't done much hitting behind him. He is a good hitter and a handy man to have around a ball club."[26]

The rainouts once again gave the Yankee pitching staff time to rest. The update on Pennock was that his neuritis had improved and that he might be able to pitch on Sunday against Detroit, but Huggins was expecting to grab another pitcher before the week ended, as August 31 was the deadline to qualify for the postseason.

The Yankees' lopsided record against the Macks in 1928 was clearly in their favor psychologically. One of the veteran players commented on the upcoming series on September 9, saying, "If the Mackmen hold on that long they will be knocked off in that series. We can beat them, and they know it. We have taken thirteen out of eighteen games from the Athletics for a percentage of .722. We are quite likely to take three out of four and kill the race then and there." Reports from Philadelphia said that the Macks were quite anxious about the series.[27]

Next the Yankees tangled with the Browns for three games, followed by an off day before facing Detroit, while the Athletics had four games each against the Indians and White Sox. In the series opener, Waite Hoyt outdueled Sam Gray, and the Yankees resorted to little ball. A two-run single by Benny Bengough in the second inning proved to be the big blow. The Babe confirmed that he was now concentrating on base hits and using the entire field, scoring the third run on a single by Lou Gehrig.[28]

With rain canceling the next two games, a makeup doubleheader had to be scheduled for what was supposed to be an off day on August 24. Since the issue of Yankee dominance had subsided, there were other topics. Both New York clubs led their leagues for three straight days through August 21. The Cardinals seemed to bury the Giants for good after beating them in a fifteen-inning game at the Polo Grounds on August 5, increasing their lead to six and a half games. But the Giants fought their way to the top by beating the tough western teams and seemed to have the edge with a stretch of games coming up against the Robins, Braves, and Phillies.

In the junior circuit, the remainder of the schedule still seemed to favor the Athletics, with eight games still remaining with the Red Sox. The Yankees won nine of their last twelve games after their 6–12 slump and needed to play at a .543 rate to reach the 100-victory mark. The only team up to that point that had lost a pennant after winning one hundred games was the 1909 Chicago Cubs.[29]

In 1928, a fourth all-New York Fall Classic was on the table in New York baseball circles, and if it were to happen, it might eclipse the previous three at the beginning of the decade. Combining six postseason and city series going back to the first city series in 1910, the Giants still held a 20–10 advantage. The Yankees' only series win came in 1923. Both clubs finished in second place in 1910, which was followed by the great pennant run of the Giants and trips to the bottom of the standings for the Yankees. The Giants crushed the Yankees in the city series after the 1914 season, and again the following spring.[30]

Ruth and Gehrig swinging in the Polo Grounds, where right field was just 263 feet away, seemed to favor the Yankees. Combs and Koenig also swung from the left side and had a shot at those dimensions. Right field at Yankee Stadium was more than three hundred feet away. Fred Fitzsimmons, with a good curve and deceptive motion, and Bill Walker, were considered the only Giant pitchers capable of giving the Yankees trouble. Larry Benton was a fastball pitcher with an average curveball and might not be effective. The National League was considered a curveball league, and the American League a fastball league. None of the Giant hitters were expected to give any of the Yankees' frontline pitchers any trouble.[31]

The reality was beginning to set in for the remainder of the season: The pitching chores would be up to Pipgras, Hoyt, Johnson, and Heimach. Herb Pennock complained to Huggins about soreness in his shoulder and could not start against the Indians. He may have strained himself during his last outing, when he silenced Boston. "He may be out for just the series with St. Louis, which opens today, or he may be on the shelf for several weeks. You never can tell about these older pitchers," said Huggins. Lazzeri's bruised shoulder, which he injured in St. Louis in early July, was not healing as quickly as hoped. Although there was no pain, his arm felt dead. It was feared that it would develop into a career-ending injury.[32]

The postponement of the middle game of the series with the Browns allowed Huggins to further update everyone on the Pennock situation as of the third week of August, as well as give his views on the race in the National League:

The most I can say is that we are not satisfied with his condition. He is taking baking treatments, and a couple of doctors are working on him. But he isn't responding as fast as he might.

Sure we're trying to get another pitcher, but I can't tell you who he is. That would ruin everything. It's hard enough as it is to find a fellow in the minors who has the stuff and the experience and who could do me some good in this emergency. Kids wouldn't do. We want a fellow who knows what it's all about and can step right in.

Give me Pennock back and we'll win. If Pennock is out for a long spell—well, I don't know what would happen. If the Yanks play .600 baseball or three victories in every five games, the Athletics will have to hit a .700 clip to beat us. You can say for me that in the last week the Yanks played better baseball than in the six previous weeks.[33]

Meanwhile, Huggins was still sticking with the Giants, commenting,

Yes, sir, that's my selection. The Giants have been playing great ball against the toughest clubs in the league. I think the Cardinals are through.

They've beaten themselves. Don't overlook the Pirates. They have a fine chance. This morning they were only six games behind the Giants and coming strong, although they've been licking weak teams like the Phillies and Braves.[34]

The Yankees won a total of twenty-two games of the eighteen makeup doubleheaders played as of August 23. They swept seven, lost three, and split eight, which computed to a winning percentage of about seventy points below their current .681 percentage. Two of the sweeps and two splits came against the Athletics, while one of the whitewashes and two splits came against the Tigers. They had four additional twin bills against Washington, Philadelphia, Boston, and Detroit. Yankee pitchers were staring at thirty-five games in about a five-and-a-half-week span with Pennock's arm in a sling.[35]

The team, however, did get some needed pitching help in the person of left-hander Tom Zachary, while chopping Stan Coveleski from the roster, as he had never recovered from a sore arm. "I intend to use Zachary as a starting pitcher," said Huggins. He elaborated,

> He is a smart, clever southpaw who has had plenty of experience and is in excellent condition right now. Zachary is not through by any means. He is only thirty-one years old, and I expect him to deliver for the Yanks, not only this year, but the next. He may prove to be just the pitcher needed by my ball club at this stage of the season.[36]

Huggins was hoping to catch lightning in a bottle for the injured Herb Pennock. Both pitchers were incidentally left-handed and of the few Quaker stars in baseball. Zachary frequently roomed with Walter Johnson. The Athletics passed on Zachary in 1928, because they had no room on their roster. The Senators were hoping that no team would put in a claim so that they could move him to Minneapolis as compensation for two prospects.[37]

When Zachary arrived in Washington in 1919, his teammates took a liking to him because of his ability to be a good listener. The Yankees had no shortage of talkers or those who excelled in the art of "barbering." With the exception of Bob Meusel, there were no sounding boards to do the absorbing. Hugh Bradley of the *New York Evening Post* recalled from another writer that Zachary was a great listener, and that when he was finished listening to everyone else, he would correct or enlighten the conversation. Zachary explained how this trait originated:

> It's this way. I live outside the town of Graham, North Carolina, during the winter. Every now and then I decide I need to get posted on the topics of the day. So I hitch up the horses and go to town. Then I go into the store, and all the boys are there. I sit down, pick up a nice pine board, get

out my knife, and begin to whittle. The boys keep right on talking, and I keep right on whittling. Finally, I whittle the board away, and then I get up and drive home. But in the meanwhile I have picked up considerable knowledge in the midst of my whittling.[38]

After a two-day layoff, the Yankees were flat and the Browns sharp on a day when they played a doubleheader. In the first game, General Crowder bested George Pipgras, and then George Blaeholder—with the help of sloppy defense by the Yankees—beat Fred Heimach in the second game, only giving up two hits in seven innings. Lazzeri's solo homer in the ninth tarnished what would have been a four-hit shutout.[39]

In Philadelphia, the box score shouted "Very Nice Indeed" for the Athletics, as they completed a four-game sweep against Cleveland. Pennant fever was gripping the city, and the players, while not making any boasts, were growing increasingly confident that the Yankees would sink to second place. The deficit, which had hovered between five and a half and three and a half games since August 1, was down to an even three.[40]

The slippage continued for the Yankees into the first game of the next day's doubleheader against Detroit, but the damage was limited, with no loss of ground in the standings. The three games originally scheduled included a fourth makeup game for the July 13 rainout, and 25,000 made it to the Stadium. The Yankees trailed by nine runs as they came to bat in the ninth inning of the opener, which was a hit parade against Henry Johnson, who yielded twelve safeties and seven runs in seven innings before giving way to Myles Thomas.

Huggins' reversion of his batting order lasted just ten days. "After our boys, in the first game," wrote Harrison, "had given one of the most terrible exhibitions ever seen of bad pitching, puny hitting, and general indolence, Miller James Huggins instituted the most drastic shake-up of the last several years." Since September 20, 1926, when Ruth and Gehrig were both in the lineup, they had hit third and fourth, respectively, but for the second game against Detroit, the hotter Gehrig was in the third slot and the cooler Babe at cleanup. Joe Dugan batted first, replacing the normal leadoff man, Earle Combs, who dropped to second. Koenig dropped four notches, down to sixth, and Tony Lazzeri was benched for Leo Durocher.

The skies were still gloomy and the rain heavier as the Yankees proceeded to pound Elam Vangilder in what was a rain-shortened 7–0 victory.[41] Miller Huggins was becoming more guarded about the season:

I am not a pessimistic gloom when I say that the Yankees are in a dangerous plight right now. I do not know when Herb Pennock can pitch again, and there is no denying that the Athletics are playing the best baseball in the American League. Physicians who have examined Pennock's arm seem to be puzzled. They say he has neuritis and are treating him for that troublesome ailment. If it is as serious as Arthur Nehf's attack several years ago, Pennock may be idle for the rest of the season.

This is the first time Pennock has been crippled, and his loss at such a critical juncture indicates more trouble than I anticipated. I had relied on him to keep up his wonderful pitching to the end of the schedule. Consequently, his sudden disability, which may last for several weeks or longer, is a hard blow to the Yankees' pennant chances.[42]

Huggins was hoping that Pennock's injury was a short-term one and the Athletics would come back to earth as the Yankees did. He felt that one hundred victories was the magic number that would put Philadelphia in the World Series:

Baseball, as you know, is a funny game. It's a case of up and down. The A's may slump and the Yankees brace up on the coming western trip. Uncertainty is always a big figure in our national pastime. The baseball world knows that the Yankees, for two months, have not played as well as in April, May, and June, when they rolled up an overwhelming lead.

My club has lost ground, first because several pitchers have fallen down, second, the poor condition of Lazzeri's throwing arm and erratic work at shortstop and third base, and third, the team as a unit hasn't been hitting as it should. Wilcy Moore's ineffective pitching has been a drawback. He tells me his arm isn't lame, and some days in practice he has a world of stuff. But when he is put into a game he simply isn't there. Moore saw a tremendous success last year, his first in Major League Baseball.

Perhaps misfortunes early this season broke down his confidence. The way his delivery was batted when he felt right doubtless discouraged him. The Yankees won 110 games in the American League race and took four straight from the Pirates in the World Series. They created the national impression that nobody could beat them this season, and they strengthened it by winning thirteen of eighteen games from the A's before midsummer. Too much has been expected of my club. The players haven't been exactly overconfident, but they have read everywhere how they cannot lose.[43]

Kieran pointed out that the falling off of the play of the Yankees had much more to do with hitting than pitching. Both parts of the team suffered their share of injuries and disappointments, but the numbers bore out hitting as more of the problem. Before they hosted the western clubs after July 4, they averaged 6.36 runs per game and hit eighty-four home runs in seventy-two games. During the course of the next fifty-three games, they averaged one less run, and home runs plunged to just thirty. The team's earned run average barely budged from 3.66 to 3.68. Earle Combs, however, was at the top of his game at a time when everyone was slumping around him.[44]

When it rains it pours, as a single game on a Sunday with the Tigers was postponed and the Yankees had to refund 20,000 fans their money. The business manager could only hope that some of them would take off work to attend Monday's doubleheader, when Tom Zachary was scheduled to pitch.[45]

Tony Lazzeri's shoulder injury was a question mark going into the season's final month. At best, he would be available only as a pinch hitter. Although he was one of the team's most consistent hitters when in the lineup, Huggins did not want to risk Lazzeri's career and would make do with his reserves. He stated, "I certainly would not risk Lazzeri's value to the club for the sake of a few ball games, even now when we could use them. If Durocher does not hit, I will give the others a chance. Lazzeri's injury should clear up with rest, but a snap throw now might ruin him forever."[46]

Huggins also said,

> I don't expect Lazzeri to play regularly the rest of the season. He is practically through for this year. I gave him two weeks rest with medical treatment. Then he played a week, and now the old trouble has returned. I consider that conclusive proof that he cannot play regularly. Besides affecting his throwing, Tony's sore shoulder has interfered with his hitting and fielding. Knowing that his arm is weak, he is trying to throw the ball before he has it, resulting in fumbles. A long rest will cure him. Abuse of the shoulder might result in permanent injury.[47]

The team also announced the purchase of Bill (Rosy) Ryan from the Toledo team of the American Association, in a continuing effort to supplement their pitching. He was 11–5, with a 3.05 earned run average. Ryan formerly played for the Giants, who he joined in 1913.[48]

After taking the first six contests early in the season with the Tigers, the Yankees dropped the next five of seven games before the August 25 doubleheader, but they had to get four games in for what was originally a three-game series to ensure that any makeup games would not have to be tacked onto the season's final series in Detroit. That series already included a makeup game.

The Yankees increased their lead to four games with two additional games played after their timely sweep of the Tigers, while the Athletics and White Sox were dealing with rain. Tom Zachary came to the rescue with his best slow stuff, holding the visitors to three runs on seven hits. The Yankees and Pipgras were in control in the nightcap; it was the twenty-first win of the season for the Yankee right-hander.[49]

While the Yankees were in Hartford for an exhibition game, the Mackmen won a pair from the White Sox. Lefty Grove twirled a 1–0 masterpiece in the first game on Max Bishop's fifth home run of the year to raise his winning streak to an even dozen and become the major league's fourth twenty-game winner. George Pipgras had won his twentieth game ten days earlier, while Burleigh Grimes and Larry Benton in the National League won their twentieth games on August 7 and August 19, respectively.[50] The Athletics continued their mastery of the White Sox and Ted Lyons in the last game of that series for their fourth straight victory. The margin of difference in the American League as of August 27 stood at four games.

Failure to Harvest Hits
(August 30–September 12)

When last seen or heard from, Miller Huggins was inquiring about the temperature and depth of the East River. Colonel Ruppert had retired to Garrison-on-the-Hudson and ordered all telephone and telegraph wires cut. His ears were stuffed with cotton. Ed Barrow had settled in a corner with a sharp pair of scissors and some paper dolls. Alas and also alack! These are tense times.

—*New York Times*, September 8, 1928[1]

$\mathcal{I}$n the August 28, 1928, "Sports of the Times" column, John Kieran reminisces about the whining in the American League earlier in the season, writing, "Charitably inclined persons suggested that the esteemed Colonel give Babe Ruth back to the Red Sox, Lou Gehrig to the White Sox, Herb Pennock to the Tigers, and Waite Hoyt to the Cleveland Indians. Then there would be a pennant race in the American League."[2]

Now it was Yankee fans who were sweating. The talk earlier in the season of the team breaking records and breaking up the Yankees had evaporated. Just to match their own record of 1927, they would have to win twenty-six of their last twenty-nine games. The possibility of the Babe breaking his personal home run record was highly in doubt. Then there was the demanded retraction by Uncle Wilbert Robinson of his statement that the Yankees were the greatest team of all time, which upset his old teammates on the old Orioles. During the previous season at this time, Miller Huggins finally admitted that the race was over and began thinking about his rotation for the World Series. He stated, "We want to go into the World Series in our best form, and our job is to prevent the club from slipping too far from the fighting edge we want for the series."[3]

The Yankee slump during the previous two months, combined with the Athletic surge, had done wonders for the league's coffers, especially in Philadelphia, where weekday crowds had been numbering greater than 20,000 and more than 35,000 on Saturdays. The junior loop had already suffered the most rainouts in its history. The western clubs were miraculously resurrected to the point where they were ahead of last year's attendance figures, particularly in Detroit, where the Tigers had given the Yankees a battle in their last series. Both the Yankees and Athletics would wind up the season in the west as well.

"The Yankees' slump was worth at least a half million dollars to the American League," one of the league owners commented. "It may have cost Colonel Ruppert several headaches and Miller Huggins a few extra gray hairs, but it saved several other clubs from having worse headaches and more gray hairs when they balanced their books at the close of the season."[4]

Along with the Yankees, the Athletics had been drawing big crowds since they got back in the race. They won forty-three of fifty eight-games as they entered the final month of the season, which was just two games worse than the 45–13 start of the Yankees. The Yankees played at a respectable .550 clip during the same span. Nonetheless, the .740 pace of the Athletics allowed them to trim ten games off of the huge deficit (see table 12.1).[5]

Table 12.1.   American League Standings, August 27, 1928

Team	Won	Lost	GB	Pct.
Yankees	84	41	—	.672
Athletics	79	44	4	.642
Browns	66	60	18.5	.524
White Sox	56	67	27	.455
Senators	57	69	27.5	.452
Indians	57	70	28	.449
Tigers	56	69	28	.448
Red Sox	45	80	39	.360

The Yankees began to stumble during their trip to Detroit on July 25, losing two games, while the Athletics were taking two in Chicago. The lineup changes made by Connie Mack were a huge factor in his team's success, with his key players managing to stay injury free during their spectacular run in contrast to the ailing Yankees. Most importantly, the Athletics had a fortified pitching staff with Grove, Rommel, Quinn, Walberg, Ehmke, and Earnshaw. The Yankee additions of Zachary, Ryan, and Heimach were more or less substitutes out of desperation.[6]

The Babe paid a compliment to the Athletic pitching staff but believed that the team would come back to reality:

To my mind, the strongest point of the Athletics' success is pitching— Grove, Walberg, Ehmke, and Quinn make up a quartet of pretty fair pitchers—and when Mack stepped in and bought Earnshaw, he rounded out the pitching staff. Of course I am saying nothing new when I say it is Orwoll and Foxx who have really made the Athletics. Foxx is the best-looking young ballplayer I have seen in a long time.

I think all the Athletic members are playing over their heads, just as the Yankees did earlier in the season. There's no big-league ball club that figures to play .800 baseball consistently. I still believe that the Yankees will win the pennant. I base that on two grounds. First, I believe we have a little more punch than the Athletics. Our hitting power is better distributed from top to bottom of the batting order. The second big point in our favor is that we can beat the A's themselves. All season long we've had the Indian sign on them.[7]

Following an examination in Philadelphia, there was hope that Tony Lazzeri would be back in the lineup against the Macks for the upcoming series. Even with this latest medical report, the Yankees were requesting the delivery of Lyn Lary from Oakland to play second base, but the Oaks were still in the race in the Pacific Coast League and did not want to give him up until they were eliminated from contention.[8]

The Yankees got ready to begin the fourth and final sectional batch in Washington, beginning Thursday, August 30, for three games. They would then head home for a Labor Day doubleheader on September 3, against Boston, followed by five more games at home against Washington before the final series with the Athletics on September 9. The backlog of makeup doubleheaders for the Hugmen was three, one each at home against Washington and Philadelphia, and on the road in Detroit. The Mackmen had four doubleheaders remaining, two in Boston and one each in New York and Washington.

The Senators were an improved club, having won eight of their last thirteen games, climbing from seventh to fourth place. They were also in the thick of the battle for the final first-division slot with Detroit, Cleveland, and Chicago, which involved prize money; just eight percentage points or one game separated all four clubs.

The Senators rallied for three runs off of Waite Hoyt in the sixth inning to break a scoreless pitching duel against Sam Jones. The merry mortician had gone thirty-five straight innings without allowing an earned run, but in the fatal frame, the Senators bunched five of their ten hits for the victory. The Babe's forty-seventh home run leading off the seventh accounted for all the Yankee scoring.

There was no doubt which team Washington fans were rooting for as far as the pennant race was concerned: "The moaning of the multitude was loud and long when the scoreboard showed that the Red Sox had beaten the Athletics."[9]

With Friday off, the Babe, along with sportswriter Richards Vidmer, focused on his slowing home run pace and the Yankees' loss of ten games in the standings in a Saturday, September 1, special in the *New York Times*. Almost two months and sixty games had elapsed since the Yankees swept the Athletics in that July 1 doubleheader.

Ruth explained to reporters on a much-needed off day, when no exhibition game was scheduled, that he would swing for base hits for the rest of the season. He was mainly concerned about the team's slump in the standings, stating, "I've just been figuring if we win eighteen of the twenty-eight games we've got to play, we ought to win easily. That's not hard to do." When asked about his home run record, the Babe replied, "I'm not thinking about that now. I need fourteen more, but as long as the Athletics are close I'm going to be swinging for hits into left field. I can't hit 'em as far in that direction, but I can hit 'em seven times out of ten. That's what wins ball games."[10]

Ruth wanted to reach his goal of playing in ten World Series. He commented, "You can break a home run record with a last-place club, but you can't get into a World's Series except with a winner." Most critics, as well as the majority of the team, pointed to the hitting as the team's problem. Ruth added, "One of these days we're all going to snap out of it, and when we do it's going to be a terrible thing for the other fellows."[11] This was in contrast to his ambitious program back in spring training and as late as mid-June, when he was aiming for five hundred career home runs, sixty-one home runs in 1928, and a blast into the center-field bleachers and completely out of right field at Yankee Stadium. He also set out to bat .400 before his contract was up and finish his career at first base.[12]

Miller Huggins had a tendency to worry when things looked the brightest but rationalize and avoid pushing the panic button when the crises came, and he echoed these sentiments to Frank H. Young in the *Washington Post*:

> It would be foolish for me to pretend that we are not worried at the closeness of the present race. For we thought we were "in" some time ago, and now we find ourselves unprepared for the fight [that] the Philadelphia team is giving us. However, the race is not yet over, and I am confident that we will be in front when the last game is played. The way I figure it out, all we have to do is play .600 ball for the balance of the season to win the American League pennant.[13]

He was heartened by the fact that the team was still in first place and felt that they were overdue to break out of their hitting slump. As for the upcoming series with Philadelphia at the Stadium, he stated,

Judging from the record so far, in a team-to-team match, we have quite an edge, for we have beaten the Mackmen thirteen times in eighteen starts, and, despite our physical handicaps, this fact will give us a moral advantage when this series starts, for my men will take the field confident, while the Macks will be remembering how badly we have punished them in the past.

No, things don't look bright for us, but take my advice and don't bet against us, for we have a habit of playing our best in the pinches, and I've got a hunch that, if there is any "cracking" done, the Athletics will be the ones to do it.[14]

The normally pushover Red Sox played the Athletics tough for a second day, but the Athletics won to pull to within two games of first place as the month of August came to a close.

With Herbert Hoover among the 15,000 in attendance at Griffith Stadium, the Yankees got September off to a positive start, handing George Pipgras an early six-run lead and an 8–3 victory. A few factors caused the game to take a little more than two and a half hours. Washington used five pitchers, the Yankees two, and there was a small-scale riot in the sixth inning after the umpire called Sam Jones out after being hit with a batted ball. Bucky Harris was tossed while arguing a call at second base in the ninth inning, which added a few minutes to the game's duration.[15]

Before the game, Clark Griffith, president of the Washington Senators, told reporters that a photographer had requested that the Babe pose with Hoover. "As an earnest baseball devotee, I have long admired Babe Ruth's batting ability, and I look forward with pleasure to meeting him," said Hoover. But Ruth's refusal sparked somewhat of a controversy throughout the country. Ruth said it was a matter of politics, but Griffith was disappointed, saying, "I am at a loss to explain such unusual conduct on the part of an American League player under such circumstances. It's up to Ruth to give some explanation." Huggins tried to explain that things got a little confused, as the game was called just after the request was made.[16] Ruth explained afterward,

> Politics had nothing to do with it. The ball game was about to start; Hoover was the center of attraction, and I thought it would look odd for me to go to his box at that time. When the photographer asked me to go over to Mr. Hoover's box, I labored under a misunderstanding and deeply regret that I did not avail myself of the opportunity of meeting him. I hope Mr. Hoover will be gracious enough at some future time to permit me to present myself to him.[17]

The Babe later admitted what he really meant: "It means that I will do anything for Mr. Hoover except vote for him."[18]

Babe Ruth, Joe Dugan, and Benny Bengough were among the more stalwart Democrats on the Yankees, which had a mixed representation of both parties. With the recent flap over the Babe not posing with the Republican candidate, it was noted that they prospered much more on the field with someone from the GOP in the White House, winning five flags and two World Series.[19]

Charley O'Leary was one of the team's Democrats:

> We shoulda' won in 1920, but we went down with Governor Al Smith in the Republican landslide of that year. I'll never forget it. It nearly killed me. If the Republicans had given us any help at all, we woulda' walked in. We won in 1921, not because there was a Republican governor, but because of the work of that sterling democrat George H. Ruth.
>
> We are New Yorkers. It's New York that supports us, and we have done well under a Democratic rule of the city and state. We would be traitors if we turned on the Democrats now. Who throws out the first ball to start the season for us? Always a Democrat and generally Mayor Walker. Who gave us Sunday baseball? The Democrats. Who roots for us? The Democrats. As for those Athletics, they come from a Republican state, and when we get them at the Stadium we'll knock them clear out of the campaign.[20]

Meanwhile, the Athletics finished their regular season at Shibe Park with a lopsided victory against Boston. Lefty Grove collected three hits and a walk as he won his thirteenth straight game. Their remaining twenty-five games would be played on the road. They completed their final home stand with sixteen victories in twenty-two games, still trailing the Yankees by two games.

Fred Marberry was the Senators' star during Sunday's game with his bat and arm, as his team beat the Yankees. The pitcher singled in the only runs of the game with the bases loaded and two out in the fourth inning. Tom Zachary and Wilcy Moore held the Senators to just two runs in relief, but Marberry blanked the Yankees out on four hits. Among the 25,000 cheering fans in attendance were Connie Mack and several of his Mackmen. The deficit was now a game and a half.[21]

Huggins didn't expect Tony Lazzeri to play for the remainder of the season, but at a subsequent visit to an osteopath at the beginning of September, Lazzeri was given the green light to play. Meanwhile, the committee of Zachary, Heimach, and Ryan would have to fill the gap left by the loss of Herb Pennock.

The Yankees and Red Sox entertained a less than expected crowd of 30,000 at the Stadium on a grey, misty Labor Day. Boston had completely fallen apart after they were blanked by the Athletics on July 5. They had dropped twenty-two of thirty-six games against the western clubs and five of six to the Yankees, resulting in them once again being buried in the American League basement. Both one-run, nine-inning affairs lasted for more than two hours.

Second-line staffers Fred Heimach, Rosy Ryan, and Wilcy Moore nearly blew a seven-run lead in the opener. With the Yankees ahead by three runs in the sixth inning, neither Ryan nor Moore were effective, leaving the final three innings of pitching and a slim one-run lead to Waite Hoyt, who held Boston in check. The second match featured a near comeback by the Yankees, but Jack Russell bested Henry Johnson by a score of 4–3.[22]

The Senators continued to play the spoiler, winning both games of their holiday duels with the Athletics. Howard Ehmke pitched the first game for Jack Quinn, who woke up with a stiff neck, and lost his fourth straight decision. George Earnshaw took the loss in the nightcap, failing yet again to even his record for the year as the margin in the standings increased to two and a half games.[23]

In the September 5 installment of the *Philadelphia Inquirer*, Joe Vila wrote that the Yankees no longer compared favorably to the 1927 team in "hitting, fielding, and pitching," while the Athletics were showing "marked improvement."[24] Vila was of the opinion that it would take nothing short of a miracle by Miller Huggins to lead the Yankees to another pennant.

To pull off that miracle, Huggins would have to squeeze out of his pitching staff the wins he got out of Ruether, Shocker, and Moore in 1927. Those three pitchers won fifty games in 1927, leaving a gap of twenty-two games between the six new pitchers on the roster, plus Wilcy Moore, through September 3. Five Yankees, Ruth, Meusel, Combs, Grabowski, and Collins, had lower batting averages than in 1927. Tony Lazzeri was out of the lineup, Mark Koenig's fielding had been wanting, and Joe Dugan and Leo Durocher were slumping. The glass became half empty.[25]

The Yankees had Tuesday off, but the Athletics, behind the streaky Rube Walberg, avenged their holiday double defeat against Washington. The win avoided a split with the Senators for the season and lowered the deficit to two games.

The Mackmen had come a long way in a two-month span and could almost taste the pennant. They believed that the Yankees of September were not the same club that beat them in July and that their malaise would continue throughout the remainder of the year. Mack said the following to Hugh Bradley in the *New York Evening Post* on September 4:

> I won't deny that we have started to think about the championship. It would be foolish for me to say that we are not giving some thought to it now that we are so close to the Yankees. We are however, confining

ourselves to thinking and are not talking about our prospects. If we play every game to win, the future will take care of itself.[26]

As the Yankees got set to face the Senators, Huggins was careful not to look beyond Washington before the Athletics:

That four-game series [that] we start with the Athletics on Sunday looks very vital, but the chances are that developments of the next four days will make our five contests with the Senators even more important. You see, the Athletics have five games with Boston before they come in here for that doubleheader Sunday.

Yes, those with the Mackmen look critical for us. But we have won thirteen out of eighteen from them, and you know how those big series go. Most often it's fifty-fifty. We've got to keep winning from Washington while the Athletics are in Boston, and it is no mean job that confronts us, with our twenty-third doubleheader today. By the time this season is over, we will have set a new mark for playing two games with one admission.

You know, whenever I get a bad dream it takes the form of a doubleheader with pitchers running out of the bull pen faster than I can call them in. I've stopped eating bedtime snacks. Only last night, I dreamed that I had to drag in poor Shocker from the pen. Man, that was a real nightmare. Yes, those games with the Athletics are going to be important, but don't let anybody kid you about the scraps with the Senators.[27]

The twenty-fifth doubleheader of the year, held on September 5, drew a midweek crowd of 30,000, who witnessed a draw. One of the games of the upcoming five-game series was a makeup of the nightcap of the Memorial Day doubleheader that had been cancelled with the Yankees ahead by seven runs in the second inning. Would it play a part in costing the pennant?[28]

Sam Jones beat the Yankees and George Pipgras in the first game for his fourth victory over his old mates in 1928. Fred Heimach followed with a victory for the Yankees in the nightcap. With the Athletics idle, both teams had played 132 games, with the Yankees up by exactly two.

The momentum clearly favored the Athletics. "The Yankees are not the roysters of the springtime," wrote Gordon Mackay in the *Philadelphia Public Record*, "so jubilant, so carefree, and so cocksure." He continued,

They have been beaten and reviled by enemies whom they spurned with contempt in the days of their affluence and ease. . . . It is manifestly urgent that the Athletics win three out of the four battles in the BIG series, which starts on Sunday. On the other hand, this baseball series will be a test of GUTS. The team with the better abdominal garnishment will bring home the bacon.[28]

The Yankees' hitting began to tail off around July 2, when the team's batting average dipped from .310 to .298, and their slugging percentage from .497 to .457. Through July 1, they averaged about twelve home runs per ten games and six runs per game. From that point through September 5, the home runs were down to five for every ten games and five runs per game. Being granted permission to the services of Lyn Lary and Jimmy Reese was no longer an option for the remainder of the 1928 season.[29]

The game with Washington on Thursday, September 6, was postponed, as was the Athletics' game at Boston. The scheduled doubleheader at Fenway Park could have had strategic consequences for the final standings. The Mackmen worked out for almost two hours, hoping that the downpours would let up. They were slated to play five games in Boston, beginning with a single match on September 6, but this had to be reduced to the two previously scheduled doubleheaders in two days, thus risking a game being lost for good in the standings.[30]

In the meantime, more than five thousand fans stood in the pouring rain in front of the Yankee offices on Forty-Second Street during that morning to purchase a limited number of reserved seats. The line extended to Eighth Avenue. When the news was delivered that the 18,000 tickets were sold out, police reserves from the West Thirtieth Street Station had to calm the crowd after the people decided to stampede the Yankee offices. Police reserves were needed for the entire day as fans had to be turned away while continuing to request the choice seats. Among those turned away was Leo Durocher, who was mistaken for a fan.

There was confusion that 80,000 seats would be offered, when, in fact, that was for Sunday, when 40,000 grandstand and 20,000 bleacher seats were to go on sale. Many orders for tickets were filled through the mail, especially from fans in the Philadelphia area, not to mention requests from as far away as Florida and Illinois. Tickets were going for as much as ten dollars in the secondary market.[31]

Bucky Harris was thoroughly enjoying the Senators' role as spoiler after Wednesday's draw:

> I predict that you are going to see a lot of fun around here. Well, it's going to be a very tough finish for the Yankees, and no mistake about it. Yes, it's going to be rough going for the Yankees. In fact, I might say that if they are passed, they won't have the pitching with which to catch anybody. How are the Yankees going to win the pennant if they can't even beat us? Right now we haven't a ball club to brag about. And yet we have managed to win three out of our last five games with the Yankees. That's no way to head for a championship. Yes, you're going to see a lot of fun around here.[32]

Harris also commented on his club beating the Athletics on Labor Day, after being questioned about whether they were worse than the Yankees:

> No, they aren't worse. Last Monday the Washington club got two of the most brilliantly pitched games I have watched this year. Don't blame the Philadelphia boys for dropping that pair. It was just a tough break.
>
> The Yankees are feeling the loss of Lazzeri and Pennock more and more as the race tightens and the goal gets closer. Any other ball club losing the services of two such players at this stage would have been wrecked. But the Yankees manage to stay up there and fight back. Mind, I am not predicting that the Yankees cannot win, but I do say that if the Athletics pass them you're bound to see a lot of fun around here.[33]

"The Yankees piled up their victories over Cornelius McGillicuddy's hired help when Pennock's arm was free of neuritis, when Tony Lazzeri was appearing daily at second base, and when Babe Ruth was knocking home runs to all fields," wrote John Kieran. "Some of the New York victories were chalked up when Speaker and Cobb were in the outfield for the Athletics, and Al Simmons was on the bench, a situation [that] has since been reversed with considerable advantage to the Mackmen."[34]

Both teams were about equal in team and individual statistical categories. The Athletics seemed to have the slight advantage. "Ruth and Miller are hitting on the same level in right field," dissected Kieran. He added,

> but the Babe lands the heavier blows; Combs is hitting higher than Haas in center; Simmons is higher than Meusel in left; Gehrig is above any first baseman Mack can produce; Bishop has the honors at second with Lazzeri out; Koenig tops Boley; Foxx leads Dugan; Cochrane heads up the catchers.[35]

The Macks clearly had the advantage in pitching and defense with Pennock injured, Moore ineffective, and the Yankee infield in somewhat of a state of disarray all year.

Huggins did not want to alter his rotation for the Athletics, but he was aware of the circumstances:

> At this time it looks as if we will shoot George Pipgras and Freddy Heimach at the Athletics on Sunday, but there may be a change where we send Waite Hoyt into the opening program. It is possible that I will use Hoyt against the Senators anyway and depend on Henry Johnson for one of the Sunday games. I just don't know myself.
>
> You see we've got to keep winning while the Athletics win up in Boston. If we should win against Washington while the Philadelphians are dropping a game against the Red Sox, I would be inclined to do some gambling

and shoot Myles Thomas and Wilcy Moore at Bucky Harris. But if the Athletics keep right on winning, or we should lose, it will be Pipgras and Heimach, and don't think that they can't handle the job the way it should be handled. It looks like a merry fight. And it is a serious fight.

We have found no trouble in beating the Athletics in the past, but with Tony Lazzeri and Herb Pennock on the shelf, and the Babe in a hitting slump, we may not look so extra tough to the Mackmen, and they may decide to knock us over. Do I put any stock in stories that the Athletics aren't so aggressive against us? That's the bunk! To come right out in the open, you mean to ask if the Athletics aren't game. Well, I am sure they are. And anybody who believes that a club [that] has accomplished what the Philadelphians have achieved could possibly be deficient in grit just doesn't know this game of ball. I am ready for the fight of the year.[36]

With the Athletics' doubleheader against Boston postponed on September 6, and the Yankees single game in Washington as well, a not so slight wrinkle was thrown into the race. The Yankees and Athletics were even in games played, with 132, as of that date. The Yankee doubleheader backlog was reduced to the makeup games with the Senators on September 7, the Athletics on September 9, and a makeup in Detroit on September 27.

Assuming no further postponements, the Yankees would be able to play all remaining twenty-two games. The Athletics, however, were able to play just twenty-one games because of a lack of open dates from the Boston series. Thanks to a nor'easter, the five games in three days in Boston were reduced to two doubleheaders on Friday and Saturday. The Athletics feasted on Boston all year, winning thirteen of seventeen matches.

Since both cities still honored Sunday blue laws, there were no dates available after Saturday, September 8. Mack commented on this development as follows:

I don't like to see any games go. But this rainy day may prove a blessing in black glasses and false whiskers. It solves some of my pitching problems, and I can start the series Sunday in New York in much better shape for flingers. I am this much relieved. If the four pitchers I have decided to start the remaining games here go through, I can wait until Saturday night to select my curvers for the doubleheader Sunday.[37]

Some of the Athletic players felt that the Yankee series was overblown. One player commented on the matter:

If we leave New York three games in the rear, we will win the pennant because we will win far more games on the road than the Yanks. That's what we did on the last western trip, and we are going to do the same thing. Just remember it was our wonderful work on that western trip that enabled us to tear down that so-called irresistible Yankee lead. If the Yanks believe that they have won the pennant, if they should take the coming series from us, they are in for a shock. We will prove otherwise against the western teams.[38]

With just about all medical options exhausted, Pennock decided to have five of his molars yanked following a dentist's advice and hopefully get back on the mound. Getting back in action this season was not looking good, however, for Tony Lazzeri. "We need Tony's hitting," said Huggins, "but I don't want to ruin this fine young player." Huggins elaborated,

Lazzeri has had all sorts of treatment, but in my opinion, he has a torn ligament in his shoulder, an injury [that] only time can cure. Lazzeri can't throw overhanded, and his injury has hurt his playing. He now is overanxious and tries to hurry his plays, with the result that balls were getting by him [that] were easy for him before his shoulder was hurt.[39]

The Yankees still clung to a two-game lead going into their September 7 doubleheader against Washington. Before being swept by the Senators, the Yankees were indeed looking forward to the upcoming series with the Athletics, where they felt confident they would take three of four and settle the pennant right then and there.[40] Then the worst of all outcomes took place as the Mackmen swept Boston decisively at Fenway and the Senators crushed the Yankees twice at the Stadium. The champions were outscored 17–1 in the two games, and what had the earmarks of a historic collapse finally appeared to come full circle.

Tom Zachary did not exactly exact revenge on his former mates, losing 11–0 to Washington's Bump Hadley. The Yankees managed just three hits, two from Ruth and one from Gehrig, while the Senators tagged Tom Zachary and Rosy Ryan for sixteen safeties. With the lead down to a single game, Miller Huggins had no choice with regards to who to call on to stop the bleeding. Waite Hoyt followed up by pitching poorly in a 6–1 defeat to the invincible Fred Marberry. The Yankees, in desperation, added another pitcher from Oklahoma City, Fay Thomas, who was formerly property of the Giants.[41]

There was also no doubt where the sentiments of the baseball world lay. The Fenway crowd was rooting for their hometown hero, as described by James Isaminger following the double win:

The uninterrupted advance of the Athletics has electrified the whole baseball world, and now everybody has jumped into the Connie Mack bandwagon and is predicting that he will win the pennant with games to spare.

Mack, the master manager of baseball, was surrounded by Boston friends and strangers at the end of the long program today. Hundreds followed him as he trailed out of Fenway Park and sought his automobile. The cheers were so loud and the greeting so cordial that he was compelled to bow to the fans in acknowledgement.

His face beamed with smiles as he accepted the congratulations of friends and the stray sport lover, who always admires a hero. The lean leader did not recede from his policy not to make any claims.[42]

"It was a wonderful day for the Athletics," said Mack, "and we are now on even terms with the Yanks and are prepared to fight it out to the finish. My boys deserve every credit for closing the gap."[43]

Connie Mack was described by Sam Otis of the *Cleveland Plain Dealer* as the "kindly manager" of the Athletics, slaying the wealthy Goliath that was the Yankees. Otis wrote, "It is almost like a dream to behold the prospects of an end to Yankee domination of the American circuit . . . every red-blooded observer of the national pastime is pulling for the Philadelphians to march on through to the championship.[44]

By contrast, Vidmer put things in perspective for the Yankees, commenting, "The sun comes up every morning and sets at evening time. Breezes blow and birds sing in the treetops. Flowers bloom and their fragrance fills the air. Rivers still run downhill and winter follows the fall. But, alas! No longer are the Yanks in a class by themselves."[45]

The results of the September 7 doubleheaders wiped out what was left of the fourteen-game lead in the Barnard circuit. The Yankees and Athletics had identical 87–47 records. During the recent two-month span, the Athletics nearly duplicated what the Yankees did through July 1, winning forty-eight of their last sixty-five games.

Despite Bill Carrigan's intentions, the Yankees would not get any help from the Red Sox, who, along with the Browns, were the Macks' whipping boys in 1928. Boston was swept again at Fenway on September 8 by the Athletics, who moved into sole possession of first place while the Yankees were winning a single game against the Senators. Connie's rookie hurlers achieved much success, with Ossie Orwoll winning the first game and George Earnshaw the nightcap.

This marked the first time that the Athletics had been in first place this late in September since they won the pennant fourteen years previously. There was concern of some tiring on the pitching staff, and the strain was getting to Mickey Cochrane's arm and his hitting as well. He was batting .241 with no home runs but nineteen runs batted in since August.[46]

The Yankees had Lazzeri back at second base, even though Huggins stated that he would rather lose the pennant than lose Lazzeri permanently to injury. But when push came to shove, he succumbed. After seeing as many as five doctors, Lazzeri was still having trouble throwing. Lary or Reese were still options.[47]

Around the middle of August, Connie Mack felt so confident that the games on Sunday, September 9, would be important that he telephoned the following request to Ed Barrow: "I want you to send me 700 reserved seats for that doubleheader we will have with you on Sunday, September 9. We're organizing a little celebrating party here and will go in a special train." Both Barrow and Huggins were amused, as Barrow replied, "What will 700 Philadelphians want at Yankee Stadium on September 9? I'm tickled to sell the tickets, but your folks won't be interested much in baseball by that time." Mack answered, "Well that's all very interesting, but send me those 700 tickets. We'll use them. By the time that doubleheader is played, we will have caught you. Don't worry about our not using the seats. Why those 700 Philadelphians will wind up in the aquarium or the Bronx Zoo." Thousands of Philadelphia fans were expected.[48]

"If they'll only fire Lefty at us, we'll give 'em such a lacing that we'll get 'em on the run," said the Babe. It was a very strange set of affairs that the Yankees were able to totally block out what the great Lefty was doing to the rest of the league. Not only the Babe, but the entire club, had an overall confidence that they had his number. Grove had lost only one game in twenty-three decisions, not counting the five losses against the Yankees, and if the mite manager lived by the law of averages, something had to give soon. There was one game left in the season against the crack lefty.[49]

An article in the *Philadelphia Public Record* read, "How to get a ticket to the first game of the big series was worrying more Philadelphians last night than how to get a drink, now that the town has ratified the Eighteenth Amendment. And that's saying a lot." It was estimated that up to 10,000 fans in attendance for the games on Sunday would be from the Philadelphia area, as the highways were crowded with motor vehicles headed for Yankee Stadium. The Pennsylvania and Reading railroads were packed with people and ready to supply extra cars if needed.[50]

The Maulers from Manhattan, unstoppable and invincible two months earlier, were now reeling and in second place. Momentum and psychology were decisively on Philadelphia's side. A close race was what everyone, including Miller Huggins, expected all along. For the first time since April 29, the Yankees were looking up in the standings.

The final showdown with the Athletics and the final regular home appearance for the Yankees on Sunday also included single games on Tuesday and Wednesday, after which both teams would then head west. The September 9 doubleheader would be the fourth in the span of twelve days for both clubs. The enlarged grandstand at Yankee Stadium had increased capacity to 78,000, with room for an additional 7,000 standees. The Yankees had to turn away thousands of requests for tickets for the 18,000 reserved and box seats for each of the three days as early as September 6, and the 40,000 grandstand and 20,000 bleacher seats were to go on sale at 10:30 on the morning of each game for $1.00 and $.50, respectively.[51]

A World Series atmosphere was anticipated at the Stadium. Scalpers were asking $25.00 for $2.00 box seats and between $8.00 and $10.00 for $1.50 reserved seats. A filled Yankee Stadium, let alone the largest crowd in the history of baseball, was not something that the Colonel expected during the remainder of the regular season. "There will be 85,000 persons in the Stadium for the doubleheader between the Yankees and Athletics on Sunday," Ed Barrow announced on Friday. "There will be close to 65,000 unreserved seats first-come, first-served, and those who have not been able to obtain reserved seats should not feel that they are at a disadvantage on the fact that from the standpoint of the spectator, we have the best plant in the country."[52]

The chief inspector for the Bronx, John O'Brien, made the necessary preparations as far as police presence was concerned for the anticipated crowd. Officials for the Interborough Rapid Transit Company announced additional service beginning at 10:00 a.m. for the Jerome Avenue and East Side subway lines, as well as continuing service as needed after the game. Large crowds of between 50,000 and 60,000 were also anticipated for the next two games. The Yankees ramped up their staff of ushers and ticket sellers. The caterers made additional preparations as well.[53]

The final estimate was 85,265, bringing in receipts of $115,000; the previous record was believed to be 72,641, set on July 4, 1927. Thousands of fans from the Keystone State were expected to make the trip to the Bronx, and they did so by the trainload, along with Connie Mack admirers from New England. The dollars, however, were way below last year's record of $209,665 for the World Series game on October 7, which realized much higher ticket prices. The top ticket fetched about $2.00, as opposed to $6.00 for the World Series.[54]

According to the Setpember 10 edition of the *New York Times*, fans waited as much as twenty hours to see the two games:

> And they came early, so early, in fact, that three men were in line at six o'clock Saturday evening, armed with soap boxes, sandwiches, and soda pop, prepared for the all-night vigil. . . . An hour and a half after midnight there were sixty or seventy persons, including one woman, on the scene anxiously awaiting the morning sale of unreserved seats.
>
> Two hundred policemen were on duty under Deputy Chief Inspector O'Brien, and they did a fine job of policing. There were twenty mounted

men, ten sergeants, four lieutenants, and two captains, under the direct supervision of Inspector Joseph Thompson of the Seventh Inspection District. Captain Richard O'Connor of Traffic D took care of traffic arrangements. Inspector George C. Liebers of the Eighth Inspection District volunteered his services and took a hand in the work.[55]

The gates opened an hour and a half early, with 60,000 in the park by noon. This should have been enough to make Jacob Ruppert smile, but additional fans were actually turned away. People were pouring in by the thousands without tickets. The weather cooperated as well, with barely a cloud in the sky. Just before game time, at 2:05, New York's mayor, Jimmy Walker, a Yankees fan, received a huge ovation. Because of the importance of the series, league prexy Ernest Barnard assigned the World Series quota of four umpires to make the calls.[56]

The big crowd was not disappointed. Following two sweeps in as many days against Boston, the Macks had some of the air taken out of their sails. The pitching matchups for the day slightly favored Philadelphia, with Jack Quinn (16–5) facing George Pipgras (22–11), and Rube Walberg (15–10) twirling against Fred Heimach (2–3). Lefty Grove, Ed Rommel, and Jack Quinn had been Connie's hottest pitchers during the blistering pace set since they hit bottom in early July. Walberg had been streaky, losing five straight, winning three, losing three, and then winning his last four decisions. Quinn was trying to work off soreness in his neck muscles. His last victory came against the Indians on August 21, with a no decision against the White Sox a week later. Quinn was proving to be the most fruitful of the antique collection, with Collins, Speaker, and Cobb long since on the bench. His contract before the season called for a bonus if he won more than fifteen games.[57]

The first game was scoreless through the first five and a half innings, with Quinn more in control, giving up only three hits. Then the magical three-run sixth inning started with singles from Combs and Koenig. After Gehrig's double scored Combs, Ruth was intentionally passed to load the bases. Meusel's deep fly to Bing Miller on the warning track scored Koenig and moved Gehrig to third; Lazzeri then scored Gehrig on a single to right.

Ed Rommel came on in relief and shut the Yankees down until he was removed for a pinch hitter in the eighth inning. Pipgras got out of a bases-loaded, two-out jam during that same inning by fanning the nineteen-year-old Jimmie Foxx. In the Yankee half, Orwoll was hit hard by Gehrig, Ruth, Meusel, and Lazzeri for two more runs, which put the finishing touches on a 5–0 victory.

It appeared that the Athletics would gain a split after taking a two-run lead and Rube Walberg a one-hitter into the bottom of the seventh inning during the nightcap. That one hit was a triple by Combs leading off the game, from which he scored on an infield out. Heimach was not pitching badly, except for a two-run blast by Al Simmons, his fourteenth, in the sixth inning, which put the Athletics in front by one run. The Mackmen scored again in the next inning on a single by Simmons to take a two-run lead. Koenig led off the seventh inning with a walk and was forced by Ruth. Meusel followed with an infield hit. After Lazzeri popped to Boley at shortstop, the inning looked like a hiccup for Walberg, but Ben Paschal pinch-hit for Dugan and singled to right to score Ruth. Walberg then lost the plate, walking Gazella—batting for Bengough—and Collins—batting for Moore, who relieved Heimach—to force in the tying run. Ed Rommel relieved Walberg and kept the score tied at three. Hoyt held the Macks in the eighth inning, setting the stage for the coming dramatics. Koenig led off the bottom half with a single to right, and Gehrig followed with a double, followed by an intentional pass to the Babe. That brought up Bob Meusel with the bases loaded.

As Vidmer wrote in the September 10 copy of the *New York Times*,

> From the grandstands and the bleachers, from the boxes and the runways, came a scream of delight from the frenzied thousands. Hats were hurled onto the field—old straw hats, new felt hats, derbies, and caps, torn and tattered. Score cards fell in flakes and covered the diamond like dust. Pandemonium reigned, and a hoarse shout couldn't be heard more than a foot away.[58]

Bob Meusel's tenth home run of the year was a devastating momentum changer, and the Yankees were back in first place. He was mobbed by his teammates in the clubhouse after the game. Waite Hoyt won his nineteenth game, while Ed Rommel suffered his first losing decision since July 23.[59]

The Babe spoke for the entire team, declaring, "We broke their hearts today. And we gave that greatest crowd in baseball history some real baseball."[60] Mark Roth congratulated Huggins, who said,

> We ought to play them every day. Things would be easier then. They were two great games to win, but beyond that I won't say a word. The season isn't over yet, and everything I say is misinterpreted or places a jinx on the team anyway. So I'll not say anything beyond that we're doing pretty well considering the setback the team is suffering through the condition of Pennock and Lazzeri.[61]

Meusel, one of the day's heroes, explained, "I hit a curveball, about the fastest he could throw."[62] The lean leader left the dugout and went back to his hotel without making any statement.

The Yankee locker room resembled that of a college football team, as all the pent-up emotions were let go. A completely different and inspired

Yankee team emerged out of the doubleheader from the team that could only score one run against the Senators in eighteen innings just two days before. The Babe said,

> We can beat those Athletics any old time and they know it, and act as if they knew it. If this pennant depends on licking those birds, we're in already. They can't stop us, and that goes for Bob Grove or any other pitcher. The Red Sox might beat us. The Senators have stepped on us. But the Athletics! No! We've got the Indian sign on them—just a lot of "cousins."[63]

There was one event that put a damper on the festive atmosphere of the day. The Yankees were sorrowed when they learned of the death of Urban Shocker, who passed away in a Denver hospital from a combination of pneumonia and heart disease. He was attempting a comeback with a Denver semipro club when he was knocked out of the box on August 6 by a Cheyenne team. Shocker was admitted to St. Luke's hospital one week later.[64]

The baseball schedule left New Yorkers without a home game to watch, with the Yankees idle, the Giants in Boston, and the Robins in Philadelphia, but the previous day's doubleheader was the talk of the town. Miller Huggins was all smiles, saying, "By golly, I'm beginning to think it was all fixed and I wasn't in on it. The way the boys snapped into it when the crises came amazed even me. That's the kind of ball team you're proud of."[65]

The great Yankee collapse was put on hold, and whether a temporary or not remained to be seen. The team that had been humiliated in a doubleheader two days before and knocked out of first place the next day showed why it had gained a reputation as a great money team.[66]

With a tight race now on in the American League, the business manager of the Yankees, Ed Barrow, did not want to put the jinx on:

> That's a fine kettle of fish. That thing they play after the season is scheduled to start in a certain American League park on Wednesday, October 3. How is a certain business manager going to handle the ticket situation if a certain ball club doesn't clinch the pennant until the grand finale? Well, there is no other way out of it. The Yanks will have to win soon so a certain business manager can handle the job the way it should be handled. Otherwise a certain business manager will have to go into Times Square and toss all the tickets into the air and let the fans scramble for them.[67]

"It will be Grove tomorrow," said Connie Mack. "He's our hope for checking the Yanks and keeping us up there. If he can hold them our chances will be very bright. It'll let us go west within striking distance of the lead."[68]

The lean leader was not sure who would pitch the final game of the series and was naturally disappointed, especially with the outcome of the second game. "The Yanks didn't look right," said Mack, "they didn't look like the same team that we faced earlier in the season. But somehow or other, I don't know why it is our boys just can't seem to play their regular game against them.

"The second game was sad," he continued. "We had that one until Walberg lost his control. All Rube had to do was get the ball over the plate to lick them. He had more speed than he has had at any time this year and he had them stopped."[69] There was some possibly legitimate griping about a called third strike that was reversed by umpire Brick Owens during the seventh inning, which would have left the Yankees trailing by a run. Gazella, who walked, was originally called out on strikes, and Walberg and Cochrane began walking to the bench when Owens changed his mind and called them back.[70]

Huggins decided to use Henry Johnson against Lefty Grove in front of a midweek crowd of 50,000. The Yankees had an amazing run of success against Grove in 1928, handing him five of his six losses on the season. Working in Grove's favor was that he was the hottest pitcher in baseball, winning fourteen-straight decisions and not losing a game since June 27. It was Grove who was mainly responsible for keeping his team in the race, and he was the year's most dominant pitcher.

Grove's record of 22–6 meant that his only other defeat came at the hands of the St. Louis Browns back on June 7. The rookie, Henry Johnson, was treading water with the rest of his team, but it was Johnson who last beat Grove, and in head-to-head matchups that year, he was unbeaten in three decisions.

Lazzeri was inserted into the lineup by Huggins to give the team some much-needed inspiration, especially to shortstop Mark Koenig. "I would be overjoyed if Lazzeri could stay at second base right to the finish. I am persuaded that perhaps Tony and the success of this season are intertwined. But there is no way of telling how long he will last," said Huggins, adding, "We're up there now. And I imagine it will be a little harder this time to knock us down. Did you note the dash of the club on Sunday? Did you note how the boys scampered all over the lot, backed up each other, ran out every opportunity?" Lazzeri told Huggins that he was fine but was actually playing in a lot of pain.[71]

The game turned out to be another late, come-from-behind thriller, and another tough loss for the Athletics. Grove shut out the Yankees on two hits, and Philadelphia held a three-run lead going into the seventh inning. Johnson, with four of the Yankee victories against the Athletics, was hit for two runs in the first inning on a walk to Haas, a triple by Cochrane, and a sacrifice fly by Simmons. In the fifth, the Mackmen loaded the bases, helped by a walk and an error, but the damage was limited to one run on a sacrifice fly.

The Yankees began to chip away at the Athletic lead by scoring a run in the seventh, when Lazzeri scored on an infield out. That set the table for the eighth inning, with the Yanks still trailing by two runs. Combs lead off the inning with a walk, and Koenig beat out an infield hit in the direction of Jimmy Dykes, whose wild throw on the play put runners on second and third. A wild pitch by Grove scored Combs, and then an excuse-me single to left by Gehrig scored Koenig to tie the game.

Still not hitting Grove hard, Mack allowed him to pitch to Ruth. The Babe attempted a bunt that rolled foul by just a few inches. Leaving finesse aside, the Babe then took one of Grove's fastballs out of the park for his forty-ninth home run of the year, putting a cap on the 5–3 victory.[72]

Regarding his domination of Grove, the Babe commented,

Grove cannot beat us anymore than any other fastball pitcher can stop us. Grove knows that he is our cousin. He knows that he has pitched the greatest ball of his life against us this season and yet has been beaten five times. We don't fear any of the Philadelphia pitchers—Walberg, old Jack Quinn, Ehmke, Earnshaw, or Rommel. That gang knows that we just won't take defeat from the Athletics.[73]

Referring to Johnson, Huggins stated,

That kid has the nerve of a brass monkey. He's got crust. He takes all the time he wants between pitches and nothing bothers him. He is the same with men on bases as when the bases are empty. I never have seen a young pitcher worried less by having men on bases. He has sublime faith in himself, which is a great thing in his favor, and the team plays with all kinds of confidence behind him.[74]

Tony Lazzeri's presence in the lineup for the Philadelphia series gave an unmistakably huge lift to the team, especially Mark Koenig at shortstop, who played with more confidence with Tony at second base. Both players came up with the Yankees together, roomed together, and were from the San Francisco area.

Huggins explained whether Lazzeri was capable of remaining in the lineup:

He is if he can keep conquering the pain, which very evidently marks his work. I saw on Saturday that while Durocher was playing great and Koenig lacked a balanced wheel, and the club as a whole needed the force and the inspiration [that] Lazzeri gives it on the attack, I decided to take a big chance and asked Tony if he could jump in. He was tickled silly. I would be overjoyed if Lazzeri could stay at second base right to the finish.

I am persuaded that perhaps Tony and the success of this season are intertwined. But there is no telling how long he will last. He will tell you that he feels no pain. He'll tell you that he is getting over his injury. But you watch him closely out there and see how he grits his teeth. It is up to Lazzeri to give the word when he wants to go out.

He shouldn't be playing, but we had reached an impasse and had to do something drastic to regain the lead. We're up there now, and I imagine it will be a little harder this time to knock us down. Did you notice the dash of the club on Sunday? Did you notice how the boys scampered all over the lot, backed up each other, ran out every opportunity?[75]

Lazzeri was believed to be the most versatile player in the game, thought by some to be better than Gehrig, Koenig, or Dugan at their positions. He was pressed into becoming a second baseman during spring training in his rookie year, having played more games at third base and shortstop in the minors. Luckily, Huggins stuck with him, having been a second baseman himself, even as he struggled there. Said Lazzeri, "Guess I might have been sent back if manager Huggins had not been a star second baseman in his day. He knew how second ought to be played and he coached me until I became familiar with the work." Tony added, "My previous work in a boiler shop gave me the power to hit the ball, but it was Miller Huggins who made me a Big-League second baseman."[76] Experts thought that the Yankees were taking too big a gamble on him, paying $65,000. Lazzeri also admitted that his minor-league numbers were inflated in the thin air at Salt Lake City of the Pacific Coast League, where he twice had to be sent down.[77]

"Tony Lazzeri is a great ballplayer," said Huggins. Huggins went on, stating,

I've seen a few better second baseman, but not many. He has a phenomenal set of hands and a great throwing arm, and he covers acres of ground. Eddie Collins was the perfect second baseman, Lajoie was great, and Hornsby of course. But I think this fellow will cover more ground. Besides, he has a great disposition for a ballplayer. He had to work hard in his younger days and appreciates what baseball has done for him. He's a great ballplayer now, but he'll improve.[78]

Connie Mack and his entourage would not see his club put the coup de grace on the Yankees. The Babe's home run completed the momentum shift, but it would still be a dogfight to the end of the season. The Athletics would again show the ability to bounce back from another series of humiliating defeats at the hand of the Yankees.

In the next game of the series, the pitching matchup appeared to favor the Yankees, as Howard Ehmke opposed Waite Hoyt. The Mack starter had lost his last five decisions since August 14.

With the Athletics leading by a run in the eighth inning, a brawl almost ensued after Athletic starter Ehmke hit Meusel, which loaded the bases. Meusel started toward the mound, but no fighting resulted. After one pitch to Lazzeri, Ehmke limped off the field with a twisted ankle and was lost for the remainder of the season. He would not get a decision in this game, as Orwoll held the Yankees in the ninth inning, but Ehmke had kept his team in the game.[79] What could truly be called the "showdown series" ended with a two-out solo home run in the ninth inning by second baseman Max Bishop, which untied a three-all score and gave the Athletics a victory in what was basically a must-win situation.

The Mackmen had a name for Bishop's home run. "I'll tell you what, boys," one of the veterans said, "Bishop's homer this afternoon was a $100,000 smack. That's what you'll have to call it. It puts us up there. Only a game and a half now! Not so bad."[80]

There was a fair amount of trash talking during the three games, with Walter French getting under the Yankees' skin and Leo Durocher yelling back for the Yankees. Different versions of the barbs and scuffling between the players have been written. The main combatants during the middle game of the series were Howard Ehmke and Tony Lazzeri. The former's version was that just before the two players came to blows, Mickey Cochrane stepped in to collar Lazzeri, and the Babe grabbed Ehmke and both were dragged to separate clubhouses. The other was that Ehmke was given a going over before they were separated.[81]

It was on Tuesday, September 13, 1927, of the previous year, to be exact, that the Yankees had clinched the pennant in a doubleheader against the Indians. The dual 5–3 victories increased their lead to seventeen games, with fifteen to play. The team caucus that put the 1928 race to bed during the third week of May seemed like a long time ago; the Yankees still had much work to do.

Both rivals had two days off before they headed west for the last swing of the season. The Athletics, who had dominated the Red Sox all year, chose not to use this last open date to make up the September 6 postponement. Instead Connie Mack chose to play an exhibition game in Albany. As a result, the game could no longer be made up.[82]

Credit was given to the managing of Miller Huggins in the face of key injuries, although he still held out hope that Pennock, like the hobbled Lazzeri, might make a comeback before the season ended. It was Joe Vila, in the *Philadelphia Inquirer*, who sang the praises of the Yankee manager:

> Making the fight to hold first position without the assistance of Pennock and Lazzeri has demonstrated the managerial skill of Huggins. He has

had to contend with other misfortunes—the prolonged ineffectiveness of Wilcy Moore, for instance. Several Yankees have batted far below normal figures. Others have fielded poorly, while, barring Hoyt, each regular pitcher has been erratic. Huggins, never for a moment discouraged, has handled the Yankees with keen judgment, making few, if any, tactical errors and reviving the flagging spirits of several important players.[83]

Consideration was given to the fortune of Connie Mack in having his main stars still intact. Where would the Athletics be without Bishop and Grove? The player who was stepping up for the Yankees was Lou Gehrig; while the rest of the team seemed tight, the first baseman was loose and relaxed.[84]

The 180,000 fans that attended the series was a record, even for a World Series, and the crowd averaged 60,000 for each day. A total of 170,000 attended the seven games for the 1920 World Series between Brooklyn and Cleveland. The four games of the 1927 series averaged about 50,000 fans. The year before, the Yankees and Cardinals had set a record, with about 328,000 fans for the seven games. The attendance of more than 85,000 at the Stadium was astounding, even to those who were aware of the great increase in the popularity of baseball during the decade. It also raised the question of whether teams should study the advantages of increasing the size of stadiums in the future.[85]

"As a magnet for the fans," noticed Bill Dooley, "the Yankees–Athletics series drew rooters from all over the country. Sports who make it a habit to travel thousands of miles to attend the World's Series added another jaunt to their travels this year just to see the Mackmen tangle with the champions." Dooley added, "Hardly without exception they were for the Athletics. The whole country is rooting for Connie Mack."[86]

For the Yankees, the final push began with four games in St. Louis, three in Chicago and Cleveland, and five in Detroit. The Athletics had three games each with Cleveland, Detroit, and St. Louis, and then finished the season with four in Chicago. The Yankees led by a game and a half, but the Athletics typically fared better against the west, where both teams would finish out the schedule. The Athletics would not have to face the Yankees again in 1928.[87]

As fate would have it, the Yankees arrived in St. Louis for the funeral of Urban Shocker at All Saints Church. The service was attended by 1,000 people. The deceased's teammates, Gene Robertson, Waite Hoyt, Mike Gazella, Lou Gehrig, Earle Combs, and Myles Thomas, acted as pallbearers, and the rest of the team as honorary pallbearers.[88]

Won or Lost in the West
(September 15–September 30)

There is something very hollow about a victory when it comes on a day a team is eliminated from the race.

—*Philadelphia Inquirer*, September 29, 1928[1]

*T*hroughout the season, the Athletics showed a remarkable ability to bounce back following their defeats at the hands of the Yankees, and they felt that their reaction would be no different this time. The American League pennant would be won or lost in the west, an observation made by James Isaminger in his September 16 "Tips from the Sport Ticker" column. Aside from stating the obvious, Isaminger expounded on why the Athletics felt confident that they would pass the Yankees before the season-ending series in Detroit. The Athletics had taken fourteen of nineteen clashes with the Indians, while the Yankees barely managed to eke out a winning record against the Browns. For the rest of the swing, it was felt that the Yankees' troubles would continue, having lost eight of their last fifteen games with the White Sox and Indians. The Athletics would play three fewer games than the Yankees in the month of September.[2]

The Athletics had handily beaten the Browns and Tigers thus far in the season, winning twenty-seven of thirty-eight games, but one psychological angle still working against Connie Mack as he faced these teams a final time was the Cobb factor. There were many players left on the Tigers, as well as former Tigers on the Browns, who reportedly held a grudge against their former teammate and manager and wanted to keep him out of the World Series. It may have stemmed from the scandal that broke around Cobb and Tris Speaker after the 1926 season, suggesting that both players had thrown an important game seven years earlier.[3]

Table 13.1.   American League Standings, September 14, 1928

Team	Won	Lost	GB	Pct.
Yankees	91	48	—	.655
Athletics	90	50	1.5	.643
Browns	77	63	14.5	.550
White Sox	66	74	25.5	.471
Senators	65	75	26.5	.464
Tigers	62	78	29.5	.443
Indians	59	81	32.5	.421
Red Sox	49	90	42	.353

Table 13.2.   National League Standings, September 14, 1928

Team	Won	Lost	GB	Pct.
Cardinals	84	55	—	.604
Giants	83	56	1	.597
Cubs	82	58	2.5	.586
Pirates	77	62	7	.554
Reds	73	64	10	.533
Robins	70	70	14.5	.500
Braves	44	93	39	.321
Phillies	42	97	42	.302

There was no necessity for the lean leader to experiment with young, unproven pitchers. With Howard Ehmke out injured, the chores down the stretch fell to the other three pitchers Mack had depended on since spring training, plus the addition of George Earnshaw with Ed Rommel, and Ossie Orwoll coming out of the bull pen. The Yankees were not as fortunate with the injury to Herb Pennock and the ineffectiveness of Wilcy Moore. There were doubts that the likes of Fred Heimach, Henry Johnson, and Tom Zachary could step up and supplement Waite Hoyt, George Pipgras, and the ailing Pennock. It was very much a possibility that the Yankees would have to win more than nine of the remaining fifteen games to clinch the flag. The four games for the Hugmen in St. Louis, three each in Chicago and Cleveland, and five in Detroit would be played without any postponements beginning on September 15, with two off days on September 19 and September 26.[4]

The final push did not get off to a good start for the Yankees. General Crowder outpitched George Pipgras as the Browns outscored the Yankees, 6–5.[5] The playing field at Sportsman's Park, where both the Browns and Cardinals played, was possibly the worst in baseball. "There is hardly a blade of grass growing in the infield, and the outfield is as rough as a brickyard," wrote Isaminger. "The field is so uneven that balls often take a false bound. Kress, a good shortstop, has stacked up a lot of errors because of the field."[6]

The Athletics beat the Indians to pull back to within half a game of the Yankees. Jack Quinn was superb as he and his team opened the final swing of the season by shutting out Cleveland.

Ty Cobb's final at bat as a player came as a pinch hitter on September 11, against the Yankees. One week later, he announced his retirement:

> Never again after the finish of the present pennant race will I be an active player in the organization to which I have devoted twenty-four seasons of what for me was hard labor. I make the announcement today because of the many inquiries constantly coming to me concerning my future plans. I will leave Connie Mack and my present team, the Athletics, with sincere regret.
>
> Why, I scarcely know my children, and they are now getting to the stage where they must soon marry. My work was in summer when they had their vacation. When the baseball season ended and I went home, my children were sent to school for the winter, so to a great degree I lost contact with them. I will be forty-two years old next December 17, and I think it is time to stop, for I might get some serious injury on the baseball field that might lessen my life.[7]

A huge crowd of 30,000 showed up at Sportsman's Park on Sunday, as the Yankees came back with Henry Johnson against George Blaeholder, and neither man was sharp. Johnson got credit for his twelfth victory. He gave up three hits and didn't make it through the sixth inning, issuing six walks and a hit batsman. Huggins did not wish to take any chances with the rookie's control and had Tom Zachary warm up after every walk. Earle Combs led off the game with a triple; he was almost stranded, but the swift center fielder stole home on a double steal, with Ruth taking second.

Five consecutive singles in the second inning, starting with the bottom of the order, Robertson, Bengough, Johnson, Combs, and Koenig, put the Yankees in the lead by four runs. Gehrig hit a solo home run in the fifth inning, his twenty-fourth, and Koenig smacked his fourth, a two-run shot in the sixth inning, to account for the team's seven runs in a 7–5 victory.[8]

After having his winning streak broken at fourteen, Lefty Grove bounced back nicely for the Athletics against Cleveland. The Tribe managed just four hits in the 7–1 drubbing. They could do nothing with Grove, who faced the minimum number of batters through the first five innings.[9]

The Yankees gained a half game on the idle Macks to lead by a full game behind Waite Hoyt as they defeated the Browns in front of 20,000 on Ladies' Day on Monday. "The only trouble with Ladies' Day is that the fair fans show no discretion. They scream at the sight of a strike out, they cheer mightily when a foul ball is hit, and a good solid pop fly throws them in a high state of hysterics," wrote Richards Vidmer. None of the pitchers were helped by the six errors in the rough infield at Sportsman's Park.[10]

The team finally acquired George Burns, even though he would not be eligible for the World Series. "I claimed Burns for use as a pinch hitter mainly," explained Huggins, "but also to safeguard myself on first base if anything happens to Gehrig. I'm not going to be caught in the same position I was with Lazzeri this year."[11]

Unlike Clarence Mitchell's move from the Phillies to the Cardinals, the thirty-five-year-old Burns was not at all excited about leaving a floundering team to play with a pennant contender. Burns was voted Most Valuable Player in the American League in 1926, his thirteenth season, garnering 63 votes on 64 ballots, with 4 home runs and 114 runs batted in, with a record 64 doubles. He did not wish to report to the Yankees and instead wanted his outright release as a ten-year man and wished to be a free agent.[12] Burns explained, saying,

> I have no personal dislike to the Yankees nor Miller Huggins, but I do not seek a job with the club. In fact, I feel that I have several years yet remaining as a ballplayer, and while able to play I would like to step out of the big leagues and take over some minor-league club as a player-manager. I have had this in mind some time now and feel that I could certainly make good in this line. If I go to the Yanks now I will be used only as a pinch hitter and relief man. For I could not get Lou Gehrig's job, and I would probably be shifted to some New York minor-league club next spring.[13]

Burns unequivocally favored the Athletics to prevail in the race with the Yankees. He was born in Niles, Ohio, but attended Central High School, in Philadelphia, and considered himself a Philadelphia boy.[14] But he later changed his decision not to report to the Yankees and expressed that he was willing to report to the team after a satisfactory reassurance of his status from the team.[15]

"Burns is still a good ballplayer and will be a fine substitute for Gehrig next year in case any such accident that befell Lazzeri this season should hit Lou," Huggins explained. He added,

> In the meanwhile, I can get a lot of good service out of him this season as a right-handed pinch hitter. He isn't eligible for the World Series, as we got him after September 15, the deadline on World Series eligibles, but he will be a handy man to have around while we are trying to sew up the American League pennant.[16]

Wilcy Moore finally departed for his farm in Oklahoma and was placed on the voluntarily retired list, unavailable for the rest of the year because of a sore arm. The favored right-hander could never regain his sinkerball. It was not a permanent retirement as much as a feeling of uselessness and being a liability to the team. "The difference between the Yankees of 1927 and the Yanks of 1928 is Cy Moore," said Huggins. "He was in fifty games for us last year, and he finished with a record of nineteen victories and seven defeats."[17]

In the span of three years, Moore went from a virtual unknown to a World Series hero to out of baseball, from nineteen victories to just four. The credit for the discovery of Moore went to Ed Barrow, who noticed Moore's record of thirty wins in thirty-four decisions at Greenville, in the Sally League, while reviewing minor-league stats in his office during the winter of 1927. He was also a workhorse, pitching 305 innings, with an earned run average of less than three. It was Moore who relieved Hoyt in the first game of the World Series, getting credit for a save, and he clinched the series with a complete-game victory in game four. He gave up just one earned run in ten and two-thirds innings.[18]

Moore's index finger on his throwing hand was shorter than usual, which aided his sinkerball. He never had to work at developing the pitch. "So far as I know, that's the whole secret of what you fellers call the sinker," Moore once said.[19] In his last outing in St. Louis on September 15, he gave up two runs on as many hits and two walks in one and one-third innings.

It was not a permanent banishment, as Huggins informed reporters, stating,

> He'll report at St. Petersburg next spring. He'll also get his full World Series share if we win the pennant this year. He is a hard worker and tried his best to win for us, but he simply couldn't do it with that lame wing of his. I think it is a smart thing for him to lay off and not try to pitch. It will bring his arm back, that rest, if anything will. It is my opinion that he will be as good as ever next year.[20]

Many Yankee players felt that he was through for good and did not anticipate a successful comeback.[21]

Huggins needed to use four of his starting pitchers against the Browns in the final game in St. Louis, Heimach for one and a third innings, Hoyt for two innings, Pipgras for a third of an inning, and Johnson for five and a third innings, but the pitching was overshadowed by the Yankees pounding of Wiltse, Blaeholder, and Strelecki for eighteen hits and fourteen runs. "Both teams looked like a couple of bush clubs in a bad slump," wrote Rud Rennie of the *New York Herald Tribune* in describing the performances.[22]

Both the Yankees and Browns scored in each of the last three innings in what ended as a 14–11 win for the Yankees. The Babe for the Yankees and Otis Brannan for the Browns were the only players who failed to hit safely.

After utterly dominating the Browns, the Yankees narrowly took the season series from Dan Howley's men twelve games to ten, but more importantly, they still led the pennant race by two games.[23]

Meanwhile, the memo above the box score for the Athletics aptly read, "This Was Tough," describing their setback in their third game with the Indians as Rube Walberg took the loss against Walter Miller.[24] The Indians scratched across the deciding runs in the seventh inning already leading by a run. With John Hodapp on third base and two out, reserve outfielder Luther Harvel doubled to left. The next batter, reserve infielder Ed Montague, hit a scorcher to Sammy Hale, which he ended up kicking into center field to allow Cleveland's third run.[25]

The American League had a scheduled day off, giving pause for the Yankees to reflect on the state of their physical health before they faced Chicago. Tony Lazzeri was playing in severe pain with a sore shoulder, possibly risking his career. Mark Koenig had an injured heel and missed the last game with the Browns. Joe Dugan was out of the lineup with what was described by Vidmer as a "seemingly incurable batting slump." He was batting .203 in 133 at bats since July, with one just home run and six runs batted in. The fact that Miller Huggins was using Gene Robertson at third base regularly probably meant the end for "Jumping Joe." Dugan's average had steadily declined from .357 on June 13 to .284 on September 9. Last year's relief ace, Cy Moore, was out for the rest of the year, and Herb Pennock was still bothered by neuritis. Waite Hoyt, who had worked in four of the last seven games, and George Pipgras, who was active in the last three out of five, were being overworked.[26]

Representatives from all six contenders outlined plans for the postseason. The World Series was set to open on October 4, with the first two games on American League soil and the next three in the National League team's park. The Yankees had asked that the series open on a Thursday instead of the customary Wednesday after the regular season because it did not give them enough time to prepare for the anticipated large crowds. The bleachers would fetch $1.00, general admission $3.00, reserved seats $5.50, and box seats $6.60. The games would begin at 1:30 p.m., except for the Sunday game in New York, which would have a start time of 2:01 p.m. The Athletics began accepting requests for tickets on September 19.[27]

The Yankees opened the next series in Chicago, on September 20, having gained a half game on the Athletics during the final swing, with eleven games remaining. Several players were picking up with the bat where the Babe had left off. Against the Browns, Bengough hit .461, Koenig .417, Meusel .375, Gehrig .354, Lazzeri .313, and Robertson .308. The Babe was trailing at a .118 clip.[28]

Connie Mack felt that the issue with his Athletic club was more psychological and that the players were still focusing on the Yankees. He commented,

> It is not too late yet even if the season is nearing the end, and I feel that the team will play out the string to the end. It will be of immense help if we can mop up the series in Detroit, for I feel that the Yanks may meet some disappointment in Chicago. There is a chance that the coming series will result in the Athletics tying or getting ahead of the Yankees.[29]

Mack explained that he would rather have seen his team go down to the wire and lose the pennant on the last day of the season rather than drop out of the race before then:

> But don't think I am not disappointed by this first section of the western trip. I thought we should go out of Cleveland tied with New York. I figured we would take three straight and that St. Louis would break even with New York. Yesterday's game with Cleveland was a big disappointment. So was the showing of the Browns.
>
> New York is not getting the pitching, but they are hitting. We are getting grand pitching, but the hitting is terrible. The outlook is just this: We can count on our pitching to be good every game we have left on the schedule.
>
> It won't hurt me deeply if we lose the pennant in Chicago, but if our last chance gets away from us here in St. Louis, I will feel that we failed when we should not have failed. Those six games in three days, two doubleheaders with Boston and one with New York, took a lot out of them physically. A few of them were quite haggard after that overwork, but the rest in between New York and this trip seemed to put them on their game again. But yesterday they were just a lifeless ball club.
>
> This is my best team, and I'll go down with the ship and with the crew just the way it is. The lineup, just as it is, is the one that will win or lose the pennant, and if they lose it in Chicago, the season will satisfy me, championship or no championship.[30]

In the National League, with eleven games remaining, the Giants (86–57) had four games left with the Cardinals (88–55), four with the Cubs (85–59), and three with the Reds (75–66). The Cardinals finished with four games in Brooklyn and three games in Boston. There was one game with the Giants scheduled as a stand-alone game to end the season.[31]

Thirty-nine-year-old Red Faber, with still almost 800 innings remaining in his arm, pitched a complete-game, twelve-inning victory for the White Sox, helping them top the Yankees. Faber broke into professional baseball in 1909, at the age of twenty, with Dubuque in the Three-I League. Coming into the 1928 season, Faber and team manager Ray Schalk were the last remaining links to the World Series championship team of 1917. Faber had beaten the Giants three times in that year's postseason. He was also tough on the Yankees, managing a winning record against them during their six pennant-winning years.[32]

The loss cut the Yankee lead to one game. George Pipgras started the game instead of Zachary, as originally planned, and the big right-hander weakened in the eighth inning with the Yankees ahead by a run.[33] Pipgras was sailing along, allowing the White Sox just four hits, but in the eighth inning he gave up three straight singles to Alex Metzler, Willie Kamm, and Bill Hunnefield, which tied the game. Extra innings were not something the stretched Yankee pitching staff needed; nonetheless, Waite Hoyt had to be summoned once again for his third straight appearance, and the fifth of the last eight games. The White Sox won in the twelfth inning, when Carl Reynolds beat out an infield hit, stole second, went to third on a sacrifice, and scored on a sacrifice fly by Karl Swanson.[34]

Jack Quinn got the Athletics back on track in front of a crowd of 2,000 during their series opener in a foggy, chilly Detroit. The spitballer recorded his eighteenth victory, along with a game winning single.[35]

The Yankees had won three of five games in their pennant-deciding western trip, with little hitting from the Babe. He had just two hits in twenty-two at bats but drove in six runs, walked four times, and scored three runs. One of the hits was a home run, in his first at bat in St. Louis. The team scored thirty-three runs in their three wins in St. Louis, with only one hit in seventeen plate appearances from Ruth.[36]

For the first time in twenty years, it appeared that both races were going to go down to the wire, but baseball was still wary about scandals. Would one of the teams still in the hunt be subjected to bribes? "Baseball's integrity [was] at stake during the dying moments of both races in the major leagues. . . . Because of past scandals, baseball . . ., like Caesar's wife, [had] to be above suspicion." This year it was the Boston Braves dropping eight games to the Giants that was fueling doubts.[37]

In the Yankees' next game against the White Sox, it was Tom Zachary who stepped up to the plate with a two-run blast in the eighth inning, giving the Yankees a much-needed lift. The victory over Chicago, coupled with a Tigers win over the Athletics, lifted the lead back to two games. Incidentally, both pitchers were slow workers, which resulted in the game taking a little more than two hours to complete.[38]

Huggins was not confident with emergency replacements Heimach, Zachary, and Ryan. He explained the work that remained ahead for his team:

> Well, I'm kind of shivery here, but it's the cold weather rather than ap-
> prehension [about] the ball games. If the team keeps on hitting the way it

did in St. Louis, we ought to be all right. But you can't tell about the Yanks this year. They have been so inconsistent.

It looks now as if Koenig might not be able to start against the White Sox at short. The trainer tells me Mark's bruised heel is worse. It's just enough to cut down his speed in fielding, and I may have to rely on Durocher. Shortstop is where Leo belongs, so I am not much worried about the defense end of the situation that this latest accident has brought up. But we will miss Koenig's hitting if he cannot play, for he has always batted pretty briskly at Comiskey Park.

In view of all this I can't say yet whether we will win. We need most imperatively to take two games here out of the three. We can't afford to drop two. There will be the problem of manipulating what pitching we have to get the best results. Zachary simply has to win me a couple of games during the final three series to take some of the burden off the other boys. I will open with either Zachary or Pipgras against the White Sox, and I suppose they will give us a battle, with either Faber and Adkins both available.[39]

The Athletics, behind Lefty Grove, were beaten at Navin Field in Detroit on "two long, whistling hits." One was a grand slam by center fielder Harry Rice off of Grove, and the other an inside-the-park homer by left fielder John Stone off of Orwoll with two runners on base. Grove retired the first nine batters but took his eighth loss of the year. The ace and stopper for Connie throughout the year lasted just one out into the fifth inning. Elam Vangilder went the distance for Detroit and evened his record on the season.[40]

The White Sox won their final game against the Yankees, 5–2, against the Yankees, with the winning pitcher, Tommy Thomas, striking out eight and giving up eight hits. Four runs in the bottom of the fourth inning resulted in the undoing of Henry Johnson.

Only three Yankee regulars—Gehrig, Meusel, and Combs—could be considered healthy. Al Shealy, who had nobly filled in for Hoyt earlier in the year, was recalled from St. Paul to do the same for Pennock. Babe Ruth was batting .075 on this trip through the Chicago series. At the midpoint of their jaunt through the west, the Yankees had gained a half game on Philadelphia.[41]

Tiger fans had mixed feelings about their team's showing so far against the Athletics. In the September 23 edition of the *Philadelphia Public Ledger*, Bill Brandt wrote, "All afternoon a Detroit crowd cheered and exhorted the efforts of the A's to cling to the rim of the pennant race."[42] The Athletics, who could not afford to lose any more games, blew a chance to pull back to within a game of first place. The box score said it all, reading, "Lost Opportunity," as the Athletics kicked the game away. Sammy Hale's second fielding miscue at third base in the third inning landed him on the bench. He was replaced by Foxx, with Hauser shifting to first base.[43] "The multitude strug-gling out the exits seemed as depressed as any Shibe Park assemblage could have been," added Brandt.[44]

The Yankees still clung to a two-game lead, with ninety-five wins and fifty-one losses, to the Athletic's ninety-three wins and fifty-three losses, with eight games remaining for the Yankees and seven for the Athletics as of September 22.

The team announced World Series ticket prices at $6.60 for box seats and $5.50 for reserved seats. The 25,000 grandstand seats and 20,000 box seats would go on sale at 10:00 a.m. the day of games one, two, and six of the series for $1.00 and $3.00 apiece, respectively. Only certified checks or money orders would be accepted.[45]

The recent hot hitting from Benny Bengough was a timely development for Huggins. Throughout the Chicago series, he had been batting nearly .500, raising his average to .289 for the year. George Pipgras and Waite Hoyt pitched in all but two of the first seven games. Joe Dugan was still benched, but his decent postseason record would give him a chance to see action in the World Series.

The next to last series of the season in Cleveland began on a Sunday. Waite Hoyt pitched a clutch four-hit shutout against the Indians to win his twentieth game of the season, inching the Yankees ever closer to a third consecutive pennant. The Brooklyn mortician was doubling as the team's top starter and reliever, appearing in four of the team's last six games. A score-less tie was broken in the fifth inning when Lazzeri singled home Gehrig from second after a double. The next inning, the slumping Babe doubled and scored on Gehrig's triple. Singles by Hoyt in the final two innings played a part in the last three runs.[46]

The Athletics broke out the lumber against the Browns to remain two games back. The sixteen-hit, eleven-run attack included home runs from Foxx, Hauser, and Dykes.

The Yankees now had two games remaining in Cleveland, and they would then finish with five at Navin Field. The Athletics had two more with the Browns and four with the White Sox and were still confident that they would pick up another game in St. Louis and overtake the ailing and tired Yankees with a weaker opponent in Chicago.[47]

In his September 23 "Tips from the Sport Ticker" column, James Isaminger wrote about where sentiments lay in the pennant race:

> Beyond any shadow of doubt, it has been demonstrated that the American League baseball followers, outside of New York, want the Athletics to win the pennant. The applause they received in visiting cities since they have become real contenders has been inspiring to Mack's players. They had

all of the best of the rooting in Washington and Boston, and they had a
wonderful break even from the fair-minded fans in New York.

On that Sunday, in which 85,000 persons saw the doubleheader
between the Yanks and Athletics, the largest crowd ever known since
Abner Doubleday put the sport forth in Cooperstown, New York, the
spectators gave the Athletics almost as much encouragement as they did
their own Yanks.

In Cleveland, the Athletics had every encouragement from the partisan
followers there. The Athletics won the first two games and lost the third.
This was a bitter fight in which the Macks were nosed out, 3–2.

The same thing happened in Detroit. The spectators whooped it up
for the Athletics in every game. . . . Everybody in baseball seems to
want the Athletics to win the pennant, and that ought to be a source of
encouragement to the players who now have their backs to the wall with
odds against 'em.[48]

Another all-New York World Series was a worst-case scenario. "Who
wants to see a fourth all-New York World Series?" asked Sam Otis. Otis
elaborated, stating,

Most folks shudder to think of such a possibility, yet it strongly exists.
Truth it is that the baseball world is fed up [with] New York superiority.
Everybody would be happy to see both the Yankees and Giants edged
out. A World Series next month between the Mackmen and either the
St. Louis Cardinals or Chicago Cubs would come as a welcome relief.[49]

Both teams were running out of gas. The Yankees were tired and crippled by injuries, and the Athletics were simply suffering from fatigue. Homer
Thorne, a staff correspondent for the *New York Evening Post*, noticed:

The downtrodden, crippled Yankees are falling all over the field. They
can't field, they can't hit, yet they can't drop out of first place. For pure
downright inconsistency, this 1928 Yankee club takes all the prizes. It
drops from the ridiculous to the sublime overnight. The players can't do
the same thing twice the same way. You never can tell what is going to
happen from one inning to the next.[50]

The Yankees could not figure out Cleveland lefty Walter Miller, managing just five hits in front of a sparse crowd on a chilly afternoon by the
lake, with business manager Billy Evans providing blankets and hot coffee to
members of the press. The Yankees overcame a two-run deficit in the fifth
inning, when Combs doubled, Koenig walked, Ruth's double scored Combs,
and a sacrifice fly scored Koenig. The Indians broke the tie off of George
Pipgras with a run in the sixth on a single by John Hodapp and a triple by

Luke Sewell that acted like a pinball to the Babe in right field. Fred Heimach was summoned in the sixth inning to hold the damage, but the Yankees could not mount a comeback.[51]

Bibb Falk was "Shoeless Joe" Jackson's replacement following the infamous Black Sox scandal of 1919, and he was one of the senior members of the White Sox. He shared his thoughts on the pennant race:

> Those Yankees have been so much stronger than any other club in the league for a season and a half that they have forgotten how to scramble for a tight game. Their test will come when a slump and a flock of injuries hit them at the same time. I think they'll come through, because I know them, and I know they can fight.[52]

A hitting slump did indeed occur, and so did the injuries, with Lazzeri's shoulder, Koenig's ankle, Ruth's knee, and Pennock's neuritis.[53]

In the September 25 issue of the *Philadelphia Inquirer*, the box score of the Athletics game against the Browns reads, "A Costly Defeat," which left the deficit for Philadelphia at two games. Jack Quinn, with eighteen wins, was let down by his defense and lost a chance at a twenty-win season; instead, it was General Crowder who won his twentieth game.[54]

The Yankees were increasingly in control of their own destiny and worked it to their advantage by leaving Cleveland with a 10–1 victory and maintaining a two-game lead with five to play. Yankee bats took some pressure off Zachary in the first inning, racking up six runs off of George Grant. The only other threat came in the third inning, when what appeared to be game-threatening storm clouds resulted in mere drizzle. The Yankees would finish the season in Detroit with five games, where three wins would guarantee their sixth pennant in eight years.[55]

"Sticking Close" is the message accompanying the box score in the September 26 installment of the *Philadelphia Inquirer*, referring to the Macks' victory over the Browns. There was little margin for error with four games remaining to the Yankees' five. The Macks needed a sweep in Chicago and for the Tigers to take three of five from the Yankees.[56]

In the Tuesday, September 25, edition of the *Philadelphia Inquirer*, Joe Vila reminded readers of the game that the Athletics elected not to play with the Red Sox, a team they beat so handily during the year, when they had a chance to make up the game. The final series with Boston was on September 6, 7, and 8, at Fenway, with five games scheduled. The rainout on the sixth resulted in two doubleheaders during the next two days, with the fifth game unable to be replayed.[57]

In the National League, it came down to the Cardinals at the Braves for three games and the Cubs at the Polo Grounds for four games with the Giants. The Cardinals then met the Giants in the season's final game in New York. The Cubs had beaten the Giants eleven of eighteen times going into their series.

A collective effort was keeping the Giants in contention, with Freddy Lindstrom taking lead honors at third base. Jimmy Welsh and Francis Hogan, who had been acquired from the Braves, were contributing, along with Travis Jackson at shortstop. Mel Ott, Lefty O'Doul, and Bill Terry were also getting timely hits. Larry Benton, Fred Fitzsimmons, and rookie Carl Hubbell were carrying the pitching load.[58]

The Cardinals were still in first place, and the demand for World Series tickets was almost four times the available 23,000 reserved and grandstand seats. The club received 40,000 letters with applications for tickets. The payments enclosed were estimated at $1 million, and nine bank clerks were given the job of randomly selecting the lucky ones.

Jim Tierney, secretary of the Giants, explained that his team was not yet counting their lucky stars, saying, "When and if the Giants clinch the pennant, we will begin to accept reservations, if accompanied by a certified check or money order. Until that time, there is nothing stirring. No, we're not superstitious. But there's no use counting your chickens until they're hatched."[59]

The magic number was three for the Yankees, and a sweep of Detroit in the final makeup doubleheader, coupled with a Chicago victory over the Athletics, would give the Hugmen their third straight flag. Following an off day from the Cleveland series, Waite Hoyt and Henry Johnson would have the honors on Thursday, September 27, in the season's final makeup doubleheader. Hoyt, in particular, had been a workhorse on the final western trip, fully justifying his holdout during spring training.

The Yankees had limped west with a lead of a game and a half, and they increased it by half a game by winning three of four in St Louis, one of three in Chicago, and two of three in Cleveland. The Athletics played copycat, with the half-game difference coming from one less game played in the Cleveland series. The injured Yankees still included Pennock, Lazzeri, Koenig, Dugan, and Ruth. Among the healthy were Gehrig, Combs, Meusel, and Durocher.[60]

The Athletics won only five of the nine games, and although their confidence was beginning to wane, they were still somewhat upbeat. Manager Mack didn't think twice about it, as Grove would get the ball on Thursday and Sunday, with Jack Quinn and Rube Walberg throwing in between. Jimmie Foxx took over third base, leaving Sammy Hale on the bench. Jimmy Dykes remained at shortstop for Joe Boley, who was still out with an injured hand. The White Sox were in a race of their own for the last spot in the first division, trailing Washington by two games.[61]

The magic number to clinch the pennant was suddenly down to one, and the Yankees did not want to rely on any help from the White Sox with the pennant hanging by a thread. The Yankees never trailed in either game of the final doubleheader of the year, winning both games by scores of 4–3 and 8–5.

The Babe, bandaged knee and limping, hit his fifty-first and fifty-second home runs in his first times at bat in each game. The Tigers started Owen Carroll in the first game. The second run off of the Tiger righty in the third inning broke a one-all tie on a walk to Combs, a single to Koenig, and two infield outs. In the fifth inning, Gehrig drove in the third and fourth runs with a double. The Tigers chipped away at a three-run deficit with runs off of Hoyt in the seventh and eighth but could come no closer.

In the nightcap, the Yankees ended the season as they began it, by scoring early and often against Vic Sorrell. The trio of vulnerables—Heimach, Shealy, and Johnson—came through; Heimach was spotted a six-run lead going into the Tiger third inning but was batted around for three runs. Shealy got the final out of the inning before being rescued by Johnson in the fifth. Incredibly, Waite Hoyt was up in the bull pen and may have entered the game had it not been called after seven innings on account of darkness. Ben Paschal finished the game for the Babe in left field. The win was a costly one, however. Earle Combs ran into the left-field wall and fractured a bone in his right wrist. He would not be able to play in the series and would lose out on some exhibition game money following the postseason.[62]

Philadelphia's ace, Lefty Grove, continued his mastery of the White Sox for his twenty-fourth win against eight defeats. In a rare statistical anomaly, each player in the Athletic lineup had exactly one hit. Grove's hit was a solo home run to right field in the top of the third inning.[63] "Well, I hear New York won the second game," said Connie Mack. "It doesn't look so good, does it? No, it looks kind of bad for us. But they still have to win another. I hope we can force them to win that one. That's what we must do now." The players, however, were singing a different tune. They had the pennant handed to them only to blow it. They began making their plans for the offseason.[64]

Not counting on or relying on the Athletics to back them into the postseason, the Yankees won their one hundredth game to clinch the pennant. With their 11–6 victory over the Tigers on Friday, September 28, they reached the century mark in wins against fifty-two losses to the Athletics ninety-seven wins and fifty-four losses. Even if the Yankees lost their last two games and the Athletics won their remaining games, it would not matter, thanks to the game the Athletics elected not to make up earlier in the month against Boston. Miller Huggins had now won more pennants than Connie Mack, and Waite Hoyt was free to take his mortician's exam in Buffalo. It was now a matter of who would win the pennant in the National League to face the Yankees in the twenty-fifth World Series.

George Pipgras was given the duties for the clincher, and he held the Tigers to one run on three hits through six innings, while enjoying a seven-run lead. The Babe homered his last time at bat with Koenig on base in the eighth inning, his fifty-third of the year and third round-tripper in two days. They knocked Detroit starter Sam Gibson out in the first inning, scoring four runs on singles by Meusel and Robertson after the bases were loaded, and then added seven more runs against three additional Tiger hurlers.[65]

There was a fitting eulogy by Isaminger for the 1928 Philadelphia Athletics:

> It took the Philadelphians to make a race in the American League, when, in early July, New York was out in front by thirteen games. With seven owners in the Barnard loop lamenting over the absence of a race and attendance thinning [throughout] the circuit, the Athletics started one of the most dramatic drives in the history of the junior circuit. They demolished everything before them for weeks, and the climax was reached on September 8, in Boston, when the Macks took both sections of a doubleheader and moved into first place by the margin of a half game.[66]

Ty Cobb and Tris Speaker made their final bow, as both antiques were given permission to depart when the race was settled. Cobb left for Detroit for a visit to the dentist, and Speaker for Wyoming to go hunting. Neither player would be back with the Athletics. Some of the other players also asked for permission to leave with one game left to play.[67]

Vila sung the praises of the managerial ability of Miller Huggins. For 1928, he had not had the luxury of merely making up a lineup card and sitting back to enjoy the season. He had been required to actively manage through multiple injuries to pitchers and everyday players. The mite manager had to manage around the incapacitation of pitchers Moore, Pennock, and Shocker, and injuries to Lazzeri, Dugan, and Meusel. Going into the postseason, there was also the extended slump from the Babe and the loss of Earle Combs:

> No manager of a championship team in the history of baseball has overcome so many obstacles as Huggins has encountered during the last three months. In view of everything, he has scored a great personal triumph and has won the admiration of baseball fans everywhere. But Huggins, patching up his creaking machine to the best of his ability, went through the ordeal, never giving up hope or overlooking a trick. Misinformed persons who once clamored for the release of Huggins, who, in their opinion, wasn't a real major-league manager, should hide their heads in shame. Hug surely has performed a baseball miracle.[68]

"The baseball season couldn't have been a greater success if it had been staged by Belasco and played by George M. Cohan," wrote John Kieran. "Five teams in the American League are entitled to at least a kind word for their efforts, and six teams in the National League did well enough to merit a measure of applause."[69] In the junior circuit, aside from the Yankees and Athletics, Kieran was referring to the stellar work by Dan Howley moving the Browns from seventh to third place, the recovery of the Senators in their final thirty games of the season, and the appearance of a nucleus of good players in Boston engineered by Bill Carrigan. All the clubs in the senior circuit deserved praise, with the exception of the Braves and Phillies.[70]

The Athletics' deficit proved to be too much to overcome, primarily due to the fact that the Yankees avoided collapsing themselves, playing .570 baseball since their largest lead and winning the crucial series at the Stadium in September. In the end, Bill McKechnie and Miller Huggins prevailed.

> The Yankees and Cards, veteran teams, did not burn themselves out under the inspirational urge of driving managers. Bill McKechnie and Miller Huggins are quiet plodders, content to let veterans solve their own problems. When the Cards were in their worst slump, hanging on by a thread to the first-place rung, McKechnie's only comment was, "Our slump can't last forever, and when the boys snap out of it we'll win." Huggins' comment was something similar when the Yankees were sliding down the ladder. "It had to come sometime, by the law of averages," remarked the mite manager.[71]

Baseball Magazine had probably the most accurate description of Miller Huggins in November 1928:

> A peculiar chap this Huggins—a man with the cool aloofness of a banker; the keen analytical sense of a trained engineer; the shrewd trading instinct of a David Harum; the eye for small detail of a watch maker; and the pessimism of a jilted lover! There is nothing bombastic about Huggins. He is not, cannot be, a driver of the McGraw type; the inspirational methods of a McCarthy or the coaxing wheedling art of a Robinson are not for him. He lacks the color of a Howley and the friendly effervescence of a Hendricks. He is as cold as an arctic iceberg; as methodical as a milkman; and about as much given to enthusiasm as a hitching post. Huggins approaches his baseball problems as a mathematician approaches an algebraic equation—and his campaign is planned with a mathematical precision that permits of variety or novelty only in its ratio to the human equation with which he is forced to deal.[72]

An early assessment of the World Series was that the Yankees were no match for the Cardinals and presented a lesser challenge than in 1926. The only healthy arm appeared to be Waite Hoyt, with George Pipgras appearing overworked. Heimach and Zachary would be no match for the National League champs.[73] The Yankee roster for the Fall Classic appears in table 13.3.

Table 13.3. Yankee Roster for the Fall Classic

Pitchers	Catchers	Infielders	Outfielders
Herb Pennock	Ben Bengough	Lou Gehrig	Bob Meusel
Waite Hoyt	Pat Colliins	Tony Lazzeri	Earle Combs
George Pipgras	John Grabowski	Mark Koenig	Babe Ruth
Fred Heimach	Bill Dickey	Joe Dugan	Ben Paschal
Henry Johnson		Mike Gazella	Cedric Durst
Tom Zachary		Leo Durocher	
Myles Thomas		Gene Robertson	
Rosy Ryan			

In the final game of the season, it was only fitting for the Babe to go deep for his fifty-fourth home run and for Waite Hoyt to be credited with his twenty-second victory. For whatever reason, twenty-two victories was the number that the Colonel had pulled out of the air to award Hoyt a bonus—$2,000 if he attained that number. It was officially Hoyt's twenty-third victory. The Yankees got a scare when Gehrig had to be taken out of the game after being hit in the face on a ground ball by Tiger left fielder John Stone.[74] When a groggy Gehrig arrived in New York the next day, his upper lip was swollen to twice its normal size, and he would need to have bridgework done. A female fan fainted when she witnessed the blood running down Gehrig's face.[75]

In the final analysis, it came down to pitching, which was the main concern for the Yankees going back to March in St. Petersburg. The saving grace ended up being the fourteen additional wins from George Pipgras. Newcomers Al Shealy, Hank Johnson, Arch Campbell, Fred Heimach, Stan Coveleski, Tom Zachary, and Rosy Ryan won thirty-two games in 1928, just one short of the thirty-three won by Shawkey, Ruether, and Shocker in 1927. Pennock and Hoyt were minus one victory, whereas Wilcy Moore and Myles Thomas came up twenty-one victories short.

The 1928 New York Yankees tried to defy the law of averages and actually top their performance of the previous year. In that regard, as the manager would have fully expected, the law of averages won.

IV

THE POSTSEASON

· *14* ·

Just the Way the Colonel Likes It

Here is advice from the very first page of the *Book of Pitching Truth*: Be ready to duck if you throw 'em wrong to Gehrig, or Meusel, or Ruth.

—*New York Herald Tribune*, October 6, 1928[1]

The 1928 World Series would be, officially counted, the twenty-fifth. The baseball world was hoping to see a rematch of the 1913 series between Connie Mack and John McGraw but had to settle instead for a rematch of the series from two years before. This World Series was somewhat of an anticlimax for both clubs and is described in the *Washington Post* as the "stagger series," since both teams were tired and worn, especially the Yankees, after the regular campaign.[2]

The series was scheduled to begin in New York, on October 4 and 5, before moving to St. Louis for three games on October 7, 8, and 9. If necessary, the sixth and seventh games would move back to New York, without an off day, on October 10 and 11. The games would begin at 1:30 p.m. local time. The umpires from the National League were Charles Rigler and Cy Pfirman, and Charles Owens and Bill McGowan from the American League. The official scorers were Burton Whitman of the *Boston Herald*, Sid Keener of the *St. Louis Times*, and Richards Vidmer of the *New York Times*. Graham McNamee and Phillips Carlin had been selected to broadcast the games for more than forty stations for the National Broadcasting Company, and Major J. Andrew White and Ted Husing for twenty-three stations for the Columbia Broadcasting Company.[3]

The Cardinals became the de facto favorite in the National League when the Pirates stumbled badly early in the season, and they became the clear favorite to beat the Yankees in the World Series. When it was officially

219

announced that Earle Combs was out of the postseason, the odds went to 5–3 on the Cardinals, with a chance to rise to 2–1.[4]

Albert Keane, sports editor for the *Hartford Courant*, dissented and predicted that the Yankees would win, writing,

> Common sense, logic, and the arguments advanced by experts from many sections of the realm of baseball may refute our belief, but once you have a hunch that one team will be a winner it is hard to shake it. That's how we stand on the Yankees. And maybe this hunch of ours lies in the fact that the Yankees, to use the Queen's English, have guts. The Cards are not a bit gamer than the New York team.[5]

Dan Daniel agreed:

> Those Yankees are hitters. They are great money players. They are quite likely to develop pitching strength almost on a par with that of the St. Louis club, which builds its hopes largely on it hurling potentialities. Beset with hurts, apparently forsaken by fortune, pursued by the relentless Athletics, the Yankees had to be quite a ball club to win the American League pennant. That New York ball club looks strong enough to retain the world championship. The issue very likely will be stretched out to the limit of seven games.[6]

Walter Johnson was an American Leaguer who had pitched for the Senators for twenty years. His prediction was dire for the Yankees:

> As the time nears for the start of the blue banner classic of baseball tomorrow, I have not changed my views in the slightest regarding the outcome. To me, the St. Louis Cardinals should make short work of the New York Yankees. It has been said often that Colonel Ruppert's team is what is known as a money team, meaning probably that they will produce for their admirers when they have to. In the long run, however, percentage counts, and it favors the Cards. As I said before, I will be pulling for the Yanks, but I cannot pick them to win.[7]

Among the reasons given by the "Big Train" were the "greater opposition" faced by the Cardinals throughout the year in the National League. The loss of Lazzeri, Combs, and Pennock would also be too much for the Yankees to overcome. Dugan and Koenig had suffered subpar years as well.[8]

"How do I figure this series with the Cardinals the favorites?" asked Huggins. "Well, how is anybody going to figure a World Series? How is anybody to predict a wild pitch like Miljus, a home run with a few on, a shift in weather that might ruin your star pitcher?"

He would be managing against a slightly different Cardinal team than that of 1926. Frank Frisch was now at second base for Rogers Hornsby, Jimmie Wilson was the new catcher for Bob O'Farrell, and Wattie Holm was at third base in place of Lester Bell.[9] And the Cardinals were not without injuries to key players. They had lost the services of outfielder Wally Roettger, who had been batting .341, on July 4, against the Cubs, and Tom Thevenow, their young shortstop, was out with a broken ankle. The injury occurred in Cincinnati, while sliding into second base, even though the ball was thrown to another base.[10]

Huggins discussed his pitching rotation for the series:

> I will start with Waite Hoyt, who just has passed his examination as an official and qualified undertaker and first-class embalmer. He'll do his stuff. I plan to use Pipgras on Friday and Zachary in St. Louis on Sunday. If Combs is out, Koenig will be the leadoff man. I am not counting on Combs, so if he comes around I will be all the happier. Benny Bengough will catch the entire series. At third we will alternate Dugan against left-handers and Robertson against right-handers.
>
> Will I pitch Henry Johnson? Yes, but not away from the Stadium. As a matter of fact, I have given no thought to the pitching beyond the third game. By that time we may be so far in front that it won't matter much who will go in the fourth. Maybe it will be Hoyt. He may work three times in this series on account of those days of rest spent in jumping to and from St. Louis.[11]

Pennock would not see any action but would stay in the Yankee dugout throughout the series, with the pain in his left arm worsened to the point where he could barely lift it to eat.[12] The Cardinals used left-hander and twenty-one-game winner Bill Sherdel to open the Series.

Bill McKechnie and Miller Huggins, along with some players, wrote articles—many ghostwritten—carried in several newspapers, doping the series immediately after the regular season. The Cards' skipper boasted about his infield, starting with his first baseman. "Bottomley, the sunny one; Frisch, the brilliant and one of the best base runners the world has ever seen; Maranville, the mighty one, who, after fourteen years, comes back as a regular in another World Series; the painstaking High, mentally alert and ever trying. You know, the longer I look at it, the better it looks. Perhaps, you'll think so, too."[13] The regular outfield of the Cardinals consisted of the lesser-known Chick Hafey, Taylor Douthit, and George Harper. The reserves were super subs Ernie Orsatti and Pepper Martin, along with reserve outfielder Ray Blades.

"Some people think our defeat by the Cardinals two years ago will affect Yankee play in this series," penned the Yankee manager. "I don't think so.

Two years ago, when we played the Cardinals, the Yankees were a young club, inexperienced and green. Three men on that 1926 infield, for instance, were playing their first season of big-league baseball and their first World Series."[14]

Huggins further explained his pitching and hitting situations:

> Strange as it may seem to the casual observer, I am not worried about my pitching. True, I have not Pennock, and Pennock is the greatest World Series pitcher I ever saw. But I have known for a long time that Pennock wouldn't be in there—and I've made the best of it. In Hoyt, Pipgras, and Zachary I believe we have three men capable of making trouble for any ball club.
>
> My hitting ought to be strong. The Yankees, following a slump of six weeks, have been hitting with power during the last two weeks and seem to be nearing the crest of their slugging power once more. I believe they will go into the series hitting just as well as they have the last two weeks.[15]

In the October 1 installment of the *Hartford Courant*, Lou Gehrig wrote,

> In the first place, the series this year, regardless of who may win the pennant, will bring together two teams that are tired and worn out by the tough season's play. It will bring together two teams that have been straining for weeks to win, teams that will probably be on the verge of cracking. I look to see a series that is hard fought, a series that goes six and possibly seven games before it is decided.[16]

"A battle?" said the Babe. He continued,

> Huh, they figure to be easy for us this time. Hoyt ought to take two himself. You notice we're hitting again. That's what counts these days. When we're hitting we hit 'em all. And speaking of hitting, those fifty-four homers weren't so bad for me, after all. Hadda pretty good year. This makes my ninth World Series. Try and tie that one. There's more than one way to set a record.[17]

GAME 1: THURSDAY, OCTOBER 4, 1928; ATTENDANCE 61,425; TIME 1:49

It was a beautiful, clear day in the Bronx for the opening game. Scalpers, with an oversupply of tickets, saw prices plunge from as much as $15.00 down to $2.00 in the span of a half an hour as game time approached. It was a much more orderly scene than what occurred in the May and September series against the Athletics. There were 61,000 fans in and out, who watched Waite Hoyt perform without one bead of perspiration.[18]

"The timely hitting of Koenig, Ruth, and Gehrig of the Yankees' top file of hitters, aided in a prodigious measure by a home run by Meusel, sent the New York runs over the plate, and the gorgeous pitching of Waite Hoyt kept the Cardinals from sending runs over the plate," said W. B. Hanna of the *New York Herald Tribune*.[19] The only hint of the crippled Yankees was Durocher's replacement of Lazzeri at second base in the seventh inning. Just as in both teams' initial workouts, the Cardinals seemed tight and the Yankees loose.

Hoyt retired the Cardinals in order in the first inning. Taylor Douthit rubbed his hands with a little dirt, got behind in the count, and grounded to Lazzeri. Andy High filed out to Cedric Durst, and Frank Frisch grounded to Mark Koenig. Bill Sherdel got Paschal and Koenig to fly to Chick Hafey in left field, but Ruth and Gehrig followed with back-to-back doubles to score the first run in the 1928 Fall Classic.

Jim Bottomley led off the second inning with a walk, but Waite Hoyt retired the next ten Redbirds, until George Harper's single in the fifth inning. Sherdel got the Yankees in order in the second and third innings, but Meusel homered to the opposite field after a Ruth double to put the Yankees up by three runs. Hoyt remained in control, only yielding a walk to Douthit in the sixth inning. In the seventh, Bottomley got the second Cardinal hit of the day. The Babe just kept his hands on his knees and didn't bother to move, a home run almost in the same spot as Meusel's to cut the Yankee lead to two runs. Hafey followed with a long fly ball, which Meusel made a great catch on, and Harper fouled out to Dugan.

McKechnie looked to his bench in the eighth inning. After Jimmie Wilson lined out to Ben Paschal, Ernie Orsatti hit for Rabbit Maranville and drew a walk, but Wattie Holm, batting for Bill Sherdel, skied to center field, and Taylor Douthit struck out. The Cardinals argued that Douthit had stepped out of the batter's box on one of the strikes, but to no avail. Tom Thevenow replaced Maranville at shortstop, and Syl Johnson was the new pitcher. After Johnson retired Hoyt and Paschal, there were three straight hits by Koenig, Ruth, and Gehrig, adding another run to make it a 4–1 lead. The Cardinals had the heart of their order up in the ninth inning. High fouled off two pitches and swung and missed at a third. Frisch nearly had an infield hit, but Koenig made a great play to nab him at first. Bottomley got the Cardinals' third hit off of Hoyt, but Hafey recorded the final out of the game by flying out to Ruth.[20]

Bill McKechnie commented after the loss:

> That was an easy game to lose. Waite Hoyt pitched a marvelous game. There was nothing we could do about it. He was just in there, and right, and that's all there was to it. Little Lefty Sherdel pitched a great game too, and his own brand of hurling would have won nine out of ten contests. Hoyt deserves to win. Don't think this series is on the chutes, though. The

Yankees won the first game of the 1926 series, too, but the Cardinals won the championship. Pete Alexander will be in there tomorrow, and there'll be another story.

The first game of a World Series is a good one to win. I'd have liked to have won it. But it does not mean everything. We're not discouraged. We have a hustling club.[21]

The Yankees and their famed slugger took the opening victory in stride: "Looks like the cripples did pretty well," said the Babe, as he tried to beat a teammate to the showers. Elated about his three hits, he added, "I was sure due for some. That first double off Sherdel was a fastball over the outside corner, the second a nice slow ball inside. I guess that Sherdel is a cousin of mine after all.[22]

"My knee began to bother me along toward the end of the game," said Ruth. "But as long as it does not pop on me I'll be alright. Sherdel pitched a good game, but Hoyt was even better. What we've got to do now is win the next three."[23]

Hoyt reflected on his performance, stating, "I suppose I did pitch a good game, but I did better when I shut out the Giants in the second game of the 1921 series. But did you stop and see that throw Koenig made on Frankie Frisch in the ninth inning? Greatest play I ever saw."[24] Hoyt continued,

I did not get physically tired, but I was going along, and they weren't hitting me hard, so I was becoming mentally careless. Along about the seventh inning my mind strayed from its concentration upon Bottomley, and I pitched a fastball straight through the middle. There is no excuse for it. It did not get away from me. It went for a home run. That hit served to bring my mind back on the job. I had a lot of luck getting past Hafey. He didn't hit any today, but that doesn't mean he won't hit next time. Mark Koenig made a great play on Frisch's grounder. I thought sure that was a hit. The boys played a nice game. We hit and they didn't. But they've got a good ball club.[25]

"Hoyt was great," said Huggins. "My men played a nice game. Our hits were timely. Tomorrow, I'll either pitch Pipgras or Zachary. I haven't made up my mind. I've told them both to be ready to pitch tomorrow."[26]

Sherdel wished that he could have that one pitch to Meusel back, commenting, "All day I fed Meusel low balls on the outside, except just once. My control slipped, and I tossed him a curve that broke high on the outside. You saw what he does to that kind of a ball. Those Yankees are a troublesome club."[27] He later added,

I was in the hole too often today. They had me so that I couldn't fool around with my slow ball. I don't throw that up there for them to hit.

I throw it for them to tease them and make them swing. The ball that Meusel hit was too high and too far outside. I won't say it got away from me. It was just in the wrong place, that's all. And he socked it. That second ball Ruth hit wasn't a well-hit ball. Like every team, we play him for a right-field hitter, and it was just too bad he had to hit it into center field. If anybody else had to hit it Douthit would have been there to catch it. It was a good game, but it was tough that their hits should have been bunched as they were.

It looks like I am not supposed to win one. But I'm not discouraged. All I ask is that I hold them to four hits next time. I'll win. That's the third close game I've lost to this team.[28]

GAME 2: FRIDAY, OCTOBER 5, 1928;
ATTENDANCE 60,717; TIME 2:04

The crowd was slightly less than the one that had gathered for the first game, and speculators were disappointed at the low demand for tickets. The lines were shorter than expected for bleacher and unreserved seats, with less than fifty people in line for tickets at 7:00 a.m. and about two hundred people an hour later, leaving almost 230 policeman on duty with nothing to do.[29]

The box score and results of the second game resembled something from earlier in the season, when the Yankees used to put the Colonel at ease by scoring early and often. The mite manager made two lineup changes, inserting Durst in center field against the righty Alexander, and giving Gene Robertson the start at third base. McKechnie used the same lineup against the righty George Pipgras.

There was a realization that McKechnie's decision to give the ball to Alex was based on sentiment as much as baseball sense, but he had pitched regularly all year and chalked up more than 240 innings on an average of between four and five days' rest. The forty-one year old immortal knew his arm was fading but was confident he could win.[30]

Alexander was quite assured about pitching to Ruth and Gehrig, as he wrote before the World Series:

> One question that was pumped at us pretty often before the 1926 World Series has been absent from the list this year, and I guess that's because the fans remember what we did then and know that we certainly will follow the same procedure. That is the old question as to whether we are going to pitch to Babe Ruth and Lou Gehrig. Of course we are going to pitch to both of them. We stopped those sluggers in 1926, except in one game, where young pitchers put the ball in the wrong spot and the Babe slammed it out of the park. We have a better chance of stopping them this year, for

neither Ruth nor Gehrig is as dangerous as he was last year or the year before. Ruth has tumbled far down—for him—and we'll treat him just as we would any other hitter.[31]

The Cardinals threatened in their first at bat, when Pipgras walked High and Frisch after retiring the leadoff batter. But, after going to a full count, he got the dangerous Bottomley to foul out to Bengough and then struck out left fielder Chick Hafey to end the inning.

The Yankees struck Alexander for three runs in their first at bat. Durst led off with a screaming single off of Frisch's glove, Koenig flied out to left field, and Ruth walked on four pitches. With one swing, Gehrig smashed one deep into the right-field stands to give the Yankees a three-run lead. Alex fanned Meusel, and Lazzeri hit back to the box.

The bottom of the order for the Cardinals came back to tie the game in the second inning. George Pipgras walked George Harper, who was sixth in the lineup. Wilson doubled, scoring Harper, and Maranville's single sent Wilson to third. Lazzeri then threw wild to first base on a ground ball hit by Alexander, scoring Wilson and sending Maranville to third. The Rabbit scored the tying run on a double play, Koenig to Lazzeri to Gehrig. High fouled out to Robertson to end the inning.

The great Alexander faced the bottom of the Yankee lineup in their half and got Robertson to ground out to Bottomley but walked Bengough on four pitches. Bengough then went to second base on a Pipgras sacrifice. The leadoff man, Cedric Durst, singled to center field to score Bengough and put the Yankees back in the lead.

The back-and-forth battle appeared to continue as Frisch led off the third inning with a single and stole second. Bottomley failed to advance the runner by striking out, but Hafey's groundout moved Frisch to third. Harper went down on strikes, leaving the deficit at one.

It all came apart for Alex in the Yankee third inning against the heart of the order. The Babe led off with a single, and Lou followed with a walk on five pitches. Meusel's ground-rule double scored Ruth and sent Gehrig to third. High, at third, made a great play on a short hop grounder by Lazzeri, and the runners had to hold. With one out, the next four batters consisted of two reserves and the weak-hitting battery, but Bengough's pop fly to short right field scored Gehrig and reloaded the bases for Pipgras.

With his team trailing, 6–3, McKechnie replaced his Hall of Fame veteran with the thirty-seven-year-old lefty Clarence Mitchell, who plunked Pipgras in the stomach and then gave up a single to Paschal, hitting for Durst. The base hit put the Yankees ahead by five runs, but Bengough was out at the plate on Paschal's single. Then Mitchell got Koenig to pop out to end the inning.

George Pipgras got better as the game progressed. He was sensational in the next four innings after making an adjustment in his release point and throwing more curveballs than usual—and for strikes. The only Redbird to reach base was Maranville on an error by Koenig. A single by Frisch in the eighth inning and a walk to Maranville in the ninth were the only hiccups for the rest of the game. Joe Dugan's pinch-hit sacrifice fly in the seventh scored Meusel to round out a Game 2, 9–3 victory. [32]

In the October 6 edition of the *New York Herald Tribune*, Don Skene wrote the following, referring to Miller Huggins: "The Singer midget of the big baseball show, when pressed for a statement, finally admitted with quivering lip and doleful eyes that the Yankees had won and had a chance to win the series."[33]

"We got the hitting today," said Huggins. "When our club is hitting we win ball games. That's all there is to it. How many hits did the Cardinals get? Four, you say? Well, that just goes to show that you can't win without hitting."[34]

"You can't win ball games without base hits," reaffirmed McKechnie. "We aren't licked yet. The club is still full of fight and pepper, and we are eager to get at the Yanks again on our home grounds. I think we'll start hitting that ball when we get home. I think we'll come back to New York in the lead."[35]

Alexander was searching for answers, saying the following:

> I pitched to the Yanks just exactly as I did two years ago, and I was putting the ball just where I wanted to put it. But they hit everything I had. I put everything I had into the pitch that Gehrig hit for a home run. I wanted to give him a low "screwball" on the outside corner. When the ball left my hand, I knew it was headed for the exact spot that I aimed it at and that I felt was Gehrig's weak alley. But he stepped into it and hit it a hundred miles. I can't understand why everything went wrong out there for me. I guess it was just one of those days when you can't win no matter what you do.[36]

"I'm making no predictions," said Huggins. "We're just going along playing ball. But I'll say this, we're going to be tough to beat from now on. We're getting the hitting."[37]

George Pipgras thought that he was more prepared for this game than last year against the Pirates. He commented,

> I don't know where my control went to in the first innings. I was letting the ball go too soon or something. It got better as I went along. Most of my trouble was in controlling a half-speed ball, the one I just wanted to get across the plate in a pinch. Jim Bottomley and Frisch were swinging at

curves all afternoon. The only things I can really control anyway are very fast balls and fast curves.[38]

The Cardinals felt that they were still not a beaten team and were optimistic about coming back in St. Louis. The Yankees, however, feared them much less than they had the Pirates the previous year at this same point. "We will not return for another game in New York," announced Meusel over breakfast the next morning, as the Babe nodded in agreement. "There is no pepper in that outfit," said another Yankee. "It misses a scrapper like Hornsby. You can feel it out there in the field and at the plate. They stand out there like a lot of cigar store Indians, waiting for something to happen, and praying that when it does happen it will help dear old St. Louis."[39]

GAME 3: SUNDAY, OCTOBER 7, 1928; ATTENDANCE 39,602; TIME 2:00

There was a huge homecoming planned for the Cardinals on Saturday, even though they were down two games in the series. There were eighteen automobiles, with the first carrying the mayor, the team's owner, Sam Breadon, and Branch Rickey, the vice president. The second contained the commissioner and presidents of both leagues, while the third carried members of the Cardinals' front office. Manager McKechnie, team captain Frisch, and the team physician rode in the fourth, while the remaining cars carried the players.[40]

Coming to within an eyelash of landing in the minor leagues a few weeks before, Tom Zachary now loomed as the wild card of the World Series. He was the Yankees' third pitcher, after Hoyt and Pipgras. "I am a greater pitcher now than I ever was," said Zachary. "I ain't figuring the Cardinals any different from any other ball club. They can be stopped just like any other team. There's some pretty good hitters in the American League, and I've stopped them."[41]

Zachary was confident that he would get the ball against the Cardinals; he was undefeated in World Series play, beating the Giants twice in 1924, but only used for two innings by Harris against the Pirates the next year, being a left-hander. "Where I got it on these other pitchers in a World Series game," he said, "is I don't get nervous. All batters look alike to me. I don't get scared in a pinch. When there's men on bases and the going gets tough, that's when I get good."[42]

The Cardinals had to return 75,000 requests, or 40,000 letters, for 27,000 reserved seats at Sportsman's Park for the World Series. Almost everyone who mailed a letter wanted two seats.[43] No team to this point had ever come back to win a World Series after dropping the first two games. The situation for the Cardinals was not hopeless, but they were no doubt disappointed that they couldn't come away with a win against either Hoyt or Pipgras and come home to Sportsman's Park tied against the softer part of the Yankee staff. Their hottest pitcher, right-hander Jesse Haines, would face southpaw Tom Zachary. McKechnie inserted the righty-swinging Wattie Holm in right field for George Harper. Huggins stuck with Gene Robertson at third base and the lefty-swinging Cedric Durst against the Cardinals' righty.[44]

Haines retired the side in order in the first inning, but Zachary got off to a shaky start. After Douthit hit back to the box, High singled, Frisch singled, and Bottomley tripled both runners home for the Cardinals' first lead of the series. But Bottomley was stranded after Hafey grounded to Lazzeri and Holm struck out.

Gehrig quickly got a run back with a leadoff home run in the top of the second. He drove a high, inside fastball off of the roof in right field and into the street. Zachary managed to escape damage in the pitted infield in the bottom half by recording two strikeouts and a fly-ball out. The Cardinals could not take advantage of errors on ground balls to Robertson and Lazzeri.

The Yankees went into the fourth inning still trailing by a run. Ruth singled after Koenig grounded to first base. Center fielder Taylor Douthit tried to make a shoestring grab of Gehrig's line drive, but the ball went under his feet and into center field for an inside-the-park home run and a 3–2 lead. The Cardinals tied the score in the fifth inning, when Zachary hit the leadoff batter, Douthit, who scored on High's double. Frisch sacrificed High to third base, but Bottomley fouled out to Bengough, and Hafey lined out to center field.

Jesse Haines would face eight Yankees in the sixth inning, and the Cardinals were suddenly staring at a three-run deficit in what was an unconventional rally. Koenig led off with a single but was forced out by Ruth. Haines then elected to walk the red-hot Gehrig, but the Cardinal defense betrayed their pitcher. The next batter, Meusel, grounded to High at third base, who began what he hoped would be an inning-ending double play. Instead, Gehrig, although out on a force play, crashed into Frisch, whose throw to Bottomley at first was wide. The Babe attempted to score from third, but the throw to the catcher, Wilson, had him beat, leaving no other option but to force a collision. The 220-pound Ruth made impact on the 200-pound Wilson, and the catcher dropped the ball. When he recovered, he threw wild trying to catch Meusel at second, who then took third base. Haines walked Lazzeri. With runners at the corners and two out, the Yankees pulled a double steal, as Meusel stole home and Lazzeri second. Robertson's single scored Lazzeri, but Haines got Bengough to fly out to Holm in right field.

"If he hits me any other way than he did, why, then, he's out," said Jimmie Wilson about his collision with Ruth during the inning. "But he kicked the side of my head first, then struck my chest protector here, and I went over. You are bound to spread when a 225-pound guy falls on top of you. I want to have the ball in my duke and be ready for Mr. Ruth if he gets a chance to come ea-ing into the plate tomorrow."[45]

Zachary retired the Cardinals in the bottom of the sixth inning in order. The Yankees got to Syl Johnson, who replaced Jesse Haines, for another run in the seventh inning when Cedric Durst reached second base on Chick Hafey's error in right field and was driven home on a two-out single by Ruth. Johnson struck out Meusel after walking Gehrig to end the inning with the Cardinals trailing by a score of 7–3. This would be the final score.

Ray Blades led off the Cardinal seventh as a pinch hitter for the pitcher and struck out. After a single by Douthit, a fly-ball out by High, and walk to Frisch, Zachary got Bottomley to ground to Gehrig. Flint Rhem was the third Cardinal pitcher of the game, and he retired the Yankees in order in the eighth and ninth innings.

Hafey and Holm started the Cardinal eighth, with their club still trailing, 7–3, with singles, but Jimmie Wilson grounded into a 6–4–3 double play, and Maranville fouled out to end the threat. It was a difficult double play turned by Durocher, who had just replaced Lazzeri that inning. Zachary struck out pinch hitter Ernie Orsatti to begin the ninth inning, Douthit grounded to short, and High lined out to Ruth in left field. The gloom began to set in for Cardinal fans.[46]

"I'll be doggoned if they look like a pennant-winning club to me," said Lazzeri. "I can't understand how the Cardinals managed to win out. They must have played better ball than they have shown us. Didn't they look terrible today? We'll beat them tomorrow and go home."[47]

The Cardinals could not believe that they were staring at a 3–0 deficit but understood why. "We are terrible," said McKechnie. The manager elaborated:

> In that sixth inning, when we were throwing the ball around, they made three runs when they should not have made any. That was the turning point of the game. They didn't beat us; we beat ourselves. There's nothing I can say. We're simply terrible. There's no use talking to the men. What can they say?[48]

"They got the breaks of the game, that's all," continued McKechnie. "But if they can win three games in a row, we can do the same thing. I expect to start either Sherdel or Alexander tomorrow. I am not naming anybody, but some of our players have played better ball this season than we showed today."[49]

The Yankees knew what formula was working for them: Their twenty-two hits in the three games had resulted in twenty runs. "We are hitting well," said a smiling Huggins, "and getting the most out of our hits. Durocher's double play in the eighth was the best fielding play of the game. It broke up the ball game. They had two men on and none out, and it stopped the Cardinals in their tracks. It will either be Hoyt or Johnson tomorrow." [50]

Lou Gehrig had driven in eight runs so far on five hits, for a total of fifteen bases. "The first one I hit was a knuckleball. The second one was a fastball," said Gehrig. "Believe me, I ran. I was almost on top of the Babe when I crossed the plate. So far, great. I tol' ya we could beat these guys."[51]

The quiet hero of the day was Tom Zachary, who said, "Wal, I ain't kicking. I might a done worse. And then again, I might a done better. But we won; so it's okay. Looks like we got 'em on the run. It was purty warm out there today. I begun to get tired in the legs toward the finish. Yas, sir, purty warm."[52]

GAME 4: MONDAY, OCTOBER 8, 1928; POSTPONED

After a series of thunderstorms barreled through the city of St. Louis during the morning with no sign of clearing, the commissioner of baseball ordered Game 4 postponed. Landis was roundly criticized, but he explained his decision. "The field is unplayable," he said. "As the left field is still underwater and the other outfields are wet and slippery, it would be unfair to either team to play. Even if the rain had stopped early this morning and I found the ground in the condition it is in, I would not permit playing." Sportsman's Park drained very slowly. The field was caked in mud, with no real, modern system for drying the field. With an extra day of rest, Henry Johnson would have to put his first World Series start on hold. This was the first postponement for the Yankees after twenty-nine consecutive World Series games.[53]

It was an opportunity for the Babe to visit a boy at St. Luke's Hospital who was reportedly dying with a broken neck. The Babe was there at 11:00 a.m. and gave the youngster an autographed ball and promised him a season pass for Sportsman's Park the next year.[54]

GAME 4: TUESDAY, OCTOBER 9, 1928;
ATTENDANCE 37,331; TIME 2:25

The emotions of Cardinal fans suddenly went from feelings of hope to feelings of despair. The former was in the air before the third game, with nearly

40,000 fans in a sea of Cardinal red and clanging cowbells. The stands were once again packed for Game 4 on what was a hot and hazy day in St. Louis.[55]

Bill McKechnie shook up his lineup for the fourth game. He inserted Ernie Orsatti in center field to try and light a spark and Earl Smith as catcher for Jimmie Wilson. He also went back to George Harper in the outfield. With an extra day, Miller Huggins went to the man who had held out during spring training, Waite Hoyt. It was up to the merry mortician to bury the Cardinals in a rematch of Game 1. Huggins continued to play lefty, righty in center field, with the righty-swinging Ben Paschal against the lefty Bill Sherdel. Joe Dugan got the start at third base.

The game remained scoreless until the bottom of the third inning, when the leadoff hitter, Orsatti, stretched a single into a double, as Paschal was playing too deep. Orsatti took third on High's bunt single. Frisch's fly ball to center field was deep enough to score Orsatti. The rally stopped at one run after Bottomley fouled out to Bengough and Harper struck out on Hoyt's curveball; however, the lead was short-lived, as Sherdel served up a long drive to deep right field, to the Babe, in the top of the fourth.

The Cards, desperate to grab some kind of momentum, retook the lead in their half of the fourth inning. Earl Smith led off with his second single but was forced out at second base. Koenig threw wild to first base on Maranville's grounder, with Maranville taking second. Sherdel skied to center field for the second out. Hoyt struck out Orsatti, but not before he threw wild attempting to pick off Maranville at second base, allowing the go-ahead run.

The Yankees threatened in the fifth after leadoff singles by Hoyt and Paschal but came away empty after a pop-fly out by Koenig and groundouts by Ruth and Meusel. The Yankees also wasted two leadoff singles in the next inning, as Sherdel retired Bengough, Hoyt, and Paschal. The Cards wasted a walk and single in their half of the sixth inning, leaving the score in their favor, 2–1.

The seventh inning was a terrible one for the Cardinals. The Yankees scored four runs to take a three-run lead. Sherdel got Koenig to pop out to short, but he could not get the twin killers. The Babe appeared to face two strikes, but the second called strike was reversed to a ball by home plate umpire Cy Pfirman since the Babe was not in the batter's box. The Cardinals argued vehemently. After Sherdel threw two more out of the strike zone, the Babe took him out over the right-field roof.[56] Lou followed with a home run that touched the roof. After Meusel smashed a single, McKechnie replaced Sherdel with Alexander. Lazzeri greeted him with a double—or more of a misplay by Orsatti and Hafey—and Meusel stopped at third base. Gene Robertson had replaced Dugan at third base, and his ground ball scored Meusel, who beat the throw to the plate. Earle Combs pinch-hit for Bengough and drove the ball to right field, deep enough to score Lazzeri with the fourth run of the inning.

Pat Collins took the backstop position, Leo Durocher replaced Tony Lazzeri at second, and Cedric Durst was the new center fielder as Waite Hoyt retired the side in order in the seventh inning. The fans got into the act when Gehrig was bumped going for Frisch's pop-up, but he grabbed his second foul for the third out.

The Yankees continued to exact revenge on old Alex. Durst led off the eighth inning with a home run. After Koenig's groundout, the Babe followed with his third straight circuit clout. The Cardinals were down to their final six outs, trailing 7–2. The Babe was greeted with a shower of pop bottles as he went out to left field. Bottomley led off the inning with his second strikeout, and then a single by Hafey was quickly wiped out by a double play.

Now down to their last three outs, catcher Earl Smith began the ninth with his third single. Pepper Martin was inserted as a pinch runner and took second base on a defensive indifference call. Maranville popped to Koenig for the first out. Wattie Holm pinch-hit for Alexander and grounded to Koenig for the second out as Martin scored the Cardinals' third and final run. Hoyt then gave up singles to Orsatti and High with two outs and the bases empty. Leaving it up to the "Fordham Flash," Frank Frisch hit one foul down the left-field line, which landed in the glove of Babe Ruth, who grabbed it on the run and sprinted into the Cardinal dugout to avoid the fans.[57] The Yankees had won the World Series, after almost following their great season in 1927, with what to this day would still have been considered one of the greatest collapses in the history of American team sports!

"I never saw such a game," said Huggins. "What a ball club! Don't talk to me, because I don't want to say anything. We won and I'm glad."[58]

"I was terrible," said a more withdrawn Waite Hoyt. "They had me in a hole all afternoon. But once the wrecking crew went to work it was all over. It's good to have Ruth playing with you instead of against you. I never saw him have such a good time playing a ball game."[59]

The Babe set or tied several records, with three home runs in one game and thirteen lifetime in the World Series. He hit three home runs during Game 4 in the 1926 World Series in the same park. He tied a record for total bases, with twenty-two, and set a record with nine runs scored. Lou Gehrig broke Bob Meusel's record, with nine runs batted in, and his five consecutive walks was a record. The Babe's .625 average, with ten hits in sixteen at bats, was also a record.

Bill McKechnie lamented, "Give them all the glory they deserve. They beat us, and we looked terrible. But what can you do when you don't make hits?"[60]

In the October 10 issue of the *New York Herald Tribune*, Grantland Rice wrote,

> By winding up this series in four straight games, the Yankees proved that when it comes to a money series, they have no equals in history. A year ago they wrecked the Pirates four days in a row. This last season they beat the Athletics, their only rivals, sixteen games out of twenty-two. They faced the Cardinals with their star pitchers and one of their best outfielders crippled and out, with Ruth limping, Lazzeri lame, and others injured or hurt.[61]

Ruth and Gehrig, together in the four games, had a total of sixteen hits and forty-one total bases. Hoyt's clincher was a record for most World Series games won, with six.[62]

"I sent them where I wanted to," said Bill Sherdel of his pitches. "I hated to see them sail out of the park, but a ball game is a ball game. Ruth is just a great, terrible hitter. More power to him. I'm glad he ain't in the National league."[63]

The total players' pool was a record $419,736.60, of which $293,815.62 was awarded on a 60–40 basis to the two pennant winners. The Yankees' share was $176,289.37, the Cardinals' $117,526.25. Each Yankee regular was awarded $5,531.91, with approximately $4,800 appropriated to various other team personnel and the widow of Urban Shocker. Two players who had joined the team late in the season, Tom Zachary and Fred Heimach, as well as Wilcy Moore, were voted full shares. Stan Coveleski was voted half a share. The Cardinals received $4,197.37 in twenty-eight shares. The remaining $125,920.98 went to the teams who had finished the regular season in the first division.[64]

Miller Huggins was weaned during the Deadball Era, but he left any fondness of those days in the past:

> This Yankee club is the most destructive in the history of baseball. Is this the best of all the great Yankee clubs? Why, there is no question about it. I know that some of the older players, with a fine regard for pitching strength, point to the 1923 team, which had Hoyt, Pennock, Mays, Bush, Shawkey, and Jones in the box, and Pipp, Ward, Scott, and Dugan in the infield, as the greatest.
>
> But they have the wrong angle. Give me destructive ability—the faculty for going out and crashing the opposition down. There never was a club like this, with hitters like Ruth and Gehrig. They overawe, they knock

down, they accomplish the seemingly impossible, and they do the most unaccountable feats in the face of seemingly impossible handicaps.[65]

Regarding the World Series, Huggins stated,

> When the Cardinals saw their standby driven out by a home run barrage after having failed with Sherdel, they realized all was lost. They knew that Alexander was done as a starter in this series. They began to have their doubts about Sherdel, and I don't think they were so awfully sure about Haines.
>
> The second most important break of the series was that home run by Babe Ruth in the seventh inning yesterday, his second of the game. This blow tied the score, and it so upset Sherdel that he put one over for Gehrig to drive over the roof, too.
>
> Just as soon as Gehrig hit that ball and gave us one to spare, I knew that the series was over. But above everything else stood the knockout over Alexander last Friday. It hurt the Cardinals incurably, and it gave us a tremendous psychological edge.
>
> That game yesterday, with Ruth hitting those three home runs, gave me the greatest thrill of my whole baseball career. The Cardinals again were at a big disadvantage. Once more they were forced from the start to play defensive ball, and again many of them were too tense. They went to bat and swung at anything.[66]

Incidentally, Bill McKechnie did not make the many strategic mistakes with which he has been charged. His critics have judged his tactics from the calm outlook of the man in the stands, whereas he had to work against big odds all the way.[67]

Waite Hoyt added the following:

> I did not have my speed, and I did not have my stuff, but I was helped by an unlooked-for aid. That damp, slick dirt got on the ball a lot and made it do all sorts of tricks for me. The Cards kept hollering that the ball was sailing, and Pfirman kept showing them that there were no abrasions on it. On top of it all, the Cardinals were overanxious and ready to hit at almost anything. And there were seven left-handers in that revised batting order, with Orsatti and Smith. Great credit belongs to Huggins, the best manager in the business.[68]

The Yankees set or reset numerous team records. They broke the Cubs' record of six World Series wins in a row, with eight; and the Yankees' five home runs in Game 4 was a record, along with nine in the series. Moreover, Miller Huggins tied Connie Mack and John McGraw with three World Series titles.[69]

Hundreds of fans greeted the Yankees at Grand Central Station on Thursday, October 11. The crowd grew to more than 1,000 as the team deboarded and marched toward the Biltmore Hotel to be greeted by Governor Smith. It was a display of hero worship, with the largest applause reserved for the Babe, who was preceded by the World Series' other stars, Waite Hoyt and Lou Gehrig.[70]

Afterword

$\mathcal{O}$n his forty-ninth birthday and thirtieth year in professional baseball, Miller Huggins confided to sportswriter Dan Daniel, at the end of April 1928, that his first choice in baseball was to be in some kind of ownership capacity. He recounted his career from the beginning, when he looked at a bar of soap and adopted the name "Proctor" so that his father would not find out he was playing baseball on Sunday. Said Huggins,

I speak from the angle of a man who not only loves baseball but likes financial success and ease in the years past fifty. I really have no cause for complaint. I have achieved success under a liberal ownership, which has made me happy and content. But from way back, I have nursed ideas of financial independence on my fiftieth birthday—ideas of being my own boss, without worries of any kind. Had I followed my inclination to become an owner, I would now be on that Easy Street about which I dreamed.

I saw this coming—plants like Yankee Stadium and the Polo Grounds. I saw it, and yet my love for playing the game was so great that it kept me from cashing in on that vision. Had I grabbed that Minneapolis chance, I would be a millionaire now. In recent years I have had the opportunity to reform. I have had a chance to become a manager-owner in the majors. But Colonel Ruppert and I seem to be definite partners in this Yankee enterprise. It is too late to start building all over again somewhere else.

I see stadiums seating 100,000 [throughout] the big circuits. And it won't be very long before this dream will become a reality. Baseball is a big business now, but it will become twice as big in the next twenty years. That's why I tell the young player with brains to save and to build his ambitions for the future on the business side of baseball.

The progress made by baseball since I joined the St. Paul club at $125 a month in 1901 is amazing. Just imagine paying $150,000 for two

237

youngsters like Lary and Reese who never have been tested! Imagine major-league clubs worth millions and millions as compared with the $125,000 [that] Charley Murphy paid for the Chicago Cubs in the comparatively modern era. It's staggering. When I was sold by St. Paul to the Cincinnati Reds in 1904, I held out for the princely salary of $3,000 a year and a piece of the purchase price.[1]

Miller Huggins wrote about the stages of building a winning ball club in the November 1924 edition of *Baseball Magazine* as the Yankees were going for their fourth straight pennant and were in a tight race with the Senators. Huggins said, "The first stage of baseball success is all fireworks and general celebration. The second stage comes when you have won so long that people are tired of seeing you win. Then your job is pure hard work, with the obstacles growing heavier all the time and public favor rapidly diminishing."[2]

The Yankees were in the second stage, having completed their second pennant three-peat in the last eight years in 1928, along with their first World Series repeat. But their future decades-long dominance of baseball was not a foregone conclusion. The team's one World Series in the next seven years looks like a hiccup in the team encyclopedia, but it was their worst stretch until the twelve-year drought that followed the 1964 season.

They did not fall by the wayside after the 1928 season, although it may have seemed that way. "Miller Huggins was left sitting in the midst of the most expensive baseball wreckage the baseball world has seen. The Yankee powerhouse was all wet," said Ralph McGill of the *Atlanta Constitution* shortly before Huggins's death in September 1929.[3]

The Colonel wanted to see his club become only the second team to win four straight pennants, but, on September 3, 1929, Huggins conceded the pennant to Connie Mack after a third straight loss at Shibe Park buried them for good, thirteen and a half games behind the pace. The Athletics led the Yankees by nine and a half games on July 4, 1929. The lead increased to seventeen games on Friday, September 20, which was the day Miller Huggins entered St. Vincent's Catholic Medical Center for erysipelas, a skin infection.

Huggins had not been in good health since the spring and had suffered from severe headaches during the team's last western swing in mid-August. He died five days later, on September 25, at 5:15 in the evening. Blood transfusions may have been the cause of blood poisoning from an infection beneath his left eye from a week before. There were also complications from high fever and influenza. He was fifty years old and passed away with his sister, with whom he was very close, and brother at his side. All games in the American League were called off the next day.[4]

What continued in the American League was yet more race suicide. The Athletics blew the race wide open during the first week of June 1929, the last week of July 1930, and the third week of July 1931. Lefty Grove and George Earnshaw blossomed as the best pitching tandem in baseball, with consistent contributions from Rube Walberg and Ed Rommel. The nearly $400,000 investment, almost entirely in eight players, finally broke a fifteen-year drought for Connie Mack.[5]

The Athletics, however, slipped to second place in 1932, as the Yankees, under Joe McCarthy, won the World Series. Then the familiar dismantling of the last Mack machine began with the sale of Al Simmons, Jimmy Dykes, and Mule Haas to the White Sox. In 1933, Mack sold Mickey Cochrane to the Tigers, and Lefty Grove, Rube Walberg, and Max Bishop to Tom Yawkey, the new owner of the Red Sox.[6] Falling attendance, renovations, and a depressed economy necessitated payroll reductions, factors that would beset another owner of the Athletics in a different time zone more than four decades later.[7]

Postscript

$\mathcal{O}$n December 5, the Baseball Writers' Association of America announced the All-Star team for 1928. The three pitchers were Waite Hoyt, Larry Benton of the Giants, and Lefty Grove—one of the flingers had to be a lefty. The Babe got enough votes to be placed in either right or left field, but he was placed in left field, with Heinie Manush of the Browns in center field and Paul Waner of the Pirates in right field. The others honored were Lou Gehrig, Mickey Cochrane, Rogers Hornsby, and Fred Lindstrom and Travis Jackson of the Giants.[1]

Appendix

Summary of Postponements

Note: Does not include four regularly scheduled doubleheaders: Patriot's Day in Boston; Independence Day in Washington, DC; and Memorial Day and Labor Day at the Stadium.

Schedule information was taken from the Official American League Schedule *for 1928 from the February 9 edition of the Sporting News, page 2.*

Date Postponed	Opponent	Makeup Date	Note
12 April	@ Philadelphia	24 May	
14 April	@ Philadelphia	25 May	
17 April	@Boston	30 June	
22 April	Philadelphia	20 June	
23 April	Washington	29 May	
27 April	Boston	21 May	
28 April	Boston	23 June	
9 May	Cleveland	15 July	
18 May	St. Louis	7 July	
19 May	St. Louis	8 July	
30 May	Washington	5 September	Second game of scheduled DH
4 June	@Detroit	25 July	
5 June	@Detroit	26 July	
8 June	@Cleveland	28 July	
19 June	Philadelphia (2)	20 June	
21 June	Philadelphia	1 July	Second game of scheduled DH
22 June	Philadelphia	9 September	

Date Postponed	Opponent	Makeup Date	Note
6 July	St. Louis	9 July	
10 July	Detroit	11 July	
13 July	Detroit	25 August	
14 July	Cleveland (2)	16 July	
27 July	@Detroit	27 September	
17 August	Cleveland	19 August	
22 August	St. Louis	24 August	Scheduled off day
23 August	St. Louis (2)	24 August	Scheduled off day
26 August	Detroit	27 August	
6 September	Washington	7 September	

Notes

PREFACE

1. John Mosedale, *The Greatest of All: The 1927 Yankees* (New York: Dial, 1974), 19–20.

2. Marc Egnal, *Clash of Extremes* (New York: Hill & Wang, 2010), 2–3.

INTRODUCTION

1. J. Newton Colver, "Are the Yankees the Strongest Club of Baseball History? Part III," *Baseball Magazine* 40, no. 2 (January 1928): 362.

2. This information was gathered from the various team encyclopedias and the "Seasons" tab from the www.baseball-reference.com website. This is the case for much of the statistical information in this book.

3. Bertram Reinitz, "Baseball Plays a Golden Anniversary," *New York Times*, 8 February 1925, SM5.

4. Harold Seymour, *Baseball: The Early Years* (New York: Oxford University Press, 1960), 275.

5. J. C. Kofoed, "Baseball Changes of Forty Years," *Baseball Magazine* 32, no. 2 (January 1924): 365.

6. Ford Sawyer, "Style of Baseball Play Changed in Past Decade," *Boston Daily Globe*, 27 August 1925, A11.

7. Dan Daniel, "Colonel Convinced Yanks Will Repeat This Season," *New York Telegram*, 15 March 1928, 13.

8. Ty Cobb, as told to C. William Duncan, "Baseball Then and Now," *Washington Post*, 3 June 1928, SM4.

9. Dan Daniel, "Daniel's Dope," *New York Telegram*, 13 March 1928, 14.

10. Jim Nasium, "The Golden Age of Baseball, Jim Nasium Wonders What Earlier Day Stars Would Be Worth at Current Salaries," *Sporting News*, 3 November 1927, 3. There were actually seven twenty-game winners and six nineteen-game winners in 1927. Ruth, Hornsby, and Cobb were making $70,000, $60,000, and $50,000, respectively, as compared to $5,000 for the old-time stars.

11. John B. Sheridan, "Back of the Home Plate," *Sporting News*, 29 September 1927, 4.

12. Gordon Mackay, "Is Zat So," *Philadelphia Record*, 27 May 1928, S5.

13. Dan Daniel, "Daniel's Dope," *New York Telegram*, 18 July 1927, 13. Robinson had been manager of the Brooklyn Dodgers since 1914.

14. Irving Vaughan, "Uncle Robbie Lauds Yankees," *Los Angeles Times*, 24 July 1927, A6.

15. "M'Graw Is Honored, Picks Great Stars," *New York Times*, 16 July 1927, 6.

16. Edward Hanlon, "Yanks? Huh! You Should 'A' Seen the Orioles!" *New York Telegram*, 30 July 1927, 9.

17. C. M. Gibbs, "Hanlon Watches Yankees Win; Brands Old Orioles Best Ever," *Baltimore Sun*, 14 August 1927, 2.

18. Dan Daniel, "Daniel's Dope," *New York Telegram*, 26 March 1928, 13.

19. Dan Daniel, "Daniel's Dope," *New York Telegram*, 26 March 1928, 13.

20. Alan Schwarz, *The Numbers Game: Baseball's Lifelong Fascination with Statistics* (New York: Thomas Dunne Books, 2004), 21, 50.

21. Grantland Rice, "Sportlight," *Boston Daily Globe*, 13 April 1925, 1.

22. J. Newton Colver, "Are the Yankees the Strongest Club of Baseball History? Part I," *Baseball Magazine* 39, no. 6 (November 1927): 557–58.

23. Colver, "Are the Yankees the Strongest Club of Baseball History? Part I," 558.

24. Colver, "Are the Yankees the Strongest Club of Baseball History? Part I," 558; J. Newton Colver, "Are the Yankees the Strongest Club of Baseball History? Part II," *Baseball Magazine* 40, no. 1 (December 1927): 309–10; Colver, "Are the Yankees the Strongest Club of Baseball History? Part III," 362. Each article contains rather complicated analysis of rankings and weightings that would do an Excel spreadsheet of today proud.

25. Colver, "Are the Yankees the Strongest Club of Baseball History? Part III," 362.

26. MacLean Kennedy, "Boston Red Stockings, 1871–75, Greatest Ball Teams of History," *Sporting News*, 27 October 1927, 6. The Cardinals were known as the Browns in the American Association and had no relation to the later Browns teams of the American League. Kennedy's series, which ran weekly through February 2, 1928, was excerpted from his book published in 1928, *The Great Teams of Baseball*. It features sixteen clubs; the Detroit Tigers of 1907–1910 were left out of the *Sporting News* series, but the series was later updated through the 1928 season. Kennedy's career as a writer began in Michigan in 1905. MacLean Kennedy, *The Great Teams of Baseball* (St. Louis, MO: Charles C. Spink & Son, 1928).

27. Grantland Rice, "The Ace of Clubs," *Collier's, The National Weekly* 80, no. 7 (13 August 1927): 22–23.

28. Rice, "The Ace of Clubs," 22–23.

CHAPTER 1

1. Rosalind Shepard, "Durant Cites Era Optimism: Friday Morning Club Hears Philosopher in Talk, Speaker Tells of Confidence in World Progress, Younger Generation Lauded as History's Finest," *Los Angeles Times*, 8 January 1928, C31.

2. Waldemar Kaempfert, "Wizard Science Is Annihilating Space: Airplane, Televisor, and Radiophone Are Signs of Wonders Yet to Come," *New York Times*, 15 April 1928, 78.

3. Daniel R. Levitt, *The Bulldog Who Built the Yankees' First Dynasty* (Lincoln : University of Nebraska Press, 2008), 10–11.

4. Edward Grant Barrow, with James M. Kahn, *My Fifty Years in Baseball* (New York: Coward-McCann, 1951), 11.

5. Norman L. Macht, *Connie Mack and the Early Years of Baseball* (Lincoln: University of Nebraska Press, 2012), 19.

6. Connie Mack, *My 66 Years in the Big Leagues: The Great Story of America's National Game* (Philadelphia, PA: John C. Winston Company, 1950), 3–4.

7. "Full Text of Hoover's Speech Accepting Party's Nomination for the Presidency," *New York Times*, 12 August 1928, 2. The year 1928 would be the last election of this country's fourth-party system and would end the ascendancy of the Republican Party since 1896.

8. "107 Radio Stations Linked for Hoover," *New York Times*, 11 August 1928, 12; "Hoover Outlines Policies in Acceptance Speech," *Washington Post*, 12 August 1928, M4.

9. Evans Clark, "America's Prosperity Reaches New Heights," *New York Times*, 27 November 1927, XX4.

10. Evans Clark, "In the Onward March of Production, Marked by Mergers and Billion-Dollar Corporations, Agriculture Construction, Railroads, and Textiles Take the Lead: How They Rank in Importance," *New York Times*, 25 March 1928, 141.

11. "See Auto Industry behind Prosperity: A. P. Sloan and R. D. Chapin Assert '$5,000,000,000 Annual Business Leads Nation,'" *New York Times*, 13 January 1928, 16; William Ullman, "Auto's Popularity Forces Expansion of Road Programs," *Washington Post*, 25 March 1928, A2.

12. Giuseppe M. Bellanca, "The Era of Transocean Flying Opens," *New York Times*, 12 June 1927, XX1.

13. Lauren D. Lyman, "Big Business Swings to the Aid of Aviation," *New York Times*, 8 January 1928, 127.

14. Kaempfert, "Wizard Science Is Annihilating Space," 78.

15. "Television Is Evolving at Slow but Sure Pace," *New York Times*, 22 April 1928, 145; "Sees Television in 1928 in Everyday Operation," *Boston Daily Globe*, 7 January 1928, 19.

16. "Electricity in Homes: General Electric Dealers Told 4,000,000 Await Refrigeration," *New York Times*, 27 March 1928, 39; "Users of Electricity Continue to Increase: Foshay Survey Shows Rise in Number of Patrons Is Faster Than Population Increase," *New York Times*, 2 September 1928, 29.

17. "Use of Electricity Spreads into Small American Towns," *New York Times*, 2 December 1928, 182.

18. "National City's Small Loan Department Six Months Old," *Bankers' Magazine* 117, no. 6 (December 1928): 1,042; John Walker Harrington, "Big Banks and Small Personal Loans," *Bankers' Magazine* 116, no. 6 (June 1928): 895.

19. "Saving to Travel," *Literary Digest* XCVII, no. 4 (28 April 1928): 67.

20. "Coming: A Five-Day Work Week," *Literary Digest* 96, no.13 (31 March, 1928): 12; Daniel J. Tobin, "Labor Gain Seen in Five-Day Week," *New York Times*, 13 March 1927, X15.

21. Clark, "America's Prosperity Reaches New Heights," XX4.

22. Charles A. Selden, "Changing Wall Street: New Frontiers," *New York Times*, 22 April 1928, 82.

23. Selden, "Changing Wall Street," 82; "Huge Appreciation in General Motors," *New York Times*, 11 March 1928, 37. This article is not clear as to whether the author computed the appreciation of General Motors stock from 1908 or 1918.

24. D. Grier Stephenson, Robert J. Bresler, Robert J. Friedrich, and Joseph J. Karlesky, *American Government* (New York: Harper & Row, 1988), 257–58; Ellen M. Kozak, *The U.S. Constitution Book* (Avon, MA.: Adams Media, 2011), 244–45.

25. Don Marquis, "Youth's Questionnaire, Submitted to the Older Generation by the Intelligent Flapper and Her Boy Friends," *Outlook Magazine* 149, no. 5 (30 May 1928): 177.

26. Helena Huntington Smith, "We Look at the Older Generation," *Outlook and Independent* 150, no. 11 (14 November 1928): 1,166.

27. Betty Kirk and Jacob Ruppert, "Born Bachelor, Sees Day Coming with Marriage Extinct," *New York Telegram*, 13 June 1928, 9.

28. "Organized Sports Now Rank as Big Business: Games and Contests for the Public to Watch Involve the Outlay of Hundreds of Millions of Dollars—Sporting "Industry" Is Still Growing," *New York Times*, 3 April 1927, XX13.

29. "Colonel Ruppert Values the Major Leagues at $50,000,000; Doak Leaves the Robins," *New York Times*, 13 March 1927, S3.

30. "Colonel Ruppert Values the Major Leagues at $50,000,000," S3.

31. Gordon Cobbledick, "Barnard Finds Baseball Most Vigorous Since War," *Cleveland Plain Dealer*, 28 March 1928, 22.

32. "Carry of 500 Feet Hailed as Sensation in Earlier Day," *New York Telegram*, 28 March 1928, 13.

33. Cobbledick, "Barnard Finds Baseball Most Vigorous Since War," 22.

34. Cobbledick, "Barnard Finds Baseball Most Vigorous Since War," 22.

35. "Baseball Revival Planned among Boys of the Nation," *New York Times*, 1 April 1928, 133.

36. C. William Duncan, "Baseball: Then and Now," *Washington Post*, 3 June 1928, SM4.

37. "Spalding Sales, Profits Larger," *Wall Street Journal*, 19 August 1929, 5; "A. G. Spalding to Split Common Stock 5 for 1," *Wall Street Journal*, 7 January 1929, 2; "Another Record Year Looms for A. G. Spalding," *Wall Street Journal*, 11 November 1927, 3.

38. James M. Gould, "When the Diamond and Gridiron Clash," *Baseball Magazine* 34, no. 2 (January 1925): 357–58; Herbert L. McNary, "Is There a Growing Demand for Professional Football?" *Baseball Magazine* 36, no. 2 (January 1926): 359.

39. Grover Theis, "The Game of Hockey Finds Supporters in New York," *New York Times*, 4 November 1928, 147.

40. Walter Trumbull, "The Listening Post," *New York Evening Post*, 2 June 1928, 13.

41. Robert W. Peterson, *Cages to Jump Shots: Pro Basketball's Early Years* (Lincoln: University of Nebraska Press, 2002), 48, 80.

42. John Kieran, "Sports of the Times," *New York Times*, 10 January 1928, 37. The National Basketball Association was still more than twenty years in the future.

43. "Third League Embraces Six Cities," *Washington Post*, 28 December 1926, 13; "Third League Reports Hinted in Cobb–Speaker Case," *Washington Post*, 22 January 1927, 15; "Talk of Third League Foolish, Says McGraw," *Washington Post*, 30 December 1926, 13.

CHAPTER 2

1. "Yankee Deals for Players in Sight: Boston, Cleveland, and St. Louis Clubs May Trade or Sell Men to New York," *New York Times*, 3 February 1915, 12.

2. Daniel R. Levitt, *The Bulldog Who Built the Yankees' First Dynasty* (Lincoln: University of Nebraska Press, 2008), 178–80.

3. "Ban Johnson Must Strengthen Yanks," *New York Times*, 19 December 1914, 11. This was a time well before teams had outright ownership of a chain of minor-league teams, and well before the modern system of free agency.

4. "Yankees Not Yet in Ruppert's Hands," *New York Times*, 24 December 1914, 7.

5. "Ready to Close Deal: Col. Ruppert Wants Good Manager before Buying the Yankees," *New York Times*, 21 December 1914, 10. Here is an excerpt from the *New York Times* regarding the pending purchase by Ruppert and Huston. Johnson should have been careful of what he wished for the American League. "Every club owner in the American League is taking an interest in the sale of the Yankees, at President Johnson's request, as the organization is anxious to build up a strong team and make New York one of the best cities in the circuit...President Johnson is said to have put the matter up to the other club owners, and they are willing to do everything they can to aid the new owners in strengthening the club." "Yankees Not Sold, Johnson Goes Away," *New York Times*, 14 December 1914, 9.

6. "Ruppert and Huston Buy the Yankees," *New York Times*, 1 January 1915, 12.

7. "Mack Not Coming Here," *New York Times*, 10 December 1914, 11; "Connie Mack May Manage Yankees," *New York Times*, 9 December 1914, 11; "Mack Owns Half the Club," *New York Times*, 17 November 1912, S4.

8. "Wild Bill" Donovan was hired as manager of the Yankees for the 1915 season from the Providence team in the International League on a recommendation from the owner of the Boston Red Sox, Joseph Lannin. "'Wild Bill' Talks with Yanks' Owners," *New York Times*, 3 January 1915, S1.

9. Levitt, *The Bulldog Who Built the Yankees' First Dynasty*, 182–83. Even though the teams in his circuit were individually owned, Johnson was granted an unusual number of long-term contracts as league president, and he was involved by way of the league's constitution in each team's internal affairs and decision-making process. In 1901, Johnson was given a ten-year contract, and each club was required to submit the leases on their grounds and 51 percent of their stock to him in trust. "American League Baseball," *New York Times*, 28 January 1901, 5; "Baseball Plans," *Boston Daily Globe*, 29 January 1901, 5.

10. "Huggins Signed as Manager of Yanks," *New York Times*, 26 October 1917, 16; I. Sanborn, "New Yanks' Manager Moves to Strengthen League in New York," *Chicago Daily Tribune*, 27 October 1917, 13.

11. "Miller Huggins May Succeed O'Day as Reds' Manager," *Fort Worth Star-Telegram*, 2 August 1912, 13.

12. "Bresnahan Lets Cat Out of Bag, Discloses Woman Owner as Cause for Failure of Club," *Fort Worth Star-Telegram*, 17 August 1912, 3; Frederick G. Lieb, *The St. Louis Cardinals: The Story of a Great Baseball Club* (New York: G. P. Putnam's Sons, 1944), 34–45.

13. Al Munro Elias, "Miller J. Huggins," *Baseball Magazine* 20, no. 2 (March 1918): 433–34.

14. "Huggins Offered Big Money to Stay Put," *San Francisco Chronicle*, 27 October 1917, 8. The New York American League club fielded seven different managers before Huggins. Clark Griffith, who later became president of the Senators, was the Yankees first manager in 1903, and he lasted partially through the disastrous 1908 season. Incidentally, Griffith moved on to manage the Reds, where he benched Huggins and cut his salary, resulting in bad blood between the two men. "Fur Will Fly between Pair Miller Huggins and Clark Griffith, Not on Good Terms," *Duluth News-Tribune*, 25 November 1917, 3.

15. J. R. McDermott, "Miller Huggins, the Midget Manager," *Baseball Magazine* 11, no. 6 (October 1913): 59–67.

16. Henty L. Farrell, "Huggins Has Hermit Role," *New York Telegram*, 23 August 1928, 13.

17. Levitt, *The Bulldog Who Built the Yankees' First Dynasty*, 177.

18. Levitt, *The Bulldog Who Built the Yankees' First Dynasty*, 12–17.

19. Jim Nasium, "Unsung Heroes of Baseball, Barrow Had Big Part in Making Yankees Famous," *Sporting News*, 5 January 1928, 3.

20. Nasium, "Unsung Heroes of Baseball," 3.

21. "The Official Directory of Organized Baseball," *Sporting News*, 26 April 1928, 5.

22. Levitt, *The Bulldog Who Built the Yankees' First Dynasty*, 203.

23. "Huston to Sell Yank Interests for Huge Price," *Chicago Daily Tribune*, 12 December 1922, 24.

24. "Ruppert to Be Sole Owner of Yankees," *New York Times*, 13 December 1922, 30.

25. "Ruppert to Be Sole Owner of Yankees," *New York Times*, 13 December 1922, 30.

26. "Ruppert Completes Deal for Yankees," *New York Times*, 22 May 1923, 15.

27. Fred Lieb, "Cutting the Plate with Fred Lieb," *New York Evening Post*, 14 September 1927, 18.

28. "Yanks and Boston Close Big Trade," *New York Times*, 16 December 1920, 26.

29. "Yankees Get Dugan from the Red Sox," *New York Times*, 24 July 1922, 17.

30. "Yankees' Catcher Goes to Red Sox," *New York Times*, 4 January 1923, 16; "Yanks Get Pennock from the Red Sox," *New York Times*, 31 January 1923, 16; James O'Leary, "Pennock, Last of Old Guard, Let Out," *Boston Daily Globe*, 31 January 1923, 1.

31. "Huggins Returns with Good Tidings: Babe Ruth Agrees to Yankees' Terms and Will Play in the Right Garden. Ruth Not in Movies. Clubs Not Anxious to Sell," *New York Times*, 23 January 1920, 14.

32. "Yanks Sign Gehrig, Colombia Slugger: Cazella of Lafayette and Vanderbach of Fordham Also Accept Terms," *New York Times*, 12 June 1923, 16; "Collegians Pet Peeve of Huggins," *Los Angeles Times*, 20 May 1928, A6.

33. "Louisville Star Bought by Giants: Wayland Dean Comes to National League Champions for Cash and Players," *New York Times*, 6 January 1924, S1; "Outfielder Combs Bought by Yanks: Sum Believed to Exceed $50,000 and Two Players Paid for Louisville Star," *New York Times*, 8 January 1924, 28.

34. "Louisville Gets Five Players," *New York Times*, 8 January 1924, 28; "Combs Joins Yanks at Training Camp: $50,000-Outfielder Reports to Manager Huggins and Shines in Workout. Slight Rain Mars Drill; Bad Weather and Indigestion Keep Ruth Out of Uniform—Snow Predicted for Today," *New York Times*, 14 March 1924, 13. Dean would not fare so well in the majors, winning twenty four games and losing thirty-six throughout four seasons.

35. "Eddie Collins, Bibb Falk, and Sam Rice Are Coming to Yankees in Big Three-Corne," *New York Herald Tribune*, 11 December 1922, 12; John Kieran, "Collins Deal Sure to Go Through and Will Be Three-Man Swap between Yanks and White Sox," *New York Herald Tribune*, 19 December 1922, 15; "Collins to Remain with Chicago Club," *New York Times*, 20 February 1923, 14.

36. "Deal for Collins Revived by Yanks," *New York Times*, 2 February 1924, 8; "White Sox Demand Ward for Collins," *New York Times*, 5 February 1924, 18.

37. The Cardinals and Giants each won nineteen pennants; the Dodgers won eighteen and the Athletics fourteen.

38. "The Official Directory of Organized Baseball," 5.

39. John Heidenry, *The Gashouse Gang: How Dizzy Dean, Leo Durocher, Branch Rickey, Pepper Martin, and Their Colorful, Come-from-Behind Ball Club Won the World Series—and America's Heart—during the Great Depression* (New York: Public Affairs, 2007), 335–42.

40. Earl Obenshain, "Majors Spend Vast Sum for Minor Talent," *Sporting News*, 15 December 1927, 6; Hugh Bradley, "Farm Plank Inserted in Baseball by Rickey," *New York Evening Post*, 17 September 1928, 17.

41. James R. Harrison subbing for John Kieran, "Sports of the Times," *New York Times*, 11 December 1927, S2.

42. John Kieran, "Sports of the Times," *New York Times*, 4 May 1929, 23.

43. Edward Grant Barrow, with James M. Kahn, *My Fifty Years in Baseball* (New York: Coward-McCann, 1951), 8.

44. "Connie Mack and John McGraw Stand Firm as Many Managers Move On," *Hartford Courant*, 14 February 1927, 10.

45. "Baseball Titles Costly; But They Seem Worth It," *Chicago Daily Tribune*, 14 February 1927, 23; Frederick G. Lieb, *Connie Mack: Grand Old Man of Baseball* (New York: G. P. Putnam's Sons, 1945), 28. The Giants' payroll was estimated to be between $145,000 and $200,000 in 1927.

46. "Connie Mack, 64 Today, Wants 65th Year to Be His Very Best," *Boston Daily Globe*, 23 December 1926, A8; "Mack Predicts A's Will Win 1927 Pennant," *Chicago Daily Tribune*, 25 December 1926, 16.

47. Irving Vaughan, "Athletics as Good as in Now," *Los Angeles Times*, 20 March 1927, A2.

CHAPTER 3

1. Frederick G. Lieb, *The Baseball Story* (New York: G. P. Putnam's Sons, 1950), 226.

2. "Yankees Overjoyed Over Clean Sweep," *New York Times*, 9 October 1927, S5.

3. "'We Like to Destroy the Enemy,' Ban Johnson Wires Ruppert," *New York Times*, 9 October 1927, 54.

4. Dan Daniel, "Owner of Pirates Prepares for Battle with Magnates," *New York Telegram*, 11 October 1927, 15.

5. Daniel, "Owner of Pirates Prepares for Battle with Magnates," 15.

6. Joe Williams, "Colonel Ruppert—Champion Fan," *New York Telegram*, 5 January 1928, 13.

7. Williams, "Colonel Ruppert—Champion Fan," 13.

8. Alan J. Gould, "Yanks Making Runaway of Race," *Los Angeles Times*, 30 May 1928, B1.

9. Dan Daniel, "Over $150,000 Going Back to Buyers of Series Tickets," *New York Telegram*, 13 October 1927, 15.

10. "Ten Records Broken in World's Series, Most of Which Are Shattered by Ruth," *New York Times*, 10 October 1927, 18; John Drebinger, "Yankees Disburse, Four to Barnstorm," *New York Times*, 10 October 1927, 18.

11. "Ruth and Gehrig Get All-Star Posts," *New York Times*, 30 November 1927, 18.

12. John Drebinger, "Baseball Heads Gather Here Today," *New York Times*, 12 December 1927, 27.

13. Pat Robinson, "Johnson Quits as League Head after Meeting," *New York Telegram*, 8 July 1927, 1; Harold Seymour, *Baseball: The Golden Age* (New York: Oxford University Press, 1971), 398.

14. Brian Bell, "Barnard, American League Head, Knows Few Players in Big Tent," *Washington Post*, 6 November 1927, M23; Irving Vaughan, "Barnard Signs 3 Yr. Contract as President of A.L.," *Chicago Daily Tribune*, 3 November 1927, 21.

15. "E. S. Barnard Taking Charge of American League, Sees Johnsonian Policies as Enduring Influence," *Sporting News*, 10 November 1927, 3.

16. "Howard Ehmke Says Yankees Won't Repeat 1927 Victory," *Los Angeles Times*, 15 January 1928, A6.

17. Joe Williams, "Connie Mack Sees Trouble Ahead for Yankees," *New York Telegram*, 21 March 1928, 13. The Athletics finished third after winning the pennant in 1910 and 1911.

18. Herbert S. Allan, "Infinite Variety of Yanks Is Responsible for Club's Sustained Drawing Power," *New York Evening Post*, 5 May 1928, 10.

19. Dan Daniel, "'Meusel Fixture, Trades Stress Pitching'—Huggins," *New York Telegram*, 10 December 1927, 10. Ed Barrow believed that the team would be taking a gamble on Uhle, a premier pitcher who was plagued by a sore arm in 1927, but Huggins thought that he was well worth getting.

20. Daniel, "'Meusel Fixture, Trades Stress Pitching'—Huggins," 10.

21. Daniel, "'Meusel Fixture, Trades Stress Pitching'—Huggins," 10.

22. James R. Harrison, "Trade Winds Blow as Magnates Meet," *New York Times*, 13 December 1927, 35; John Drebinger, "Major Leaguers Meet This Week," *New York Times*, 11 December 1927, S1; Daniel, "'Meusel Fixture, Trades Stress Pitching'—Huggins," 10.

23. Dan Daniel, "Huggins Stays on Sidelines as Other Clubs Bid for Men," *New York Telegram*, 15 December 1927, 13.

24. Dan Daniel, "Daniel's Dope," *New York Telegram*, 19 December 1927, 14.

25. Daniel, "Daniel's Dope," 14. The $25,000 figure quoted by Daniel for Combs may have been a misprint. Per Baseball-Reference.com, he was traded by Louisville (American Association) to the New York Yankees for Elmer Smith, $50,000, and a player to be named. "Earle Combs," *Baseball-Reference.com*, http://www.baseball-reference.com/players/c/combsea01.shtml#trans (accessed 29 January 2014).

26. "New York Club Not Approached on Fletcher by Cleveland," *New York Telegram*, 10 December 1927, 10.

27. James R. Harrison, "Human Spark Plug to Ignite Yankees," *New York Times*, 2 March 1927, 21.

28. "Huggins's Latest Move Indicates Need of Some Yankee Pugnacity," *Sporting News*, 4 November 1926, 1.

29. "Moriarty Has Made Good on a Promise," *Sporting News*, 23 February 1928, 1.

30. "Barnard Has No Fear of Yankees Running Away with His League," *Sporting News*, 26 January 1928, 2.

31. James R. Harrison, "Yanks Pay $125,000 for Lary and Reese," *New York Times*, 5 January 1928, 35; Dan Daniel, "Lary and Reese Will Join Club on 1929 Training Trip," *New York Telegram*, 4 January 1928, 13.

32. "Chalmer Cissell Sold to Chicago White Sox for $123,000 in Cash and Ballplayer," *Los Angeles Times*, 6 November 1927, A6; "Yankees Dominate Player Market, Controlling 3–5 of Minors' Stars," *Washington Post*, 6 January 1928, 13.

33. Dan Daniel, "Colonel Won't Let Reese and Lary Slip; Thinks Yankees Are Good for Five Years," *New York Telegram*, 28 December 1927, 13.

34. James R. Harrison, "Huggins Is Seeking Gehrig Understudy," *New York Times*, 2 February 1928, 24. In reaction to the Yankees' purchase of three top minor leaguers and a drastic fall off in attendance in 1927, the Senators voted not to pay a

dividend at their annual meeting, instead purchasing nineteen players for $139,000, mostly young prospects for future use. At the top of the shopping list, however, was thirty-five-year-old George Sisler, who cost the team $15,000. He was replacing Tris Speaker, whose purchase the year before they took a bath on. Frank Young, "Griffith Builds Team for Future," *Washington Post*, 8 January 1928, 23.

35. In the June 1928 issue, *Baseball Magazine* lists, to the best of their knowledge, the current state of the major- and minor-league relationships from the "absolute ownership to a general but pretty definitively understood working agreement." Each major-league team was listed with at least one affiliation, ranging from the Yankees to St. Paul of the American Association. Ira Irving, "The 'Chain Store' Idea Invades Baseball," *Baseball Magazine* 41, no. 1 (June 1928): 315.

36. James R. Harrison, "Huggins to Return to City Tomorrow," *New York Times*, 27 January 1928, 17.

37. Harrison, "Huggins Is Seeking Gehrig Understudy," 24. The Yankees offered Joe Dugan for George Burns and backup infielder Rube Lutzke; when the latter was sent to the minors, the Yankees did not want to give up Dugan for Burns alone.

38. Murray Tynan, "Ruth and Gehrig to Accompany First Group of Yankees to St. Petersburg," *New York Herald Tribune*, 19 February 1928, C2.

39. "Ruth, Gehrig Leave for Florida Camp," *New York Times*, 25 February 1928, 18.

40. "Yank Squad Rolls Southward in Rain," *New York Times*, 26 February 1928, 152.

CHAPTER 4

1. Pat Robinson, "Joe Dugan and Combs Only Yanks Hitting True Stride," *New York Telegram*, 29 March 1928, 13.

2. James R. Harrison, "Only Five Yankees Still Are Unsigned: Thirty-two Already Have Come in the Fold," *New York Times*, 9 February 1928, 22; James R. Harrison, "Yanks Sign Gehrig to Three-Year Contract," *New York Times*, 7 January 1928, 9. Player contracts with a length of greater than one year were considered long-term and risky for the owner.

3. "Ruppert in Game for Pleasure But It Isn't Much Fun Just Now," *Sporting News*, 24 February 1927, 1.

4. "Combs Joins Yanks and Ruth Returns," *New York Times*, 18 March 1927, 17; "Ruth Right-Handed Signing for $210,000," *New York Times*, 5 March 1927, 9; "Ruth Here Today; Will See Ruppert," *New York Times*, 2 March 1927, 21; "Pennock Signs for Three Years; All Yanks Are Now in Fold," *New York Times*, 27 March 1927, S1; James R. Harrison, "Bob Meusel Signs on the Dotted Line," *New York Times*, 17 March 1927, 19.

5. Dan Daniel, "Yankee Payroll Approaches $300,000 Mark for 1928," *New York Telegram*, 9 January 1928, 10.

6. Dan Daniel, "Yank Ace Returns Papers to Col. Ruppert Unsigned," *New York Telegram*, 20 January 1928, 13.

7. James R. Harrison, "Veterans Will Bow to Yankee Youths," *New York Times*, 6 March 1927, S1.

8. Harrison, "Only Five Yankees Still Are Unsigned," 22; "Shawkey, Ruether Dropped by Yanks," *New York Times*, 29 November 1927, 23. In 1928, Reuther went on to lead the Pacific Coast League with twenty-nine wins against seven losses while pitching for the San Francisco Seals.

9. "Shocker to Learn to Fly; Says He Has Quit Baseball," *New York Times*, 22 February 1928, 26; Dan Daniel, "Huggins Not Worrying Over Pitchers, Even If Shocker Does Quit Baseball," *New York Telegram*, 20 February 1928, 13.

10. Richards Vidmer, "Yankees to Start Training on Feb. 26; Ruth and Gehrig Will Head the First Delegation to Arrive at St. Petersburg. Dugan and Bengough Sign, But Hoyt Is Still a Holdout—Huggins Will Return to Florida Today. The First Detachment. Huggins Leaves Today," *New York Times*, 7 February 1928, 31.

11. Dan Daniel, "Babe Ruth Takes 48 Bats to Camp in Starting Campaign for 61 Homers This Season," *New York Telegram*, 28 February 1928, 13.

12. Daniel, "Babe Ruth Takes 48 Bats to Camp in Starting Campaign for 61 Homers This Season," 13.

13. Daniel, "Babe Ruth Takes 48 Bats to Camp in Starting Campaign for 61 Homers This Season," 13.

14. James R. Harrison, "Yankees Will Play 22 Games in Spring," *New York Times*, 4 January 1928, 28.

15. James R. Harrison, "Yanks Find Camp Better Than Ever: Huggins Calls Crescent Lake Park Finest Grounds He Has Seen for Training," *New York Times*, 2 March 1928, 36.

16. Harrison, "Yanks Find Camp Better Than Ever," 36.

17. Dan Daniel, "Joe Dugan May Be Forced to Yield Hot Corner Job," *New York Telegram*, 1 March 1928, 14.

18. Ibid.

19. Dan Daniel, "Shortstop Durocher First 1928 Recruit to Win His Spurs with Champion Yankees," *New York Telegram*, 29 February 1928, 13.

20. Dan Daniel, "Yanks Will Start 1928 Season with Old Lineup," *New York Telegram*, 3 March 1928, 9.

21. Daniel, "Yanks Will Start 1928 Season with Old Lineup," 9.

22. James R. Harrison, "Huggins Will Use Oratory on Rebels," *New York Times*, 5 March 1928, 33.

23. Harrison, "Huggins Will Use Oratory on Rebels," 33.

24. Harrison, "Huggins Will Use Oratory on Rebels," 33.

25. Dan Daniel, "Puts Force on Swing," *New York Telegram*, 7 March 1928, 13.

26. Daniel, "Puts Force on Swing," 13.

27. "Huggins, Believing Golf Corrupts Players, Issues Absolute Ban," *New York Telegram*, 3 February 1928, 13

28. Harrison, "Huggins Will Use Oratory On Rebels," 33; "Huggins, Believing Golf Corrupts Players, Issues Absolute Ban," 13; Dan Daniel, "Daniel's Dope," *New York Telegram*, 7 March 1928, 14.

29. James R. Harrison, "Lazzeri Is Signed for a Two-Year Term," *New York Times*, 6 March 1928, 22.

30. Dan Daniel, "Tony Lazzeri Signs Two-Year Contract, Leaving Only Hoyt and Shocker Holdouts," *New York Telegram*, 5 March 1928, 11.

31. Dan Daniel, "Shealy and Johnson Appear Fixtures on Hurling Staff of World Champions," *New York Telegram*, 2 March 1928, 15; Eugene Murdock, *Baseball between the Wars: Memories of the Game by the Men Who Played It* (Westport, CT: Meckler, 1992), 250.

32. James R. Harrison, "Shocker Lets Fall a Hint He May Sign," *New York Times*, 8 March 1928, 18.

33. Dan Daniel, "Tardy Star in Condition," *New York Telegram*, 10 March 1928, 9; Dan Daniel, "Hug Makes Decision after New Wire from Pitcher," *New York Telegram*, 8 March 1928, 13.

34. "Huggins Trades Five Players to Get Pratt for the Yankees," *New York Times*, 23 January 1918, 6.

35. "Shocker a Yankee; Traded for Bush," *New York Times*, 18 December 1924, 26.

36. W. B. Hanna, "Odds and Ends of Sport," *New York Herald Tribune*, 16 September 1928, 1.

37. "Yanks Wash Hands of Urban Shocker," *New York Times*, 9 March 1928, 29.

38. Dan Daniel, "Hoyt Called into Huddle," *New York Telegram*, 9 March 1928, 13; Daniel, "Hug Makes Decision after New Wire from Pitcher," 13.

39. Ibid.

40. Harrison, "Lazzeri Is Signed for a Two-Year Term," 22.

41. Ibid.

42. Dan Daniel, "Minor League Record Set in Bid for Henry Johnson," *New York Telegram*, 27 December 1927, 14.

43. Daniel, "Shealy and Johnson Appear Fixtures on Hurling Staff of World Champions," 15.

44. Dan Daniel, "Daniel's Dope," *New York Telegram*, 8 March 1928, 13.

45. Ed R. Hughes, "Baseball Gossip," *San Francisco Chronicle*, 11 August 1928, H3; Herb Pennock, "Breaking into the Big Show," *New York Telegram*, 13 March 1928, 13.

46. Dan Daniel, "Daniel's Dope," *New York Telegram*, 27 March 1928, 13.

47. Joe Williams, "Hoyt Sees Yankees," *New York Telegram*, 19 January 1928, 13; James R. Harrison, "Ruppert to Talk Terms with Hoyt," *New York Times*, 12 March 1928, 26.

48. Dan Daniel, "Flatbush Mortician Holds Out for Salary of $20,000," *New York Telegram*, 13 March 1928, 14.

49. Daniel, "Flatbush Mortician Holds Out for Salary of $20,000," 14.

50. Daniel, "Flatbush Mortician Holds Out for Salary of $20,000," 14.

51. James R. Harrison, "Hoyt Still Delays on Yankees' Offer," *New York Times*, 15 March 1928, 21.

52. Fred Lieb, "Cutting the Plate with Fred Lieb," *New York Evening Post*, 21 July 1927, 14.

53. Daniel, "Yank Ace Returns Papers to Col. Ruppert Unsigned," 13.

54. Daniel, "Yank Ace Returns Papers to Col. Ruppert Unsigned," 13; Harrison, "Hoyt Still Delays on Yankees' Offer," 21.

55. James R. Harrison, "Hoyt and Ruppert Chat, But in Vain," *New York Times*, 14 March 1928, 32.

56. Harrison, "Hoyt and Ruppert Chat, But in Vain," 32.

57. "Hoyt Signs Two-Year Contract with Yanks; Terms Said to Call for $16,000 per Season," *New York Times*, 16 March 1928, 26.

58. Dan Daniel, "Flatbush Mortician Makes Sixth Yankee to Sign Long-Term Contract This Year," *New York Telegram*, 16 March 1928, 13.

59. Harrison, "Ruppert to Talk Terms with Hoyt," 26.

60. Joe Williams, "No Captain for Champion Yankees," *New York Telegram*, 14 March 1928, 13.

61. "Did Babe Overwork?" *New York Telegram*, 16 March 1928, 14.

62. "Ruth Sends for Big Bertha—Seeks Harder Punch," *New York Telegram*, 17 March 1928, 9.

63. Dan Daniel, "Colonel Convinced Yanks Will Repeat This Season," *New York Telegram*, 15 March 1928, 13.

64. Dan Daniel, "Daniel's Dope," *New York Telegram*, 13 March 1928, 14.

65. Dan Daniel, "Yankees All Set to Maul Exhibition Opponents Now," *New York Telegram*, 19 March 1928, 11.

66. Daniel, "Yankees All Set to Maul Exhibition Opponents Now," 11.

67. James R. Harrison, "Yanks Get Eleven Hits But Lose to Cards," *New York Times*, 17 March 1928, 16; James R. Harrison, "Yanks Lose, 4 to 2, on Two Wild Throws," *New York Times*, 21 March 1928, 23.

68. Dan Daniel, "Yanks Near Form Again," *New York Telegram*, 21 March 1928, 13.

69. Daniel, "Yanks Near Form Again," 13.

70. Frederick G. Lieb, "Officials of Club Believe That Shocker May Return and Solve Mound Puzzle," *New York Evening Post*, 23 March 1928, 18.

71. Lieb, "Officials of Club Believe That Shocker May Return and Solve Mound Puzzle," 18.

72. Dan Daniel, "Spitballer Satisfied Comeback Is Real," *New York Telegram*, 23 March 1928, 13.

73. "Only Six Active Hurlers Remain Out of Seventeen Granted Immunity When Freak Deliveries Were Outlawed by Majors," *Detroit Free Press*, 20 March 1928, 16.

74. Dan Daniel, "Yankee Ace Works Out," *New York Telegram*, 14 March 1928, 13.

75. Daniel, "Spitballer Satisfied Comeback Is Real," 13.

76. Daniel, "Spitballer Satisfied Comeback Is Real," 13.

77. James R. Harrison, "Dugan Shows Way to Yankee Victory," *New York Times*, 22 March 1928, 20.

78. Dan Daniel, "Dugan Shows Pep of Youth as Hugmen Shoo Losing Jinx," *New York Telegram*, 22 March 1928, 13.

79. "Yanks Drop Final Despite Two Homers," *New York Times*, 23 March 1928, 16.

80. Pat Robinson, "Huggins Has Big Problem," *New York Telegram*, 26 March 1928, 11.

81. "Cy Enjoys Relief Job," *New York Telegram*, 20 March 1928, 13.

82. L. H. Addington, "Wilcy Moore's 'Nanny' Once a Fleeting Thing," *Sporting News*, 27 November 1927, 8.

83. Pat Robinson, "Cy Now Has Curveball," *New York Telegram*, 27 March 1928, 11.

84. James R. Harrison, "Pitching Disclosed as Yank Weakness," *New York Times*, 25 March 1928, 165.

85. Richards Vidmer, "Golf and Fishing Divert the Yanks," *New York Times*, 26 March 1928, 16.

86. "Fans of New York Feel Pretty Well Fed Up on Alibi Stuff," *Sporting News*, 29 March 1928, 1.

87. Richards Vidmer, "Yanks Leave Camp; Start Trek Home," *New York Times*, 31 March 1928, 15.

88. Robinson, "Joe Dugan and Combs Only Yanks Hitting True Stride," 13.

89. Robinson, "Joe Dugan and Combs Only Yanks Hitting True Stride," 13.

90. Vidmer, "Yanks Leave Camp; Start Trek Home," 15; Pat Robinson, "Gazella Latest Yankee Considered in Deal for Pitcher Miller of Cleveland Indians," *New York Telegram*, 31 March 1928, 10.

91. Pat Robinson, "End of Long Slump Seen," *New York Telegram*, 6 April 1928, 11.

92. Richards Vidmer, "Ruth and Gehrig Clout Two Apiece," *New York Times*, 7 April 1928, 16.

93. Pat Robinson, "End of Long Slump Seen," *New York Telegram*, 6 April 1928, 11.

94. Pat Robinson, "Champions Begin Clouting, with Bambino Setting Pace," 13.

95. Robinson, "End of Long Slump Seen," 11.

96. "Ruppert Believes Yanks Will Repeat," *New York Times*, 8 April 1928, S3.

97. "Robins Rout Yanks at Stadium, 12 to 5," *New York Times*, 8 April 1928, S1; "Yankees' Three Homers Defeat Robins, 7–3," *New York Times*, 9 April 1928, 25; "Four Sacrifice Drives Conquer Robins, 3–2," *New York Times*, 10 April 1928, 24; John Drebinger, "Robins Turn Back Yanks in Final, 7–2," *New York Times*, 11 April 1928, 37.

98. Westbrook Pegler, "Spring Line of Ballyhoo for Major Baseball Clubs Is Best in Years," *Chicago Daily Tribune*, 8 April 1928, A2.

99. Pegler, "Spring Line of Ballyhoo for Major Baseball Clubs Is Best in Years," A2.

CHAPTER 5

1. F. C. Lane, "Baseball's Burning Question, 'How's the Weather?'" *Baseball Magazine* 39, no. 1 (June 1927): 303–4. There were seventy-three games postponed as of May 31, 1927, forty-two in the National League and thirty-one in the American League. "73 Games in Majors Put Off; Six for Giants, Five for Yanks," *New York Times*, 31 May 1927, 26.

2. Lane, "Baseball's Burning Question," 303–4.

3. "Disaster Record of 1927 One of Worst," *Boston Daily Globe*, 6 November 1927, A54.

4. "Zeroless Winter Likely, the Weather Man Says," *New York Times*, 6 March 1928, 1; "Heaviest Snowfall of Winter Hits City," *New York Times*, 10 March 1928, 1.

5. "Says Coolidge Tires of Cares of Office," *New York Times*, 25 February 1928, 2.

6. "Senate to Recess for Ball Opening," *New York Times*, 13 April 1926, 20.

7. Shirley L. Povich, "18,000 Brave Cold; See Nats Beaten in Opening Game, 7–5," *Washington Post*, 11 April 1928, 1.

8. Povich, "18,000 Brave Cold," 1.

9. Alan J. Gould, "Eyes on Yanks as Season Starts," *Washington Post*, 11 April 1928, 13; "Opening Tilts Draw Crowds of 227,660," *Boston Daily Globe*, 13 April 1927, 27; "205,000 See the Season Open, 36,000 Less Than Last Year," *New York Times*, 12 April 1928, 20.

10. James R. Harrison, "Barnard Orders Snappier Games; American League Bars Dawdling," *New York Times*, 19 March 1928, 25.

11. "Umps Call Ball on Seaton; Phillies Protest Game Lost Because Klem Hurried Play," *Morning Oregonian*, 7 May 1913, 8.

12. Dan Daniel, "Daniel's Dope," *New York Telegram*, 19 March 1928, 12; Dan Daniel, "Daniel's Dope," *New York Telegram*, 22 March 1928, 14.

13. Ibid.

14. George B. Underwood, "Fanning with the Fans," *New York Morning Telegraph*, 8 September 1928, 6.

15. Frank Wallace, "Huggins Half Hopes Yanks Will Slump Now. And Get It Over before the World Series," *New York Evening Post*, 19 August 1927, 12.

16. Wallace, "Huggins Half Hopes Yanks Will Slump Now," 12.

17. Dan Daniel, "Daniel's Dope," *New York Telegram*, 24 March 1928, 12.

18. Joe Williams, "No Captain for Champion Yankees," *New York Telegram*, 14 March 1928, 13.

19. John P. Gallagher, "High-Salaried Speaker and Cobb May Cause Dissension in Athletic Ranks," *Los Angeles Times*, 11 March 1928, A5; "Dissension Is Rumored in Ranks of Mack's Athletics," *Los Angeles Times*, 8 April 1928, A7.

20. Dan Daniel, "Daniel's Dope," *New York Telegram*, 27 March 1928, 13.

21. Dan Daniel, "Ty to Confer with McGraw in Augusta Training Camp," *New York Telegram*, 8 February 1928, 11; "Will Join Mackmen Monday, Says Ty in Denying Retirement," *Philadelphia Inquirer*, 31 March 1928, 24.

22. "Records Shattered on Stock Exchange," *New York Times*, 1 April 1928, 43.

23. "Will Join Mackmen Monday," 24.

24. "Simmons Patient in Hospital; Out of Athletics' First Game," *New York Times*, 6 April 1928, 29; "Mack a Bit Grumpy at Way His Men Muddled through Training," *Sporting News*, 5 April 1928, 1; "Fortune Frowns as Macks Start It Off," *Sporting News*, 19 April 1928, 1.

25. Ford Frick, "Back of the Stars That Shine," *Baseball Magazine* 41, no. 6 (November 1928): 545–46.

26. "Athletic Fan Braves Cold, Reaches Park at 7:45 A.M.," *New York Times*, 12 April 1928, 21.

27. Richards Vidmer, "Yanks Get Off Fast; Trim Athletics, 8–3," *New York Times*, 12 April 1928, 20. Details for Yankee and Athletic games were taken from daily

reporting in the *New York Times* and *Philadelphia Inquirer*, and from http://www.baseball-reference.com.

28. James Isaminger, "Hugginsmen Regain Stride to Send Athletics Sprawling," *Philadelphia Inquirer*, 12 April 1928, 22.

29. Vidmer, "Yanks Get Off Fast," 20.

30. James Isaminger, "City Series Close-Ups," *Philadelphia Inquirer*, 1 April 1928, S3.

31. "'A' Replaces Elephant on Mack's Uniform," *Philadelphia Public Ledger*, 3 April 1928, 10; "Sports Editorial," *Philadelphia Public Record*, 27 May 1928, S7; Frederick G. Lieb, *The Baseball Story* (New York: G. P. Punam's Sons, 1950), 31.

32. "Grove Masters Slow Ball," *Los Angeles Times*, 4 March 1928, A6.

33. Vidmer, "Yanks Get Off Fast," 20; Isaminger, "Huggensmen Regain Stride to Send Athletics Sprawling," 22.

34. "Ice and Snow Halt March of the Yanks," *New York Times*, 13 April 1928, 20.

35. James Isaminger, "Ed Rommel to Face Yankee Foes Today," *Philadelphia Inquirer*, 13 April 1928, 20.

36. "Ice and Snow Halt March of the Yanks," 20.

37. Hugh Bradley, "Advance in Price of Ivory Cause of Extra Precaution Exercised by Players," *New York Evening Post*, 30 April 1928, 12.

38. Richards Vidmer, "Gehrig's Home Run Lights Yankee Fuse," *New York Times*, 14 April 1928, 14; James Isaminger, "Hauser Cracks Two Homers and Triple," *Philadelphia Inquirer*, 14 April 1928, 24.

39. James R. Harrison, "Rain Forces Giants to Postpone Game," *New York Times*, 15 April 1928, 157.

40. John Kieran, "Sports of the Times," *New York Times*, 16 April 1928, 31.

41. Hugh Bradley, "Weather Qualifies Hugmen as Hardy Arctic Explorers on Expedition into Boston," *New York Evening Post*, 16 April 1928, 14.

42. "Bill Carrigan Going into the Banking Business," *Boston Daily Globe*, 17 November 1916, 1. Eminent Red Sox historian Ellery H. Clark Jr., in his book *Red Sox Forever*, separates the first seventy-five years of the Red Sox into five periods. The fourth period, from 1923 through 1933, was a "Decade of Despair." The second period, during which Carrigan managed, from 1912 to 1918, was the "Golden Age at Fenway Park." Ellery H. Clark Jr., *Red Sox Forever* (New York: Exposition Press, 1977), chapters 2 and 4; "Carrigan, Talking of Baseball, Surprised Himself by Signing Up," *Boston Daily Globe*, 2 December 1926, 1.

43. "Carrigan Not for Chain Store Idea," *Sporting News*, 2 February 1928, 1.

44. "Quinn Tells Why His Red Sox Are Better," *Sporting News*, 29 March 1928, 1.

45. "Carrigan Tells of First-Year Errors," *Sporting News*, 9 February 1928, 1.

46. Ford Sawyer, "Yankees Pound Out Game, 7–2," *Boston Daily Globe*, 17 April 1928, 27; Richards Vidmer, "Yanks Rout Red Sox; Homer for Gehrig," *New York Times*, 17 April 1928, 23.

47. "Cold Keeps Giants, Yanks, Robins Idle," *New York Times*, 18 April 1928, 21.

48. Tabulations taken from daily standings from the *New York Times*.

49. "Live Tips and Topics," *Boston Daily Globe*, 17 April 1928, 25.

50. Richards Vidmer, "Yanks Spray Hits to Repel Red Sox," *New York Times*, 19 April 1928, 17; John J. Ward, "A Rival For Babe Ruth?" *Baseball Magazine* 29, no. 2 (July 1925): 350.

51. James O'Leary, "Sox Victors, 7–6, Yankees Win, 7–21: Ruth's First Home Run of Year Delights 35,000; Home Team Flashes Late Rally for Morning Triumph," *Boston Daily Globe*, 20 April 1928, 1; Richards Vidmer, "Yanks Divide Day; Ruth Hits His First," *New York Times*, 20 April 1928, 27.

52. Hugh Bradley, "Meusel Seems to Have Hit Stride; Should Have One of Best Years with Yanks," *New York Evening Post*, 18 April 1928, 12.

53. "Population of Borough of the Bronx Has Passed the Million Mark," *New York Times*, 4 March 1928, 167; Charles E. Reid, "Bronx Still Holds Housing Record," *New York Times*, 15 January 1928, 154.

54. "Wind Lashes City, Many Hit by Debris," *New York Times*, 20 April 1928, 1; Frederick G. Lieb, "Ruth and Company in Peak Form for Local Debut," *New York Evening Post*, 20 April 1928, 1.

55. Dan Daniel, "World Champs Celebrate Twenty-Fifth Anniversary," *New York Telegram*, 20 April 1928, 13.

56. Dan Daniel, "Left-Field Line Will Be Stretched Out at Stadium," *New York Telegram*, 9 December 1927, 15.

57. Fred Lieb, "Cutting the Plate with Fred Lieb," *New York Evening Post*, 14 April 1928, 14; "Yanks and Giants to Test Plan Monday of Starting All Their Games at 3 O'clock," *New York Times*, 11 April 1928, 37.

58. Richards Vidmer, "Mayor among 55,000 Who See Yanks Bow to Athletics in Home Debut," *New York Times*, 21 April 1928, 12.

59. John Kieran, "Sports of the Times," *New York Times*, 24 April 1928, 23.

60. Dan Daniel, "Breaks Giving A's Victory Don't Alarm PeeWee Pilot," *New York Telegram*, 21 April 1928, 10. The one break Huggins was referring to was catcher Pat Collins's misplay of a foul pop by Max Bishop with two outs in the sixth inning.

61. Richards Vidmer, "Athletics Humble Yankees by 10 to 0," *New York Times*, 22 April 1928, 151; W. B. Hanna, "Walberg Gives Yankees First Shutout of '28," *New York Herald Tribune*, 22 April 1928, 2.

62. James Isaminger, "Yanks Dropped First Home Series Since '26," *Philadelphia Inquirer*, 23 April 1928, 16. It is interesting how Isaminger called the demise of Moore so soon in the season. On the same day, April 20, 1927, Moore had an ERA of 8.22, with seven earned runs in 7.2 innings pitched. In 1928, he had an ERA of 6.30, with seven earned runs in ten innings pitched.

63. Richards Vidmer, "Rain Halts Yanks, Giants, and Robins," *New York Times*, 23 April 1928, 26.

64. Richards Vidmer, "Huggins's Ultimatum to Shocker Will Expire Today," *New York Times*, 24 April 1928, 20; Richards Vidmer, "Yanks Set May 23 as Shocker's Limit: Huggins Fixes Time When the Pitcher Must Be Ready," *New York Times*, 28 April 1928, 14; "Shocker Signs with Yankees; Salary Begins When He Is Fit," *New York Times*, 25 April 1928, 21; "Huggins Still in Dark on Shocker's Return; Says He Has Received No Word from Pitcher," *New York Times*, 10 April 1928, 24.

65. "Shocker Is Back in Fold," *New York Telegram*, 25 April 1928, 13.

66. "Shocker Is Back in Fold," 13.

67. Dan Daniel, "Pilot of Senators Predicts Hard Sledding for Champs," *New York Telegram*, 24 April 1928, 11.

68. Daniel, "Pilot of Senators Predicts Hard Sledding for Champs," 11; James R. Harrison, "Trouble For Yanks Visioned by Harris," *New York Times*, 11 March 1928, 157. The Washington Senators won back-to-back pennants in 1924 and 1925, and finished the 1927 season with a respectable 86–69 record. Many of the team's key players from the championship years still remained, including Goose Goslin and Muddy Ruel, and they were still led by their second basemen and manager. The pitching staff had been almost completely overhauled.

69. Richards Vidmer, "Ruth Wallops Two; Senators Bow, 4–0," *New York Times*, 25 April 1928, 21.

70. Dan Daniel, "Tough Break in Luck Gives Harris Hopefuls Three Hits," *New York Telegram*, 25 April 1928, 13.

71. Daniel, "Tough Break in Luck Gives Harris Hopefuls Three Hits," 13.

72. "$1,000 Bet Laid Ruth Will Not Hit 50 homers; Yanks and Cards Picked to Win," *Philadelphia Inquirer*, 24 April 1928, 20.

73. Dan Daniel, "Champions Hand Senators Dose of Old-Time Clouting," *New York Telegram*, 26 April 1928, 13.

74. Richards Vidmer, "Hugmen Hit Hard; Rout Senators, 12–4," *New York Times*, 26 April 1928, 21.

75. Fred Lieb, "Cutting the Plate with Fred Lieb," *New York Evening Post*, 7 May 1928, 14.

76. Daniel, "Champions Hand Senators Dose of Old-Time Clouting," 13.

77. Daniel, "Champions Hand Senators Dose of Old-Time Clouting," 13.

78. Frank Graham, "Pipgras Once Cost Minor Club 60 Cents," *Sporting News*, 20 October 1927, 7.

79. Richards Vidmer, "Yanks' Siege Guns, Batter Boston, 9–4," *New York Times*, 27 April 1928, 19.

80. Dan Daniel, "Eighth-Inning Rally Gives Shealy His First Victory," *New York Telegram*, 27 April 1928, 13.

81. Daniel, "Eighth-Inning Rally Gives Shealy His First Victory," 13.

82. Daniel, "Eighth-Inning Rally Gives Shealy His First Victory," 13.

83. Daniel, "Eighth-Inning Rally Gives Shealy His First Victory," 13.

84. Vidmer, "Yanks Set May 23 as Shocker's Limit," 14; Frederick G. Lieb, "Durocher, Durst, Paschal Rise to the Occasion as Stars Grace Hospital List," *New York Evening Post*, 27 April 1928, 12.

85. James R. Harrison, "Rain Pelts Giants with Double Bills," *New York Times*, 29 April 1928, 1.

86. "Scribbled by Scribes," *Sporting News*, 3 May 1928, 4.

87. "Scribbled by Scribes," 4. Following two years of adverse weather, it was decided to begin the 1929 regular season one week later, around April 16, and end it on October 6, even though it would conflict with football. "Baseball Season to End Week Later," *New York Times*, 14 December 1928, 35.

88. Fred Lieb, "Cutting the Plate with Fred Lieb," *New York Evening Post*, 1 May 1928, 12.

89. James Isaminger, "Macks Must Play Eleven Games in Eight Days," *Philadelphia Inquirer*, 28 April 1928, 21. There were seven reasons given by Isaminger in the *Philadelphia Inquirer* for the turnaround of the Athletics: 1) the vital and consistent hitting of Ty Cobb and Tris Speaker; 2) the audacious fielding and heavy batting of shortstop Joe Boley; 3) the airtight pitching of Lefty Grove, Rube Walberg, and Jack Quinn; 4) the dramatic thumping of Sammy Hale, topped by his sound fielding; 5) the daredevil fielding of Max Bishop; 6) the demonical catching and timely hitting of Gordon [Mickey] Cochrane; and 7) the all-around excellence of Bing Miller.

90. James Isaminger, "Mack Disturbs Stock Market Players' Dope," *Philadelphia Inquirer*, 29 April 1928, S.

91. Frank H. Young, "Harris Sees Long Rest Ahead," *Washington Post*, 27 April 1928, 15; Frank H. Young, "Hapless Nats Try Again Today," *Washington Post*, 28 April 1928, 13.

92. "They Do Quite Well for Hospital Crew," *Sporting News*, 26 April 1928, 2.

93. Richards Vidmer, "Ruth's Fourth Puts Senators to Rout," *New York Times*, 30 April 1928, 15; Shirley L. Povich, "20,000 Watch Drive Off Lisenbee Clinch Victory for Yankees," *Washington Post*, 30 April 1928, 11.

94. F. C. Lane, "The New Ace of the Washington Hurling Corps," *Baseball Magazine* 40, no. 2 (January 1928): 359. The Senators' hopeful would suffer the same fate as his sinker-balling counterpart on the Yankees, Wilcy Moore. Both had excellent years in 1927, but their ineffectiveness would not allow either to finish the season. Lisenbee was given his fare to Minneapolis in early July after a poor showing against the White Sox. The Senators lost thirteen of sixteen games he appeared in, and he lost six of eight decisions. They were one-pitch pitchers, and for that reason Lisenbee was turned down by McGraw.

95. Richards Vidmer, "Yanks Triumph, 8–4, Their Fourth in Row," *New York Times*, 1 May 1928, 36.

96. Richards Vidmer, "Ruth's Fifth Sends Yanks Marching On," *New York Times*, 2 May 1928, 20; Shirley L. Povich, "Ruth Hits Fifth Home Run in Victory," *Washington Post*, 2 May 1928, 13.

97. Richards Vidmer, "Jones Writes Finis to Yankees' Streak," *New York Times*, 3 May 1928, 32.

98. Hugh Bradley, "Worrying Over Moundsman Who Will Turn Back Yanks Represents Wasted Energy," *New York Evening Post*, 1 May 1928, 12.

99. Frank H. Young, "Nats Seeking Seasoned Material," *Washington Post*, 3 May 1928, 13.

100. "6,000 See Yankees Win at West Point," *New York Times*, 4 May 1928, 30.

CHAPTER 6

1. John Kieran, "Sports of the Times," *New York Times*, 3 May 1928, 36.

2. Homer H. Metz, "Inclement Weather Again Holds Back Giants, Yanks," *New York Morning Telegraph*, 29 April 1928, 10.

3. "Casual Comment, by the Observer," *Sporting News*, 26 April 1928, 4.

4. Frederick G. Lieb, "Secret of Team's Success Lies in Its Ability to Win from Second Division Clubs," *New York Evening Post*, 4 May 1928, 17.

5. Lieb, "Secret of Team's Success Lies in Its Ability to Win From Second Division Clubs," 17.

6. Hugh Bradley, "Yankees' Heavy Slugging Has a Bad Effect upon Batters Opposing Hugmen," *New York Evening Post*, 2 May 1928, 12.

7. "Athletics Move at a Fast Clip," *Boston Daily Globe*, 2 May 1928, 16.

8. Edward Burns, "Up or Down, They're Our White Sox," *Chicago Daily Tribune*, 28 March 1928, 23.

9. Don Maxwell, "Speaking of Sports," *Chicago Daily Tribune*, 5 May 1928, 23. The White Sox, in fifth place, were champions of the second division three years running. There were thought to be some bright spots, the most legitimate being the pitching tandem of Ted Lyons and Tommy Thomas. "White Sox Again Pin Hopes on Arms of Lyons, Thomas," *Chicago Daily Tribune*, 19 February 1928, A5; "How About Yanks?" *Chicago Daily Tribune*, 28 March 1928, 23.

10. Irving Vaughan, "Yanks Drop Sox to Last Place, 10–4," *Chicago Daily Tribune*, 5 May 1928, 23.

11. James S. Collins, "Almost the Naked Truth," *Washington Post*, 4 January 1929, 13.

12. "City Crowds Lured Outdoors by Balmy Day Throng Beaches, Parks, and Sports Fields," *New York Times*, 6 May 1928, 3; Richards Vidmer, "55,000 See Yanks Beat White Sox; Reds Down Giants; Robins Divide with Cards," *New York Times*, 7 May 1928, 18.

13. Richards Vidmer, "Yanks Win, 8–5, and Sweep Series," *New York Times*, 7 May 1928, 20; John Kieran, "Sports of the Times," *New York Times*, 6 May 1928, 152.

14. As of May 7, the Yankees and Athletics had played nineteen games and fifteen games, respectively, while the Tigers and Browns had played twenty-six and twenty-five, respectively.

15. John Kieran, "Sports of the Times," *New York Times*, 10 May 1928, 25.

16. "Cleveland's House Is Put into Order," *Sporting News*, 1 December 1927, 7; "Arthur Fletcher Named Cleveland Manager," *Washington Post*, 8 December 1927, 17; Gordon Cobbledick, "Pitchers May Land Indians in Fourth," *Cleveland Plain Dealer*, 8 April 1928, 2C.

17. Eugene Murdock, *Baseball between the Wars: Memories of the Game by the Men Who Played It* (Westport, CT: Meckler, 1992), 5, 8.

18. Dan Daniel, "Increase in Salaries Has Pepped Up Cleveland Club," *New York Telegram*, 9 May 1928, 13; Dan Daniel, "Daniel's Dope," *New York Telegram*, 13 March 1928, 14; "Indian Outlook Not So Drear When One Lists Tribe Pitchers," *Sporting News*, 16 February 1928, 1; Cobbledick, "Pitchers May Land Indians in Fourth," 2C.

19. Frederick G. Lieb, "Huggins's Tossers Believe That Indians' Early Start Is Just a Flash in the Pan," *New York Evening Post*, 10 May 1928, 12.

20. Dan Daniel, "Hug Can See A's Only Foe," *New York Telegram*, 10 May 1928, 17.

21. Daniel, "Hug Can See A's Only Foe," 17.

22. Gordon Cobbledick, "Yankee Hurling Staff May Find It Tough When Doubleheader Come Along," *Cleveland Plain Dealer*, 8 May 1928, 3B.

23. Kieran, "Sports of the Times," 10 May 1928, 25; John J. Ward, "From Sandlots to the Majors," *Baseball Magazine* 31, no. 4 (September 1923): 453.

24. "Yanks Shut Out by the Indians, 3–0," *New York Times*, 9 May 1928, 29. Details for Yankee and Athletic games were taken from daily reporting in the *New York Times* and *Philadelphia Inquirer*, and from http://www.baseball-reference.com.

25. "Indians Don Paint and Go on War Path," *Sporting News*, 17 May 1928, 1.

26. "Eight Doubleheaders Loom for Yanks: Weather Causes Addition to List of Scheduled Games with the Indians," *New York Times*, 10 May 1928, 23. This was a tentative schedule.

27. Vidmer, "Yanks Win, 8–5, and Sweep Series," 18.

28. Dan Daniel, "Huggins's Plea Rouses Yanks to Break Grip of Ohio—Wow," *New York Telegram*, 11 May 1928, 13; Richards Vidmer, "Ruth's Seventh Homer Wins for Yanks, 4–2," *New York Times*, 11 May 1928, 28.

29. John Kieran, "Sports of the Times," *New York Times*, 9 May 1928, 32.

30. John P. Gallagher, "Yankees Spoiling Race for Rest of American Clubs," *Los Angeles Times*, 13 May 1928, C6; Irving Vaughan, "Boston Drops White Sox Back in Cellar, 4–3," *Chicago Daily Tribune*, 12 May 1928, 21.

31. "Harry Rice Proves Salvation of Tigers," *Sporting News*, 10 May 1928, 1. Detroit fans took pride in their team's seventeen batting titles, a dozen by Ty Cobb, four by current Tiger Harry Heilmann, and one for Manush, but they were now two years removed from the Ty Cobb era and almost three decades away from the three consecutive pennants under the recently mourned Hughie Jennings. Harry Bullion, "Tigers Rule with Bat," *Detroit Free Press*, 4 March 1928, S; Dan Daniel, "Moriarty Insists Detroit Is Best Club in the West," *New York Telegram*, 12 May 1928, 9.

32. Richards Vidmer, "Ruth's Eighth Aids in Subduing Tigers," *New York Times*, 13 May 1928, 145.

33. Richards Vidmer, "50,000 See Yankees Conquer Tigers, 7–2," *New York Times*, 14 May 1928, 25; James Isaminger, "Uhle Allows Macks But Single Base Hit," *Philadelphia Inquirer*, 14 May 1928, 16.

34. Dan Daniel, "Champs Perk Up with Bat as Lazzeri Gets in Form," *New York Telegram*, 15 May 1928, 11.

35. Richards Vidmer, "Ruth Hits Two More; Yanks Sweep Series," *New York Times*, 16 May 1928, 29.

36. "St. Louis Fans Convinced Browns Will Build from the Bottom Up," *Sporting News*, 22 December 1927, 1; Gordon Cobbledick, "Ball Seems Smart in Scrapping Vets," *Cleveland Plain Dealer*, 29 April 1928, 3B.

37. "Good Ones Often Enter Back Door," *Sporting News*, 19 January 1928, 1. Ski Melillo remained with the team as a backup for Brannan.

38. Martin J. Haley, "Two Recruits in Infield, Added Speed, and Punch Buoy Hopes of Browns," *Washington Post*, 29 March 1928, 13; John Drebinger, "Howley Is Building a New Browns Club," *New York Times*, 24 March 1928, 12; Cobbledick, "Ball Seems Smart in Scrapping Vets," 3B.

39. "Yankees Run Season's Wins Over St. Louis Browns to Twenty Straight," *Los Angeles Times*, 10 September 1927, 10.

40. Dan Daniel, "Home Run Derby Continues, Though Hit Total Is Curbed," *New York Telegram*, 28 July 1927, 13.

41. Dan Daniel, "Daniel's Dope," *New York Telegram*, 29 July 1927, 16.

42. Dan Daniel, "Urban May Face Old Team in Stadium Battle Sunday," *New York Telegram*, 19 May 1928, 11.

43. Dan Daniel, "Depleted Heaving Ranks Puts Burden on Attack," *New York Telegram*, 18 May 1928, 15.

44. Irving Vaughan, "Grove Gives Sox Two Hits; Macks Win, 2–0," *Chicago Daily Tribune*, 20 May 1928, A1; "Mack Snaps," *Philadelphia Inquirer*, 20 May 1928, S.

45. Daniel, "Depleted Heaving Ranks Puts Burden on Attack," 15.

46. Richards Vidmer, "Yanks Win by 9–3 for Eighth Straight," *New York Times*, 21 May 1928, 16; "Shocker Ban Lifted to Reinforce Yanks; Landis Reinstates the Veteran Hurler, Who Was a Holdout Until He Signed April 25," *New York Times*, 19 May 1928, 15.

CHAPTER 7

1. Stan Baumgartner, "42,000 Mad Fans Perch Everywhere," *Philadelphia Inquirer*, 25 May 1928, 20.

2. James Isaminger, "Tips from the Sporting Ticker," *Philadelphia Inquirer*, 20 May 1928, S7.

3. John Kieran, "Sports of the Times," *New York Times*, 22 May 1928, 25.

4. Fred Lieb, "Cutting the Plate with Fred Lieb," *New York Evening Post*, 22 May 1928, 12.

5. Richards Vidmer, "Yanks Feel March to Flag Is Easy," *New York Times*, 20 May 1928, 147.

6. "Between Macks and Yanks Says Ruppert," *Philadelphia Inquirer*, 23 May 1928, 20.

7. Dan Daniel, "Urban May Face Old Team in Stadium Battle Sunday," *New York Telegram*, 19 May 1928, 11.

8. Richards Vidmer, "Yanks and Red Sox Split Double Bill," *New York Times*, 22 May 1928, 22. Details for Yankee and Athletic games were taken from daily reporting in the *New York Times* and *Philadelphia Inquirer*, and from http://www.baseball-reference.com.

9. James Isaminger, "Shores Is Enigma to Griffs, Who Bow, 4–2," *Philadelphia Inquirer*, 24 May 1928, 22.

10. Frederick G. Lieb, "Ruth, Far Ahead of Record, Adds Two More Home Runs, Making Sixteen for Season," *New York Evening Post*, 26 May 1928, 12.

11. Fred Lieb, "Cutting the Plate with Fred Lieb," *New York Evening Post*, 29 June 1929, 17.

12. Richards Vidmer, "Yanks Break Even; Ruth Clouts No. Fourteen," *New York Times*, 25 May 1928, 18.

13. Baumgartner, "42,000 Mad Fans Perch Everywhere," 20.

14. Baumgartner, "42,000 Mad Fans Perch Everywhere," 20.

15. James Isaminger, "Shibe Park Shorts," *Philadelphia Inquirer*, 26 May 1928, 20.

16. Baumgartner, "42,000 Mad Fans Perch Everywhere," 20.

17. "Quaker Fans Have Their Brief Thrills," *Sporting News*, 31 May 1928, 1.

18. "Quaker Fans Have Their Brief Thrills," 1.

19. "Thousands of Frenzied Fans Storm Shibe Park to See Athletics Battle Yankees," *Philadelphia Public Record*, 25 May 1928, 11; Baumgartner, "42,000 Mad Fans Perch Everywhere," 20.

20. Frederick G. Lieb, "Connie Mack Still Trying for Seventh Championship as Huggins Draws Nearer," *New York Evening Post*, 24 May 1928, 12. The six pennants won by Mack include the year 1902.

21. Vidmer, "Yanks Break Even; Ruth Clouts No. Fourteen," 18; James Isaminger, "Record Crowd In, Around, and On Top of Stands as Macks Split with Yanks," *Philadelphia Inquirer*, 25 May 1928, 20.

22. "Expert Working on Wilcy to Restore Snap to Arm," *New York Telegram*, 25 May 1928, 14.

23. "Sports Editorial," *Philadelphia Public Record*, 25 May 1928, 12.

24. Frederick G. Lieb, "Yankee Ace Relief Hurler Likely to Be of Little Help to Club for Rest of Season," *New York Evening Post*, 25 May 1928, 12; "Expert Working on Wilcy to Restore Snap to Arm," 14.

25. Fred Lieb, "Cutting the Plate with Fred Lieb," *New York Evening Post*, 25 May 1928, 12.

26. James Isaminger, "Babe Hits Fifteenth and Sixteenth, Dugan Socks Pair as Yanks Trip A's in Twin Bill," *Philadelphia Inquirer*, 26 May 1928, 20; Stan Baumgartner, "Paper Shower Rivals Homer Deluge at A's," *Philadelphia Inquirer*, 26 May 1928, 20; Richards Vidmer, "Yanks Win Twice; Ruth Hits Two More," *New York Times*, 26 May 1928, 10.

27. "Baseball Mad," *Washington Post*, 26 May 1928, 6.

28. "Sports Editorial," *Philadelphia Public Record*, 26 May 1928, 12.

29. James Isaminger, "Tips from the Sport Ticker," *Philadelphia Inquirer*, 27 May 1928, 9.

30. John M. McCullough, "30,000 Hearts Sad as Collins Whiffs," *Philadelphia Inquirer*, 27 May 1928, S2.

31. James Isaminger, "Yankees Heavy Guns Send Mackmen Down," *Philadelphia Inquirer*, 27 May 1928, S2; Richards Vidmer, "Athletics Beaten by the Yankees, 7–4," *New York Times*, 27 May 1928, 141; James Isaminger, "Athletics Lose Another to Yankees," *Philadelphia Inquirer*, 27 May 1928, S.

32. James Isaminger, "Athletics Lose Another to Yankees," S.

33. Dan Daniel, "Daniel's Dope," *New York Telegram*, 23 January 1928, 13; "Yankee Siege Guns Crush York, 9–2," *New York Times*, 28 May 1928, 29.

34. Joe Vila, "Series with Yanks Has Netted A's Big Profit," *Philadelphia Inquirer*, 27 May 1928, 9.

35. James Isaminger, "Hadley Gives Macks Fourth Loss in a Row," *Philadelphia Inquirer*, 28 May 1928, 14.

36. James Isaminger, "Yanks Hit at Merry Clip and Beat Athletics, 11–4," *Philadelphia Inquirer*, 29 May 1928, 20; Richards Vidmer, "Yankees Win Again; Take Five in Six," *New York Times*, 29 May 1928, 19.

37. Frederick G. Lieb, "Mack Feels Failure of A's Acutely; Was Sure Hurlers Would Still Hugmen's Bats," *New York Evening Post*, 28 May 1928, 12.

38. Gordon Mackay, "Is Zat So," *Philadelphia Public Record*, 28 May 1928, 11.

39. John Kieran, "Sports of the Times," *New York Times*, 29 May 1928, 23.

40. Kieran, "Sports of the Times," 29 May 1928, 23.

41. James Isaminger, "A's Land Earnshaw by Trading Shores," *Philadelphia Inquirer*, 29 May 1928, 20. Earnshaw was not at the top of his game when he came to Philadelphia, as he was not expecting to be sold by Jack Dunn during the current season. He based his judgment on the length of time it took Jack Ogden and Joe Boley to be moved. He was in the worst shape of his career and had won only three of seven when the Athletics came calling. Bill Dooley, "Three and Two," *Philadelphia Public Record*, 24 June 1928, S4.

42. Dan Daniel, "Yanks After New Record," *New York Telegram*, 29 May 1928, 10.

43. Daniel, "Yanks After New Record," 10.

44. Richards Vidmer, "Yankees Take Two from the Senators," *New York Times*, 30 May 1928, 14. This doubleheader included the makeup game from the April 23 postponement.

45. Alan J. Gould, "Yanks Making Runaway of Race," *Los Angeles Times*, 30 May 1928, B1.

46. Frank H. Young, "Yanks Reciprocate in Ruether Deal by Transferring Pair," *Washington Post*, 31 August 1926, 13; James R. Harrison, "Braxton Subdues White Sox in Debut," *New York Times*, 24 September 1925, 20; "Yankees Buy Springfield Pitcher," *New York Times*, 21 August 1925, 9; Richards Vidmer, "Senators and Rain Ruin Day for Yanks," *New York Times*, 31 May 1928, 29.

47. "Pickups and Putouts," *New York Times*, 1 June 1928, 20; Richards Vidmer, "Ruth Slams Nineteenth; Yankees Win, 4–0," *New York Times*, 1 June 1928, 20.

48. Frederick G. Lieb, "Huggins's Southpaw Marvel Places Ball at Exact Spot He Desires in Blanking Nats," *New York Evening Post*, 1 June 1928, 16.

CHAPTER 8

1. Hugh Bradley, "Yankees Coin New Slogan to Revive Ebbing Spirits of Fearful Club Owners," *New York Evening Post*, 13 June 1928, 17.

2. John Kieran, "Sports of the Times," *New York Times*, 31 May 1928, 34; Bill Dooley, "Three and Two," *Philadelphia Public Record*, 3 June 1928, 4S.

3. Joe Vila, "Let Other American League Clubs Go Out and Buy Players as We Have Done, Says Barrow in Answering General Yelp," *Philadelphia Inquirer*, 1 June 1928, 21.

4. Pat Robinson, "Yanks See Race Cinch," *New York Telegram*, 2 June 1928, 11.

5. "World Champs Invade West Seven and a Half Tilts Ahead," *New York Telegram*, 1 June 1928, 13.

6. Hugh Bradley, "Study of Statistics Shows Yanks Are Winning Repute as Sterling Fielding Club," *New York Evening Post*, 4 June 1928, 12.

7. Hugh Bradley, "Yanks Don't Mind Losing Regular Stars from Team; They Win Just the Same," *New York Evening Post*, 2 June 1928, 12.

8. James R. Harrison, "Rain Again Balks Yankees in Detroit," *New York Times*, 6 June 1928, 19.

9. Ty Cobb, with Al Stump, *My Life in Baseball: The True Record* (Lincoln: University of Nebraska Press, 1993), 200–201.

10. Harrison, "Rain Again Balks Yankees in Detroit," 19.

11. James R. Harrison, "Yanks' Three in Tenth Beat Detroit, 5–2," *New York Times*, 3 June 1928, S1.

12. James R. Harrison, "40,000 See Yankees Tame Tigers, 7–2," *New York Times*, 4 June 1928, 23; Pat Robinson, "Huggins Not in Any Deals," *New York Telegram*, 5 June 1928, 12.

13. Harrison, "40,000 See Yankees Tame Tigers, 7–2," 23; Robinson, "Huggins Not in Any Deals," 12.

14. Pat Robinson, "Injured Ankle May Keep Bambino Out for Few Days," *New York Telegram*, 4 June 1928, 14.

15. Dan Daniel, "Yanks Have A's Scared," *New York Telegram*, 20 June 1928, 13.

16. "Can This Be True? Babe Slipping!" *Los Angeles Times*, 17 June 1928, A6.

17. Homer George, "Babe Could Hit Hundred Home Runs," *Los Angeles Times*, 10 June 1928, A4.

18. James R. Harrison, "Huggins Thinks Giants Will Win," *New York Times*, 5 June 1928, 25.

19. Robinson, "Huggins Not in Any Deals," 12.

20. Hugh Bradley, "Yanks Stretch Their Hits into Extra-Base Safeties by Daring, Speedy Running," *New York Evening Post*, 5 June 1928, 12.

21. Ibid.

22. R. L. Duffus, "Our Changing Cities: Opulent Cleveland," *New York Times*, 1 May 1927, SM10. The city had a forty-nine-year history in Major League Baseball in three leagues. The one flag came under Tris Speaker in 1920; before that, as the Spiders, from 1892 through 1896, they were led by manager Patsy Tabeau and pitcher Cy Young. Those clubs finished in second place three times, third place, and sixth place. Joe Vila, "Cleveland, with Teams in Three Leagues, Had One Flag Winner in 49 Years," *Philadelphia Inquirer*, 10 May 1928, 24.

23. Pat Robinson, "Dugan Sets Dizzy Pace," *New York Telegram*, 8 June 1928, 13.

24. "Scribbled by Scribes," *Sporting News*, 7 June 1928, 4.

25. James R. Harrison, "Record of Old Cubs Imperiled by Yanks," *New York Times*, 9 June 1928, 11; Alan J. Gould, "Yanks Making Runaway of Race," *Los Angeles Times*, 30 May 1928, B1.

26. Hugh Bradley, "Huggins Certain His Yanks Will Go Way of All Ivory, but Hardly This Season," *New York Evening Post*, 9 June 1928, 12.

27. Homer H. Metz, "Stars of Yankees Are Worth Nearly a Cool Million in Baseball Market," *New York Morning Telegraph*, 2 September 1928, 8.

28. Charles C. Alexander, *Spoke: A Biography of Tris Speaker* (Dallas, TX: Southern Methodist University Press, 2007), 271.

29. Pat Robinson, "Wilcy's Arm Is OK Again," *New York Telegram*, 9 June 1928, 8.

30. Hugh Bradley, "Prophet Ruth's Prediction of 40 Wins and 10 Losses Faces Acid Test in Chicago," *New York Evening Post*, 12 June 1928, 14.

31. James Isaminger, "Tips from the Sporting Ticker," *Philadelphia Inquirer*, 10 June 1928, S10. The inability of the American League to generate a three- or four-team pennant race in recent years was termed the "race suicide" or even the "race problem"—not to be confused with the later issue of breaking the color barrier.

32. James R. Harrison, "Ruth's Two Homers Fail to Save Yanks," *New York Times*, 11 June 1928, 15.

33. James R. Harrison, "Yankees Humbled by White Sox, 6–1," *New York Times*, 12 June 1928, 21.

34. Hugh Bradley, "Durocher May Have Talked Himself into Regular Job in Miller Huggins's Infield," *New York Evening Post*, 12 June 1928, 18.

35. James R. Harrison, "Yankees Bombard White Sox, 15–7," *New York Times*, 13 June 1928, 21.

36. Hugh Bradley, "Yankees Coin New Slogan to Revive Ebbing Spirits of Fearful Club Owners," 17.

37. James R. Harrison, "Yanks Win Again and Divide Series," *New York Times*, 14 June 1928, 33.

38. Joe Williams, "Snappy Platter by Mr. Hendricks," *New York Telegram*, 7 June 1928, 16.

39. Williams, "Snappy Platter by Mr. Hendricks," 16.

40. Joe Williams, "One of Those Futile Debates," *New York Telegram*, 9 June 1928, 8.

41. Williams, "One of Those Futile Debates," 8; Dan Daniel, "Colonel Won't Let Lary and Reese Slip; Thinks Yanks Are Good for Five Years," *New York Telegram*, 28 December 1927, 13.

42. John Kieran, "Sports of the Times," *New York Times*, 13 June 1928, 25.

43. Williams, "One of those Futile Debates," 8; Daniel, "Colonel Won't Let Lary and Reese Slip," 13.

44. John Kieran, "Sports of the Times," *New York Times*, 6 June 1928, 21; John Kieran, "Sports of the Times," *New York Times*, 15 July 1928, S2; John Kieran, "Sports of the Times," *New York Times*, 13 July 1928, 22.

45. "Scribbled by Scribes," *Sporting News*, 14 June 1928, 4.

46. R. L. Duffus, "Our Changing Cities: Sturdy St. Louis," *New York Times*, 3 April 1927, SM8.

47. "Editorial Page," *Sporting News*, 14 June 1928, 4.

48. Hugh Bradley, "Browns Are Having Trouble Living Down Poor Repute Gained in Second Division," *New York Evening Post*, 15 June 1928, 17.

49. Hugh Bradley, "Great Days for California with Lazzeri and Hoover Making Good in Big-Time," *New York Evening Post*, 14 June 1928, 4.

50. James R. Harrison, "Ruth's 24th Fails to Check Browns," *New York Times*, 16 June 1928, 20.

51. Hugh Bradley, "Pitching Problems Worry Huggins Despite Big Lead of Yanks Over Other Clubs," *New York Evening Post*, 16 June 1928, 10.

52. Robinson, "Wilcy's Arm Is OK Again," 8.

53. James R. Harrison, "Browns' Onslaught Levels Yanks, 7–5," *New York Times*, 17 June 1928, 139.

54. James R. Harrison, "Ruth Hits No. 25; Yanks Stop Browns," *New York Times*, 18 June 1928, 14.

CHAPTER 9

1. "Live and Tips Topics Dope on Baseball Race Good," *Boston Daily Globe*, 30 May 1928, 9.

2. "The Two Leagues," *Washington Post*, 18 June 1928, 4.

3. Dan Daniel, "Daniel's Dope," *New York Telegram*, 18 June 1928, 12.

4. J. P. Gallagher, "Yankees Spoiling Race for Rest of American Clubs," *Los Angeles Times*, 13 May 1928, C6; "Navin Adamant When Detroit Fans Demand Moriarty's Head," *Sporting News*, 14 June 1928, 1; "Scribbled by Scribes," *Sporting News*, 28 June 1928, 4.

5. "Navin Adamant When Detroit Fans Demand Moriarty's Head," 1.

6. "All Not Paved Road for Yanks in West," *Sporting News*, 21 June 1928, 1.

7. "Marvels at Finding Way to Lose Games," *Sporting News*, 21 June 1928, 3.

8. Dan Daniel, "Pilot Credits Reserves for Yankee Breeze in the West," *New York Telegram*, 19 June 1928, 12.

9. Daniel, "Pilot Credits Reserves for Yankee Breeze in the West," 12.

10. Daniel, "Pilot Credits Reserves for Yankee Breeze in the West," 12.

11. Daniel, "Pilot Credits Reserves for Yankee Breeze in the West," 12.

12. Hugh Bradley, "Travel Broadens Yankees and Widens Open Spaces between Hugs and Macks," *New York Evening Post*, 18 June 1928, 12.

13. Hugh Bradley, "Figures Show Why Race Lacks Heat," *New York Evening Post*, 19 June 1928, 12.

14. J. Roy Stockton, "The Star of the Late World's Series," *Baseball Magazine* 40, no. 1 (December 1927): 293–94.

15. Fred Lieb, "Cutting the Plate with Fred Lieb," *New York Evening Post*, 19 June 1928, 12.

16. Lieb, "Cutting the Plate with Fred Lieb," 12.

17. James Isaminger, "Macks Must Clean Up to Remain in Race," *Philadelphia Inquirer*, 20 June 1928, 22.

18. Homer H. Metz, "Hugmen and Athletics Clash in Double Bills Today and Tomorrow," *New York Morning Telegraph*, 20 June 1928, 7.

19. Metz, "Hugmen and Athletics Clash in Double Bills Today and Tomorrow," 7.

20. Dan Daniel, "Yanks Have A's Scared," *New York Telegram*, 20 June 1928, 13; Isaminger, "Macks Must Clean Up to Remain in Race," 22.

21. Frederick G. Lieb, "Huggins Believes Yankees Must Win Over 100 Games to Retain Championship," *New York Evening Post*, 20 June 1928, 12.

22. Lieb, "Huggins Believes Yankees Must Win Over 100 Games to Retain Championship," 12.

23. "Yankees After Victory Record Made by Cubs," *Los Angeles Times*, 24 June 1928, A5; "American League Owners Unorthodox in Business," *Hartford Courant*, 25 June 1928, 14; "All-Star Cast Suggested as Opponent for Yankees," *Washington Post*, 6 June 1928, 11; "Profits Scarce in American League," *Washington Post*, 9 June 1928, 11; "The Two Leagues," 4; "Billy Evans Says Yankees Greatest Ball Club of All," *Hartford Courant*, 17 June 1928, C1; Albert Keane, "Calling 'Em Right," *Hartford Courant*, 22 June 1928, 14; Richards Vidmer, "Yanks Feel March to Flag Is Easy," *New York Times*, 20 May 1928, 147.

24. James R. Harrison, "Yankees' Dual Bill Ends in Even Break," *New York Times*, 21 June 1928, 20. Details for Yankee and Athletic games were taken from daily reporting in the *New York Times* and *Philadelphia Inquirer*, and from http://www.baseball-reference.com.

25. Dan Daniel, "George Pipgras Now Leads American League Pitchers," *New York Telegram*, 21 June 1928, 14. Foxx was one of baseball's "baby twins," along with Mel Ott of the Giants. Foxx was born in Sudlersville, Maryland, on October 22, 1907, and Ott in Gretna, Louisiana, on March 2, 1909. Tris Speaker and Ty Cobb were just beginning their major-league careers. "Baseball's Baby Twins," *New York Telegram*, 22 June 1928, 12.

26. Frederick G. Lieb, "Yank Pilot Nearly Ready to Admit League Pennant Is Safely within His Grasp," *New York Evening Post*, 22 June 1928, 12.

27. Gordon Mackay, "Is Zat So," *Philadelphia Public Record*, 25 June 1928, 11; James R. Harrison, "Athletics Shut Out by the Yankees; Giants Split with Braves," *New York Times*, 22 June 1928, 16.

28. James R. Harrison, "Rain Brings Yanks More Double Bills," *New York Times*, 23 June 1928, 11; Bill Dooley, "Rain Washes Out Final Yankee Fray; Mack's Meet Senators Today," *Philadelphia Public Record*, 23 June 1928, 11. Two of the ten additional postponements were made up with the June 20 doubleheader.

29. Frederick G. Lieb, "Huggins' Outfit to Essay Fourth Twin Bill of Week against Boston Nine Today," *New York Evening Post*, 23 June 1928, 12.

30. Dan Daniel, "Johnson Justifies Faith Placed in Him by Huggins," *New York Telegram*, 23 June 1928, 10.

31. Daniel, "Johnson Justifies Faith Placed in Him by Huggins," 10.

32. James R. Harrison, "Ruth Hits Two Homers, but Yanks Lose Two," *New York Times*, 24 June 1928, S1; "Red Sox Trample on Yanks in Twin Bill," *Boston Daily Globe*, 24 June 1928, A18.

33. Frederick G. Lieb, "Southpaw Star Has Lost Three of Last Four Starts; Moore Slipping as Relief," *New York Evening Post*, 25 June 1928, 12.

34. James R. Harrison, "Ruth Hits Homer as Yankees Blank Red Sox, 4–0; Robins Shut Out Giants, 2–0," *New York Times*, 25 June 1928, 15; "Pickups and Putouts," *New York Times*, 25 June 1928, 15.

35. Lieb, "Southpaw Star Has Lost Three of Last Four Starts," 12. The disappointing pitching of Wilcy Moore, the status of Urban Shocker, and the slumping Herb Pennock were concerns for Huggins.

36. Pat Robinson, "Connie Mack Sees Flag Hopes Fading but Declares A's Will Fight to Finish," *New York Telegram*, 27 June 1928, 13. At the same time, Mack did not regret his purchases of Bishop, Grove, and Boley from Jack Dunn during a span of four years at a cost of $225,000. James Isaminger, "Tips from the Sporting Ticker," *Philadelphia Inquirer*, 10 July 1927, S6.

37. Frederick G. Lieb, "Hugmen Start New Series with Second-Place Macks Ten Full Games in Lead," *New York Evening Post*, 27 June 1928, 14.

38. James R. Harrison, "Yanks Rally in Eighth to Down Athletics," *New York Times*, 28 June 1928, 20.

39. Frederick G. Lieb, "Lefty Grove Proves Bust as Slayer of Hugmen for Fifth Time in Six Starts," *New York Evening Post*, 28 June 1928, 16; James Isaminger, "Henry Johnson a Nemesis Once More," *Philadelphia Inquirer*, 28 June 1928, 22.

40. Bill Dooley, "Three and Two," *Philadelphia Public Record*, 1 July 1928, 5.

41. Pat Robinson, "Yanks Lead by Twelve Tilts," *New York Telegram*, 29 June 1928, 14.

42. Robinson, "Yanks Lead by Twelve Tilts," 14.

43. James R. Harrison, "Ruth Hits Two Homers as Yanks Win, 10–4," *New York Times*, 29 June 1928, 19; James Isaminger, "Bambino Raps 29th and 30th Home Runs," *Philadelphia Inquirer*, 29 June 1928, 22.

44. James Isaminger, "Mark Koenig Clouts Homer in Ninth Frame," *Philadelphia Inquirer*, 30 June 1928, 20.

45. James R. Harrison, "Yanks Are Stopped by Athletics, 6–4," *New York Times*, 30 June 1928, 21; Frederick G. Lieb, "Pennock Hurls Courageous Game, but Skill, Control of Other Days Are Lacking," *New York Evening Post*, 30 June 1928, 12.

46. James R. Harrison, "Yankees Take Two from the Red Sox," *New York Times*, 1 July 1928, 133; James O'Leary, "Yankees Sweep Doubleheader with Red Sox," *Boston Daily Globe*, 1 July 1928, A16.

47. James Isaminger, "Gehrig and Lazzeri Crash Two Homers," *Philadelphia Inquirer*, 2 July 1928, 17.

48. James R. Harrison, "60,000 See Yanks Win Doubleheader," *New York Times*, 2 July 1928, 21; "Four of Five Leading Batsmen in American League Are Yanks," *New York Times*, 2 July 1928, 21.

49. James Isaminger, "Tips from the Sporting Ticker," *Philadelphia Inquirer*, 1 July 1928, S6.

50. Harrison, "60,000 See Yanks Win Doubleheader," 21.

51. John Kieran, "Sports of the Times," *New York Times*, 7 August 1928, 19.

52. John Kieran, "Sports of the Times," *New York Times*, 3 July 1928, 17.

53. "This Postponement Is Made Indefinite," *Sporting News*, 5 July 1928, 3.

54. "This Postponement Is Made Indefinite," 3.

55. James R. Harrison, "Ruth Propels 31st, but Yanks Bow, 4–3," *New York Times*, 3 July 1928, 14.

56. "Ruth Autographs 51 Baseballs for Military Training Camps," *New York Times*, 3 July 1928, 15.

57. Fred Lieb, "Cutting the Plate with Fred Lieb," *New York Evening Post*, 3 July 1928, 10.

58. Frank H. Young, "Yanks Face Dearth of Pitchers," *Washington Post*, 3 July 1928, 11.

59. James R. Harrison, "Yankees Win in Eleventh from Senators, 7–6," *New York Times*, 4 July 1928, 16.

60. "38 Die as 3,000,000 Jam Resorts Here," *New York Evening Post*, 5 July 1928, 1.

61. James R. Harrison, "Yanks Bow, 5 to 2, Then Beat Senators," *New York Times*, 5 July 1928, 20; Shirly L. Povich, "Barnes Wins First Game by Homer," *Washington Post*, 5 July 1928, 11.

CHAPTER 10

1. James R. Harrison, "60,000 See Yanks Win Doubleheader," *New York Times*, 2 July 1928, 21.

2. Alan J. Gould, "Yanks Luck Ascribed to Huggins' Management," *Washington Post*, 30 June 1928, 11.

3. James R. Harrison, "Browns to Attack Yanks Here Today," *New York Times*, 6 July 1928, 17. Frederick G. Lieb favored giving a split season of seventy-seven games a tryout for one year. It was tried once in the National League in the 1890s. Frederick G. Lieb, "Would Make Little Change in American League Chase, But Very Much in National," *New York Evening Post*, 3 August 1927, 12.

4. "Baseball Prospects," *Washington Post*, 1 July 1928, S1; "No Fat Checks Come from Detroit Visits," *Sporting News*, 5 July 1928, 1.

5. Dan Daniel, "Hug Wants Bigger Lead," *New York Telegram*, 5 July 1928, 13.

6. "Suburbs Hit by Downpour as Heat Is Routed," *New York Herald Tribune*, 7 July 1928, 5.

7. Frederick G. Lieb, "Victory in Forty-One Tilts Would Give Huggins' Clan Better Record Than in 1926," *New York Evening Post*, 6 July 1928, 12.

8. Lieb, "Victory in Forty-One Tilts Would Give Huggins' Clan Better Record Than in 1926," 12.

9. Dan Daniel, "Yanks in Three Twin Bills with Browns in Three Days," *New York Telegram*, 7 July 1928, 9.

10. Daniel, "Yanks in Three Twin Bills with Browns in Three Days," 9. The previous year, Huggins was increasingly at ease with his pitching situation as the season progressed. The three young hurlers giving him growing confidence were Myles Thomas, who was small and crafty; Wilcy Moore, a big, powerful sinker baller; and George Pipgras, who was a lot like Moore but was thought to need more seasoning. "Young Yankee Hurlers Star," *New York Telegram*, 7 July 1927, 13.

11. Daniel, "Yanks in Three Twin Bills with Browns in Three Days," 9.

12. Frank H. Young, "Yankees Again in Reach of .700 Winning Season," *Washington Post*, 8 July 1928, 19.

13. Frederick G. Lieb, "Yankees, Back from West, Almost Certain of Flag, Now Seek to Break Marks," *New York Evening Post*, 26 July 1927, 12.

14. Albert Keane, "Calling 'Em Right," *Hartford Courant*, 11 July 1928, 13. Only catcher Wally Schang and third baseman Frank O'Rourke remained from the regular lineup from 1927.

15. James R. Harrison, "Yanks Lose Twice as Ruth Hits 32nd," *New York Times*, 9 July 1928, 19. Meusel missed twenty-three games from May 29 through June 26.

16. "Rain Halts Yanks-Tigers; Postponement Causes Doubleheader to Be Listed for Today," *New York Times*, 11 July 1928, 25. Details for Yankee and Athletic games were taken from daily reporting in the *New York Times* and *Philadelphia Inquirer*, and from http://www.baseball-reference.com.

17. "Heat Kills Six, Fells Twenty-Four Here; Cool Wind and Showers Due," *New York Herald Tribune*, 10 July 1928, 1.

18. "Rain Breaks Heat after Forty-Five Die Here," *New York Evening Post*, 10 July 1928, 1.

19. "No Fat Checks Come from Detroit Visits," *Sporting News*, 5 July 1928, 1.

20. Dan Daniel, "Tigers Lose Old Morale," *New York Telegram*, 11 July 1928, 12.

21. Fred Lieb, "Cutting the Plate with Fred Lieb," *New York Evening Post*, 26 July 1927, 14.

22. Frederick G. Lieb, "Hugmen to Play Fourth Successive Double Bill on Stadium Field Today," *New York Evening Post*, 11 July 1928, 12.

23. James R. Harrison, "Ruth Hits Thirty-Third as Yanks Break Even; Giants and Robins Win," *New York Times*, 12 July 1928, 25.

24. James R. Harrison, "Yankees Again Bow to the Tigers, 4–2," *New York Times*, 13 July 1928, 20.

25. Beginning in 1918, all teams finishing in the first division were given a share in the World Series money. In August, at a meeting of both leagues, it was originally decided to give all sixteen clubs a share, but it was narrowed down to the top four finishers in each league. "Each Member of Winning Team to Receive $2,000, Losers $1,400, Under New Plan," *New York Herald Tribune*, 1 January 1918, 17.

26. James Isaminger, "Worst Is Now Over, Says Geo. Moriarty, Speaking of Tigers," *Philadelphia Inquirer*, 15 July 1928, 2. Carl Hubbell won ten games for a poor Beaumont team in the minors and was not one of the Tiger prospects taken north with the team by manager George Moriarty. On July 13, the Giants announced that they paid the largest sum ever for the Texas League player when they purchased the contract of the twenty-three-year-old left-hander. Ty Cobb was unfairly blamed for releasing Hubbell before he left Detroit in 1926. "Giants Pay Record Price For Hubbell," *New York Evening Post*, 13 July 1928, 13; Ty Cobb, with Al Stump, *My Life in Baseball: The True Record* (Lincoln: University of Nebraska Press, 1993), 211.

27. Dan Daniel, "Daniel's Dope," *New York Telegram*, 12 July 1928, 15.

28. James R. Harrison, "Yanks and Indians Stopped by Rain," *New York Times*, 15 July 1928, S2.

29. Frederick G. Lieb, "Myles Thomas Scheduled to Succeed Wilcy Moore as Leading Relief Hurler," *New York Evening Post*, 14 July 1928, 12.

30. Dan Daniel, "Postponement Gives Yanks Another Chance to Rest Up," *New York Telegram*, 14 July 1928, 8.

31. Daniel, "Postponement Gives Yanks Another Chance to Rest Up," 8.

32. James R. Harrison, "Ruth Clouts Thirty-Fourth as Yanks Win Two," *New York Times*, 16 July 1928, 20.

33. John P. Gallagher, "Yanks' Supremacy Causes Race Suicide in Majors," *Los Angeles Times*, 15 July 1928, A4.

34. "Split Season in American Might Prove Beneficial: With the New York Yankees Putting on Their Runaway Act Last Season and Again This Year, Division Should Help Keep Up Interest," *Hartford Courant*, 15 July 1928, C7.

35. Bill Dooley, "Three and Two," *Philadelphia Public Record*, 15 July 1928, S6.

36. James R. Harrison, "Yankees Take Two; Ruth Drives No. 35," *New York Times*, 17 July 1928, 16.

37. "Schalk Is Popular with Sox Players," *Sporting News*, 25 November 1926, 3.

38. Dooley, "Three and Two," S6; Dan Daniel, "Bambino Expected to Pull Whole Team to New Mark," *New York Telegram*, 21 July 1928, 9; "White Sox Pepping Up," *New York Telegram*, 16 July 1928, 10.

39. James R. Harrison, "Yanks Win When Ruth Hits Homer in Ninth; Robins Lose Two," *New York Times*, 19 July 1928, 15.

40. Dan Daniel, "Bam Blasts Thomas' Hope of Victory Over Yankees," *New York Telegram*, 20 July 1928, 11.

41. Daniel, "Bam Blasts Thomas' Hope of Victory Over Yankees," 11.

42. Daniel, "Bam Blasts Thomas' Hope of Victory Over Yankees," 11.

43. James R. Harrison, "Yankees Win 7th in Row as Ruth Smashes 37th and 38th; Robins Blank the Pirates," *New York Times*, 20 July 1928, 13.

44. James R. Harrison, "Yankees Equal Pace They Set Last Year," *New York Times*, 21 July 1928, 14.

45. Dan Daniel, "Daniel's Dope," *New York Telegram*, 20 July 1928, 12.

46. Daniel, "Daniel's Dope," 12.

47. James R. Harrison, "Ruth's 39th Brings Walsh's Downfall," *New York Times*, 22 July 1928, 123. This was the farthest ahead of his 1927 home run pace Ruth would reach before beginning to tail off and fall behind.

48. Daniel, "Bambino Expected to Pull Whole Team to New Mark," 9.

49. Bill Brandt, "Grove and Quinn Triumph on Mound, Streak Now Seven in Row," *Philadelphia Public Ledger*, 22 July 1928, S1.

50. James R. Harrison, "Faber's Hit Beats Yankees by 6–4," *New York Times*, 23 July 1928, 20.

51. James R. Harrison, "Ruth Hits His 40th as Red Sox Win, 8–3," *New York Times*, 24 July 1928, 15.

52. Pat Robinson, "Yanks Again Crash West," *New York Telegram*, 25 July 1928, 11.

53. James R. Harrison, "Yankees Win, 12–1; Then Yield, 13–10," *New York Times*, 27 July 1928, 15.

54. "Indians Brace Up When They Hear Peck Stays with the Team," *Sporting News*, 2 August 1928, 1.

55. James R. Harrison, "Yanks Beat Indians, 6–2, Then Lose, 9–4," *New York Times*, 29 July 1928, S1.

56. James R. Harrison, "Yankees Swamped by Indians, 24–6," *New York Times*, 30 July 1928, 20.

57. James Isaminger, "A's Continue Dizzy Stride, While Yanks Retain Seat on Toboggan," *Philadelphia Inquirer*, 31 July 1928, 18.

58. James R. Harrison, "Yanks Lose Again; Drop Third to Indians," *New York Times*, 31 July 1928, 24.

59. Isaminger, "A's Continue Dizzy Stride," 18.

60. "Sports Editorial," *Philadelphia Public Record*, 30 July 1928, 12.

61. John J. Ward, "The Greatest Leadoff Man in the American League," *Baseball Magazine* 40, no. 1 (December 1927): 317.

62. Ward, "The Greatest Leadoff Man in the American League," 317.

63. "Who Said There Would Be No Race in the American League?" *Sporting News*, 2 August 1928, 1.

64. James R. Harrison, "Yanks Rout Browns as Ruth Slams 42nd," *New York Times*, 2 August 1928, 15. Crowder dropped to 11–4 from 11–1 on the season.

65. James R. Harrison, "Yanks Lose in 15th; Lead Is 4 1/2 Games," *New York Times*, 3 August 1928, 12.

66. Harrison, "Yanks Lose in 15th," 12.

67. James R. Harrison, "Gray Blanks Yanks for Browns, 8 to 0," *New York Times*, 4 August 1928, 15.

68. James R. Harrison, "Yanks Win in 10th; Ruth Hits His 43rd," *New York Times*, 5 August 1928, 129.

69. Bill Nowlin, "Fred Heimach," *Society for American Baseball Research*, http:// sabr.org/bioproj/person/9e7d80e7 (accessed 5 February 2014); James Isaminger, "Rain Shortens A's Series with Chisox," *Philadelphia Inquirer*, 6 June 1928, 22; "Yanks Get Heimach of St. Paul by Lending Shealy, Campbell," *New York Times*, 5 August 1928, 129; "Yanks Alarmed by Mack's Rush to Buy Freddy Heimach," *Philadelphia Inquirer*, 5 August 1928, 14.

70. James R. Harrison, "Yanks Lose, 5 to 4; Lead Is 3 1/2 Games," *New York Times*, 6 August 1928, 23.

71. James Isaminger, "Grove Whiffs Eleven, Permits Three Swats," *Philadelphia Inquirer*, 6 August 1928, 12.

72. John Kieran, "Sports of the Times," *New York Times*, 7 August 1928, 19.

73. Kieran, "Sports of the Times," 7 August 1928, 19.

74. James R. Harrison, "Yanks Take Brace; Rout White Sox, 6–3," *New York Times*, 8 August 1928, 22.

75. Harrison, "Yanks Take Brace," 22.

76. "Who Said There Would Be No Race in the American League?" 1; James Isaminger, "A's Pare Down Lead," *Philadelphia Inquirer*, 28 July 1928, 15.

CHAPTER 11

1. John Kieran, "Sports of the Times," *New York Times*, 31 July 1928, 26.

2. Frederick G. Lieb, "Recent String of Defeats Worries Midget Manager More Than He Will Admit," *New York Evening Post*, 5 August 1927, 12.

3. James Isaminger, "Mack Refuses to Talk Pennant, Is Silently Hopeful," *Philadelphia Inquirer*, 9 August 1928, 14.

4. George Moriarty, "Connie Mack's Original Plans for Season Upset," *Los Angeles Times*, 2 August 1928, 2.

5. John Kieran, "Sports of the Times," *New York Times*, 9 August 1928, 17.

6. James R. Harrison, "Heimach Victor, 7–1, in Debut as Yank," *New York Times*, 10 August 1928, 18. Details for Yankee and Athletic games were taken from daily reporting in the *New York Times* and *Philadelphia Inquirer*, and from http://www.baseball-reference.com.

7. James R. Harrison, "Yanks Rally in Ninth; Upset Red Sox, 5–2," *New York Times*, 12 August 1928, S1.

8. James R. Harrison, "Pennock Shuts Out Boston with Three Hits," *New York Times*, 13 August 1928, 17.

9. James R. Harrison, "Gehrig's Home Run Wins for Yanks, 5–2," *New York Times*, 11 August 1928, 7.

10. James R. Harrison, "Yanks Today Start Final Home Stand," *New York Times*, 14 August 1928, 18.

11. Homer H. Metz, "Yankees, Once Heroes, Now Mere Team to Fans," *New York Morning Telegraph*, 13 August 1928, 6.

12. James R. Harrison, "Ruth hits 44th as White Sox Beat Yanks; Cubs Routed by Giants; Robins Lose," *New York Times*, 15 August 1928, 23.

13. "Ruth Hits 45th as Yanks Lose to White Sox; Giants Halted," *New York Times*, 16 August 1928, 19.

14. Joe Vila, "Mack Figures Layout of Remaining Games Will Help His Team," *Philadelphia Inquirer*, 15 August 1928, 18.

15. James R. Harrison, "Yanks End Slump, Rout Chicago, 11–1," *New York Times*, 17 August 1928, 20.

16. John Kieran, "Sports of the Times," *New York Times*, 18 August 1928, 16.

17. Kieran, "Sports of the Times," 18 August 1928, 16.

18. James Isaminger, "Simmons, Foxx Lead Slaughter of Tigers," *Philadelphia Inquirer*, 17 August 1928, 16.

19. James Isaminger, "Mackmen Expect to Add to Their Run," *Philadelphia Inquirer*, 18 August 1928, 12.

20. James R. Harrison, "Yanks and Indians Kept Apart by Rain," *New York Times*, 18 August 1928, 14.

21. Joe Vila, "Athletics Will Grab Pennant, Says Old Fox," *Philadelphia Inquirer*, 18 August 1928, 12.

22. Vila, "Athletics Will Grab Pennant," 12.

23. James R. Harrison, "Yanks' Early Lead Beats Indians, 8–5," *New York Times*, 19 August 1928, 130.

24. James R. Harrison, "65,000 See Yanks and Indians Divide," *New York Times*, 20 August 1928, 21.

25. James R. Harrison, "Yanks and Browns Will Clash Today," *New York Times*, 21 August 1928, 24; Fred Lieb, "Cutting the Plate with Fred Lieb," *New York Evening Post*, 16 August 1928, 16.

26. Frederick G. Lieb, "Mackmen Become Normal Again as the Law of Averages Asserts Itself Once More," *New York Evening Post*, 21 August 1928, 13.

27. Homer H. Metz, "Twin Bill Today Will Wind Up St. Louis Series," *New York Morning Telegraph*, 24 August 1928, 6.

28. James R. Harrison, "Yankees Sweep On; Subdue Browns, 3–1," *New York Times*, 22 August 1928, 24.

29. Fred Lieb, "Cutting the Plate with Fred Lieb," *New York Evening Post*, 22 August 1928, 12; Joe Vila, "M'grawmen Have Braced in Splendid Style, While Cardinals Appear Stale," *Philadelphia Inquirer*, 22 August 1928, 16.

30. Lieb, "Cutting the Plate with Fred Lieb," 13.

31. Homer H. Metz, "Yank–Giant World Series Would Be Interesting Clash," *New York Morning Telegraph*, 19 August 1928, 12. On August 19, the Giants had just completed a three-game sweep of the first-place Cardinals in St. Louis, by identical scores of 3–2, to pull to within a half game of the top. Benton had a record of 21–4. His last defeat had come against the Pirates on July 7.

32. Homer H. Metz, "Huggins Trying to Land New Flinger from Minors," *New York Morning Telegraph*, 21 August 1928, 6.

33. James R. Harrison, "Yanks and Browns Are Halted by Rain," *New York Times*, 23 August 1928, 22.

34. "Huggins Picks Giants to Win; Says Cardinals Are Through," *New York Times*, 23 August 1928, 22. As of August 28, the Pirates had a record of 70–54, from a record of 32–40 as of July 6. The 1928 season had gotten off to a terrible start for the Bucs, beginning during their preseason training in Paso Robles, in northern California. They were beset by two weeks of bad weather on their way cross-country, which resulted in injuries and illnesses to several players. "Pirates Show Need of More Training," *Sporting News*, 19 April 1928, 2.

35. Fred Lieb, "Hugmen Don't Fare Well in Bargain Day Warfare; Probe of Contests Show," New York Evening Post, 23 August 1928, 14. Lieb included the regularly scheduled doubleheader against the Senators on July 4 but left out the makeup doubleheader of May 29.

36. "Yankees Purchase Zachary, Southpaw," *New York Times*, 24 August 1928, 19.

37. "Yankees Purchase Zachary, Southpaw," 19; Joe Vila, "Faltering Hill Staff Is Worrying Huggins in Heat of Play Race," *Philadelphia Inquirer*, 26 August 1928, 14; Dan Daniel, "Lucky to Land Veteran Southpaw, Players Declare," *New York Telegram*, 24 August 1928, 10.

38. Hugh Bradley, "Zachary to Earn Spurs by Being Best Listener," *New York Evening Post*, 29 August 1928, 18.

39. James R. Harrison, "Yankees Lose Two; Lead by Three Games," *New York Times*, 25 August 1928, 16.

40. James Isaminger, "Cochrane's Single in Third Wins for Macks," *Philadelphia Inquirer*, 25 August 1928, 14.

41. James R. Harrison, "Yanks Break Even; Keep Three-Game Lead," *New York Times*, 26 August 1928, 135; Rud Rennie, "Yankees Lose, 9–3, to Tigers; Win Second, 7 to 0," *New York Herald Tribune*, 26 August 1928, C1.

42. Joe Vila, "Hug Says Macks Are Playing Best Ball," *Philadelphia Inquirer*, 26 August 1928, 6.

43. Vila, "Hug Says Macks Are Playing Best Ball," 6.

44. John Kieran, "Sports of the Times," *New York Times*, 26 August 1928, 136.

45. James R. Harrison, "Lazzeri Forced Out for Rest of Season," *New York Times*, 27 August 1928, 20.

46. Frederick G. Lieb, "Italian Star Again Retired to Bench; Shoulder Hurt to Keep Him Out for Year," *New York Evening Post*, 27 August 1928, 13.

47. Harrison, "Lazzeri Forced Out for Rest of Season," 20.

48. "Yanks Buy Bill (Rosey) Ryan, Ex-Giant, from Toledo Club," *New York Times*, 25 August 1928, 16.

49. James R. Harrison, "Yankees Win Two; Lead by Four Games, *New York Times*, 28 August 1928, 27; Rud Rennie, "Zachary and Pipgras Triumph, Former in Debut as New Yorker," *New York Herald Tribune*, 28 August 1928, 21.

50. James Isaminger, "Grove, Bishop, Miller Prove Mackian Aces," *Philadelphia Inquirer*, 29 August 1928, 16.

CHAPTER 12

1. Richards Vidmer, "Two Defeats by Senators Drop Yanks into First-Place Tie with Athletics," *New York Times*, 8 September 1928, 19. Details for Yankee and Athletic games were taken from daily reporting in the *New York Times* and *Philadelphia Inquirer*, and from http://www.baseball-reference.com.

2. John Kieran, "Sports of the Times," *New York Times*, 28 August 1928, 29.

3. Frank Wallace, "Yanks, with Flag Certain, Prepare to Return Home and Groom for Big Series," *New York Evening Post*, 27 August 1927, 10. Ruth had forty-seven home runs as of September 1, 1928, compared to forty-three at the same time in 1927, but he would have to hit fourteen during the month of September to break his 1927 record.

4. Fred Lieb, "Cutting the Plate with Fred Lieb," *New York Evening Post*, 28 August 1928, 12.

5. James Isaminger, "Tips from the Sporting Ticker," *Philadelphia Inquirer*, 9 September 1928, S7.

6. Joe Vila, "Mackmen Have Grabbed Off 46 Out of Last 58 Games," *Philadelphia Inquirer*, 30 August 1928, 16. The Athletics had actually won forty-three of their last fifty-eight games as of the 126th game of the season on August 29.

7. Babe Ruth, "Addition of Earnshaw Make Staff Equal to Any in League," *St. Louis Post-Dispatch*, 21 August 1928, 13.

8. "Yanks Seek Lary at Once to Take Place of Lazzeri," *Washington Post*, 30 August 1928, 13. There were conflicting reports on Lary and Reese, namely that the Yankee owner had soured on both players' performance during 1928 in the PCL, and wished to drop his option on them. "Lary and Reese Not to Join Yankees, Is Report," *New York Herald Tribune*, 29 August 1928, 18.

9. James R. Harrison, "Senators Beat Yanks, 3–1; Athletics Bow to Red Sox, 3–2," *New York Times*, 31 August 1928, 20; James Isaminger, "Ehmke Falters in Ninth and Red Sox Score Winning Runs," *Philadelphia Inquirer*, 31 August 1928, 18. Ruth's forty-seventh home run came during the 126th game of the season. His next home run would not come until nine games later, on September 8, by which time he had fallen exactly one game behind his 1927 pace.

10. Richards Vidmer, "Ruth Aims for Hits, Not Home Run Mark," *New York Times*, 1 September 1928, 14.

11. Vidmer, "Ruth Aims for Hits, Not Home Run Mark," 14.

12. Pat Robinson, "Ruth Aiming for Records," *New York Telegram*, 18 June 1928, 11.

13. Frank H. Young, "Huggins, Undismayed, Sure Yankees Will Finish Ahead," *Washington Post*, 1 September 1928, 13.

14. Young, "Huggins, Undismayed, Sure Yankees Will Finish Ahead," 13.

15. Richards Vidmer, "Hoover Sees Yanks Beat Senators, 8–3," *New York Times*, 2 September 1928, 115.

16. "Babe Ruth Refuses to Pose with Hoover," *New York Times*, 2 September 1928, 3.

17. "Hoover and 'Babe' Friends, They Say," *Washington Post*, 3 September 1928, 1.

18. "Hoover and 'Babe' Friends, They Say," 1; John Kieran, "Sports of the Times," *New York Times*, 6 September 1928, 29.

19. John Kieran, "Sports of the Times," *New York Times*, 4 September 1928, 37.

20. "Babe Ruth Refuses to Pose with Hoover," 3.

21. Richards Vidmer, "Yanks Beaten, 2–0; Lead Is One Game," *New York Times*, 3 September 1928, 14.

22. Richards Vidmer, "Yanks Break Even; Gain on Athletics," *New York Times*, 4 September 1928, 32. Fred Heimach was credited as the winning pitcher in the box score of the article. Because he pitched just three and one third innings as the starter, the win was later revised to Waite Hoyt, who pitched the final three and one third innings of the game.

23. James Isaminger, "Griffs Lift Goblet of Defeat Twice to Lips of Connie Mack," *Philadelphia Inquirer*, 4 September 1928, 16.

24. Joe Vila, "Yankees Have Lost Power Everywhere," *Philadelphia Inquirer*, 5 September 1928, 18.

25. Vila, "Yankees Have Lost Power Everywhere," 18.

26. Hugh Bradley, "Connie Mack Reveals Yen for League Flag," *New York Evening Post*, 4 September 1928, 14.

27. Dan Daniel, "Five Games with Harris Tribe Vital to Champs," *New York Telegram*, 5 September 1928, 12.

28. Gordon Mackay, "Is Zat So," *Philadelphia Public Record*, 6 September 1928, 15.

29. According to a report printed in the *Cleveland Plain Dealer*, Lary refused a request by Huggins to report to the Yankees on Sunday, September 7. This information was provided by players of the Sacramento team, who said that Lary demanded $10,000 of the proceeds of his sale price. Lary was upset that he was not let go before the August 31 deadline, which would have qualified him for a share in any World

Series money. "Lary Disregards Miller Huggins' Orders to Report," *Cleveland Plain Dealer*, 12 September 1928, 25.

30. Bill Dooley and Joe Dugan, "Hold Grove and Walberg for Yanks; Quinn Also Ready; Rain Gives Schedule Jolt," *Philadelphia Public Record*, 7 September 1928, 11; Joe Vila, "Mack's Neglect to Play Postponed Game with Red Hose May Prove Costly," *Philadelphia Inquirer*, 25 September 1928, 20.

31. Richards Vidmer, "Yankee–Athletic Ticket Rush Brings Police to Quell Riot," *New York Times*, 7 September 1928, 24.

32. Dan Daniel, "Predict Victory for A's If Champions Are Passed," *New York Telegram*, 6 September 1928, 12.

33. Daniel, "Predict Victory for A's If Champions Are Passed," 12.

34. John Kieran, "Sports of the Times," *New York Times*, 8 September 1928, 23.

35. Kieran, "Sports of the Times," 8 September 1928, 23.

36. Dan Daniel, "Yankees Looking Forward to Crucial Tests with A's," *New York Telegram*, 7 September 1928, 12. Lazzeri dominated Athletic pitching in 1928, with thirty hits in sixty-three at bats and six of his ten home runs, along with twenty-one runs batted in.

37. "Rain Abbreviates A's Schedule in Boston," *Philadelphia Inquirer*, 7 September 1928, 18.

38. "Rain Abbreviates A's Schedule in Boston," 18.

39. "Yankee Southpaw Flinger Hopeful Visit to Dentist Will Restore Pitching Arm," *New York Evening Post*, 7 September 1928, 12.

40. Richards Vidmer, "Yankees-Senators in Twin Bill Today," *New York Times*, 5 September 1928, 37.

41. Vidmer, "Two Defeats by Senators Drop Yanks into First-Place Tie with Athletics," 19; "Yanks Buy Fay Thomas," *New York Times*, 8 September 1928, 19.

42. James Isaminger, "Mack Aces Trump Hose Deuces and A's Share First-Place Pot," *Philadelphia Inquirer*, 8 September 1928, 20.

43. Isaminger, "Mack Aces Trump Hose Deuces and A's Share First-Place Pot," 20.

44. Sam Otis, "Pulling for Athletics," *Cleveland Plain Dealer*, 8 September 1928, 19.

45. Vidmer, "Two Defeats by Senators Drop Yanks into First-Place Tie with Athletics," 19.

46. "Orwoll, Earnshaw Prove Men of Hour as Macks Climb to Top," *Philadelphia Inquirer*, 9 September 1928, S; John Kieran, "Sports of the Times," *New York Times*, 9 September 1928, 148.

47. Kieran, "Sports of the Times," 6 September 1928, 29.

48. "Connie Mack Predicted He'd Catch Yankees Three Weeks Ago," *New York Telegram*, 8 September 1928, 8.

49. George B. Underwood, "Fanning with the Fans," *New York Telegraph*, 8 September 1928, 6.

50. "Fans on Edge as A's Take League Lead," *Philadelphia Public Record*, 9 September 1928, S.

51. "85,000 to See Yanks Sunday; All Reserved Seats Are Sold," *New York Times*, 6 September 1928, 25.

52. "$25 for $2 Seats Asked by Scalpers for Games Today," *New York Times*, 9 September 1928, 147; Kieran, "Sports of the Times," 9 September 1928, 148; "Sunday Doubleheader between Huggins and Mack Clans," *New York Telegram*, 7 September 1928, 12.

53. "Extra Police Ready for Stadium Jam," *New York Times*, 8 September 1928, 19.

54. "Crowd of 85,265, Baseball Record, Sees Yanks Win Two," *New York Times*, 10 September 1928, 1.

55. "Crowd of 85,265, Baseball Record, Sees Yanks Win Two," 1.

56. "Crowd of 85,265, Baseball Record, Sees Yanks Win Two," 1.

57. Isaminger, "Tips from the Sporting Ticker," 9 September 1928, S7; Dooley and Dugan, "Hold Grove and Walberg for Yanks," 11; Gordon Mackay, "Jack Quinn Passed Fifteen Victories; Dean of Curvers, He Leads His Team; Has Owned Rich Experience and Life," *Philadelphia Public Record*, 2 September 1928, S2.

58. Richards Vidmer, "Yankees Win Twice and Pass Athletics," *New York Times*, 10 September 1928, 26.

59. Vidmer, "Yankees Win Twice and Pass Athletics," 26.

60. "The Same Old A's, Chant the Yankees," *New York Times*, 10 September 1928, 26.

61. "Yank Players Emulate Rah! Rah! Boys in Victory," *New York Evening Post*, 10 September 1928, 15.

62. Frederick G. Lieb, "Inspired Hugmen Again Champions in Deed and Name," *New York Evening Post*, 10 September 1928, 15.

63. Dan Daniel, "Mackmen Again Victims of Champs' Indian Sign," *New York Telegram*, 10 September 1928, 12.

64. "Urban Shocker Dies in Denver Hospital; Former Yankee Pitching Star Passes Away After an Illness of Several Weeks," *New York Times*, 10 September 1928, 27.

65. Richards Vidmer, "Johnson to Pitch for Yankees Today," *New York Times*, 11 September 1928, 22.

66. Lieb, "Inspired Hugmen Again Champions in Deed and Name," 15.

67. Dan Daniel, "Tony Necessary to Hold Hug's Infield in Balance," *New York Telegram*, 11 September 1928, 12.

68. Bill Dooley, "Lefty Grove Faces Yankees Today to Keep His Winning Streak and Mates in Hunt," *Philadelphia Public Record*, 11 September 1928, 11.

69. Dooley, "Lefty Grove Faces Yankees Today to Keep His Winning Streak and Mates in Hunt," 11.

70. Dooley, "Lefty Grove Faces Yankees Today to Keep His Winning Streak and Mates in Hunt," 11.

71. Daniel, "Tony Necessary to Hold Hug's Infield in Balance," 12.

72. Richards Vidmer, "Ruth's Homer Puts Athletics to Rout," *New York Times*, 12 September 1928, 31.

73. Dan Daniel, "Champs Lack Old Punch But Spirit to Win Remains," *New York Telegram*, 8 September 1928, 8.

74. Ed R. Hughes, "Baseball Gossip," *San Francisco Chronicle*, 11 August 1928, H3.

75. Daniel, "Tony Necessary to Hold Hug's Infield in Balance," 12.

76. "Tony Lazzeri, Spark Plug of Yanks, Poison to A's," *Hartford Courant*, 6 January 1929, C7.

77. "Tony Lazzeri, Spark Plug of Yanks, Poison to A's," C7.

78. F. C. Lane, "A Great Natural Ballplayer Is Tony Lazzeri," *Baseball Magazine* 40, no. 1 (December 1927): 305.

79. Stan Baumgartner, "Ehmke in Hospital, Is Out for Season," *Philadelphia Inquirer*, 14 September 1928, 20; "Yanks Bow in Ninth, 4–3, on Bishop's Homer—Five Ex-Champions Lose at Brae Burn," *New York Times*, 13 September 1928, 34. It was almost five years ago to the day that Ehmke had almost made baseball history pitching for the Red Sox. On September 7, 1923, he pitched a no-hitter at Shibe Park. Fans thought that they were witnessing another no-hitter four days later at Yankee Stadium, when Whitey Witt reached on an error to lead off the game. The play was scored a hit, which gave Ehmke a one-hit shutout, at 3–0. The scorer on the play was Fred Lieb. F. C. Lane, "The Toughest Break a Pitcher Ever Had," *Baseball Magazine* 31, no. 6 (November 1923): 551.

80. Bill Dooley, "Three and Two," *Philadelphia Record*, 16 September 1928, S2.

81. Ed R. Hughes, "Baseball Gossip," *San Francisco Chronicle*, 28 September 1928, H3.

82. Vila, "Mack's Neglect to Play Postponed Game with Red Hose May Prove Costly," 20.

83. James Isaminger, "Pennock Expects to Aid Yankees on Western Trip," *Philadelphia Inquirer*, 12 September 1928, 18.

84. Isaminger, "Pennock Expects to Aid Yankees on Western Trip," 18.

85. Sam Otis, "Limit Not Yet Reached," *Cleveland Plain Dealer*, 12 September 1928, 25.

86. Dooley, "Three and Two," 16 September 1928, S2.

87. John Kieran, "Sports of the Times," *New York Times*, 15 September 1928, 28.

88. "Last Tribute to Shocker; Entire Yankee Team Attends Funeral of Former Pitcher," *New York Times*, 16 September 1928, 149.

CHAPTER 13

1. James Isaminger, "Mack Close-Ups," *Philadelphia Inquirer*, 29 September 1928, 22.

2. James Isaminger, "Tips from the Sporting Ticker," *Philadelphia Inquirer*, 16 September 1928, S4.

3. Westbrook Pegler, "Pegler Says: Detroit Ballplayers Torn between Two Desires in Series with Athletics," *San Francisco Chronicle*, 22 August 1928, H3.

4. During the month of September, Huggins would rely on Hoyt, Pipgras, Johnson, Zachary, and Heimach to start games and serve in relief roles. Hoyt started six games and appeared in five others, working on one day's rest four times. Pipgras started seven games, with three relief stints. Heimach, Johnson, and Zachary each

started five games and were summoned from the bull pen seven times between them. Moore, Shealy, and Ryan were only used sparingly.

5. Richards Vidmer, "Yanks Lose, 6 to 5; Lead Is Half Game," *New York Times*, 16 September 1928, 147; Rud Rennie, "Yanks' Lead Cut to 1/2 Game as Browns Win," *New York Herald Tribune*, 16 September 1928, 2.

6. James Isaminger, "Mack Close-Ups," *Philadelphia Inquirer*, 26 September 1928, 20.

7. "Ty Cobb to Retire This Fall after 24 Years of Service," *Philadelphia Inquirer*, 18 September 1928, 24.

8. Richards Vidmer, "Yanks Jolt Browns; Hold League Lead," *New York Times*, 17 September 1928, 25. Details for Yankee and Athletic games were taken from daily reporting in the *New York Times* and *Philadelphia Inquirer*, and from http://www.baseball-reference.com.

9. James Isaminger, "Grove Invincible as A's Pound Victory," *Philadelphia Inquirer*, 17 September 1928, 16.

10. Richards Vidmer, "Yanks Trip Browns; Lead by Full Game," *New York Times*, 18 September 1928, 23.

11. Homer Thorne, "Departure of Cy Moore May Presage Shakeup in Ranks of Huggins' Outfit," *New York Evening Post*, 18 September 1928, 16.

12. "Thirteenth Year Is George Burns's Best," *Sporting News*, 21 October 1926, 3.

13. "George Burns, Sent to Yanks, Refuses to Join New Yorks," *Philadelphia Inquirer*, 16 September 1928, 24.

14. "George Burns, Sent to Yanks, Refuses to Join New Yorks," 24.

15. "Burns Will See Huggins; Willing to Play with Yanks, but Wants to Know His Status," *New York Times*, 20 September 1928, 38.

16. "Burns Is New Yank," *New York Telegram*, 18 September 1928, 12.

17. Vidmer, "Yanks Trip Browns," 23; Thorne, "Departure of Cy Moore May Presage Shakeup in Ranks of Huggins' Outfit," 16. Moore made his last appearance on September 15, against St. Louis, giving up two runs in one and one-third innings. He finished the season with four wins and four losses and a 4.18 earned run average.

18. Ed Pollack, "Playing the Game," *Philadelphia Public Ledger*, 20 September 1928, 15.

19. "Here's the Secret of Moore's Famed Sinker," *New York Telegram*, 9 April 1928, 13.

20. "Burns Is New Yank," 12.

21. Pollack, "Playing the Game," 15.

22. Rud Rennie, "Yankees Increase Lead, Taking Slugfest from Browns, 4 to 11," *New York Herald Tribune*, 19 September 1928, 25.

23. Richards Vidmer, "Yanks Stop Browns; Lead Now Two Games," *New York Times*, 19 September 1928, 38.

24. James Isaminger, "Miller Masters A's, Who Fail in Pinches," *Philadelphia Inquirer*, 19 September 1928, 18

25. Bill Brandt, "Tucker's Homer and Costly Break on Grounder in Seventh Spoil Walberg's Fine Work," *Philadelphia Public Ledger*, 19 September 1928, 14.

26. Richards Vidmer, "Yanks Open Series at Chicago Today," *New York Times*, 20 September 1928, 38.

27. "World's Series Set to Open on Oct. 4," *New York Times*, 18 September 1928, 24; "Athletics Accept Bids Today for World's Series Tickets," *New York Times*, 20 September 1928, 38.

28. Vidmer, "Yanks Open Series at Chicago Today," 38.

29. "Tall Tutor Explains Team's Big Weakness," *Philadelphia Inquirer*, 20 September 1928, 19.

30. Bill Brandt, "Athletics to Stand or Fall on Lineup as Now Arranged, Avers Mack as Team Rests," *Philadelphia Public Ledger*, 20 September 1928, 14.

31. John Kieran, "Sports of the Times," *New York Times*, 20 September 1928, 40. The Cardinals were in first place, two games ahead of the Giants and three and a half games ahead of the Cubs, as of September 19.

32. Fred Lieb, "Cutting the Plate with Fred Lieb," *New York Evening Post*, 16 August 1928, 15.

33. Homer Thorne, "Silence of Babe Ruth's Bat Continues as Macks Climb to within One Game of Top," *New York Evening Post*, 21 September 1928, 16.

34. Richards Vidmer, "Yanks Lose in 12th; Lead Cut to a Game," *New York Times*, 21 September 1928, 39.

35. "Quinn Quells Tigers; Haas Batters Homer," *Philadelphia Inquirer*, September 21, 1928, 20.

36. Thorne, "Silence of Babe Ruth's Bat Continues as Macks Climb to within One Game of Top," 16.

37. "Sports Editorial," *Philadelphia Public Record*, 22 September 1928, 13.

38. Richards Vidmer, "Yanks Win, 5–2; Take Two-Game Lead," *New York Times*, 22 September 1928, 21.

39. "Koenig Out of Sox Tilt," *New York Telegram*, 20 September 1928, 13.

40. James Isaminger, "Tiger Homers Send A's Two Games to Rear," *Philadelphia Inquirer*, 22 September 1928, 22.

41. Richards Vidmer, "Yanks Beaten, 5–2; Hold Two-Game Lead," *New York Times*, 23 September 1928, S1.

42. Bill Brandt, "Earnshaw Pitches Great Game after Relieving Walberg," *Philadelphia Public Ledger*, 23 September 1928, S1.

43. James Isaminger, "Walberg Blows as A's Err and Drop Another to Tigers," *Philadelphia Inquirer*, 23 September 1928, S.

44. Brandt, "Earnshaw Pitches Great Game after Relieving Walberg," S1.

45. Richards Vidmer, "World's Series Ticket Plans Announced by Yankee Office," *New York Times*, 23 September 1928, S1.

46. Richards Vidmer, "Hoyt Allows Four Hits and Blanks Indians," *New York Times*, 24 September 1928, 15. The September 5 doubleheader against the Senators was the twenty-fifth of the 1928 season for the Yankees. This included three of the four regularly scheduled doubleheaders. The nightcap of the Memorial Day twin bill was cancelled. The Yankees would play twenty-eight in total.

47. James Isaminger, "Foxx, Hauser, and Dykes Deliver Crushing Blows to Down Brownies, 11–7," *Philadelphia Inquirer*, 24 September 1928, 18.

48. James Isaminger, "Tips from the Sporting Ticker," *Philadelphia Inquirer*, 23 September 1928, 12.

49. Sam Otis, "Too Much New York," *Cleveland Plain Dealer*, 17 September 1928, 22. Reference should be made to W. A. Phelon, "The New York Clubs against the Field," *Baseball Magazine* 33, no. 4 (September 1924): 455. Phelon discusses New York's domination of baseball, saying, "How the pennant race has degenerated into a contest between the two New York clubs and the fourteen contenders."

50. "Huggins Just about Ready to Give Up All Attempts to Lose League Pennant," *New York Evening Post*, 24 September 1928, 18.

51. Richards Vidmer, "Yanks Are Beaten; Hold Two-Game Lead," *New York Times*, 25 September 1928, 42.

52. John Kieran, "Sports of the Times," *New York Times*, 25 September 1928, 47.

53. Kieran, "Sports of the Times," 25 September 1928, 47.

54. James Isaminger, "Disastrous Sixth and Four Costly Boots Ruination of Quinn," *Philadelphia Inquirer*, 25 September 1928, 20.

55. Richards Vidmer, "Yankees Win, 10–1; Keep Two-Game Lead," *New York Times*, 26 September 1928, 30.

56. James Isaminger, "Walberg, Dykes are Mack's Men of Hour," *Philadelphia Inquirer*, 26 September 1928, 20.

57. Joe Vila, "Mack's Neglect to Play Postponed Game with Red Hose May Prove Costly," *Philadelphia Inquirer*, 25 September 1928, 20.

58. John Kieran, "Sports of the Times," *New York Times*, 27 September 1928, 39. Welsh and Hogan came to the Giants from the Braves in the controversial Hornsby trade in January 1928.

59. "40,000 Ask Cards for Series Tickets," *New York Times*, 26 September 1928, 30.

60. Richards Vidmer, "Chance to Win Flag Faces Yanks Today," *New York Times*, 27 September 1928, 35.

61. James Isaminger, "Lefty Grove to Hurl Twice against Sox," *Philadelphia Inquirer*, 27 September 1928, 18.

62. Richards Vidmer, "Yanks Win Two, Need One Victory for Flag," *New York Times*, 28 September 1928, 30; "Combs Out of World's Series; Fractured Wrist in Collision," *New York Times*, 29 September 1928, 20. Heimach once again was credited with the victory in the box score having started and pitched just two and two thirds innings. Henry Johnson was later credited with the victory after pitching the final two and two thirds innings of the game.

63. James Isaminger, "Grove's Arm and Bat Down White Hose," *Philadelphia Inquirer*, 28 September 1928, 22.

64. Bill Dooley, "Three and Two," *Philadelphia Public Record*, 30 September 1928, S5.

65. Richards Vidmer, "Yanks Clinch Flag; Defeat Tigers, 11–6," *New York Times*, 29 September 1928, 20.

66. James Isaminger, "A's Overthrow Sox for Hollow Triumph," *Philadelphia Inquirer*, 29 September 1928, 22.

67. Isaminger, "A's Overthrow Sox for Hollow Triumph," 22.

68. Joe Vila, "Critics of Huggins Now Remain Silent after His '28 Feat," *Philadelphia Inquirer*, 30 September 1928, S2.

69. John Kieran, "Sports of the Times," *New York Times*, 29 September 1928, 24.

70. Kieran, "Sports of the Times," 29 September 1928, 24.

71. "The Old Sport's Musings," *Philadelphia Inquirer*, 1 October 1928, 16.

72. Ford Frick, "Back of the Stars That Shine," *Baseball Magazine* 41, no. 6 (November 1928): 545–46.

73. "The Old Sport's Musings," 1 October 1928, 16.

74. Richards Vidmer, "Gehrig Is Injured as Yanks Win Final; Struck in Face by Batted Ball and Knocked Unconscious—Forced from Game," *New York Times*, 1 October 1928, 26.

75. "Gehrig Joins Cripple List," *New York Telegram*, 1 October 1928, 12.

CHAPTER 14

1. Don Skene, "Alexander Puzzled at Yankees Murdering His Favorite Hooks," *New York Herald Tribune*, 6 October 1928, 18.

2. "Series Sidelights," *Washington Post*, 5 October 1928, 18.

3. "Facts and Figures for World Series," *Hartford Courant*, 4 October 1928, 15; "Umpires and Scorers Selected for Series," *New York Herald Tribune*, 2 October 1928, 26; "Two Radio Chains Will Broadcast World Series," *New York Herald Tribune*, 4 October 1928, 25.

4. Dan Daniel, "Earle Combs Out, Odds Rise against Yanks," *New York Telegram*, 3 October 1928, 1.

5. Albert Keane, "Calling 'Em Right," *Hartford Courant*, 4 October 1928, 15.

6. Dan Daniel, "Champions' Hitting Power and Gameness Should Win," *New York Telegram*, 3 October 1928, 12.

7. Walter Johnson, "Little Hope for Yankees Seen by Walter Johnson," *Washington Post*, 4 October 1928, 13.

8. Johnson, "Little Hope for Yankees Seen by Walter Johnson," 13.

9. Paul B. Zimmerman, "1926 Heroes Replaced by New Stars," *Washington Post*, 30 September 1928, M19.

10. Joe Williams, "This Dizzy Game of Baseball," *New York Telegram*, 2 October 1928, 12.

11. Dan Daniel, "Leadoff Star of Champs Expects to Get in Series," *New York Telegram*, 2 October 1928, 12.

12. Daniel, "Leadoff Star of Champs Expects to Get in Series," 12.

13. William McKechnie, "Cardinals' Infield Will Not Crack, Says McKechnie: Veterans Occupy All Four Places; Manager Gives Plenty of Praise to 'Fordham Flash'; Says Maranville Good for Several More Seasons," *Hartford Courant*, 1 October 1928, 14.

14. Miller Huggins, "Huggins Entering Series with No Illusions," *St. Louis Post-Dispatch*, 3 October 1928, 21.

15. Huggins, "Huggins Entering Series with No Illusions," 21.

16. Lou Gehrig, "Teams Tired and Worn in Flag Fight, Says Yank Star," *Hartford Courant*, 1 October 1928, 14.

17. Babe Ruth, "Mr. Ruth Takes a Look at the Big Series," *New York Telegram*, 2 October 1928, 13.

18. Frank H. Young, "Weather Is Most Unusual Feature of Series Opening," *Washington Post*, 5 October 1928, 15; "Series Sidelights," 5 October 1928, 18; Westbrook Pegler, "Orderly Game and Quiet, Is Verdict," *Washington Post*, 5 October 1928, 15.

19. W. B. Hanna, "Play-by-Play Description of First World Series Game," *New York Herald Tribune*, 5 October 1928, 26.

20. Hanna, "Play-by-Play Description of First World Series Game," 26.

21. Edward J. Neil, "Both Teams Satisfied, They Say," *Washington Post*, 5 October 1928, 15; Rud Rennie, "Players of Both Teams Give All Credit to Hoyt," *New York Herald Tribune*, 5 October 1928, 26.

22. Neil, "Both Teams Satisfied, They Say," 15.

23. Rennie, "Players of Both Teams Give All Credit to Hoyt," 26.

24. Neil, "Both Teams Satisfied, They Say," 15.

25. Rennie, "Players of Both Teams Give All Credit to Hoyt," 26.

26. Rennie, "Players of Both Teams Give All Credit to Hoyt," 26.

27. Neil, "Both Teams Satisfied, They Say," 15.

28. Rennie, "Players of Both Teams Give All Credit to Hoyt," 26. Sherdel lost Game 1 and Game 5 of the 1926 World Series to Herb Pennock by scores of 2–1 and 1–0.

29. "Series Games Fail to Draw Former Crowd," *New York Herald Tribune*, 6 October 1928, 18.

30. "Series Sidelights," *Washington Post*, 6 October 1928, 16.

31. Pete Alexander, "Of Course We'll Pitch to Ruth, Writes Old Pete," *St. Louis Post-Dispatch*, 3 October 1928, 21.

32. W. B. Hanna, "Play-by-Play Description of Second World Series Game," *New York Herald Tribune*, 6 October 1928, 19.

33. Skene, "Alexander Puzzled at Yankees Murdering His Favorite Hooks," 18.

34. Skene, "Alexander Puzzled at Yankees Murdering His Favorite Hooks," 18.

35. Skene, "Alexander Puzzled at Yankees Murdering His Favorite Hooks," 18.

36. Skene, "Alexander Puzzled at Yankees Murdering His Favorite Hooks," 18.

37. Edward J. Neil, "Victors Happy in Revenge for 1926," *Washington Post*, 6 October 1928, 13.

38. Neil, "Victors Happy in Revenge for 1926," 13.

39. Skene, "Alexander Puzzled at Yankees Murdering His Favorite Hooks," 18; Dan Daniel, "Champs Expect to Clean Up Series in St. Louis," *New York Telegram*, 6 October 1928, 5.

40. "Cardinals to Ride in Open Autos at Parade Saturday," *St. Louis Post-Dispatch*, 4 October 1928, 3.

41. George Kirksey, "Zachary Anxious to Work; Says He Can Beat Cards," *Washington Post*, 4 October 1928, 13.

42. Kirksey, "Zachary Anxious to Work," 13.

43. "Cards Returning 75,000 World Series Requests," *New York Herald Tribune*, 3 October 1928, 28.

44. Haines finished the year with a 20–8 record, while winning his last nine decisions.

45. Charles W. Dunkley, "Ruth Kicked the Ball Out of My Hand, Says Jim Wilson," *St. Louis Post-Dispatch*, 8 October 1928, 13.

46. W. B. Hanna, "Third Series Game Won and Lost in Sixth Inning as Yankees Launch Three-Run Assault," *New York Herald Tribune*, 8 October 1928, 20; Grantland Rice, "Yankees Win 3rd in Row, 7–3, as Gehrig Hits Two Home Runs," *New York Herald Tribune*, 8 October 1928, 1.

47. Dunkley, "Ruth Kicked the Ball Out of My Hand, Says Jim Wilson," 13.

48. Rud Rennie, "Gloom Pervades Cards Quarters after Third Straight Defeat," *New York Herald Tribune*, 8 October 1928, 20.

49. Dunkley, "Ruth Kicked the Ball Out of My Hand, Says Jim Wilson," 13.

50. Rennie, "Gloom Pervades Cards Quarters after Third Straight Defeat," 20.

51. Rennie, "Gloom Pervades Cards Quarters after Third Straight Defeat," 20.

52. Rennie, "Gloom Pervades Cards Quarters after Third Straight Defeat," 20.

53. Albert Keane, "Landis Criticized for Postponing Fourth Game of World Series after Deluge," *Hartford Courant*, 9 October 1928, 13; James R. Harrison, "Yanks-Cards Idle; Fourth Game Today," *New York Times*, 9 October 1928, 38; "Yankees Meet Their First Postponement after 29 World's Series Games in Row," *New York Times*, 9 October 1928, 38.

54. Dan Daniel, "Rain Postpones World Series Game for Today," *New York Telegram*, 8 October 1928, 1.

55. Ralph H. Turner, "Loyal St. Louisans Abandon All Hope," *Washington Post*, 8 October 1928, 1.

56. "Ruth's Second Homer Is Turning Point of Game, Coming after Third Strike Is Disallowed," *New York Herald Tribune*, 10 October 1928, 27.

57. W. B. Hanna, "Play-by-Play Description of Final World Series Game," *New York Herald Tribune*, 10 October 1928, 27.

58. Rud Rennie, "Huggins Sings as Yankees Go Wild with Joy," *New York Herald Tribune*, 10 October 1928, 27.

59. Rennie, "Huggins Sings as Yankees Go Wild with Joy," 27.

60. Rennie, "Huggins Sings as Yankees Go Wild with Joy," 27.

61. Grantland Rice, "Yanks Sweep Series; Ruth Hits Three Homers in Final, 7 to 3," *New York Herald Tribune*, 10 October 1928, 1.

62. Rice, "Yanks Sweep Series," 1.

63. "Ruth Forgets Home Runs in Pride Over His Great Catch," *Boston Daily Globe*, 10 October 1928, 24.

64. "Yankee Regulars to Get $5,531.91 Each," *Boston Daily Globe*, 10 October 1928, 24.

65. Dan Daniel, "Huggins Rates Yankees Most Destructive Team," *New York Telegram*, 11 October 1928, 16.

66. Dan Daniel, "Hugmen Prove Superiority in Trimming Handed Cards," *New York Telegram*, 10 October 1928, 6.

67. Daniel, "Hugmen Prove Superiority in Trimming Handed Cards," 6.

68. Daniel, "Hugmen Prove Superiority in Trimming Handed Cards," 6.

69. James O'Leary, "Flock of Records Broken in Series," *Boston Daily Globe*, 10 October 1928, 24.

70. "Throng at Station Welcomes Yankees," *New York Times*, 11 October 1928, 29.

AFTERWORD

1. Dan Daniel, "Pilot of Champions Sees Great Future in Game," *New York Telegram*, 28 April 1928, 11.

2. Miller Huggins, "The Danger of Too Much Success," *Baseball Magazine* 33, no. 6 (November 1924): 543.

3. Ralph McGill, "Yanks Have Expensive Baseball Wreckage," *Atlanta Constitution*, 21 September 1929, 21.

4. "Huggins of Yankees Is Critically Ill," *New York Times*, 23 September 1929, 40; "Miller Huggins Dies; Many Pay Tribute," *New York Times*, 26 September 1929, 1; "Miller Huggins," *Wikipedia.org*, http://en.wikipedia.org/wiki/Miller_Huggins (accessed 10 February 2014).

5. "Mack Paid Out Fortune to Form Winning Team," *Los Angeles Times*, 15 September 1929, 1.

6. Frederick G. Lieb, *Connie Mack: Grand Old Man of Baseball* (New York: G. P. Putnam's Sons, 1945), 252.

7. Rev. Jerome C. Romanowski, *The Mackmen: Reflections on a Baseball Team* (Camden, NJ: Graphic Press, 1979), 108.

POSTSCRIPT

1. "Baseball Writers Pick All-Star," *New York Times*, 6 December 1928, 42.

Bibliography

Alexander, Charles C. *Spoke: A Biography of Tris Speaker*. Dallas, TX: Southern Methodist University Press, 2007.

Barrow, Edward Grant, with James M. Kahn. *My Fifty Years in Baseball*. New York: Coward-McCann, 1951.

Bragden, Henry W., Samuel P. McCutchen, and Donald A. Ritchie. *History of a Free Nation*. Westerville, OH: Macmillan/McGraw-Hill, 1992.

Clark, Ellery H., Jr. *Red Sox Forever*. New York: Exposition Press, 1977.

Cobb, Ty, with Al Stump. *My Life in Baseball: The True Record*. Lincoln: University of Nebraska Press, 1993.

Egnal, Marc. *Clash of Extremes*. New York: Hill & Wang, 2010.

Eskenazi, Gerald. *The Lip: A Biography of Leo Durocher*. New York: William Morrow and Company, 1993.

Goldstein, Warren. *Playing for Keeps: A History of Early Baseball*. Ithaca, NY: Cornell University Press, 1989.

Golenbock, Peter. *Wrigleyville: A Magical Mystery Tour of the Chicago Cubs*. New York: St. Martin's Griffin.

Hardy, James D., Jr. *The New York Giants Baseball Club*. Jefferson, NC: McFarland, 1996.

Heidenry, John. *The Gashouse Gang: How Dizzy Dean, Leo Durocher, Branch Rickey, Pepper Martin, and Their Colorful, Come-from-Behind Ball Club Won the World Series—and America's Heart—during the Great Depression*. New York: Public Affairs, 2007.

Hynd, Noel. *The Giants of the Polo Grounds*. Dallas, TX: Taylor Publishing, 1988.

Kennedy, MacLean. *The Great Teams of Baseball*. St. Louis, MO: Charles C. Spink & Son, 1928.

Kozak, Ellen M. *The U.S. Constitution Book*. Avon, MA: Adams Media, 2011.

Levitt, Daniel R. *The Bulldog Who Built the Yankees' First Dynasty*. Lincoln: University of Nebraska Press, 2008.

293

Leuchtenberg, William. *The Perils of Prosperity, 1914–1932*, 2nd ed. Chicago: University of Chicago Press, 1993.

Lieb, Frederick G. *The Baseball Story*. New York: G. P. Putnam's Sons, 1950.

———. *Connie Mack: Grand Old Man of Baseball*. New York: G. P. Putnam's Sons, 1945.

———. *The St. Louis Cardinals: The Story of a Great Baseball Club*. New York: G. P. Putnam's Sons, 1944.

Macht, Norman L. *Connie Mack and the Early Years of Baseball*. Lincoln: University of Nebraska Press, 2012.

McGillicuddy, Cornelius. *My 66 Years in the Big Leagues: The Great Story of America's National Game*. Philadelphia, PA: John C. Winston Company, 1950.

Merz, Charles. *And Then Came Ford*. Garden City, NY: Doubleday, Doran & Company, 1929.

Morris, Peter. *A Game of Inches: The Story Behind the Innovations That Shaped Baseball*. Chicago: Ivan R. Dee, 2010.

Mosedale, John. *The Greatest of All: The 1927 Yankees*. New York: Dial, 1974.

Murdock, Eugene. *Baseball between the Wars: Memories of the Game by the Men Who Played It*. Westport, CT: Meckler, 1992.

Peterson, Robert W. *Cages to Jumpshots: Pro Basketball's Early Years*. Lincoln: University of Nebraska Press, 2002.

Reiss, Steven A. *Sport in Industrial America, 1850–1920*. Wheeling, IL: Harlan Davidson, 1995.

Robinson, Ray. *Iron Horse: Lou Gehrig and His Time*. New York: Harper Perennial, 1991.

Romanowski, Jerome C., Rev. *The Mackmen: Reflections on a Baseball Team*. Camden, NJ: Graphic Press, 1979.

Schwarz, Alan. *The Numbers Game: Baseball's Lifelong Fascination with Statistics*. New York: Thomas Dunne Books, 2004.

Seymour, Harold. *Baseball: The Early Years*. New York: Oxford University Press, 1960.

———. *Baseball: The Golden Age*. New York: Oxford University Press, 1971.

Shindo, Charles J. *1927 and the Rise of Modern America*. Lawrence: University Press of Kansas, 2010.

Solomon, Burt. *Where They Ain't: The Fabled Life and Untimely Death of the Fabled Baltimore Orioles*. New York: Free Press, 1999.

Spatz, Lyle, and Steve Steinberg. *1921: The Yankees, the Giants, and the Battle for Baseball Supremacy in New York*. Lincoln: University of Nebraska Press, 2010.

Stephenson, D. Grier, Robert J. Bresler, Robert J. Friedrich, and Joseph J. Karlesky. *American Government*. New York: Harper & Row, 1988.

Surdam, David. *The Postwar Yankees*. Lincoln: University of Nebraska Press, 2008.

Wallace, David. *Capital of the World: A Portrait of New York City in the Roaring Twenties*. Guilford, CT: Lyons Press, 2011.

White, G. Edward. *Creating the National Pastime: Baseball Transforms Itself, 1903–1953*. Princeton, NJ: Princeton University Press, 1996.

Index

About the Author

Charlie Gentile is a first-time author and business analyst with a bachelor of science in accounting. He is a lifelong Yankees fan, as well as a fan of each of the four major North American team sports. He is a member of the Society for American Baseball Research (SABR).